ORIGEN

ORIGEN

HENRI
CROUZEL

Translated by A. S. Worrall

1817

Harper & Row, Publishers, San Francisco

Printed in Great Britain by Billing & Sons Ltd., Worcester

For information address
Harper & Row, Publishers, Inc., 10 East 53rd Street, New York, NY 10022.

Published simultaneously in Canada by Fitzhenry & Whiteside, Limited, Toronto.

First Edition

Library of Congress Cataloguing-in-Publication Data

Crouzel, Henri
  Origen
  Translation of Origène.
  Bibliography: p.
  1. Origen. 2. Theology, Doctrinal – History – Early
church, ca.30–600. 3. Bible – Criticism, interpretation,
etc. – History – Early church, ca.30–600. I. Title.
BR1720.0707613 1989   270.1'092'4 [B]   88–45985
  ISBN 0–06–061632–6

89 90 91 92 93 XXX 10 9 8 7 6 5 4 3 2 1

Contents

Translator's Preface

I am indebted to the Author, Father Crouzel, and to my daughter, Professor Frances Young, Head of the Department of Theology in Birmingham University, each of whom has read the typescript and made valuable suggestions. Footnotes indicated by figures are the Author's. The small number of additional notes indicated by letters are mine, either to acknowledge the use of published English translations of the Father's, where extended quotations occur, or, very occasionally, to comment on debatable points of translation.

A.S.W.

Foreword
In signum cui contradicetur

Eighteen centuries ago, probably in 185, Origen was born, it seems, at Alexandria. He would not have thought much of celebrating the anniversary of his birth, since, if we are to believe Homily VIII on Leviticus,[1] only the wicked keep their birthdays, Pharaoh[2] and Herod Antipas, who on his had John the Baptist beheaded.[3]

During these eighteen centuries Origen has been the most astonishing sign of contradiction in the history of Christian thought. Of course, no one has denied the greatness of his genius and the breadth of his influence: the nickname Adamantios, man of steel or of diamond, etymologically the Untameable, was certainly given to him not long after his death: Eusebius seems to think that he even bore it in his lifetime.[4] His only peers are Augustine and Thomas Aquinas and he remains the greatest theologian the Eastern Church has produced. But his posthumous history was to be one of ups and downs. In spite of the attacks made on him at the turn of the 3rd and 4th centuries by Methodius of Alexandria and Eustathius of Antioch – Origen was at that time defended by Pamphilus of Caesarea —, he is the uncontested master, barring a few reservations, of the great doctors of the 4th century, the golden age of the Fathers. He is 'the stone which sharpens us all', to use a phrase of Gregory of Nazianzus reported by the Souda, and 'the Master of the Churches after the Apostle', to quote Didymus the Blind, copied by Jerome. But the formulation, by certain monastic circles in Egypt and Palestine in the second half of the 4th century, of a system based on certain aspects of his thought and on the suppression of all that counterbalanced those aspects, unleashed at the turn of the 3rd and 4th centuries a violent quarrel, both in the East, where Epiphanius of Salamis, with the support of the patriarch Theophilus of Alexandria, let himself go against bishop John of Jerusalem, and in the West, where Jerome, recovering from his past enthusiasm for Origen, overwhelmed his former friend Rufinus in a war of pamphlets written from his convent in Bethlehem. A second crisis broke out in the first half of the 6th century on account of the doctrines, more those of Evagrius than of Origen, held

[1] §3.
[2] Gen. 40, 20.
[3] Matt. 14, 6; Mk 6, 21.
[4] *Ecclesiastical History* VI, XIV, 10.

by some Palestinian monks. The result was a condemnation of Origen in 543 by the emperor Justinian and his domestic synod and another condemnation attributed to the fifth Ecumenical Council, the second of Constantinople in 553. The historical value of the latter is virtually nil as regards Origen, for it was really aimed at the Origenists of the day, called Isochristes, and the anathemas that express it, drawn in part from Evagrius's work, do not appear in the official Minutes of the Council.

If from this date the East seems to have made up its mind that Origen was a heretic, the West, which knew him through the Latin translations of Rufinus and Jerome, was to be often divided and perplexed about him. In a chapter of the first volume of his *Exégèse Médiévale*[5] Henri de Lubac has made a close analysis of the attitude towards him of authors of the high Middle Ages. St Bernard reproduces some of his explanations of the Song of Songs but seems at the same time anxious to blur their provenance. He was hardly ever read in the scholastic period, his Platonism being at variance with the prevailing Aristotelianism. At the Renaissance Origen was to inspire some of the greatest humanists, like Pico della Mirandola[6] and Erasmus.[7] In the 16th century there began an effort to publish his works, the quality improving as standards of criticism became more exacting, and alongside this a more historical and systematic study of his work which has not yet entirely put an end to the fundamental differences of opinion about his thought.

The most recent general book about Origen is that of Jean Daniélou,[8] published in 1948. The present work cannot, any more than his, claim to be exhaustive in dealing with the considerable breadth of Origen's thought and work. So we shall talk about the points that seem to us the most important and these will often be different from those chosen by Daniélou. Nor can we, without excessively lengthening this book and distorting its purpose, pause on the controversial points – and they are numerous. For that we refer the reader to our *Bibliographie Critique d'Origène*[9] with its *Supplément I:*[10] the indexes in these two works will enable the reader quickly to find the literature on the point he wishes to pursue.

[5] Paris, 1959, pp. 221–304.
[6] H. de Lubac, *Pic de la Mirandole*, Paris, 1971; H. Crouzel, *Une controverse sur Origène à la Renaissance; Jean Pic de la Mirandole et Pierre Garcia* (*De Pétrarque à Descartes* XXXVI), Paris, 1977.
[7] A. Godin, *Erasme lecteur d'Origène*, Geneva, 1982.
[8] Origène, Collection 'Le génie du christianisme', Paris.
[9] Collection *Instrumenta Patristica* VIII, Abbaye de Steenbrugge, The Hague, 1971.
[10] Same collection VIII A. Ibid. 1982.

Bibliographical Note

The following works of Origen have been published in the collection *Sources Chrétiennes* (Paris, Editions du Cerf, abbreviated SC). Most of these have the Greek or Latin text; all have a French translation, introduction and notes.

Commentaire sur l'Évangile de saint Jean I–XX: 120 (1966), 157 (1970), 222 (1975), 290 (1982): Cécile Blanc.

Commentaire sur l'Évangile de saint Matthieu X–XI: 162 (1970): Robert Girod.

Contre Celse: 132 (1967), 136 (1968), 147 (1969), 150 (1969), 227 (1976): Marcel Borret.

Entretien avec Héraclide: 67 (1960): Jean Scherer.

Homélies sur la Genèse: 7 (1943) without the Latin text, 7 bis (1976): Henri de Lubac, Louis Doutreleau.

Homélies sur l'Exode: 16 (1947) without the Latin text: Henri de Lubac, Jean Fortier. New edition with the Latin text: 321 (1985): Marcel Borret.

Homélies sur le Lévitique: 286–287 (1981): Marcel Borret.

Homélies sur les Nombres: 29 (1951) without the Latin text: Andre Mehat. A new edition with the Latin text (29 bis) is in preparation.

Homélies sur Josué: 71 (1960): Annie Jaubert.

Homélies sur le Cantique: 37 (1953 and 37 bis (1966): Oliver Rousseau.

Homélies sur Jérémie: 232 (1976), 238 (1977): Pierre Husson and Pierre Nautin.

Homélies sur l'Evangile de saint Luc: 87 (1962): Henri Crouzel, François Fournier, Pierre Périchon.

Lettre à Africanus: 302 (1983): Nicholas de Lange.

Lettre à Grégoire le Thaumaturge: 148 (1969): Henri Crouzel.

Philocalie: 1–20: 302 (1983): Marguerite Harl.

Philocalie: 21–27 226 (1976): Eric Junod.

Traité des Principes: 252 and 253 (1978), 268 and 269 (1980), 312 (1984): Henri Crouzel and Manlio Simonetti.

Commentaire sur le Cantique: in preparation.

We mention additionally:

La Chaîne Palestinienne sur le Psaume 118 (which includes numerous fragments from Origen): 189 and 190 (1972): Marguerite Harl and Gilles Dorival.

Gregory Thaumaturgus: *Remerciement à Origène*: 148 (1969): Henri Crouzel.

Eusebius of Caesarea: *Histoire Ecclésiastique* tome II, books V–VIII (Book VI relates the life of Origen): 41 (1955 and 1965): Gustave Bardy.

Not in *Sources Chrétiennes*, with text and translation:

Origène, 2nd volume *Sur la Pâque*, Collection *Christianisme antique* 2 by Octave Guéraud and Pierre Nautin, Paris (Beauchesne) 1979.

Not in *Sources Chrétiennes*, in French translation only:

Origène, *De la Prière*, Exhortation au Martyre, by Gustave Bardy (Paris, Lecoffre-Gabalda) 1932.

Origène, *La Prière*, by A. G. Hamman, collection '*Les Pères dans la Foi*' *(Desclée de Brouwer)* 1977 (not complete).

The texts of Origen and other authors which have not been published in *Sources Chrétiennes* are cited by reference to the following collections or reviews:

J. P. Migne: *Patrologiae cursus completus; series graeca* (PG).

J. P. Migne: *Patrologiae cursus completus; series latina* (PL).

Die Griechischen Christlichen Schriftsteller (Berlin corpus) (GCS): the volume number quoted relates to the works of Origen or of the author concerned, not to the whole series.

Corpus Scriptorum Ecclesiasticorum Latinorum (Vienna corpus) (CSEL).

Corpus Christianorum, Turnhout (CChr).

Collection des Universitiés de France (CUFr).

Journal of Theological Studies (Oxford) *(JThs)*: for fragments on Pauline epistles.

When the work of Origen quoted has appeared in *Sources Chrétiennes* we indicate only the interior divisions of the text. When it has to be sought in other collections, we note the volume. Page, line, or column are only noted when the interior divisions of the text do not suffice for easy tracing of the passage.

The exegetical works of Origen are denoted by the following abbreviations: the title of the biblical book abbreviated according to the system of the Jerusalem Bible is preceded by:

Com: Commentary.

Hom: Homily.

Ser: Commentariorum series.

Fragm: Fragments.

Sel: Select.

Exc: Excerpta.

For the non-exegetical works:

CCels: Contra Celsum.

EntreHer: Dialogue with Heraclides.

Epist: Letter.

ExhMart: Exhortation to Martyrdom.

PArch: Peri Archon or Treatise on Principles.

PEuch: Peri Euches or Treatise on Prayer.

Philoc: Philocalia of Origen.

PPasch: Peri Pascha or On the Passover.

Resur: Treatise on the Resurrection.

Strom: Stromateis of Origen.

Sources for the life of Origen are:

Rem Orig: the Address of Thanks (Panegyric) of Gregory Thaumaturgus.
HE: Ecclesiastical History of Eusebius of Caesarea (see above).
ApolPamph: *Apology for Origen* by Pamphilus of Caesarea (PG 17, 521–616).
Bibl: *Bibliotheca* of Photius ed. René Henry (CUFr).
VirIll: *On illustrious men* by Jerome (PL 23, 602–720).
Epist: *Letters of Jerome*, ed. Jérôme Labourt in 8 volumes (CUFr).
Adult: *De Adulteratione* by Rufinus, ed. Manlio Simonetti (CChr XX, 7–17).
ApolRuf: *Apology against Rufinus*, ed. Pierre Lardet (SC 303).

The Author has supplied for this edition the following list of English translations of writings of Origen:

In *Ante-Nicene Christian Library* (ANCL) edited by A. Roberts and J. Donaldson, Edinburgh (Clark). American edition: *The Ante-Nicene Fathers*: General editor A. Cleveland Coxe, Buffalo (ANF).

ANCL vol. X (I or Origen's works) *De Principiis, Correspondence with Africanus, Letter to Gregory, Book I of Contra Celsum* (Fr. Crombie) 1869.

ANCL vol. XXIII (II of Origen's works) Books II to VIII of *Contra Celsum* (Fr. Crombie) 1872.

The same in ANF vol. IV.

ANCL vol. XX: The works of Gregory Thaumaturgus, Dionysius of Alexandria and Archelaus: Gregory Thaumaturgus, *The oration and panegyric addressed to Origen* (S. D. F. Salmond) 1871.

The same in ANF vol. VI.

ANCL additional volume, *Epistle to Gregory* and Origen's *Commentary on the Gospel of John* (only Books I, II, IV, V, VI, X) (A. Menzies), Origen's *Commentary on Matthew* (only Books I, II, X–XIV) (J. Patrick) 1897.

The same in ANF vol. IX.

In: *Ancient Christian writers* (ACW), Westminster Maryland (The Newman Press). London (Longman and Green).

Prayer, Exhortation to Martyrdom, ACW 19 (J. O'Meara) 1954.

The Song of Songs: Commentary and Homilies, ACW 26 (R. P. Lawson) 1957.

In: SPCK-Macmillan, London–New York:

Gregory Thaumaturgus, *Origen the Teacher* (W. Ch. Metcalfe) 1907. Second edition (with title: *Address to Origen*) 1920.

Treatise on Prayer (E. G. Jay) 1954.

On First Principles (G. W. Butterworth) 1936. Republished 1966 in Harper Torchbooks, New York (Harper and Row).

Other works:

Contra Celsum, Cambridge University Press, 1953 (H. Chadwick). Twice republished.

The Philocalia of Origen, Edinburgh (Clark) 1911 (G. Lewis).

Homilies on Genesis and Exodus. In: The Fathers of the Church 71, Washington D.C. (Catholic University of America Press) 1982 (R.E. Heine).

Selected extracts:

J. E. L. Oulton – H. Chadwick, *Alexandrian Christianity*: Selected translations of Clement and Origen, London, 1954 (From On Prayer, Exhortation to Martyrdom, Dialogue with Heraclides).

R. A. Greer. Origen: *An Exhortation to Martyrdom, Prayer, First Principles* Book IV, *Prologue to the Commentary on the Song of Songs, Homily XXVII on Numbers*. The Classics of Western Spirituality. New York, Ramsey; Toronto, Paulist Press, 1979.

Origen, *Spirit and Fire*: A thematic Anthology of his writings by Hans Urs von Balthasar, translated by Robert J. Daly, Washington D.C. (The Catholic University of America Press) 1982.

Part 1

PERSONALITY

I

The Life of Origen

The life of Origen is better known to us than that of any other writer of the ante-Nicene period, with the possible exception of Cyprian of Carthage: this is due to three principal sources and to a few secondary ones, in addition to occasional autobiographical details that can be gleaned from his writings. As he left Origen's school at Caesarea, one of his students, unanimously identified by tradition with the future apostle of Cappadocia and Pontus, St Gregory Thaumaturgus, made a valuable speech of thanks which, happily, has come down to us entire in its original language, Greek. The second part of this document describes precisely the curriculum followed by the master, while the whole tells us of the relations of Origen with his students and the moving affection felt for him by Gregory. Then Eusebius of Caesarea, who was the pupil of Origen's apologist, the martyr Pamphilus, whom he succeeded as curator of Origen's library and archives preserved in that town, devoted a large part of Book VI of his *Ecclesiastical History* to Origen's biography. His main source of information was Origen's voluminous correspondence, which he gathered into volumes and kept in the library at Caesarea.[1] Of the *Apology for Origen* that Pamphilus had composed in prison with the help of Eusebius we only have Book I in a Latin translation of Rufinus of Aquileia: the preface of this book, addressed by Pamphilus to the Christians who were condemned to labour in the mines of Palestine, contains precious hints on what Origen meant and how he should be understood. We are informed about the contents of the rest of the work by the chapter 118 of the *Bibliotheca* of Photius. Other scattered items are reproduced by various authors, Jerome, the historian Socrates, Photius and others: many seem to come from the missing volumes of Pamphilus's *Apology for Origen* or from lost works of Eusebius, such as his *Life of Pamphilus*.

Before relating Origen's life as it emerges from these different sources, mention must be made of the important critical work published on this subject by Pierre Nautin in 1977[2]: but we are not in full agreement with it. While recognising that there are certainly some interesting insights in this book, we do not agree in many cases with the criticisms expressed of Eusebius and other sources, which seem to us contrived, nor with the

[1] HE VI. XXXVI, 3-4.
[2] *Origène, sa vie et son oeuvre*, Paris, 1977.

alternative solutions put forward, which would be the better if their hypothetical and debatable character was acknowledged. A critical evaluation of this work would require to be developed beyond our present scope.[3] So, without concerning ourselves overmuch with criticism of Eusebius, we shall simply reproduce what the sources say and indicate approximately the main dates of the chronology that emerges.

Three main dates in the life of Origen can be determined from Eusebius's narrative, with a possible margin of error of a year or so either way. First, his date of birth, which can be worked out from the persecution of Septimius Severus in the tenth year of his reign, that is 202. At that time Origen 'was not yet quite seventeen',[4] which gives about 185–186 for his birth. Next, that of his death, in the time of Gallus, the successor of Decius, Origen, 'having completed seventy years, less one', that is being sixty-nine: the date of his death would then be 254–255.[5] The difficulty about this is that Gallus and his son Volusian were overthrown in May 253 and that they did not reign two years.[6] So we must suppose, either that Origen died under their successor Valerian, or that he did not live for quite sixty-nine years. Given the precision of this last figure, we give more weight to the dates 254–255 than we do the mention of Gallus's reign.

A third important date is that of Origen's departure from Alexandria to settle in Caesarea of Palestine, for that divides his life into two periods. According to most manuscripts of Eusebius this event took place in the tenth year of the reign of Alexander Severus, say 231: one manuscript only gives the twelfth year, say 233.[7] Eusebius subsequently points out that shortly after the departure of Origen Demetrius, the bishop of Alexandria, died, after holding his office for fully forty-three years. Earlier he had noted the accession of Demetrius in the tenth year of Commodus,[8] that is in 190. So Alexander would have died in 233 and that

---

[3] We have only dealt critically with one point. P. Nautin would deny that Gregory Thaumaturgus, future bishop of Neocaesarea in Pontus, was the author of the *Thanks to Origen*, but without regarding this as a fake, for he sees in it the work of a disciple of Origen, whom he calls Theodore, from the original name of Thaumaturgus according to Eusebius (HE, VI, XXX). As Origen's *Letter to Gregory* was in his view addressed neither to the orator of the *Thanks* nor to the bishop of Neocaesarea, who, in spite of the evidence from his Life by Gregory of Nyssa, had never heard Origen teach, its recipient must have been a third person, a young man whom Origen had advised about his studies. In an article ('Faut-il voir trois personnages en Grégoire le Thaumaturge', *Gregorianum* 60, 1979, 287–320) we discussed and rejected P. Nautin's criticism and used evidence which he does not mention, the above-mentioned *Life of Gregory Thaumaturgus* by Gregory of Nyssa (PG48, 893–958). We have not had the opportunity to deal similarly with the other statements of P. Nautin, but, having re-read his book several times, we judge them to be, in large measure, too disputable to be the basis of the chronology he derives from them.

[4] HE VI, II, 12.
[5] HE VII, 1.
[6] HE VII, X, 1.
[7] HE VI, XXVI.
[8] HE V, 22.

date makes it more likely that Origen settled in Caesarea in 233 than in 231.

Origen's times

Origen's lifetime was a troubled period, when emperors followed in quick succession, most of them assassinated, often by those who were to succeed them. The pressure of the barbarians, Germans on the Rhine and the Danube, Persians on the Euphrates, was becoming more and more severe and most of the emperors spent their time fighting on the frontiers. The relations of the state to the Catholic Church varied successively from hot to cold to lukewarm: there were three persecutions, two periods of peace and even of a relative favour, and several periods of indifference.

Origen was born in the reign of Commodus, unworthy son of the philosopher emperor Marcus Aurelius and the last of the dynasty of the Antonines, the most remarkable in the whole history of the empire, to which it gave, Commodus excepted, a series of princes who were all great men. But, although he was a tyrant and a madman, Commodus, unlike his father, left the Christians in peace, on account of his concubine Marcia, who thought well of Christianity: she was a concubine in the Roman sense, meaning what would later have been called a morganatic wife, one with whom legal marriage was impossible because of difference in rank. The assassination of Commodus in 192 was followed by a period of disturbance, from which Septimius Severus emerged as emperor in 193, founding the dynasty of the Severi. In 202 he started a persecution which was to last for several years in Egypt under a succession of prefects. His son, Antoninus Caracalla, 211–217, who assassinated his brother and fellow-sovereign, Geta, left the Christians in peace: likewise the usurper Macrinus (217–218) and the mad young Heliogabalus, Caracalla's cousin on the female side. But his cousin and successor, Alexander Severus (222–235), influenced by his mother, Julia Mammaea, the last of those Syrian princesses to whom the Severan dynasty owed much of its brilliance, offered the Christians not only peace but favour. The empress-mother dreamed of reconciling the Christians with Roman civilisation and the emperor set up in the private sanctuary, the 'lararium' of his palace, the statues of Abraham and Jesus.

On the assassination of Alexander Severus there succeeded a rough Thracian peasant, Maximin the Thracian, who again started persecution (235–238). On his death there were several competing for the throne. Unity was re-established under the young Gordian III, who left the Christians in peace. Assassinated by his soldiers while fighting the Persians, he was succeeded by his chief general, who mounted the throne in 244 by putting to death his predecessor's young son. Now this new emperor, an Arab from the Hauran, Philip the Arabian, seems in fact to have been the first Christian emperor, in spite of the crime with which his reign began, a crime for which he was subjected to penance by the bishop of Antioch, Babylas – which suggests that he was baptised. This public penance during an Easter vigil is attested by three independent witnesses, Eusebius, John Chrysostom and the *Chronicon Paschale*.[9] Becuase of the favour he showed to the Christians, crowds joined the Church and Origen then laments in his homilies the lowering of the moral and spiritual standards that ensued. But the celebrations marking the thousandth year of the city of Rome revived patriotic sentiment and the prestige of the traditional religion. Several competitors arose against the emperor who was putting the old religion at risk by the favour he was according to Christianity. Philip overcame three of these candidates; the fourth, Decius, defeated and killed him in 249. Described in an inscription as *restitutor sacrorum*,[10] a title conferred on no others except Julian the Apostate, Decius required every subject of the empire to sacrifice to the gods in the presence of a commission that would record the act: we possess several certificates of this kind. This measure brought on the first persecution of which it could be said that it was truly universal: its repercussions on the Christians are known to us mainly through the correspondence of Cyprian of Carthage and that of Dionysius of Alexandria, preserved by Eusebius. It ended in 251 with the death of Decius, who was succeeded by Gallus and his son Volusian. They were conquered and killed in 251 and succeeded by Valerian and his son Gallienus.

Origen at Alexandria

In all probability Origen was born of parents already Christian: or if they were not so at the time of his birth, they became so shortly afterwards, for he received from his father a Christian education.[11]

Origen's father is mentioned by Eusebius in the first chapter of Book VI as one of the martyrs of the persecution of Septimius Severus. His name was Leonides.[12]

---

[9] HE VI, XXXIV: from John Chrysostom, *Panegyric of Saint Babilas*, PG 50, 539–544; for the *Chronicon Paschale*, ed. Dindorf, *Corpus Scriptorum Historiae Byzantinae* I, 1832, p. 503. On all the above H. Crouzel, 'Le christianisme de l'empereur Philippe l'Arabe', *Gregorianum* 56, 1975, 545–550.

[10] See *L'Année épigraphique* 1973, p. 63. Une inscription de Cosa (Ansedonia).

[11] It has sometimes been thought that Origen's parents were still pagans at the time of his birth because they gave their son a pagan name. Origen seems to mean 'son of Horus', an Egyptian god, son of Isis and Osiris, symbolising the rising sun: the name Horus was usually written with the rough breathing, but sometimes with the smooth. But there was no shortage of Christians in the first centuries, who, though born Christians, bore names derived from pagan deities. As for Porphyry's assertion contrasting Ammonius Saccas, born a Christian and turned Greek, with Origen, born and educated as a Greek but turned Christian (Eusebius HE, VI, XIX 7), this is contradicted by Eusebius who, on this point at least, should be considered more reliable. We shall return to this point later.

[12] Leonides, Ionian form, and not Leonidas, Dorian form: he is often called by the latter name, because the form in – as is better known on account of Leonidas of Sparta.

On this matter Eusebius uses a curious expression: 'Leonides, who is said to be the father of Origen'. Must we necessarily conclude from this as P. Nautin does, that Eusebius did not know the name of Origen's father and that he arbitrarily gave him as father a well-known Alexandrian martyr? Or should we accept G. Bardy's[13] point 'A strange formula: perhaps it arises from the fact that Leonides owed most his fame to his son?' Was Origen baptised as an infant? It is not unlikely, for he is himself one of the main witnesses for infant baptism in this period. If many known Christians of the fourth century, from Christian families, were not baptised until they were adult, there is sufficient evidence of the baptism of infants in the third century for us to be able to ask the question. But we must confine ourselves to suppositions: no source tells us anything about the age at which Origen was baptised.

Origen received from his father a double education. Hellenic and Biblical. So he went through the whole cycle of the *enkyklios paideia*, of the 'encyclical subjects' which corresponded to our secondary education and was preparatory to the study of philosophy.[14] But at the same time his father had him study the Bible, checking what he read and making him recite it, though not always having the answer to the embarrassing questions the child asked him. This passage from Eusebius,[15] which tells first of Origen's attitude at the time of his father's martyrdom – to which we shall return – and then of his upbringing by Leonides which clearly took place earlier, has been called in question by many historians, apparently unaccustomed to ancient rhetoric and thinking its highly hagiographical tone unauthentic. It is here that we read of the father's gesture when he uncovered the child's chest and kissed it as the dwelling of the Holy Spirit. But it does not follow from this hagiographical tone that we should brand as a fabrication everything that Eusebius tells us.

Leonides was certainly an important man. The fact that he was beheaded[16] seems to show that he was a Roman citizen, a status that had not yet been widely accorded throughout the empire, as it would be in 212 by the edict of Caracalla or the Antonine constitution: a Roman citizen could not be executed in any other way. Now if we are to believe the *Historia Augusta*,[17] the main aim of Septimius Severus's persecution was to prevent proselytism: the prosecution of Leonides shows that he must have played a certain part in the training of catechumens in the Church of Alexandria. Furthermore the education that he gave to his son shows that he was an intellectual who, in addition to the common Hellenic curriculum, had assiduously studied the Bible. Perhaps he was a

[13] SC 41, p. 82 note 3.
[14] Origen's *Letter to Gregory*, 2: SC 148, p. 188.
[15] HE VI, II, 1–15.
[16] HE VI, I.
[17] Severus XVII, 1.

teacher of grammar, that is of literature: it was that profession his son took up, after the father's death, to support the family.

As for Origen's mother, we do not even know her name. The only thing we know of her from Eusebius is that, dismayed by her elder son's determination to join his father in martyrdom, she hid his clothes to force him to stay indoors.[18] Aline Rousselle's article on 'The persecution of the Christians at Alexandria in the third century'[19] gives reason for thinking that she was not of the same social status as her husband: there were in fact in Alexandria three classes of freemen, the Roman citizens, the citizens of Alexandria and of the other Greek cities in Eygpt, and finally 'Egyptians', a group that comprised also Greeks not belonging to the two higher classes. It seems that children born to a marriage between parents of different classes took the lower of the two ranks and that the persecution of Septimius Severus was aimed at the two higher classes. That would explain how, with the persecution going on at Alexandria for years, Origen was able to carry on intensively catechising without being seriously harassed by the police, even daring to accompany to their execution pupils of his who were martyrs.[20] So it would seem that Origen did not share his father's status as a Roman citizen, but that of his mother who must have been an Egyptian.

Of the behaviour of the young man at the time of his father's arrest and martyrdom Eusebius reports, in addition to the episode of the clothes hidden by his mother to prevent him going out, that he wrote a letter to Leonides exhorting him to suffer martyrdom and saying 'word for word' (*kata lexin*): 'Be careful not to change your mind because of us'.[21]

After the martyrdom of Leonides the family fortune had been confiscated by the imperial exchequer and Origen, the eldest of the family, found himself at the age of seventeen with his mother and six younger brothers and sisters in want. For a few months he continued his studies, thanks to the generosity of a rich Christian lady who took him into her home. But this lady also held in high esteem a heretic – of which sect we do not know – a man from Antioch called Paul whom she treated like a son. Origen, living in the same house, never agreed, says Eusebius, to join in the prayer meetings that he organised, which were attended not only by the heretics but also by members of the Great Church. During this time he was qualifying to teach grammar (literature), and this he did at the age of eighteen at the most, thus in large part earning his own living and probably his family's.[22]

[18] HE VI, II, 5.
[19] *Revue historique de Droit français et étranger*, 1974/2, pp. 222–251: see 231–233.
[20] HE VI, IV, 1.
[21] HE VI, II, 6: Did Eusebius have in front of him, among the numerous letters of Origen that he possessed, the text of this one? It has been doubted, but the expression *kata lexin* seems to suggest that he had.
[22] HE VI, II, 12–15.

Another of Eusebius's statements is not without its difficulties: Origen, he says, was among the pupils of Clement, who succeeded Pantaenus as director of catechesis at Alexandria.[23] Some think, in spite of his observation, that the school conducted by Pantaenus and Clement was not an official church institution as Origen's was to be, but a private school as were most of those in which rhetors and philosophers taught at the time. If Origen was in truth a pupil of Clement this must have been before he was seventeen, before the prosecution of Septimius Severus, since Eusebius tells us that at that time 'no one was in charge of the catechetical teaching, but all had been driven away by the threat of persecution'.[24] So Clement must also have left Alexandria, to which, it seems, he never returned. As for the relations between Origen and Clement, certain comments need to be made. Origen never quotes Clement by name, although he does so quote several other previous Christian writers, admittedly only a few. He sometimes alludes to doctrines held by Clement, but he introduces them by such formulas as: 'as one of our predecessors said' (tis tôn pro hemôn)[25] or 'as certain authorities report' (sicut quidam tradunt).[26] Certain features of vocabulary seem to show a reaction to Clement. Thus Origen never applies to the spiritual man the adjective gnōstikos which Clement constantly uses: Origen seems more concerned than Clement to distinguish his own position from that of the 'false gnosis'. While Clement always speaks of apatheia as the essential virtue of the spiritual man, occurrences of apatheia and apathēs in Origen's writings can be counted on the fingers of one hand and his teaching is nearer to metriopatheia, the restraint to be imposed on the passions, rather than apatheia itself. It is difficult to be sure, from the facts that Origen does not quote Clement by name and that he seems to have reacted against some features of his teaching and language, whether he had been, or had not been, among Clement's hearers, for in any case he certainly knew his works.

But to the teaching of grammar which assured his livelihood and that of his family Origen would add while still young the teaching of another subject. As, according to Eusebius, all those who had been previously responsible for catechesis had left the city, certain pagans who wanted to know about the Christian faith applied to him. Eusebius mentions among the first Plutarch, who would soon become a martyr, and his brother, Heraclas, Origen's future collaborator and successor, eventually bishop of Alexandria after Demetrius. It was in this way that by the age of

---

[23] HE VI, VI.

[24] HE VI, III, 1.

[25] ComMt XIV, 2 (GCS X): reference is to the interpretation of Matt. 18, 19–20 by Clement in Stromateis III, 10, 68, 1 (GCS Clement II).

[26] ComRm I, 1 in PG 14, 839B interpretation of syzygos in Phil. 4, 3 by Clement in Stromateis III, 6, 53, 1 (GCS Clement II).

eighteen Origen 'was presiding over the school of catechesis' which had been entrusted to him by the bishop Demetrius.[27] It was thus an official office that the young man held in the Church of Alexandria.

But how long did he cope with both kinds of teaching? Eusebius does not tell us, but a moment came when he 'judged incompatible the teaching of the grammatical subjects and the exercise of the divine disciplines' and when he devoted all his energies to catechesis. Probably by that time his brothers had grown up and taken over the support of the family, setting him free for the service of the Church. At this point he sold all the manuscripts that he possessed, some of them 'transcribed with great care', perhaps Leonides's library spared by the exchequer; he was to receive from the purchaser an income of four obols a day which would have to suffice for his sustenance. Six obols were the equivalent of one denarius, which represented a very low daily wage.[28] This gesture of selling his library marks a complete renunciation of secular studies. But he was not slow to realise that secular knowledge was of great value in explaining the Scriptures and for his missionary work, and he would soon return to what he had intended to abandon.

At Alexandria the persecution continued under several prefects in succession and Origen was many times over threatened by the mob, notably when he attended Plutarch at his execution. Several of his pupils were martyred[29] and he himself lived the life of a wanted man, while still carrying out his duties as a catechist.[30] But he was not arrested by the police nor brought before the authorities: that has seemed strange to some historians and they have suspected Eusebius of manipulating the story. Aline Rousselle's article quoted above offers a credible explanation of the position.

The young teacher led a life that was in other ways extremely austere; Eusebius describes his ascetic practices in a passage that had an influence on primitive monasticism.[31] Origen takes the precepts of the Gospel so seriously, says Eusebius, that 'he performed an action which gave strong proof of an inexperienced and youthful heart but also of faith and self-control'. He in fact took literally the verse in St Matthew's Gospel 19, 12: 'There are those who have made themselves eunuchs for the sake of the

[27] HE, VI, III, 1–8.
[28] Two centuries earlier, in Matt. 20, 1–16, one denarius represented the day's wage which the lord of the vineyard gave to his agricultural workers in the Parable of the Labourers.
[29] HE VI, IV, 1–3.
[30] HE VI, III, 6.
[31] The ascetic life is twice called by the historian the 'philosophic life' following a usage found again in the *Thanks* of Gregory Thaumaturgus and common enough in primitive monasticism: Philosophy, even pagan philosophy, is not a purely intellectual exercise, but involves a man's whole way of life.

kingdom of heaven' and he performed on himself the operation in question, Eusebius does not tell us how.[32]

What were the motives of this deed? Writers of our own time, when they speak of it, often suggest reasons such as 'horror of sex', an explanation bearing indeed the stamp of our age, adducing the desire – and the illusion – of fleeing the temptations that could have assailed him at that point. In fact Eusebius, our sole informant, mentions two other motives. The first is expressed in this way: 'whether he thought to accomplish the Lord's word'. In that case he would have felt obliged to take literally a word which the tradition of the Church did not understand in that way, so in a way lining up, in his youth, with those literalists whom he contested so harshly for all the rest of his life. It is indeed intriguing to find the one who is held to be the 'prince of allegory' taking literally a verse which earlier tradition had usually understood allegorically. A sin of youth, it will be said. But the second motive suggested by Eusebius presents more difficulty: 'Whether also because, being then young, he was preaching divinity not only to men but also to women and, desiring to eliminate every pretext for shameful calumny on the part of unbelievers he was led to carry out literally the Saviour's word. 'If by this act Origen had really wanted to avoid scandal and calumny it would have been natural for him to have made it widely known. Now Eusebius, in the very sentence that we have just quoted, says that Origen took care that his action was hidden from most of the disciples that surrounded him.' This information seems to contradict the second motive. After Hadrian's time castration was prohibited under Roman law. It is incredible that the Church should have approved of it. According to Eusebius, Demetrius knew of it later and admired Origen. But at the time of the quarrel that arose between the bishop and his catechist, because of Origen's ordination to the priesthood at Caesarea of

[32] The mutilation – the only thing the general public usually knows about Origen – has been questioned by some scholars. They have noted, for one thing, that we only know about it through this passage from Eusebius (HE VI, VIII, 1–5); now *testis unus testis nullus*. But Eusebius who is an ardent supporter of Origen can be believed even more readily when he reports something to the discredit of his hero, showing that his zeal was unbalanced. These scholars, moreover, rely on the interpretation given by Origen of this verse when, in his sixties, he was composing the Commentary on Matthew (XV, 1–5, GCS X). It is true that in this writing, Origen, without alluding to his own case, vehemently blames those who understand in a literal sense the third kind of eunuchs in Matt. 19, 12, and 'dare' with more zeal than intelligence to commit such an 'outrage' on themselves: in accordance with a tradition for which there is evidence before his time, notably in Clement who often uses the word *eunouchia* to describe celibacy undertaken for the Kingdom of Heaven's sake, Origen only admits this spiritual meaning. But the explanations given by Origen in the *Commentary on Matthew* do not seem to us to allow doubt of the statement made by Eusebius. Origen has sufficient humility – humility and modesty are virtues normally attributed to him by those who have studied him seriously – to blame in his old age an act that he had committed in his youth. Furthermore he speaks of the physiological problems resulting from castration in a way that seems to derive from personal experience: these he explains in accordance with the scientific concepts of Greek physicians.

Palestine without his permission, he announced the castration publicly
and condemned it.³³ We shall have to return to this incident later.

Eusebius gives a lot of information about the teaching work of Origen
at Alexandria, which was perhaps rather different from what he would do
in Caesarea as described in Thaumaturgus's *Address of Thanks*. There
came a time when, in view of the numbers of those seeking to hear him, in
order to keep enough time for his study of the Scriptures, Origen had to
divide his school into two courses. He took as his colleague his pupil
Heraclas, the brother of the martyr Plutarch: Heraclas had already
studied philosophy at the school of the most famous Alexandrian
philosopher of the day, Ammonius Saccas, the father of Neo-Platonism.
Origen handed over to him the teaching of the catechumens in the strict
sense of the term and himself took charge of the more advanced
students.³⁴ Eusebius describes in terms of rhetorical exaggeration the
crowds that came to follow his teaching on the Scriptures: among them
were heretics and even renowned philosophers. At this time Origen went
back to the secular studies that he had renounced when he sold his
library. To the more advanced students he taught philosophy together
with the subjects preparatory to it like geometry and arithmetic: he
expounded the teaching of the different schools of philosophers,
explained their writings, to the point where he himself acquired the
reputation of being a great philosopher. To the less advanced he was
content to teach the 'encyclical subjects' because of their usefulness in
explaining the Scriptures. 'He also thought it quite necessary, even for
himself, to practise secular disciplines and philosophy'.³⁵

Origen was certainly already the head of the catechetical school when
he began to attend the lectures of Ammonius Saccas, which Heraclas had
already been doing for five years. Ammonius, a few years later, would be
the teacher of Plotinus, the founder of neo-platonism, who was twenty
years junior to Origen. Our principal source on this is chapter XIX of
Book VI of the *Ecclesiastical History*,³⁶ which first reproduces a passage
from a book written against the Christians by Porphyry, the disciple of
Plotinus,³⁷ and a passage from a letter by Origen. The difficulty of
reconciling what Porphyry there says with the same author's *Life of
Plotinus,* has occasioned among scholars who specialise in neo-platonism
and in the works of Origen, divergent opinions and attempts to reconcile
the discrepancies. It cannot be said that the questions raised by these texts
have so far come near to being answered.

After criticising the use by the Christians of allegorical exegesis, which,

³³ HE, VI, VIII, 1–5.
³⁴ HE, VI, XV.
³⁵ HE, VI, XVIII, 2–4.
³⁶ §§1–14.
³⁷ Usually published as a foreword to the *Enneads* of Plotinus (cf. ed. Bréhier CUFr).

however, he does not hesitate to use himself, for example in the case of the *Cave of the Nymphs*, Porphyry attributes this practice to Origen whom he knew, he says, when he himself was young. This was probably at Caesarea, for Porphyry was born about 233 at the time when Origen was settling in that town. Porphyry bears witness to the considerable reputation that Origen and his works enjoyed. He states that he attended the lectures of Ammonius Saccas and he draws a contrast between the conduct of Ammonius who left the Christianity in which he was born for Hellenism, which alone was lawful, and that of Origen who left the Hellenism in which he had been brought up for that 'barbarous enterprise' (*barbaron ... tolmēma*) which is Christianity, unlawful. Origen lived as a Christian and thought as a Greek. He was always reading Plato and a whole lot of philosophers whom Porphyry lists: platonist-pythagoreans like Numenius, Chronios, Longinus, Moderatus, Nichomachus, stoics like Apollophanes, Chēremon (Nero's tutor) or Cornutus who taught the Latin poet Persius. Eusebius, after reproducing this passage of Porphyry, contradicts it at several points: Ammonius did not cease to be a Christian and Origen was born and brought up a Christian. Eusebius is right on the second point, but on the first he may have confused Saccas with another Ammonius who was a Christian, the author of a book he mentions, *The Harmony of Moses and Jesus*. Eusebius then reproduces a passage from a letter of Origen's justifying to opponents his philosophical studies as a means of winning for Christ the heretics and philosophers who approached him and relying on the example of Pantaenus, who taught Clement, and of Heraclas, his own disciple, who five years before Origen had attended the lectures of the 'master of philosophical subjects', Ammonius Saccas, and who, now that he was a priest in the Church of Alexandria, always wore the philosopher's gown.[38]

We have just pointed out that this passage is difficult to reconcile with what the same Porphyry says in his *Life of Plotinus*. Without going into the details of the problem or attempting to solve it here, we shall, however, explain what it is about. It is in fact a question of Ammonius Saccas and of his more esoteric teaching, given to three of his hearers Origen, Plotinus and Herennius. Because of certain discrepancies between what Porphyry says and what is known of Origen, specialists in neo-platonism see here an Origen other than the Christian, an 'Origen the pagan' or 'the neo-platonist', and to him they attribute also the exegeses of texts of Plato which Proclus cites as being by Origen. These twin Origens, of which antiquity seems to have been unaware, were asserted for the first time in the seventeenth century by Henri de Valois in a note to his edition of Eusebius's *Ecclesiastical History*.[39] In spite of the

[38]HE VI, XIX, 1–14.
[39] Reproduced in PG 20, 563–564, note 17, corresponding to HE VI, XIX, 5–8.

reasons on which the idea is based, reasons put forward by Henri de
Valois and by the historians of neo-platonism, many students of Origen
are unconvinced. Certainly, if there was only one Origen, it has to be
admitted that Porphyry was mistaken on one point or the other, but if
there were two there are also mistakes of Porphyry's to be accepted.
Many of the characteristics which seem to those who support the dual
theory incompatible with the Christian Origen are, their opponents say,
only deemed such because they do not know enough about Origen's
thought. Besides, it seems astonishing that the same Porphyry who, in his
treatise *Against the Christians* reports that the Christian Origen listened
to Ammonius Saccas and that he was very famous, should bring into his
Life of Plotinus another Origen, learning from the same master, without
taking the trouble to distinguish between them. We make no claim to
offer in these brief notes any final solution to a problem which seems to
us still obscure.

In a chapter devoted to the composition by Origen of his *Hexapla*
Eusebius mentions in passing that Origen learned Hebrew and here are
several references, two of them in the *Treatise on First Principles*, to a
Hebrew teacher who must have been a Jewish Christian, for the exegesis
he gave to Origen of Isaiah 6, 3 'Holy, holy, holy', is Christian.[40] Was
this the one who taught him Hebrew? This knowledge on Origen's part
has been seriously questioned. Scholars have often rejected the statement
of Eusebius and have affirmed that Origen knew no Hebrew at all and
that the allusions to 'Hebrew copies' of the Bible, sometimes found in his
works, simply mean the literal Greek translation by Aquila. But there can
be all manner of levels in one's knowledge of a language. Certainly it
would be wrong to credit Origen with a knowledge of Hebrew like
Jerome's, but he must have had enough to be able to direct the
compilation of the *Hexapla*, even if the actual work was done by some
assistant.

Another objection raised to the same statement derives from the fact
that Origen always comments on the Septuagint, even where it is most
obviously wrong and where he knows full well what is in the Hebrew.
But for Origen, as for all the Fathers before Jerome, the Greek Bible of
the Seventy was the text that the Apostles had given to the Church, the
official text that Christians had to follow. If there are in it passages that
are hard to understand, they must be reckoned among those 'stumbling
blocks' which the Holy Spirit has put in the Bible in order to persuade
readers to rise to the spiritual meaning. The use made by Origen of the
Septuagint even in these cases does not mean that he was ignorant of
Hebrew but derives from a theological motive.

[40] *Hebraeus magister* in I, 3, 4; *Hebraeus doctor* in IV, 3, 14.

Anticipating for a moment the Caesarean period of his life, we note the very extensive knowledge that he had of Jewish traditions and customs, as well as of rabbinic interpretations, as a recent study has shown.[41] He got this partly from personal relations with rabbis. In the preface to his *Commentary on the Psalms* he says that he sought explanations on the title of a psalm from the patriarch Ioullos and from someone who was said to be a scholar among the Jews. This Ioullos is thought by some to be a rabbi Hillel, who was not a patriarch but the son and brother of patriarchs. It is also believed, on the evidence of Talmudic texts that he was in contact with a famous rabbi of Caesarea, Hoschaia Rabba.

It was comparatively late, between 215 and 220, that Origen began to write his voluminous works. This new activity seems to be related to the conversion of a Valentinian named Ambrose, a rich man who had gone over to heresy in the great intellectual sect of Valentinus, because he had not found in the Great Church the food for thought that it was his right to expect. When he was brought back to orthodoxy by Origen he naturally wanted to get from his master what he had previously sought in vain. He put his fortune at Origen's disposal, maintaining for him a secretariat and a publishing house with seven tachygraphers (i.e. stenographers) who took it in turn to write from his dictation, and with copyists and calligraphers. To Ambrose's zeal for study and the pressure that he exerted on Origen in the respect, Eusebius[42] and Origen himself both testify. In a fragment of the preface to Book V of the *Commentary on John* Origen calls him, with a certain irony, 'God's taskmaster' in comparison with the Egyptian taskmasters who made the Hebrews work before the Exodus[43] and in a letter[44] he gently complains of the life his collaborator leads him. It can be said that the situation exemplified in Ambrose's case was the underlying motive for Origen's writings. The major text expressing this is to be found in Book V of the *Commentary on John:*[45]

'But even now the heterodox, with a pretext of knowledge (= gnōsis), are rising up against the holy Church of Christ and are bringing compositions in many books, announcing an interpretation of the texts both of the Gospels and of the apostles. If we are silent and do not set the true and sound teachings down in opposition to them, they will prevail over inquisitive souls which, in the lack of saving nourishment, hasten to foods that are forbidden and are truly unclean and abominable.

For this reason it seems necessary to me that one who is able to intercede in a genuine manner on behalf of the teaching of the Church and reprove those who pursue the knowledge (gnōsis) falsely so-called, must take a stand against the heretical fabrications by adducing in opposition the

[41] N. de Lange *Origen and the Jews,* Cambridge, 1976.
[42] HE VI, XVII, 1 and VI, XXIII, 1–2.
[43] See SC 120, p. 372; this expression is also reported in Jerome's notice 61 of *VirIll.*
[44] Preserved by the Byzantine chronicler George Kedrenos, PG 121, 485 BC.
[45] §8: Fr translation by Blanc, SC 120, pp. 388–391.

sublimity of the gospel message, which has been fulfilled in the agreements of the common doctrines in what is called the Old Testament with that which is called the New. Therefore, because of the lack of those interceding for the better things, you yourself, because of your love for Jesus, once devoted yourself to their teachings, since you do not bear a faith that is irrational or unlearned. Later, in good time having judged them unfavourably by using the understanding which has been given you, you abandoned them.'[a]

To provide Christians who raise intellectual problems with answers in accordance with Scripture, so that they do not go and seek them in great gnōstic sects, that is one of the major aims of Origen's literary work.

To complete this depiction of the first period of Origen's life, we must mention, still using Eusebius as our source, the main journeys that he made at that time. The first, dated by Eusebius in the pontificate of Pope Zephyrinus (198–217), had Rome as its goal, Origen having, in his own words reported by Eusebius, 'wished to see the ancient Church of the Romans'.[46] Was this the time when he heard, as Jerome reports,[47] a 'homily (prosomilian) in praise of the Saviour' preached by Hippolytus in which the speaker drew attention to the presence of Origen at his sermon. It may be so, but to be sure of it we should need to know more about Hippolytus himself. This visit to Rome shows the importance of the Church, as does also the letter which Origen is said by Jerome[48] to have written to Pope Fabian denying the charges brought against him in Alexandria.

A second journey is somewhat remarkable and must have taken place, if we can rely on the chronology of Eusebius, about 215 or a little earlier. A soldier came to Alexandria with letters from the governor of the Roman province of Arabia, present day Jordan, addressed to bishop Demetrius and the prefect of Egypt: these requested that Origen be immediately sent to talk to him. Probably this governor wanted to get to know about Christianity from one of the leading personalities of the new religion. We are in the reign of Caracalla: the Christians are more or less at peace and it is known that the princesses of the imperial family, Julia Domna, widow of Septimius Severus and mother of the reigning emperor, her sister Julia Moesa and the latter's two daughters, Julia Soemias and Julia Mammaea, are very interested in religious questions, although the first three of these scarcely paid any particular attention to Christianity. Origen, says Eusebius, quickly carried out this mission and returned to Alexandria.[49]

---

[a] English translation by permission from R. Heine Origen's Commentary on the Gospel according to St John, vol. I, vv. 1–10. Dallas Christian College (not yet published at time of writing).

[46] HE VI, XIV, 10.

[47] VirIll 61.

[48] Letters 84, 10 to Pammachius and Oceanus.

[49] HE VI, XIX, 15.

But 'in the interval', that is between his departure and his return, 'a considerable war (had) broken out in the city'. The emperor Caracalla had arrived in Alexandria and had been the butt of gibes on the part of the student population which greeted him as 'Geticus', an ironical title of honour because he had assassinated his brother Geta. Caracalla in his fury put the city to sack and slaughter, closed the schools and exiled the faculty. Then it was, according to Eusebius, that Origen left the city in secret and withdrew for the first time to Caesarea of Palestine, where the bishops of the country, notably Theoctistus of Caesarea and Alexander of Aelia, that is Jerusalem, not wishing to miss the chance afforded them by the presence of so distinguished a biblical scholar, invited him to expound the Scriptures to the congregation, although he was still a layman. Back in Alexandria, Demetrius heard about this and made a protest to the Palestinian bishops, saying that it was contrary to tradition: 'It has never been heard of and it never happens now that laymen preach homilies in the presence of bishops'. Theoctistus and Alexander retorted in a letter – which is possibly later and contemporary with the great crisis of 231–233 – saying that this statement was manifestly incorrect. They quoted cases showing that 'where there are men capable of doing good to the brethren, they are invited by the holy bishops to address the people'. But Demetrius was all the same quick to recall his catechist, sending letters and deacons for the purpose.[50]

On the occasion of this first sojourn by Origen in Palestine we must say something about one of the bishops who received him and became for him a friend and protector, Alexander of Jerusalem. At the beginning of the century, at a date we cannot fix precisely, Narcissus was governing the Church of Jerusalem, or rather Aelia, to give it the official name conferred by the emperor Hadrian, after his own *gens*, to the city that he had rebuilt.[51] This Narcissus, venerated for his virtues and his miracles, became the victim of grave calumnies and, probably attacked by what we should call today nervous depression, disappeared into the wilderness, while his accusers perished miserably of accidents and sickness that they had called down on themselves as guarantee of their oaths. Then the neighbouring bishops, disturbed by the disappearance of Narcissus, appointed to the see of Jerusalem three successive bishops who only reigned a few months each. The third was still there when Narcissus re-appeared and was immediately restored to office: but advanced old age prevented him from carrying out his duties and the population of the city, at the bidding of a divine revelation, seized a bishop from Cappadocia, named Alexander, who was on pilgrimage to Jerusalem, and compelled him to assist Narcissus and then to succeed him. Eusebius reports passages of several letters that he wrote, including one to Origen in which

[50] HE VI, XIX, 16–19.
[51] HE V, XII, 2.

he mentions his past relations with Pantaenus and Clement.[52] This
Alexander founded at Jerusalem a library which Eusebius used, as well as
the one in Caesarea which originated in the library and the archives of
Origen.[53]

Another question can be asked about this first sojourn of Origen's at
Caesarea of Palestine. In his *Historia Lausiaca*, Palladius reports the
following concerning a virgin called Juliana:[54]

> It is also said that there was at Caesarea of Cappadocia a virgin named
> Juliana, of great wisdom and faith. She took in the writer Origen when he
> fled from the rising of the Greeks and hid him for three years, providing
> him with rest at her own expense and caring for him herself. All that I
> found, mentioned in Origen's own handwriting in a very old book written
> in verses. These were the words: 'I found this book at the house of the
> virgin Juliana at Caesarea when I was hiding there. She said she had got it
> from Symmachus himself, the Jewish commentator.'

Writers usually understand by this 'rising of the Greeks' the persecution
of Maximin the Thracian in 235 and accordingly suppose that at that time
Origen had to leave Caesarea of Palestine where he had settled and hide at
Caesarea of Cappadocia. Eusebius, who had also read the same note on
the manuscript which was to be found in his day in the library at Caesarea
in Palestine, reports that the commentaries of the Ebionite Symmachus –
Ebionism was a Judaeo-Christian heresy – were to be found there and
that Origen 'indicates that he had received these works with other
interpretations of the Scriptures by Symmachus from a certain Juliana,
who, he says, had inherited these books from Symmachus himself'.[55] This
passage follows the chapter in which Eusebius explains how Origen
composed the *Hexapla*:[56] Symmachus was the author of one of the four
Greek versions which were collated in it. These chapters relate to the
Alexandrian period of Origen's life.

Chapter XXVII, which relates to the Caesarean period, mentions
among Origen's hearers Firmilian, the bishop of Caesarea in Cappadocia,
who is said first to have sent for him 'for the good of the Churches in his
country' and then to have spent some time with him 'in Judaea'. So it
might be supposed that Maximin's persecution broke out at the moment
when Origen had gone to Cappadocia summoned by Firmilian and that
he had then hidden in Juliana's house to avoid pursuit. But this solution
fails to account for several silences that are difficult to explain. Why does
not Eusebius, who had also read Origen's note about Juliana, mention
this stay of two years in her home? Is that stay compatible with his
writing the *Exhortation to martyrdom* which he sent during Maximin's

[52] HE VI, IX-XI and VI, XIV, 8–9.
[53] HE VI, XX, 1.
[54] 147, PG 34, 1250 D.
[55] HE, VI, XVII.
[56] HE VI, XVI.

persecution to his patron Ambrose and to the priest Protoctetus, both threatened with arrest? Finally and especially, the *Thanks to Origen*[57] of Gregory Thaumaturgus, who arrived in Caesarea of Palestine shortly after Origen, and spent five years with him,[58] five years which covered the time of Maximin's persecution gives no hint that his master was absent for so long.

We also wonder whether it is not right to see in the 'rising of the Greeks', not Maximin's persecution, but the troubles in Alexandria when Caracalla visited the city and to suppose that Palladius confused the two Caesareas, mentioning the Cappadocian one when it should have been the Palestinian. The fact is that the note in Origen's handwriting which he read and which is the source of his information does not say which Caesarea is meant and as the manuscript which contained it was found among the books that Origin left to the library of Caesarea in Palestine, it would seem more likely that the latter is meant. However, it is possible that Palladius knew from some other source that Juliana lived in Caesarea of Cappadocia.

A final journey, very much to Origen's credit, preceded the great crisis. He accepted an invitation from the empress Julia Mammaea, the mother of Alexander Severus, who was, as we have said above, the inspiration behind her son's policy of favouring the Christians: 'As Origen's renown spread everywhere and even came to her ears, she thought it very important to be favoured with the sight of this man and to sample his understanding of divine matters which everyone was admiring. While staying at Antioch, she sent for him by some soldiers of her guard; and he stayed some time with her, expounding to her a great many things to the glory of the Lord and to the advantage of sacred studies; then he hastened to resume his usual occupations'.[59] Origen himself mentions in his *Letter to friends in Alexandria*[60] a stay in Antioch, where he had to refute the calumny of a heretic whom he had already confronted in Ephesus. The interest shown by Julia Mammaea in the Christian religion, further evidenced by the treatise on the resurrection that Hippolytus dedicated to her, does not mean that she became a Christian.

The great crisis
On the quarrel between Origen and Demetrius which forced the former to leave Alexandria for Caesarea of Palestine we are informed by several sources: Eusebius HE VI, VIII, 4–5; VI, XXIII 5; Photius in *Bibliotheca* 118[61] where he reproduces what he read in Pamphilus's *Apology for*

---

[57] V, 63.
[58] HE, VI, XXX.
[59] HE VI, XXI, 3–4.
[60] Preserved by Rufinus in Adult 8.
[61] CUFr II.

Origen; Jerome in *Letter 33 to Paula*;[62] and from Origen himself *A Letter to friends in Alexandria*, preserved in part by Jerome, *Apology against Rufinus*[63] and in part by Rufinus, *De adulteratione librorum Origenis*;[64] and the Preface to Book VI of the *Commentary on John*.[65] From these documents we can attempt to reconstruct the course of events.

In 231 or 233, depending on what has been said above, 'Origen, to meet the urgent requirements of ecclesiastical affairs, went to Greece via Palestine', reports Eusebius.[66] Photius says that he left 'for Athens without the permission of his bishop'. What were these 'ecclesiastical affairs' which necessitated this journey? The reply may be contained in the *Letter to friends in Alexandria*, probably written from Athens. As we shall see, it is about discussions that Origen held in that city with a heretic.

But we have not got there yet for Origen took, to get to Greece, the longest way round: from Alexandria to Athens going through Caesarea of Palestine is not the most direct way. Why did he make that detour? Probably – but we have no information on the subject – to visit his Palestinian friends of whom we have already spoken, Theoctistus, bishop of Caesarea, and Alexander, bishop of Jerusalem. The event would then take place which was to make Origen's quarrel with Demetrius irremediable, namely, his ordination to the presbyterate.

Eusebius[67] attributes this ordination to 'bishops who enjoyed the highest esteem and reputation in Palestine, those of Caesarea and Jerusalem'. But it does not take two bishops to ordain a priest, one is enough: that is why Photius's account is more exact: 'It was Theotecnus, the archbishop of Caesarea in Palestine who ordained Origen with his own hands, with the agreement of Alexander, bishop of Jerusalem.' Photius constantly confuses Theoctistus who was really the prelate who ordained Origen with his second successor Theotecnus, Origen's pupil.[68] As for the archiepiscopal title with which he is credited, that is clearly an anachronism: but Caesarea was the administrative capital of Palestine and it was to be the religious capital up to the moment when Jerusalem was granted the patriarchal title.

Questions arise about the reasons for this ordination of Origen by a bishop to whose obedience he did not belong. Nearly a century later Canon 16 of the Council of Nicaea declared such ordinations null (*akyros*) but this legislation did not yet exist, Eusebius simply says that the two bishops had 'thought Origen worthy of the highest reward

[62] §4; CUFr II.
[63] II, 18–19.
[64] §§6–8.
[65] I–II, 1–11.
[66] HE VI, XXIII, 4.
[67] HE VI, VIII, 4.
[68] HE VII, XIV.

(*presbeion*) and honour (*timè*)'.[69] They were, it seems, indignant that Demetrius had not given to Origen the 'honour' of the priesthood. But it seems unlikely that for that reason alone they would have exposed themselves to the foreseeable anger of the bishop of Alexandria and there must have been other reasons. Perhaps this action should be seen as related to the protests raised against them several years earlier by Demetrius when they allowed Origen to preach in church while still a layman. Or possibly they wanted to give him greater prestige for the mission he was undertaking to Greece but Origen at this time was not thinking of settling in Caesarea; once his mission to Greece had been accomplished, he would go back to Alexandria and again direct his school. Now these bishops were ordaining, without the knowledge of the bishop of Alexandria, a man who was to exercise his ministry in Alexandria! One cannot help seeing in the 'honour' of the priesthood that they sought to confer on him something very like what would later be called in the West the priestly 'character': at any rate in their thinking the presbyterate was not absolutely identified with the ministry performed in a local church, and there seems already to be a certain distinction between priesthood and ministry, of the kind that a hundred and sixty years later Paulinus of Nola will make after his enforced ordination at Barcelona, between the *sacerdotium Domini* and the *locus ecclesiae*.[70]

What was Origen's state of mind when he received this ordination? Did he ask for it, accept it, or put up with it? It is hard to say, for no historian gives an answer to this question. He might very well suspect that, given the character of Demetrius, it would not be ratified without difficulty. That we have here a more or less forced ordination is not unlikely. In the primitive Church there are several examples, later, it is true, by a hundred and fifty or a hundred and sixty years: the ordination of Jerome by Paulinus of Antioch about 377, that of Paulinus of Nola by Lampius of Barcelona at the compelling instance of the people of the city at Christmas 394, and especially, the most astonishing of all, that of Paulinian, Jerome's brother, by Epiphanius of Salamis. This is known to us through a letter of the same Epiphanius to John of Jerusalem and translated into Latin by the ordinand's brother Jerome.[71] Paulinian received deacon's orders, and then priest's, while being held down by several deacons, one of whom stopped his mouth with his hand to prevent him crying out that he was unwilling. And according to this same letter of Epiphanius similar goings on were current coin in the ecclesiastical province of Cyprus.

It is not our view that Origen could have been subjected by his friends to such violent proceedings. He must certainly have consented to be

---

[69] HE VI, VIII, 4.
[70] *Letter to Sulpicius Severus:* CSEL XXVIII.
[71] *Letter 51* in the correspondence of Jerome. §§1-2.

ordained. With a good grace, or unwillingly giving way to their pressure? We cannot tell. In any case, when he had settled in Caesarea, he would make no difficulty about performing the priestly function of preaching – we have no evidence about the others – and several times in his homilies he makes allusion to his title of priest.

While Origen, now a priest, was on his way to Athens, the news of his ordination must have fairly quickly reached Alexandria, causing a good deal of feeling among the Christians and arousing the anger of Demetrius. And what we learn of his discussions at Athens with a heretic was likely to add fuel to the flames. Our information about this comes from a letter that Origen sent, probably from Athens, to friends at Alexandria who presumably had warned him of what Demetrius thought of him. In fact the fragment that Jerome preserves which comes from an earlier part of Origen's letter than the fragment translated by Rufinus, contains disillusioned and bitter remarks about the limited confidence it is possible to have in the leaders: it is wrong to revile them or hate them; one should rather pity them and pray for them. One should not revile anyone, not even the devil, but leave it to the Lord to correct them. At this point comes a short passage which forms the end of Jerome's fragment and the beginning of Rufinus's: both translators reproduce it in similar terms, Rufinus rather more wordily. Origen is protesting against those who attribute to him something he never said, that the devil, 'the father of malice and perdition, and of those who are excluded from the kingdom of God' would be saved. Not even a madman could say that. Rufinus's fragment goes on: Origen complains that his teaching is distorted by his enemies like that of Paul in 2 Thess, 2, 1–3. And then he relates the incident which occurred in Athens and contributed in no small measure to increased animosity towards him in Alexandria. Let him speak for himself:

> I see that similar things are happening to us. For a certain heresiarch with whom I disputed in the presence of many people, in a debate that was written down, took the manuscript from the secretaries, added what he wished to add, took out what he wished to take out, and altered it as seemed to him good: now he is passing it round under our name, insulting us for what he had himself written. Indignant about that, the brethren in Palestine sent a man to me in Athens to get authentic copies from me. But at that time I had neither re-read nor corrected that text, but had lost sight of it, so that it was difficult for me to find it. However, I sent it them and, God is my witness, when I met the man who had distorted my book, I asked him why he had done it and, as if to satisfy me, he said: 'Because I wanted to improve the discussion and to correct it'. He corrected it as Marcion and his successor Apelles corrected the Gospel and the Apostle.[72] For, just as these

[72] Marcion, who was with Valentinus the principal heresiarch of the 2nd century, had, in accordance with this doctrine which separated the Creator God, just but cruel, from the Father of Jesus Christ, effectively purged the New Testament of everything in it that related to the Old. Apelles is his best known disciple.

people upset the truth of the Scriptures, so that man, taking away what had really been said, inserted false affirmations to get us accused. But, although they are heretical and impious men who have dared to act in this way, they will nevertheless have God as their judge, those who lend credence to these accusations against us.

So it was a report of the discussion, faked by his interlocutor, which caused the trouble that Origen met at Alexandria, after the news of the ordination. One of the opinions wished upon the theologian was the ultimate salvation of the devil and against this he protests before telling this story.

In the next chapter of the *Apology against Rufinus*,[73] Jerome says he had read a dialogue between Origen and a disciple of Valentinus called Candidus. The first point of the discussion concerned the unity of nature between the Father and the Son and the second was the salvation of the devil. Jerome summarises it as follows: 'Candidus asserts that the devil has a very evil nature which can never be saved. To that Origen rightly replies that it is not because of his substance that the devil is destined to perish, but that he has fallen because of his own will and that he could be saved. Because of that Candidus slanders Origen by representing him as saying that the devil has a nature that must be saved, when in fact Origen refutes Candidus's false objection.'

To understand this discussion and the at first sight suprising approval that Jerome gives to Origen's reply (*recte Origenes respondit*) it is necessary to assume the predestinarian stance of Valentinian gnōsis: there are those who are saved and others who are damned, not by the choice of their will, but as a result of the nature with which they were created. The devil, says Candidus, is of a nature destined to damnation. Origen, the supreme theologian of free will, and the constant opponent of the Valentinian determinism, replies that is is not one's nature that decides one's salvation or damnation, but the free choice of the will in accepting or refusing grace. The devil could have been saved if he had not been obstinate in his opposition to God. But Candidus, understanding Origen in terms of his own frame of reference, concludes from this that, for his opponent, the devil is saved by his nature.

Is this Candidus the man that Origen confronted at Athens and is the *Dialogue between Origen and Candidus* that Jerome read the transcript of this discussion, not the one which the heretic distorted but the one which Origen sent to the 'brethren in Palestine'? In both cases it is a question of the salvation of the devil and the opinion is attributed to Origen that the devil will be saved, and against that attribution he protests. It is quite possible that the same facts are involved, but in that case it would have been better if Jerome had made more of the link between Origen's letter which he quoted in chapter 18 and the discussion

---

[73] II, 19.

with Candidus of which he speaks in chapter 19: and it is not Jerome but
Rufinus who reproduces the part of the letter narrating the incident that
occurred at Athens. That Candidus was the heretic he met in that city
seems likely but by no means certain.

Before going on with our story we reproduce from the same letter the
account of two similar incidents which occurred, one at Ephesus and the
other at Antioch, with the same heretic in each place, and prior to this
story in Athens. The one in Antioch may have taken place during
Origen's stay in that city as the guest of Julia Mammaea. There is no other
evidence for a stay of Origen in Ephesus.

> Finally at Ephesus a certain heretic who had seen me, but had not been
> willing to meet me and had not even opened his mouth in my presence,
> without my knowing why he had not wished to do so, wrote later a
> supposed discussion between him and me as he wanted it and then sent it to
> his disciples: I learned that he had sent it to those who were at Rome and I
> have no doubt that he sent it to others as well in various places. He was
> attacking me also at Antioch, before my arrival in that city and several of
> our people knew the discussion that he brought with him. But when I was
> there I refuted it before a large audience. As he continued without shame to
> assert his falsehoods I asked for the book to be brought and that my style
> should be recognised by the brethren who know assuredly what I am in the
> habit of discussing and what is my usual teaching. But he did not dare bring
> the book and was confounded and convicted by all of falsehood; and thus
> the brethren were persuaded not to lend an ear to his accusations.

When Origen got back to Alexandria, Demetrius, according to
Photius, reproducing Pamphilus, called a synod of bishops and priests to
decide on his case. This synod concluded that Origen ought to leave
Alexandria and that he ought no longer to live or teach there, but it did
not strip him of the 'honour' of the presbyterate. What this first sentence,
a mild enough one, amounted to was this: he was ordained by the bishop
of Caesarea, not by the bishop of Alexandria; therefore he could not
exercise his ministry in Alexandria. But that did not satisfy Demetrius
who, with a number of Egyptian bishops declared Origen deprived of the
priesthood. The word used by Photius, *apokerytein,* means 'to thrust out
by public proclamation'. So it expresses here, so it seems, a deposition
and not as Canon 16 of Nicaea will indicate later, that the ordination
conferred by Theoctistus had been *akyros,* unauthorised, invalid.
According to Jerome this sentence was ratified by a Roman synod: 'Rome
herself assembled a senate against this man', and ratified again, with a
certain theoretical hyperbole, by 'the whole world', but with four notable
exceptions, 'the bishops of Palestine, Arabia, Phoenicia and Achaia,'
Achaia being the name of the province comprising Greece. In fact Origen
was to spend the second part of his life at Caesarea in Palestine, to take
parts in synods several times in Arabia (Jordan), to stay a second time at
Athens, and to die at Tyre in Phoenicia, where his tomb was to be found.

In all these places he was to act as a priest. In the *De Viris Illustribus* Jerome was to speak without restraint about Demetrius's attitude to Origen: he 'let himself go (*debacchatus est*) so wildly that he wrote about him to the whole world'.

The main reason for the measures taken against him was certainly, if we are to believe Eusebius[74] and Photius, the ordination he received from a bishop other than his own. But his castration which, Eusebius says,[75] Demetrius then made public, played a supplementary part in this, although it was only a century later than Canon 1 of the Council of Nicaea would prohibit the ordination of someone who had mutilated himself. To what extent were doctrinal motives involved? In contradiction to what is often said these are not adduced by any of the three writers who provide us with information about these events. However, it is not impossible that they played some part and there are certain signs of this: the reaction of part of the Alexandrian public to any attempt at reflection about Christianity, already shown in relation to the *Stromateis* of Clement: the arrangement of certain passages in the *Treatise of Principles* where the appendix of I, 4, 3–5, or chapters III, 5 and III, 6 take up a subject already treated, perhaps in order to reply to misunderstandings; the fragment of the Commentary on John V preserved in the *Philocalia* in which Origen answers the reproach of those who said he had written too much; the fragment quoted by Eusebius[76] of a letter written to justify his philosophical studies: the *Letter to friends in Alexandria* already studied; the letter written by Origen to Pope Fabian, as Jerome says,[77] to excuse his boldness in saying that his patron Ambrose published what was intended to remain secret. In the end Eusebius accuses Demetrius of feeling jealous of his over-brilliant catechist: 'He was subject to human feelings about him.'[78] And Jerome himself at the peak of his enthusiasm for Origen did not hesitate to write that, if Rome called a senate against him, it was not 'on account of innovations in dogma, or to accuse him of heresy, as many of these mad dogs claim nowadays, but because they could not stand the splendid effect of his eloquence and scholarship: when he spoke all were speechless'.[79] A few years later Jerome would no longer be making statements like that.

Shortly after bringing about in this way the condemnation of Origen Demetrius died after forty-four years as bishop and Heraclas was appointed his successor.[80] Origen might have hoped for better treatment

[74] HE VI, XXIII, 4.
[75] HE VI, VIII, 4.
[76] HE VI, XIX, 12–14.
[77] *Letter 84* to Pammachius and Oceanus §10: CUFr IV.
[78] VI, VIII, 4.
[79] *Letter 33* to Paula, §5: CUFr II.
[80] HE VI, XXVI.

from the new bishop, for he had converted him, instructed him and taken him as a colleague. Far from it. In a short pamphlet entitled *Ten Questions and their Answers*,[81] at Question 9, Photius reports that, according to a tradition the source of which he does not indicate, Origen, after leaving Alexandria to go to Syria (in fact Palestine) stopped at a town on the Delta called Thmuis where he was recieved by the bishop Ammonius at whose request he preached in the church. On hearing this Heraclas hastened to Thmuis and, short of deposing Ammonius completely, imposed upon him a colleague, Philip, who was to share his episcopal responsibilities.

Origen at Caesarea

> When Origen was banished from Alexandria Theotecnus (read Theoctistus), bishop of Palestine, willingly let him stay at Caesarea and allowed him complete freedom to teach.

Thus writes Photius, reproducing Pamphilus. So Caesarea was to be Origen's usual place of residence during the second part of his life, although he went on numerous journeys. To the teaching and writing he had already been doing in Alexandria he would now add a strictly priestly function, preaching. It cannot be said that his priesthood led to any deepening of the spiritual content of his writings for that was clearly evident in those of the Alexandrian period. But pastoral concerns appear and grow stronger during the second half of his life, for his priesthood and his preaching brought him into contact not only with the intellectuals with whom he still consorted but also with the generality of the Christian population.

In the preamble to volume VI of the *Commentary on John*,[82] the first book that he composed at Caesarea as soon as he could start work again, Origen, who as a rule never speaks of himself, allows the bitterness caused by the recent events at Alexandria to show. Like the Hebrew people at the time of the Exodus he has been brought out of Egypt by the Lord. In face of the 'very cruel war' waged against him, which 'raised' against him 'all the winds of Egyptian perversity', he had tried to keep calm and to exclude evil thoughts that would rage like a tempest through the soul. Now God had extinguished the many burning darts that had been aimed at him, his soul had grown accustomed to misfortune and resigned to the plots against him. So he can resume the composition of the commentary which had been interrupted by the events in Alexandria.

The sixth volume had been started in Alexandria. Origen takes it up again in Caesarea when he has recovered peace of mind and when the stenographers whom Ambrose employed for him have been able to join

[81] PG 104.
[82] II, 8–10. Fr. trans. Blanc.

him there, and probably copyists and calligraphers as well. The Caesarea period will prove even more prolific in literary output than the Alexandrian; we shall examine that work in the next chapter.

On Origen's work as a teacher in Caesarea we have a first-hand document of exceptional value, the *Address of Thanks*[b] spoken, when he left after five years of study, by a student who was to become one of the most venerated saints of the East, Gregory Thaumaturgus. As the address itself makes clear, shortly after the arrival of Origen at Caesarea,[83] there came to the same city two young men, brothers, from a far-away country on the shores of the Black Sea, Pontus, and probably from the city of Neocaesarea. They were bringing their sister to their brother-in-law, law officer to the governor of Palestine, and they intended to go on to Beirut to complete in the famous law school of that city – first mentioned in this Address[84] – the law studies that they had begun in their own country. One of them was called, Eusebius says,[85] Theodore, but he was to take, probably at his baptism, out of devotion to his guardian angel who is mentioned several times in the Address, the name of Gregory, and he is the first person known to have borne that name: *Gregorios* means in fact one belonging to the *Gregoros*, the 'Watcher' of Daniel 4, 10. The other brother was called Athenodorus.

They had been born into a pagan family and had lost their father early in life. Gregory's first contact with Christianity occurred at the age of fourteen, but it is possible that he was not yet baptised when he came to Caesarea. In that city the two brothers met Origen who had just settled there. After some hesitation they succumbed to the charm of his talk and decided to attend his school, giving up the idea of Beirut. At the end of the first part of the Address[86] Gregory describes in moving terms the fascination that the master's language had for him when he spoke of the Word and the mutual affection that grew up between them and him:

> And thus, like some spark lighting upon our inmost soul, love was kindled and burst into flame within us, – a love at once to the Holy Word, the most lovely object of all, who attracts all irresistibly towards Himself by His unutterable beauty, and to this man, His friend and advocate. And being most mightily smitten by this love, I was persuaded to give up all those objects or pursuits which seem to us befitting, and among others even my boasted jurisprudence, – yea, my very fatherland and relatives, both those who were present with me then, and those from whom I had parted. And in my estimation there arose but one object dear and worth desire, – to wit philosophy, and that master of philosophy, that divine man.[87,c]

[b] The author refers to this work as the *Discours de Remerciement*, which I translate by *Address of Thanks*. It is usually called by English scholars the *Panegyric*. The author's abbreviation *RemOrig* is used in the notes.

[83] V, 63.

[84] V, 62.

[85] HE VI, XXX.

[86] VI, 73–92.

[87] VI, 83–84;   [c] Eng. tr. by Salmond ANCL XX, p. 54.

The relations in question, 'the people here', are the sister and the brother-in-law for whose sake they had come to Caesarea: the resolve to stay on at Origen's school had probably caused a row with the highly placed pagan official. The 'philosophy' mentioned here does not mean the Greek philosophy to which the Address later refers, but, in accordance with the praise of philosophy preceding this passage[88] and with a usage often found among Christians of that time and followed by Eastern monasticism, it means the moral and ascetic life, of Christian and pagan alike.

The second part of the Address describes Origen's syllabus of teaching. It begins with exercises in logic and dialectic conducted – this is explicitly stated – in the Socratic manner.[89] Origen used next to teach the natural sciences with an eminently religious aim: he made clear to his students the action of Providence.[90] Gregory then describes at length the ethical studies, centring around the four cardinal virtues: Origen was anxious to give practical as well as theoretical training.[91] Finally, the supreme subject was that of theology. It began with selected readings by the master from pagan philosophers and poets telling of God: philosophers of every school except the atheists. Origen sought in this way to save his students from the systematising spirit that closes the minds of philosophers to what others say. God alone has the right to men's unconditional loyalty and that is why the study of the philosophers[92] is for Origen a prelude to the study of Scripture[93] which is the crowning experience to which all this teaching leads.

A peroration full of feeling brings the Address to a close.[94] Backed by many biblical quotations the author expresses the grief of farewell and weeps to leave the almost monastic life he had led with Origen and his fellow students:

> . . . where both by day and by night the holy laws are declared, and hymns and songs and spiritual words are heard; where also there is perpetual sunlight; where by day in waking vision we have access to the mysteries of God, and by night in dreams we are still occupied with what the soul has seen and handled in the day; and where, in short, the inspiration of divine things prevails over all continually.[95,d]

And at an earlier point:

> . . . leaving the good soil, where of old I knew not that the good fatherland lay; leaving also the relations in whom I began at a later period to recognise

[88] VI, 75–80.
[89] VII, 93–108, cf. 97.
[90] VIII, 109–114.
[91] IX–XII, 115–149.
[92] XIII–XIV, 150–173.
[93] XV, 173–183.
[94] XVI–XIX, 184–207.
[95] XVI, 196–197;   d Salmond p. 78.

the true kinsmen of my soul, and the house too, of him who is in truth our father, in which the father abides, and is piously honoured and revered by the genuine sons, whose desire it also is to abide therein.[96,e]

Two fragments of letters seem to show that Origen did indeed lead a common life with Ambrose and his students. In the first of these, preserved by the Byzantine chronicler George Kedrenos,[97] Origen complains gently of the life of unceasing labour that Ambrose makes him live: the whole day and part of the night are spent in collating and correcting texts and Origen concludes by speaking of a morning's work that goes 'until the ninth or sometimes even the tenth hour', that is until three or four o'clock in the afternoon.

> 'All those who want to work devote this time to the scrutiny of the divine words and to reading.' In another fragment, from a letter written by Ambrose to Origen from Athens and quoted by Jerome in Letter 43 to Marcella the writer reports 'that he never took a meal in Origen's presence without reading: that he never went to bed before one of the brethren had read aloud the sacred writings: that it went on like this day and night, so that reading followed prayer and prayer followed reading.'

There are two further points to be studied by recourse to the *Address of Thanks*: the peculiar features of the teaching given at Caesarea; the picture that Gregory draws of his master. It is not correct to describe Origen's school at Caesarea as a 'catechetical school', still less as a faculty of theology. If the teaching given there is orthodox in what it affirms and corresponds in content to what we find in the Alexandrian's own works, there are some important omissions, at first sight astonishing. The teaching leaves out almost everything peculiar to Christianity and only reproduces the doctrines that can be enunciated in philosophical terms. For example, if the passage devoted to the Logos in the first part [98] expresses with all its shades of meaning the trinitarian doctrine in respect of the relations between the Father and the Son, it never mentions the incarnation nor the names of Christ or Jesus: thus it gives only one aspect of Origen's christology, for he gives full place to the incarnation and shows such a feeling devotion to the name of Jesus. Following A. Knauber[99] we think that the school of Caesarea was more a kind of missionary school, aimed at young pagans who were showing an interest in Christianity but were not yet ready, necessarily, to ask for baptism: Origen was thus introducing these to Christian doctrine through a course in philosophy, mainly inspired by Middle Platonism, of which he offered

[96] XVI, 189; [e] Salmond p. 76.
[97] PG 121, 485 BC.
[98] IV, 35–39.
[99] 'Das Anliegen der Schule des Origenes zu Cäsarea,' *Munchener Theologische Zeitschrift* 19, 1968. 182–203. See on this subject our study 'L'Ecole d'Origène à Césarée', *Bulletin de Littérature ecclésiastique* 71, 1970, 15–27.

them a Christian version. If his students later asked to become Christians, they had then to receive catecheticial teaching in the strict sense.

But the *didascaleion* of Caesarea is above all a school of the inner life: all its teaching leads to spirituality. It is striking to note that what Gregory admires most in Origen is not the polymath or the speculative sage, but the man of God and the guide of souls. Origen seems to Gregory to have gone far on the road of spiritual progress that leads to assimilation to God,[100] so much so that he no longer has for guide an ordinary angel but already perhaps the Angel of the Great Council himself,[101] that is to say the Logos. He has received from God exceptional spiritual gifts: he can speak of God, he is the 'advocate' or 'herald' of the Word[102] and of the virtues,[103] the 'guide' of philosophy in its moral and religious applications.[104] He possesses to a unique degree the gift of the exegete, analogous to that of the inspired author; he knows how to listen to God: 'This man has received from God the greatest gift and from heaven the better part; he is the interpreter of the words of God to men, he understands the things of God as if God were speaking to him and he explains them to men that they may understand them'.[105] Among the gifts he has received from God, he has the greatest of all, 'the master of piety, the saving Word'.[106] With him the Word comes in bare-foot, not shod with an enigmatic phraseology.[107] He teaches the virtues in wise and compelling terms,[108] but above all by his example: he puts his own lessons into practice, striving to fit himself to the ideal they describe: he presents to his students a model of all the virtues, so that they come to life.[109]

God has given him the power to convince and that is how he overcame the resistance of the two brothers. His words pierced them like 'arrows': there was in them 'a mingling of grace and gentleness, persuasive and compelling'.[110] This idea of 'compelling' recurs constantly in the Address, usually with some mitigating expression indicating that Gregory means by it Origen's power of persuasion. It was 'spell-binding'. Thus the day of their first interview 'was truly for me the first of days, the most precious of all, so to speak, the one on which for the first time the true sun began to rise before me'.[111] In the vocabulary of the master the True

[100] II, 10–13.
[101] IV, 42; Isa 9, 6, LXX.
[102] VI, 82–83; XV, 176.
[103] XII, 147.
[104] VI, 84.
[105] XV, 181.
[106] VI, 82.
[107] II, 18.
[108] IX, 117.
[109] XI, 135–138.
[110] VI, 78.
[111] VI, 73.

Sun, the Sun of Justice, is the Word, whom the brothers encounter through the medium of Origen.

We said above that preaching is the only strictly sacerdotal activity on Origen's part than can be mentioned: the others have left no trace in history. The fact is that we have nearly three hundred homilies of his, a considerable number if we think how few homilies of earlier date have come down to us: only the homily called the Second Letter of Clement of Rome; the homily on Easter by Melito of Sardis, the homily of Clement of Alexandria *Quis dives salvetur*; the *De Antichristo* and a few fragments of Hippolytus. The homilies of Origen are sermons on Scripture, explaining the text verse by verse, without a trace of the rhetoric of the schools.

A sentence from Eusebius[112] has given rise to divergent interpretations: 'It is said that Origen, when he had passed the age of sixty and had acquired by his long preparation a very great facility, allowed the stenographers to take down the talks (*dialexeis*) given by him in public, something he had never allowed before'.

What were these *dialexeis*? The common view is that they were homilies, for the Greek word *homilia* from which we get homily means an 'informal talk'. The early Christian sermons commenting on Scripture were so called to express the simplicity of their diction, the absence of rhetoric. However, several meanings have been given to this passage. Some held that it meant the whole of Origen's work, which, on this view, he did not write for publication and which Ambrose then published without his knowledge: they rely on the letter sent by Origen to Pope Fabian which they think applied to all his work and not, as is probably the case, simply to the *Treatise on Principles*. This is an unlikely view first because what we have here are *dialexeis*, a word which cannot be used of formally composed works like the commentaries, and also because the whole story of Origen as told by Eusebius shows that he wrote his works for them to be published by the staff that Ambrose provided for him.

Others have wished to restrict these *dialexeis* to conversations, like the *Conversation with Heraclides* found at Toura, of which we shall have something to say below: this would exclude the homilies. But these 'talks which he gave in public'[113] are mentioned again when Eusebius reports that Theoctistus and Alexander had Origen preach in church when still a layman and that Demetrius protested. The historian uses the verb *dialegesthai*, which is from the same root as *dialexeis* and says it means 'explaining the holy Scriptures in public'. In the letter of the two bishops rejecting the protests of Demetrius the words *homilein* and *prosomilein* from the same root as *homilia* are applied to the same activity: so it is indeed homilies that are meant.

[112] HE VI, XXXVI, 1.
[113] HE VI, XIX, 16.

Besides, Eusebius's statement is easily understood if homilies are
meant, commentaries on Scripture given in the presence of the congregation
and sometimes, as we shall see, improvised, Origen not always knowing
beforehand what passage would be read in the liturgy of the word, for
him to speak about. It was only at the age of sixty that he thought his
knowledge of the Scriptures and his meditations upon them were
sufficiently sound for him to get his homilies taken down for publication
as he spoke them impromptu. We can infer from that that the greater
number of the homilies that have come down to us were delivered after
245. But not all: the *Homilies on Luke* for example seem to be of earlier
date and to have been preached at the beginning of his stay in Caesarea.
But they are of a different structure from the rest and much shorter;
perhaps they were written out by Origen before or after delivery.

The well-known homily on Saul with the witch of Endor[114] which was
harshly criticised at the beginning of the fourth century by Eustathius of
Antioch and which has come down to us in Greek begins with an
interesting dialogue between Origen and the bishop which shows that the
sermon was completely extemporary. Origen could not have known in
advance on what text he was to preach. Origen declares that four
Scripture passages have been read and he cannot comment on them all:
the context is the liturgy of the word preceding the eucharist. So he asks
the bishop to decide on what passage he should speak and the bishop
names the one about the witch. Without a moment's pause Origen begins
to expound the passage in a homily rich in theological content.

Most of the homilies must have been preached at Caesarea in Palestine.
However, we can be sure that the homily on the birth of Samuel[115] was
preached in Jerusalem before bishop Alexander, for Origen says: 'Do not
expect to find in us what you have in Pope Alexander; we recognise that
he exceeds us all in the grace of gentleness' and a little further on: 'We
have said this by way of introduction because I know that you are used to
listening to the very sweet sermons of your very tender father.'[116] *Papa*,
in Greek *Papas*, was at the time the normal way of addressing bishops.

Several journeys that Origen made during this period remain to be
noted. Firmilian, bishop of Caesarea in Cappadocia, invited him into his
country 'for the good of the Churches' and then went himself to spend
some time 'with him in Judaea . . . to improve himself in divine matter'.[117]
We saw above the problem that arises from the commonly held view that
this stay of Origen's in Cappadocia was identical with his visit to the
virgin Juliana at the time of the 'rising of the Greeks', this being taken to

---

[114] 1 Sam 28: the homily in GCS III.
[115] 1 Sam 1: the homily in GCS VIII.
[116] §1.
[117] HE VI, XXVII.

mean the persecution ordered by Maximin the Thracian. Eusebius[118]
mentions, without giving a more precise date than during the reign of
Gordian III (238–244), a second stay in Athens. This must have been of
some length, several months at least, since it was there that Origen
finished the books on Ezekiel and began those on the Song of Songs,
getting as far as the fifth book. Then, 'returning to Caesarea, he brought
them to a conclusion, that is to the tenth book'. A journey to Nicomedia,
Diocletian's future capital, near the Asian shore of the Sea of Marmara, is
attested by the conclusion[119] of the long letter he wrote to Julius
Africanus[120] in reply to the latter's objections to the authenticity and
canonicity of the story of Susanna in the Greek version of Daniel.
Eusebius mentions this before relating the end of Gordian III's reign,
thus placing it before 244. In fact it was from Nicomedia that the letter
was sent. In the greeting at the end of it there is reference to Ambrose,
who corrected the letter, to his wife Marcella and to his children;
Ambrose's children also figure in the *Exhortation to martyrdom*[121] which
is addressed to him, but the name attributed in the letter to his wife
prevents us identifying her with the Tatiana to whom, along with
Ambrose, the *Treatise on Prayer*[122] is dedicated – unless, of course, she
bore both those names. If it is true, as Jerome says,[123] that Ambrose was a
deacon, he could not have been married twice, for Origen affirms several
times[124] the 'law of monogamy' which forbade the appointment of people
married twice to the office of deacon, priest or bishop, and likewise
prevented deacons, priests and bishops from remarrying if they were
widowed. Finally, unless in the Origen mentioned in the *Life of Plotinus*
by Porphyry we are to see someone other than the Christian theologian,
we must assume that there was a further journey, not mentioned by
Eusebius, which made possible his visit to the school of his fellow
disciple.[125] This meeting must then have taken place either at Antioch or
at Rome, for Plotinus after the defeat and death of Gordian III, whose
army he accompanied on the campaign against the Persians, spent some
time in the former city and then settled in the latter.[126]

On three occasions Origen went away to carry out missions in defence
of the faith. On the first he went to see Beryllus, bishop of Bostra in the
Hauran, capital of the Roman province of Arabia, a country to which
Origen had already been at the summons of its governor during the

[118] HE VI, XXXII, 2.
[119] §15.
[120] SC 302.
[121] §XIV (GCS I).
[122] II, 1 (GCS II).
[123] VirIll LVI.
[124] Homle XVII. 10; ComMt XIV, 22 (GSC X).
[125] §14: ed. Bréhier, CUFr I.
[126] §3: ed. Bréhier, CUFr I.

Alexandrian period of his life. Eusebius,[127] who speaks of this before mentioning the end of Gordian III's reign, so placing it before 244, attributes to Beryllus a doctrine derived from both modalism and adoptionism: the former, to safeguard the divine unity, made of the Father, the Son and the Holy Spirit three modes of being of a single divine Person, while the latter thought of the Son as a man whom God adopted. Beryllus maintained that 'our Lord and Saviour had not pre-existed in a mode of his own before his dwelling among men and that He did not possess a divinity of his own, but only that of the Father which dwelt in Him'. Many bishops had discussions with Beryllus at a synod held in his own Church and they summoned Origen to it; he succeeded in bringing Beryllus round to a more orthodox opinion. Eusebius mentions the writings of Beryllus – 'letters and various collections of writings'[128] – and the minutes of the synod containing his dialogue with Origen.

A second mission, likewise to Arabia, and related to the reign of Philip the Arabian, who came from that country, was directed against the views of certain Christians known by the name of Thnetopsychites, that is people maintaining that the soul is mortal: 'They said that the human soul in the present circumstances dies with the body at the moment of decease and that it sees corruption with the body, but that one day, at the resurrection, it will live again with the body.'[129] In this case again a council was convened, Origen was summoned and the deviants were converted to orthodoxy.

The third mission was not unconnected, as regards the opinions debated, with the two previous ones. The evidence for it is found in the *Dialogue of Origen with Heraclides and the bishops his colleagues on the Father, the Son and the soul*,[130] the transcript in part of the proceedings of a synod like the former, but of which we know neither the time nor the place. But the doctrines discussed are sufficiently akin to those in debate at the other synods to suggest that this also was in Roman Arabia and at the same period. This text was discovered in a bundle of papyri containing writings by Origen and by Didymus the Blind, head of the *didascaleion* of Alexandria in the 4th century. It was found at Toura, near Cairo, in 1941, in an old quarry which the British army was fitting out as a munitions depot. It seems to have been dumped there by the monks of a near-by monastery, called St Arsenius's, after the condemnation pronounced by the Fifth Oecumenical Council, the Second of Constantinople.

The opinions of bishop Heraclides being suspect to his colleagues, the latter gathered in his episcopal city in the presence of the Christian people of the place, with Origen summoned to conduct the debates. The first

[127] HE VI, XXXIII, cf. VI, XX, 2.
[128] HE VI, XX, 2.
[129] HE VI, XXXVII.
[130] SC 67.

sentence says that the bishops present raised the question of Heraclides's beliefs, made their observations and asked their questions. Heraclides then made an orthodox profession of faith, but probably it was not precise enough on certain points. Origen then, respectfully but firmly, subjected 'pope' Heraclides to a close interrogation to get from him clear affirmations on the points of dispute. These were the divine pre-existence of Christ, the distinction between Him and the Father and at the same time their unity, the Two Natures of the Son, God and man. Then Origen develops this unity and duality of the Father and the Son and inveighs against modalism and adoptionism. Of the other subjects dealt with by Origen in what follows we mention only, as being akin to the doctrine of Thnetopsychites, though not to be confused with theirs, the question put by a certain Dionysius: 'Is the soul the blood?' and Origen's reply:

> It has come to my ears, and I speak with knowledge of the matter, that there are here and in the neighbourhood people who believe that after passing from this life, the soul is deprived of feeling and remains in the tomb in the body.[131]

This error will rear its head again several time during the early centuries. Canon 34 of the Council of Elvira, at the beginning of the 4th century, forbids the lighting of candles in the cemeteries during the day-time for fear of 'disturbing the spirits of the saints'. At the beginning of the 5th century, Vigilantius of Calagurris (St Martory en Comminges) held similar views according to the *Contra Vigilantium* of Jerome and the *Passion of St Saturninus*, written at the same period in the same country, reports the scruples of bishop Exuperes of Toulouse when he transferred the relics of the martyr-bishop into the basilica that he had just built; he was afraid of disturbing the saint's rest and was re-assured by a dream. Further on in the *Dialogue of Origen with Heraclides* a question about the doctrine of the Thnetopsychites is directly asked of Origen[132] 'Bishop Philip came in and another bishop, Demetrius, said to him: Our brother Origen teaches that the soul is immortal'. As this remark caused a certain surprise we must conclude that the immortality of the soul was not then self-evident, even to bishops.

The final testimony and the death of Origen

Origen had escaped the first two persecutions of his life-time: that of Septimius Severus which did not spare Origen's father nor later several of his disciples, and that of Maximin the Thracian, which caused anxiety to his patron Ambrose. Origen addressed to him, and also to the priest Protoctetus, his *Exhortation to Martyrdom*. Ambrose survived, since he it was who, several years later, was to ask Origen to refute *The True Doctrine* of Celsus and to him the *Contra Celsum* was to be dedicated.

[131] §10: Fr. Translation by J. Scherer.
[132] §24 Ibid.

But Origen did not escape the persecution of Decius, which we have already described as the first truly universal persecution. Its effect in the West is best known through the correspondence of Cyprian of Carthage, in the East through that of Dionysius of Alexandria, preserved by Eusebius. Dionysius, who had been Origen's pupil in the *didascaleion;* succeeded Heraclas, first as director of that school and then as bishop of Alexandria from 247/248. Since the peace enjoyed by the Church under Philip the Arabian had led to numerous conversions, there were many not yet ready to endure the trial – in homilies preached at this time Origen laments the lower moral standards resulting from this influx. Consequently there were many apostasies, often a matter more of words than of lost convictions, and the bishops found themselves afterwards face to face, on an unprecedented scale, with the problems arising over the reconciliation of the apostates.

Alexander of Jerusalem died in prison at Caesarea.[133] Origen himself was imprisoned, and several times tortured:

> As for Origen, the terrible sufferings that befell him in the persecution, and how they ended, when the evil demon, bent on his destruction, brought all the weapons in his armoury to bear and fought him with every device and expedient, attacking him with more determination than anyone he was fighting at that time – the dreadful cruelties he endured for the word of Christ, chains and bodily torments, agony in iron and the darkness of his cell, how for days on end his legs were pulled four paces apart in the torturer's stocks – the courage with which he bore threats of fire and every torture devised by his enemies – the way his maltreatment ended, when the judge had striven with might and main at all costs to avoid sentencing him to execution – the messages he left us after all this, messages full of help for those in need of comfort – of all these things a truthful and detailed account will be found in his own lengthy correspondence.[134,g]

Photius, giving an account of Pamphilus's *Apology for Origen,*[135] says there were two traditions about Origen's death. The first said 'he ended his life in an illustrious martyrdom at Caesarea itself at the time when Decius was breathing nothing but cruelty against the Christians': that would imply his death during the persecution. The second tradition is the one attested by Eusebius: 'He lived until the time of Gallus and Volusian', which Eusebius reports at the beginning of Book VII;[136] 'he died and was buried at Tyre in his sixty-ninth year'. And Photius adds: 'This version is the true one, at least if the letters which we have, written after Decius's persecution, are not forgeries.'

These are the letters written by Origen after the persecution, probably

[133] HE VI, XXXIX, 2.
[134] HE VI, XXXIX, 4. Fr. Translation G. Bardy; g Eng. tr. by G. A. Williamson, Penguin Classics, London, 1963, p. 273.
[135] Bibl. 118, 92b.: Fr. Translation R. Henry (CUFr II).
[136] HE VII, 1.

preserved like all his letters in the library of Caesarea, letters which proved to Eusebius and to Photius that Origen had survived the persecution, having been released on the death of the persecuting emperor. The judge was in no hurry to put him to death, hoping to obtain from this most celebrated of Christians an apostasy that would have had a widespread effect. That he had not apostasised is shown by the letters written after his release, for he would not in that case have written in them 'words full of value for those who needed to be strengthened'. In Photius's account, which is not very favourable to Origen, there is no question of an apostasy, but some doubt is cast, without reason stated, on the authenticity of the letters.

Jerome attests on his part that Origen died and was buried at Tyre.[137] Concerning his tomb, which was still to be seen in the 13th century, Dom Delarue gives in one of the notes he added to Huet's *Origeniana*[138] a fairly long list of medieval authors who mention it and he sums up as follows: 'From all these authors it may be concluded that Origen was buried in the wall of the cathedral of Tyre, called the Cathedral of the Holy Sepulchre; his name and epitaph, carved on a marble column and adorned with gold and precious stones, could still be read in 1283'. Clearly it was not there that the body was first buried, as the cathedral did not exist at that time. Perhaps this was the cathedral at the dedication of which a well-known sermon was preached by Eusebius of Caesarea.[139]

Eusebius mentions a letter from Dionysius, bishop of Alexandria, to Origen *On Martyrdom*,[140] probably an *Exhortation to Martyrdom* addressed to his former master when the latter was in prison. This assurance of sympathy, coming from the Church of his birth, from which he had been banished eighteen years, must have been moving to receive. A long fragment about the story of the agony of Jesus in the garden of Gethsemane, based on Luke 22, 43–48 and to be found in a Vatican MS under the title 'From Dionysius of Alexandria to Origen' is considered to be part of this letter by Harnack, Bardenhewer and the recent translator of Dionysius into German, W. A. Bienert.[141] But the English editor of Dionysius, Charles L. Feltoe,[142] hesitates to attribute this passage to Dionysius, in spite of the title and it seems that he must be considered right, for the passage is also preserved under the name of other authors. A letter from Dionysius to Origen is likewise mentioned by Photius,[143]

[137] *VirIll* 54; *Letter* 84 to Pammachius and Oceanus, §7.
[138] Cf. PG 17, 696, note 48.
[139] HE X, IV, 1–72.
[140] HE VI, XLVI, 2.
[141] *Dionysius von Alexandrien. Das erhaltenes Werk* (Stuttgart 1972) pp. 95–102 corresponding notes pp. 122–123.
[142] *The Letters and other remains of Dionysius of Alexandria*, Cambridge 1904, pp. 229–250.
[143] Bibl. 232, 291b: CUFr V.

giving an account of a book by a certain Stephen Gobar called the
Tritheist: the same is true of a letter of condolences sent by the same
Dionysius after Origen's death to Theoctistus of Caesarea, whom Photius
confuses as usual with his second successor Theotecnus: now the death of
Theoctistus is mentioned by Eusebius as occurring in the reign of
Gallienus after his father Valerian was imprisoned in 260. The two letters
of Dionysius constitute in Photius's eyes the eulogy of Origen.

But this death as a confessor of the faith and virtually a martyr gave no
pleasure to some of those who, at the end of the 4th century, during the
first Origenist crisis, denounced him as a heretic. Such is the origin of the
confused gossip that Epiphanius of Salamins (or Constantia) put at the
head of Heresy 64 of his *Panarion*[144] – the heresy of Origen – claiming
Origen had apostasised during the persecution of Decius and following
up this incident with a number of others as if that persecution had taken
place long before Origen's death. H. de Lubac[145] has analysed this
passage and shown up its incoherence and historical improbabilities. We
shall not go over this demonstration again. We shall simply emphasise
that Jerome, who after 393, in the second part of his life, had become a
bitter enemy of Origen and a friend of Epiphanius, with whom he
collaborated in the charges brought against the Alexandrian's memory,
not only in no way echoes this account by the bishop of Salamis, but
again in his *Letter 84 to Pammachius and Oceanus*,[146] in which he
pitilessly emphasises the errors he attributes to Origen, respects his
victim's virtue to the extent of writing: 'Let us not imitate the faults of
him whose virtues we cannot copy'. In spite of all his rhetoric it is
unlikely that Jerome would have expressed himself in this way about a
man whom he thought an apostate. Now when he was writing Letter 84
in 399 he could not have been unaware of the *Panarion* of his friend
Epiphanius, finished twenty-two years earlier in 377. Likewise if Origen
had been notoriously an apostate, how would he have been granted the
burial in the cathedral of Tyre described by Dom Delarue? But 'the
legend of the fall', even if it is rejected nowadays by all Origen scholars,
has none the less through the ages weighed heavily on his memory.[147]

[144] §§1–5 (GCS Epiphanius II).
[145] *Exégèse médiévale*, first part, I, Paris, 1959, pp. 257–260.
[146] §9: CUFr IV.
[147] See Hide Lubac, op. cit., pp. 257ff; and 'La controverse sur le salut d'Origène à
l'époque moderne', *Bulletin de Littérature Ecclésiastique*, 83, 1982, 5–29, 83–110.

2

The Works of Origen

The work as a whole

The literary work of Origen was substantial, indeed he may well have been the most prolific writer of the ancient world. The scale of this work was made possible by the facilities that Ambrose put at his disposal. To give some idea of the whole we shall reproduce the list that Jerome gave in his Letter 33 to Paula.[1] Those who copied the letters of Jerome did not bother to transcribe more than the opening lines of this list, but shortly before the middle of the last century it was rediscovered by Sir Thomas Phillipps in a manuscript at Arras; since then it has appeared in the editions of Jerome's *Letters*. We have re-arranged the final part, which deals with Origen's correspondence, with the help of P. Nautin's suggestions[2] and like him we translate the word *excerpta* by scholia, a literary genre which we shall explain in a moment. One book or volume represents the amount of text that could be written on a roll of papyrus of standard format. Substantial as this list is, covering probably the works that Jerome saw in the library at Caesarea, it is not complete, for several writings do not appear which we possess and whose authenticity is not in doubt, as well as others to which reference is made in the works that we possess. Here is the list:

On Genesis 13 books;[3] assorted homilies 2 books; on Exodus scholia; on Leviticus scholia; Stromateis 10 books; on Isaiah 36 books; also on Isaiah scholia; on Hosea about Ephraim 1 book; on Hosea a commentary; on Joel 2 books; on Amos 6 books; on Jonah 1 book; on Micah 3 books; on Nahum 2 books; on Habakkuk 3 books; on Zephaniah 2 books; on Haggai 1 book; on the beginning of Zechariah 2 books; on Malachi 2 books; on Ezekiel 29 books. Scholia on the Psalms from the first to the fifteenth;[4] also a book on each of the Psalms[5] 1, 2, 3, 4, 5, 6, 7, 8, 9, 10, 11, 12, 13, 14, 15, 16, 20, 24, 29, 38, 40. On Psalm 43, 2 books; on Psalm 44, 3 books; on Psalm 45, 1 book; on Psalm 46, 1 book; on Psalm 50, 2 books; on Psalm 51, 1 book; on Psalm 52, 1 book; on Psalm 53, 1 book; on Psalm 57, 1 book; on Psalm 58, 1 book; on Psalm 59, 1 book; on Psalm 62, 1 book; on Psalm 63, 1 book; on Psalm 64, 1 book; on Psalm 65, 1 book; on Psalm 68, 1 book; on Psalm 70, 1 book; on Psalm 71, 1 book; on the beginning of Psalm 72,

---

[1] CUFr II.
[2] *Lettres et écrivains chrétiens des IIe et IIIe siècles*, pp. 233–240.
[3] Eusebius says 12: HE VI, XXIV, 2.
[4] Perhaps it should be to the twenty-fifth: cf. Eusebius's lists below.
[5] The psalms are numbered according to the Greek, not the Hebrew, system.

1 book; on Psalm 103, 2 books. On the Proverbs 3 books; on Ecclesiastes scholia; on the Song of Songs 10 books and two other volumes which he wrote in his youth; on the Lamentations of Jeremiah five volumes. Also the *Monobibla*; [6] four books *On Principles*;[7] two books *On the Resurrection* and two others on the Resurrection which are dialogues; a book on certain problems of the Proverbs; the dialogue against Candidus the Valentinian; a book on martyrdom.

Of the New Testament; on Matthew 25 books; on John 32 books;[8] scholia on certain parts of John, 1 book; on Luke 15 books; on the epistle of the apostle Paul to the Romans 15 books; on the epistle to the Galatians 15 books;[9] on the epistle to the Ephesians 3 books; on the epistle to the Philippians 1 book; on the epistle to the Colossians 2 books;[10] on the first epistle to the Thessalonians 3 books;[11] on the second epistle to the Thessalonians 1 book; on the epistle to Titus 1 book; on the epistle to Philemon 1 book.

Also homilies on the Old Testament: on Genesis 17;[12] on Exodus 8;[13] on Leviticus 11;[14] on Numbers 28; on Deuteronomy 13; on Jesus, son of Navé (Joshua) 26; on the book of the Judges 9; on the Passover 8; on the first book of the Kings 4;[15] on Job 22; on the Proverbs 7; on Ecclesiastes 8; on the Song of Songs 2; on Isaiah 32; on Jeremiah 14;[16] on Ezekiel 12. A homily on Psalms 3, 4, 8, 12, 13; 3 on Psalm 15; on the Psalms 16, 18, 22, 23, 24, 25, 26, 27; 5 on Psalm 36; 2 on Psalms 37, 38, 39; 1 on Psalms 49, 51; 2 on Psalm 52; 1 on Psalm 54; 7 on Psalm 67; 2 on Psalm 71; 3 on Psalms 72 and 73; 1 on Psalms 74 and 75; 3 on Psalm 76; 9 on Psalm 77; 4 on Psalm 79; 2 on Psalm 80; 1 on Psalm 81; 3 on Psalm 82; 1 on Psalm 83; 2 on Psalm 84; 1 on Psalms 85, 87, 108, 110; 3 on Psalm 118; 1 on Psalm 120; 2 on Psalms 121, 122, 123, 124; 1 on Psalms 125, 127, 128, 129, 131; 2 on Psalms 132, 133, 134; 4 on Psalm 135; 2 on Psalm 137; 4 on Psalm 138; 2 on

[6] Etymologically: books (or Bible) only. We have no idea what that meant.
[7] The famous *Peri Archon* or *De Principiis*.
[8] 22 according to Eusebius HE VI, XXIV, 1: but we have Books XXVIII and XXXII.
[9] This figure is certainly wrong. The von der Goltz codex only speaks of five volumes covering the whole of the epistle and notes the verses commented on in each volume. See E. von der Goltz, Eine textkritische Arbeit des zehnten bezw. sechsten Jahrhundert. Texte und Untersuchungen XVII 4, Leipzig, 1899, p. 95. Jerome also mentions five books in Letter 112 to Augustine, §4.
[10] In reality 3 books of which the von der Goltz codex notes the verses on which each comments: see previous note.
[11] A long passage of the third book is quoted in Latin translation by Jerome in Letter 119 to Minervius and Alexander, §§9–10.
[12] Sixteen homilies are usually reproduced but a Homily XVII is given in PG 13, 253–262: its text is the same as that of part of the *De Benedictionibus Patriarchorum* of Rufinus and it is eliminated as unauthentic for that reason, a faker being thought to have made up a homily of Origen out of that passage of Rufinus. I confess myself sceptical about this solution and think the opposite equally plausible: the early Fathers having no idea of literary etiquette – shown in numerous cases, the typical examples being Ambrose of Milan – Rufinus may well have sent to Paulinus of Nola who was asking for a treatise one which began by reproducing a homily by Origen which Rufinus had himself translated. In Letter 72 to Evangelus Jerome mentions a homily on Melchisedec which is no longer extant.
[13] We have 13 of them.
[14] We have 16 of them.
[15] That is of Samuel.
[16] These are the 14 that Jerome translated, but we have 22 and also in the *Philocalia* fragments of homilies 21 and 39.

Psalm 139; 3 on Psalm 144; 1 on Psalms 145, 146, 147, 149, Scholia on the whole Psalter.

Homilies on the New Testament: on the Gospel of Matthew 25; on the Gospel of Luke 39; on the Acts of the Apostles 17; on the second epistle to the Corinthians 11[17] on the epistle to the Thessalonians 2;[18] on the epistle to the Galatians 7; on the epistle to Titus 1; on the epistle to the Hebrews 18. A homily on peace. A (homily) of exhortation to Pionia. On fasting. On cases of monogamy and trigamy[19] 2 homilies. At Tarsus[20] 2 homilies. Also scholia by Origen. Two books of letters from Firmilian, Gregory and various persons: the epistles of the synods of Origen's case are in Book II. Nine books of letters from him to various people; the letter in defence of his works is in Book II.

Eusebius gives the approximate date of some of these works: there are also to be found in the texts which we possess references to other writings which permit relative dating. To the Alexandrian period belong[21] the first five books of the *Commentary on John* – Eusebius says there are 22 but there are really 32 —; the first 8 books of the *Commentary on Genesis* – Eusebius says there are 12, 13 according to Jerome who says the same in Letter 36 to Damasus[22] —; the commentaries on the first 25 psalms; the *Commentaries of the Lamentations* of which Eusebius, like Jerome, knew of five volumes; the two books *On the Resurrection*; the books *On Principles (Peri Archon)* of which Eusebius does not state the number – four according to Jerome, several other witnesses and text that we possess — ; ten books of *Stromateis*. In this last work, of which the name means Tapestries and of which only fragments remain – but the *Stromateis* of Clement are well known – Origen, according to Letter 70 of Jerome to Magnus,[23] compared 'the maxims of the Christians to those of the philosophers' and confirmed 'all the dogmas of our religion by extracts from Plato and Aristotle, from Numenius and from Cornutus'.

A second list corresponds to the beginning of his stay in Caesarea:[24] the *Commentary on Isaiah* of which Eusebius knows 30 volumes, as far as Isaiah 30, 6 and Jerome knows 36 volumes; the *Commentary on Ezekiel*, finished at Athens, in 25 volumes, but Jerome says 29; finally the

---

[17] Perhaps we should read the 'first epistle', for we have numerous fragments on it published by Cl. Jenkins in the *Journal of Theological Studies* IX–X, 1908–1909. Jerome says in *Letter 48* to Pammachius §3 that Origen gave long expositions of this epistle. On the other hand we have no fragments on 2 Corinthians.

[18] First or second?

[19] These words mean in the primitive Church those who have been married once and those who have been married three times successively. Three simultaneous marriages would have been illegal in the Greco-Roman world.

[20] There is no other evidence of a stay by Origen in Tarsus. From this point on we reproduce the text as corrected by P. Nautin.

[21] HE VI, XXIV, 1–4.

[22] §9: CUFr II.

[23] §4: CUFr III.

[24] HE VI, XXXII, 1–2.

10 volumes of the *Commentary on the Song of Songs* of which the first five were compiled at Athens, the last five at Caesarea.

The third list[25] gives the works of his old age: the *Contra Celsum* in 8 books, which Jerome does not list in Letter 33 but mentions elsewhere;[26] the *Commentary on Matthew* in 25 volumes and the Commentary on the minor prophets of which Eusebius knows 25 volumes: adding up the volumes which Jerome mentions we get 26. Eusebius speaks again of letters by Origen that he has collected into volumes and which number more than a hundred: he makes special mention of the letters written to Fabian of Rome and to a great number of other church leaders about his own orthodoxy; Eusebius listed them in the sixth book that he added to Pamphilus's *Apology for Origen*. He also speaks of letters to the emperor Phillip the Arabian and to his wife Otacilia Severa.

As we saw above the list in Letter 33 is drawn up in four parts: (1) the Commentaries on the Old Testament, then (2) on the New Testament, with which are mixed collections of scholia; next (3) the homilies on the Old Testament, finally (4) those concerning the New. The works that are not directly exegetical are variously placed in (1) and after (4) there are given homilies on various subjects and letters. So three types of exegetical writing are distinguished. First the commentaries which are explanations at the 'scholarly' level of books of Scripture, verse by verse. Then the scholia, explanations of the same kind, but bearing on isolated texts, the scholia being subsequently issued in collected editions. Finally the homilies, sermons expounding a scriptural text verse by verse, but in a way better suited to the general public in Christian congregations.

There remains one work of major importance of which Letter 33 does not speak, the *Hexapla*. It is difficult to reconcile the various accounts that are given of it, those of Origen himself, of Eusebius, of Epiphanius, of Jerome and of Ruinus as well as the allusions to the *Hexapla* that are to be found in the marginal notes of several manuscripts. P. Nautin[27] has made a very thorough study of this evidence but it cannot be said that his conclusions are always satisfactory: but it could hardly be otherwise. Let us simply say that the *Hexapla*, a word meaning six columns, like the other editions named *Tetrapla* (four columns), *Heptapla* (seven columns), *Octapla* (eight columns) means an edition of the whole Old Testament in the respective number of columns: basically it consisted of the four Greek versions of Aquila, Symmachus, the Septuagint (the official version) and Theodotion, followed sometimes by two (or three) other versions called today the Quinta, the Sexta, or perhaps the Septima, of which the first two had been discovered, one at Nicopolis near Actium in Epirus, the other in a jar found in a cave near Jericho, probably one of those in which

[25] HE VI, XXXVI, 2–3.
[26] *Letter 49* to Pammachius §13: CUFr II.
[27] *Origène*, Paris, 1977, pp. 303–361.

in the 20th century the Dead Sea scrolls would be discovered. These
versions were preceded by the Hebrew text, transliterated into Greek
characters, and perhaps also by the same Hebrew text in Hebrew
characters. Critical signs, as used by the Alexandrian grammarians,
indicated in what points the official text of the Church, the Septuagint,
varied from the others. Scholars are not agreed on the motives that led
Origen to undertake such a gigantic task: to facilitate the controversy of
the Christians with the Jews by showing the former the text which the
latter accepted; to recover, behind the various mistakes of the copyists the
primitive text of the Septuagint by choosing variants from the other
versions, or even through the literal translation of Aquila and the more
literary one of Symmachus to try to get back to the primitive Hebrew text
itself.

The work that survives

The immense structure of Origen's work is now in ruins, impressive as
these are; the erosion of time and the emperor Justinian's condemnations
and proscriptions occasioned destruction or at least prevented scribes
from making further copies of these works. For the same reason the
bundle of papyri by Origen and by Didymus, another of Justinian's
victims, discovered in the ancient quarries of Toura near Cairo, had
probably been hidden there by the monks of the neighbouring convent of
St Arsenius, who would be anxious to get rid of books they thought
dangerous to their faith or a threat to their safety if they were expecting a
raid from the imperial police.

Of the *Hexapla* there only survive numerous fragments, which many
are quoted by later authors. The completed original must have been left
uncopied and have remained in the library of Caesarea until its
destruction by the Persians or the Arabs. Its text of the Septuagint,
supplemented by borrowings from the other versions to which the critical
signs drew attention, was frequently copied, notably by Eusebius who
had fifty copies made on the orders of Constantine.[28] It was translated
into Syriac by bishop Paul of Tella and we possess part of the
Syrohexaplarion. The latest edition of the surviving fragments of the
Hexapla is that of Fr. Field in two volumes, 1867/1875, re-issued
unrevised in 1960. But as numerous other fragments have been discovered
since 1875 a new edition is called for.

As regards the other works of Origen, commentaries, homilies, scholia
or writings not directly exegetical, a good deal of what remains is not
preserved in the original Greek but in Latin versions, mostly the work of
two translators of the end of the 4th century and the beginning of the 5th,
Rufinus of Aquileia and Jerome. To these must be added the unknown

---

[28] Eusebius, *Life of Constantine*, IV, 36–37.

translator of the *Commentary on Matthew* who perhaps belongs to the
end of the 5th century or to the 6th. Besides, in addition to the writings
that we possess, if not in their entirety, at least in fairly long passages, we
have a considerable number of fragments.

From the critical point of view this situation gives rise to many
difficulties, as much over the versions as over the fragments, which we
shall study later. We can judge how Rufinus and Jerome set about
translating by their own statements, their prefaces or Jerome's Letter 57
to Pammachius on the best way of translating; but it is also possible to
compare their translations with the corresponding Greek text where we
have it; thus for Rufinus chapters III, 1 and IV, 1–3 of his translation of
the *Treatise on First Principles* can be compared with the Greek preserved
in the *Philocalia*; for Jerome twelve of the fourteen homilies he translated
on Jeremiah are also available in Greek; for the anonymous translator of
the *Commentary on Matthew* the part that runs from XII, 9 to XVII has
come down to us in both languages. On the whole these are not literal
translations, even when they set out to be such, but have been composed
as independent literary works intended for the Latin public: paraphrases
rather than translations. However, apart from omissions, they render the
ideas closely enough. But, compared with the originals, they also reflect
the difference of outlook between a Greek of the persecuted minority
Church of the 3rd century and Latins of the triumphant Church of the
end of the 4th.

Of the *Commentary on John*, which may be considered Origen's
masterpiece, we possess in Greek only nine books: I, II, VI, X, XIII,
XIX, XX, XXVIII, XXXII; of these Book XIX has lost its beginning and
its end. In it Origen frequently discusses the interpretations given by a
Valentinian gnöstic, Heracleon, author of the first commentary on John;
some fragments of the latter's work Origen preserves. The first book
contains a general introduction, then goes on to expound only John 1, 1a:
'In the beginning was the Word', the second runs from John 1, 1b to 1, 7.
The other volumes get on a bit faster.

Of the *Commentary on Matthew* we have eight books in Greek, from
X to XVII, which cover from Matt. 13, 36 to 22, 33. But a Latin
translation, the work, as we have said, of an unknown translator, has
come down to us, divided in the manuscripts and the 16th-century
editions into 35 or 36 so-called homilies. It begins at volume XII chapter
9 of the Greek, at Matthew 16, 13, and continues almost to the end of the
gospel, Matt. 27, 66. Only Matthew 28 remains without exposition. Since
Dom Delarue's edition in the 18th century which Migne re-issued, this
Latin version has been published in two parts: one corresponding to the
Greek from Matt. 16, 13 to 22, 33, called the *Vetus Interpretatio*, is
printed with the Greek text in two columns, with the same divisions; the
other beginning where the Greek text ends, from Matt. 22, 34 to 27, 66, is

called *Commentariorum Series* and divided not into the lost volumes XVIII to XXV, for we no longer know where they started and finished, but into 145 chapters each corresponding to a verse or verses. A work of Origen's old age, the *Commentary on Matthew* is on the whole less mystical and more pastoral than the *Commentary on John*.

Two other commentaries are known in the Latin translations of Rufinus. Thus we have part of the *Commentary on the Song of Songs* in ten books, the first half composed in Athens, the second in Caesarea: the prologue, Books I to III and perhaps the beginning of Book IV, the commentary on Cant. 1, 1 to 2, 15. Rufinus left out allusions to the lessons of Aquila, Symmachus and Theodotion which are preserved in Greek fragments, probably because these scholarly details were of little interest to his readers. The earliest masterpiece of mystical literature, this commentary of Origen's was of considerable influence in Antiquity and the Middle Ages.

The *Commentary on the Epistle to the Romans* translated by Rufinus comprises ten books, while the original Greek showed fifteen, both versions, however, extending to the whole of the letter: Rufinus, as he says in his preface, apologises for the difficulty of many passages and for the defective state of his manuscript: accordingly he shortened it by a third. We know the subject-matter of some of the passages that he omitted: for example the historian Socrates[29] notes a passage on Mary *Theotokos* (Mother of God) which was in Origen's volume I. The discovery at Toura of fragments of Books V and VI in the Greek, interpreting Rom. 3, 5 to 5, 7, makes possible, when to it are added other fragments previously published, a fairly positive judgement of the work of Rufinus.

There remain to us, as we have said, nearly 300 homilies of Origen's, to be precise 279. Of these only 21 are preserved in Greek: 20 on Jeremiah, of which 12 also exist in a Latin translation by Jerome, and the famous homily on 1 Kings (1 Samuel) 28, Saul and the witch of Endor. Translated by Rufinus we have 16 homilies on Genesis, 13 on Exodus, 16 on Leviticus, 28 on Numbers, 26 on Joshua, 9 on Judges, 5 on Psalm 36, 2 on Psalm 37, 2 on Psalm 38; a homily on the birth of Samuel, 1 Kings (1 Samuel) 1, perhaps comes from Rufinus but not certainly. In Jerome's translation, 2 homilies on the Song of Songs, 9 on Isaiah, 14 on Jeremiah – of which 12 also exist in Greek —, 14 on Ezekiel, 39 on the Gospel of Luke. V. Peri[30] has recently given back to Origen the credit for 74 homilies on the Psalms attributed by Dom Morin to Jerome, who was in fact only their translator-adaptor. The homilies expound the sacred text in the same way as the commentaries, verse by verse, or group of verses by group of verses, but in a less learned and simpler manner.

[29] HE VII, 32.
[30] *Omelie origeniane sui Salmi. Studi e Testi* 289. Vatican, 1980.

There is in them hardly any school rhetoric for which, according to Thaumaturgus, Origen felt a certain disdain.[31] That does not prevent him attaining sometimes a very real eloquence, but it is an eloquence which, in Pascal's words, makes fun of eloquence. One of Origen's finest homilies in terms of literary merit, Homily VIII on Genesis, expounding Abraham's sacrifice, keeps almost throughout on the literal and moral plane, with a very direct appeal to the fathers in the audience.[32] But, delicately suggested like a watermark in paper, a splendid allegorical exegesis underlies the literal; Abraham, whom God first asks to sacrifice his son, sacrifices in fact, because of the angel's intervention, a ram; Abraham stands for God sacrificing his Son, not the Word in his divinity symbolised by Isaac, but the Son in his humanity, for which the image is the ram.

It is very often difficult to distinguish the scholia that have come down to us from the substantial number of fragments that still exist, mostly from lost commentaries or homilies, something on all the books of the Bible. These fragments have been transmitted in three ways. First, in two collections of selected pieces, the *Apology for Origen* and the *Philocalia of Origen*. The former, Photius[33] tells us, comprised six volumes of which the first five had been compiled in prison by the martyr Pamphilus of Caesarea (in Palestine) who had restored the school founded in that city by Origen and had preserved Origen's library: he had been assisted in this by Eusebius, the future historian, who probably used to visit him and bring him material; the sixth volume was added by Eusebius after the death of Pamphilus on 16 February 310. Of these six volumes we possess only the first, in a translation by Rufinus. After a prologue in which he explains how Origen ought to be read, Pamphilus replies to a certain number of accusations made against him solely by quoting texts. Thus the *Apology* is a collection of selected passages: the texts have the reliability that can normally be expected of Rufinus's translations.

The *Philocalia*, a word which etymologically means the love of beautiful things, is a collection of texts by Origen collected by two of the Cappadocian Fathers, Basil and Gregory of Nazianzen: it has come down to us in Greek, the authority of its editors having saved it in the days when the author's ill-repute might not have done. The first 15 chapters are about Holy Scripture, chapters 16 to 20, taken from the *Contra Celsum*, are on the controversy with the philosophers about Scripture,

---

[31] RemOrig I, 4; VII, 107.

[32] Here is what Erasmus thought of this homily: 'All that is discussed by Origen very abundantly and very elegantly, and I know not whether the reader will derive from it more pleasure or more profit: Origen goes no further than the historical meaning.' (*Ratio verae philosophiae*, in Desiderius Erasmus Rotterdamus. *Ausgewählte Werke*, in Gemeinschaft mit Annemarie Holborn, herausgegeben von Hajo Holborn. Munich, 1933, p. 189, 1. 12–14: republished 1964.)

[33] *Bibl.* 118: CUFr II.

chapters 21 to 27 deal with free will. Among these last are a passage from the *Clementine Reognitions* and another from the Treatise of Methodius about free will: the reasons for the inclusion of these among texts otherwise exclusively by Origen are a matter of debate. A discreet apologetic motive on behalf of the Alexandrian is not absent from the minds of the two Cappadocians. These are reliable texts from the critical point of view, although some cuts may sometimes have been made in them.

A great many fragments come from the exegetical *catenae*, works in which the scriptural exegeses of various early Fathers are collected as a book of the Bible is commented on verse by verse. The first such 'catenist' seems to have been Procopius of Gaza in the 6th century. On the whole Origen is well represented in these. But the fragments of *catenae* are subject to two main difficultues from the critical point of view. First the attribution to a particular author given in the catena is not always safe, for some fragments are attributed to different authors in different catenae. Next it seems in many cases that the fragments are summaries made by the catenist of longer passages: this becomes evident when they can be compared with the passage from which they are drawn, existing in Greek or in a Latin translation; the ideas are authentic but not always their expression.

Finally, fairly numerous passages are preserved as quotations in later authors, whether supportive or hostile. But it is not always certain that they are giving us the authentic and complete text of what they are quoting. Thus on his writing entitled *Aglaophon or On the Resurrection* Methodius of Olympus quoted a long passage from Origen's *Commentary on Psalm 1*. Methodius's book is only preserved in its entirety in an Old Slavonic version, but Epiphanius reproduces about half of it in Greek in his *Panarion* 64. Before copying Origen's text as Methodius gives it,[34] Epiphanius reproduces the first paragraph directly from Origen.[35] When the two texts are compared, it will be seen that Methodius has suppressed all the expressions that he thought superfluous, so as to abridge the passage, but without changing its sense; and it is probable that he did the same with everything that he reproduced. Some quotations may well be centos of a kind, taking from a text phrases here and there and making of them a consecutive passage; or perhaps a summary giving the idea such as it was or such as the compiler took it to be.

We also possess several works that are not directly exegetical, although Scripture has an important place in them. In the famous *Treatise on First Principles (Peri Archōn or De Principiis)*,[a] the cause of so much trouble

---

[34] §§12–16.
[35] §10, 2–7.
[a] The author refers to this work as *Traité des Principes* English scholars, when they do not say *Peri Archon* or *De Principiis*, call it *On First Principles*.

after its author's death, scholars have often seen a first attempt at a Summa Theologica. That is not quite correct. First of all this work belongs to a well-known category of philosophical literature that speculates on the 'principles'; these are for Origen principles in the broad sense, the Trinity, the rational creatures, the world, only the Father being a principle in the narrow sense. Next, he does not claim to speak dogmatically, but offers a theology 'in exercise', that is in research, often indicating two or three different solutions to one problem, sometimes without himself reaching a conclusion; thus he manifests in this book all the tensions that are characteristic of his theology, so much so that to derive a 'system' from it, as people have often tried to do, more than half of what he says has to be left out. In the preface he enumerates the different points of he rule of faith,[36] as his generation was aware of them, and expresses his intention to try and reply to the problems still unsolved that that rule poses, by using Scripture and reason. This aim is in accordance with what we set out above about Origen's meeting with Ambrose: Origen wants to provide for Christians who ask questions of an intellectual order answers in accordance with Scripture, so that they do not go and look for these in the great gnōstic sects. When we come to consider our author's theology, we shall see how this book must be read and understood.

The plan of the *Treatise on First Principles* does not coincide very well with its division into four volumes, which is dictated by the problems of publication, a volume being the amount of text that fills one roll of papyrus. Thus the preface sets out the rule of faith, under nine headings. Then a first part, running from I, 1 to II, 3, studies the three groups of realities which constitute the principles, the Three Persons, the rational creatures, the world. Then a second part, running from II, 4 to IV, 3 is devoted to the problems which arise from the nine points of the rule of faith set out in the preface. Chapter IV, 4, entitled *Anakephalaiosis*, that is recapitulation, is rather a *rectractatio*, that is a new treatment of the three Principles which were dealt with in the first part.

The Greek text of the *Treatise on First Principles* is lost, except for chapters III, 1 on free will and IV, 1–3, on scriptural exegesis, which are to be found in the *Philocalia* and represent about a seventh of the *Treatise of First Principles*. The book is preserved entire in a Latin translation by Rufinus of Acquileia who states in his prefaces that he suppressed some passages on the Trinity which he thought had been inserted by heretics and replaced them with other statements by Origen on the same subject: apart from this point and from a few omissions arising from a desire to abridge and to avoid repetitions, this translation deserves all we have said above about the translations of Rufinus and Jerome. Comparison of the

[36] *PArch*, Origen's preface.

texts in the *Philocalia* with Rufinus's work yields on the whole a favourable result. The fragments quoted by Jerome and in the emperor Justinian's condemnatory letter of 543 make good the gaps in Rufinus, but in interpreting them we must take account of the fact that they do not reproduce the context and that they scarcely make it plain that in many cases a discussion of various alternatives is in progress; and also that they often harden Origen's opinions by uncomprehending interpretations, as a comparison with other works by the Alexandrian will show. Fragments are quoted by other authors, Athanasius, Marcellus of Ancyra, Antipater of Bostra, John of Scythopolis, Theophilus of Alexandria; but it is important not to attribute to the *Treatise on First Principles*, as P. Koetschau does in his edition, all the opinions of later followers of Origen; for example the anathemas of 553, attributed to the Fifth Oecumenical Council, the Second of Constantinople, although they do not appear in the official Minutes of the Council, are aimed explicitly at the Origenists of that day, called Isochristes, and often literally reproduce texts by Evagrius of Ponticus.

Two short pieces preserved in Greek inform us about the spiritual life and teaching of their author, while still giving a large place to Scripture: the *Exhortation to Martyrdom* addressed to Ambrose and to the priest Protoctetus when they were threatened during the persecution of Maximin the Thracian: the *Treatise on Prayer* answering the questions of Ambrose and a Christian lady called Tatiane. This last work, later by twenty years than the book of the same name published by Tertullian and containing like the latter a commentary on the Lord's prayer, is more developed than its predecessor and of great value, not only for the history of Christian piety but also for the advice it gives about the practice of prayer. A *Treatise on Easter*, very mutilated, was found at Toura and recently published with great care by P. Nautin. We have already mentioned the *Dialogue with Heraclides*. Of Origen's important correspondence which, as we have seen, Eusebius gathered into volumes, there remain entire only a letter to Gregory Thaumaturgus preserved in the *Philocalia*, on the value of philosophy for building up Christian theology, and a long letter to Julius Africanus on the authenticity and canonicity of the story of Susanna in the Greek version of Daniel: there also survive several fragments of other letters which we have used in describing Origen's life, the longest being drawn from the letter that was addressed to friends in Alexandria.

Origen's last great work is, alongside Augustine's *City of God*, the most important apologetic writing of antiquity: the *Contra Celsum*, preserved in its entirety in Greek. It is the refutation of the first attack launched against Christianity on the intellectual plane, the *True Doctrine* of the Middle Platonist philosopher Celsus. We know scarcely anything of him, or of the time and place of his life: the theories about him are

diverse and often contradictory. Was he the friend of Lucian of Samosata
to whom the latter dedicated *Alexander or the False Prophet*? Some assert
this, others deny it. However, there is general agreement that his work
should be dated in the reign of Marcus Aurelius (161–180). Nowadays the
True Doctrine is only known in the numerous quotations that Origen
makes of it, which must reproduce the greater part of the book. In any
case he had a great influence on later anti-Christian controversialists, like
Porphyry or the emperor Julian, and even on those of the 19th and 20th
centuries. It was Ambrose who asked Origen to refute him, during the
reign of Philip the Arabian (244–249), when the book had already been
written seventy years. Perhaps the occasion was the movement in favour
of the traditional Roman religion stimulated by the celebration of the
Millenium of the city, which brought competitors into confrontation
with the first Christian emperor. This 'revival' which was to culminate in
Decius's persecution, must have alarmed Ambrose and led to the request
he made to Origen. His preface suggests that the latter was not at first
convinced of the necessity of this refutation. However, he was to take it
on and to refute Celsus systematically, passage after passage, in the same
way that he elsewhere comments on the Scriptures. But he does not stick
simply to the texts; the *Contra Celsum* is full of wide perspectives on
Christianity, the proof of it, the relations that exist between it and Greek
philosophy and culture, and even at the end of Book VIII, when Celsus
moves the question onto the political plane, the possibility of a Christian
empire.

※   ※   ※

In the face of the difficulties for the critic offered by the translations
and fragments, scholars have sometimes been tempted to confine
themselves, in reconstructing Origen's thought, to the major works
preserved in Greek: but it was customary not to leave out of account the
Treatise on First Principles, which, when Rufinus was more or less called
in question, each specialist reconstituted in his own way to reveal the
Origen of his own imagination. To act thus is to forgo much of value and
to risk a dangerous distortion of our portrait of Origen, notably because
it eliminates the great majority of his homilies and in large measure hides
the man of God, the pastor and the Christian. The right method to use is
that indicated by H. de Lubac;[37] 'In this case more than in others, the
right procedure is not to omit but to make use of on a massive scale. To
have any chance of getting at the authentic Origen, there must be a
multiplicity of quotations. Then parallel passages are a check on each
other, they show each other's meaning and comment on it, especially

---

[37] *Histoire et Esprit*, Paris, 1950, p. 42.

when we look, for example, at a sentence in the Latin of Rufinus, another in the Latin of Jerome and a third preserved in the original. Now it is not rare to be able to do that, and from these comparisons an impression of unity emerges.' To demonstrate that a text is unauthentic, external critical arguements are obviously the most sound, where those of internal criticism are often debateable, especially when they depend on a supposed incompatibility between what is in the text and what Origen says elsewhere. The fact is that his thought is full of internal tensions and no text yields his thought precisely on a given point.

3
The Man and the Writer

The man

In the preface to his collection of texts *Geist und Feuer*, translated into French with the title *Esprit et Feu*,[1] Hans Urs von Balthasar draws a quick sketch of the man and the writer: plain but fiery, modest as well. Likewise A. Hamman.[2] Other characteristics can be suggested, evident from his work and from his life.

The nickname Adamantios, the man of *adamas*, that is steel or diamond or some other material that cannot be 'tamed' (alpha privative plus *damazein*, to tame) seems to refer to his incredible capacity for work, but perhaps also to his strength of soul. This is shown from his youth up in the radical way in which he gave practical effect to his religious convictions, a radicalism which in the years of his maturity will gradually give place to a more balanced attitude. In this respect Origen's development was to be the reverse of Tertullian's, whose rigorism became progressively stricter and seems to have been the cause rather than the effect of his going over to Montanism.

We drew attention above to the youthful Origen's gesture in selling all his manuscripts when he gave up teaching grammar and we said that that meant a total renunciation of secular subjects and concentration on the study and teaching of the Word of God alone. But we also saw that he soon realised the value of those subjects for understanding the Bible and for spreading the light of the Gospel. He quickly returned to what he had abandoned; so much so that he started attending the lectures of Ammonius Saccas and acquiring a considerable competence in philosophy. The same thing can be said about his mutilation: when in his old age he came to compile his *Commentary on Matthew* and to explain Matt. 19, 12, he was to disavow unequivocally in the strongest terms, though without alluding to his own case, the act which he had performed in his youth with 'an over ardent soul, believing but not reasonable'.[3] Eusebius[4] likewise describes the harsh asceticism practised by the young Origen. However, a study of his moral theology, for example on the subject of

---

[1] Only half has been published in French: I. *Lâme*, Paris, 1959; II. *Le Christ, Parole de Dieu*, Paris, 1960.
[2] *Dictionnaire des Pères de l'Eglise*, Paris, 1977.
[3] *ComMt* XV, 3: GCS X.
[4] HE VI, III, 9–13.

chastity, shows it to be, when all is said and done, fairly balanced, more so than might be feared, given some features of his cosmology. For example, Clement is always talking about 'apathy', that is impassibility, as the fundamental virtue of the spiritual man, whom he always calls the 'gnōstic'. Origen, who never uses the word 'gnōstic' to mean the kind of person he calls, in Pauline terms, the 'spiritual' or the 'perfect', obviously feels a mistrust of the vocabulary of 'apathy'. Instead of the eradication of the passions – whatever meaning Clement gives to this – Origen's ideal is rather the moderation to be imposed on the passions, the 'metriopathy' of the philosophers. A remarkable fragment on the First Epistle to the Corinthians,[5] about the balance that is to be observed in the name of charity in conjugal relations, is a commentary on the maxim *'in medio stat virtus'*: too little can be sinful, as well as too much. There is such a thing as holy anger – the model is provided by Phineas, Aaron's grandson[6] – and the desire to secure one's posterity is praiseworthy. The natural propensities are good in themselves: sin is exceeding the limit. Evagrius of Ponticus, a remote disciple of Origen, would go back to Clement's use of *gnōstikos* and *apatheia*.

Origen always desired martyrdom and constantly made clear, in his *Exhortation to Martyrdom* as well as in his homilies, the esteem in which he held this crowning testimony to our belonging to Christ. However, he is far from being a fanatic about it. Tertullian, when a Montanist, refuses in his *De Fuga* any kind of flight from persecution, but the Alexandrian in his *Commentary on John*[7] not only condemns any courting of martyrdom but also makes it a Christian duty to escape confrontation with the authorities, if this can be done without recantation: and he enjoins this in the name of the charity a Christian ought to show to the enemies of his faith, for it saves them from committing a crime.[8] Such would be the attitude to Decius's persecution not only of Cyprian of Carthage – who would die a martyr later under Valerian – but also of the two greatest disciples of Origen, Gregory Thaumaturgus and Dionysius of Alexandria.

Man of steel: such is Origen by reason of his total devotion to his task, intellectual and apostolic, and by reason of the way in which his life was consistent with his teaching. This last point is emphasised by Gregory Thaumaturgus and by Eusebius. The former says that it is by his deeds rather than by his words that Origen motivated his students to virtue. He brought about Gregory's decision to devote himself to philosophy, that is to the ascetic life, 'by trying to be like the good man he described in his

[5] XXXIII: *JThS* IX, 1908, pp. 500–501.
[6] Nb 25, 6–15 in *HomGn* I, 17 and in *HomNb* XV, 2.
[7] XXVIII, 23 (18), 192–202.
[8] The same judgement is found in the *Dialogue of Carmelites* by Bernanos. To the sub-prior who wants to make his sisters vow not to escape martyrdom, the prior replies – not in proper terms: How can we, who entered an Order for the salvation of sinners, want men to commit a crime against us!

lectures and by himself behaving, that is what I mean, like a sage'.[9] But
Gregory is well aware that perfection is not for this world. 'So I shall not
say that he was a perfect example, but that he was very anxious to become
one: he drove himself, one might say, with all his zeal and his ardour,
beyond the limits of human strength'.[10] Eusebius writes in the same vein:
'As his word, it was said and he showed it, so his conduct; and as his
conduct, so his word.'[11]

But this man of iron is tender. His deeply felt devotion to the person of
Jesus has a tone that is unique in Christian antiquity:[12] not until the
Middle Ages, with Bernard of Clairvaux and Francis of Assisi, will it be
heard again. Gregory Thaumaturgus describes in a very moving way the
affection between himself and his master, comparing it with that of Saul's
son, Jonathan, for David.

> And so he goaded us on by his friendship, by the irresistible, sharp,
> penetrating goad of his affability and good purposes, all the good will that
> was apparent in his words themselves, when he was present with us and
> talked to us.[13]

The friendship which unites the pupil to his master, his 'true father', is
the central idea of the moving peroration in which Gregory laments, with
the support of many biblical references, all that he is about to leave: he
compares himself to Adam driven out of Paradise, to the prodigal son
reduced to eating the fodder of the swine, to the Hebrew captives refusing
to sing in a strange land, to the robbed Jew of the parable of the Good
Samaritan. And after asking his master to pray that an angel may watch
over him during his journey back to his distant land, he ends his address
as follows:

> Ask him urgently to let us return and to bring us back to thee. That alone,
> that more than anything else, will be our consolation.[14]

The rhetoric in which this peroration is couched should in no way cast
doubt on the youthful friendship and admiration that inspired it.

Another characteristic of Origen's is worthy of notice. Like many
other theologians, he is constantly obliged to be controversial: against
Jews, against heretics, against pagans like Celsus, not to speak of
Christians who are millenarian, anthropomorphite or literalist. For he is
not a man to compromise: the attitude that he showed as a young man
towards the heretic Paul of Antioch[15] was one that was his throughout his
life. But, compared with many other early Christian writers, his polemics

---

[9] RemOrig XI, 135.
[10] Ibid. XI, 136.
[11] HE VI, III, 7.
[12] See Frédéric Bertrand, Mystère de Jésus chez Origène, Paris, 1951.
[13] RemOrig VI, 81.
[14] Ibid. XVI–XIX, 184–207: quoted XIX, 207.
[15] HE VI, II, 13–14.

are usually conducted in a realtively calm and irenical spirit. In Homily
VII on Luke, preserved in a translation by Jerome and in several Greek
fragments which correspond closely to the translation and cover more
than half of it, Origen is incensed against a heretic who, probably on
account of Matt. 12, 46–50, maintained that Mary had been renounced by
Jesus for having had children by Joseph after his birth. Where Origen
simply says: 'Some one dared to say' (*etolmēse tis eipein*), Jerome
translates: 'Some one, I know not who, let himself go to such a point of
madness that he said' (*In tantum quippe nescio quis prorupit insaniae, ut
asseveret . . .'*). The contrast is striking. To be sure it happens sometimes
in the *Contra Celsum* that Origen seems to lose control of himself when
faced with the scorn ceaselessly poured by his adversary on the
Christians, a scorn which strikes at the heart. About a passage of this kind
Pierre de Labriolle[16] writes:

> Where does Origen get this animosity? He was not a man of anger, he had
> nothing about him of a Tertullian or a Firmicus Maternus. The irenical
> tendency is very marked in him. The sharpness of Origen's reaction . . . is
> born in the first place of a very warm, susceptible religious sensitivity,
> which is cut to the quick by Celsus's tone and methods.

We have already spoken of the prologue to Book VI of the
Commentary on John, written after the great trial that drove him from
Alexandria: 'The Logos (Word and Reason) exhorted me to resist the
assault (launched by the winds of Egypt) and to watch over my heart, lest
wrong arguments should be strong enough to bring a tempest to my soul,
rather than to pursue the matter at the wrong time before my intellect had
recovered its calm.'[17] The man of steel is not insensitive. But he tries with
the help of that divine person which is the Word, Son of God, to restore
his inner calm.

The writer
The literary work of Origen has three essential characteristics, often
inseparable and found, in varying degrees, in almost every writing of his:
exegesis, spirituality, and speculative theology. An important part is often
played in his work by philosophy, philology and various subjects. So we
study Origen's exegesis, spirituality and theology, and in his theology the
place taken by philosophy. But these three characteristics are not
separable from each other; he knows 'no distinction of the genres'. They
constantly interpenetrate, so that one of these aspects cannot be
understood if abstracted from the other two. Usually it is Scripture that
forms the basis of his doctrine and it is from Scripture that he derives both
his spiritual and his theological teaching, a spiritual teaching which

---

[16] 'Celse et Origène', *Revue Historique* 169, 1932, 19–20.
[17] *ComJn* VI, 2, 8–10: Fr. translation by C. Blanc.

always has theological foundations and a theological teaching from which a spiritual flavour is never lacking.

We have seen that most of Origen's writings have as their aim the interpretation of Scripture and that in those which are not directly exegetical Scripture still holds an important place. But it is not possible to understand his method of spiritual or allegorical exegesis if one does not see that it is spiritual in the strictest sense of the term. It can only be evaluated in the setting of a spiritual life, all the more so when we come to the New Testament, his interpretation of which involves the application to the Christian of all that is said of Christ, an interiorisation which is only conceivable in that context. The fire that bakes the bread of exegesis is the love of God, the inspiration that comes from the Spirit and acts both on the inspired writer and on his interpreter. The bread which the preachers cut into pieces and distribute to the crowd, as in the miracle of the Feeding of the Five Thousand, is the spiritual meaning. The oven is not only the reasoning reason of the intellectual but the higher part of the soul, the intellect, the heart or the ruling faculty, which is the seat of man's participation in the Image of God, since only like can know like. The proper setting for this exegesis is contemplation and prayer: thence it comes down like Moses from his mountain, now that Jesus has done away with the veil,[18] to reappear in the synthesis of the theologian, in the teaching of the preacher and the professor, in the struggles of the apologist, and above all in the Christian life of all who live by it.

The spiritual doctrine is abundantly present even in the cosmology of the book that is usually considered the most intellectual of his works, the *Treatise on First Principles*. The activating factor of his cosmology is the dialectic between providence or divine grace, on the one hand, and human freedom to accept or refuse, on the other. The life of the 'intelligent beings' in the pre-existence, according to Origen's favourite hypothesis, is conceived as that of an immense convent of contemplatives: they are absorbed in the contemplation of God. The original fault which is located in this pre-existence, is represented either as the cooling of their fervour and their charity which turned them from 'intelligent beings' into 'souls' (*Pyche*, soul, being linked by a dubious etymology with *psychos*, cold) or as the *koros*, in Latin *satietas*, the boredom of incessant contemplation analogous to the *acedia* which Eastern practitioners of the spiritual life consider one of the great temptations of the monks. The pre-existent 'intellect' of Jesus is from the moment of its creation united to the Word in a way which makes it absolutely incapable of sin, through the intensity of its charity, that charity which in a way transforms it into the Word, as iron plunged into fire becomes fire.[19] It is sometimes surprising to find

[18] 2 Cor 3, 4–18 interpreting Ex 34, 29–35.
[19] *PArch* II, 6.

Origen praying, not only in his homilies, but also in his scholarly commentaries, as for example the exhortation to prayer that opens Book XX of the *Commentary on John*.[20] In the *Treatise on First Principles* itself there are three doxologies which seem to be none other than ejaculatory prayers and once at least a fervent call to prayer.[21]

The food that Origen, at the instance of Ambrose, seeks to provide for the Christians who ask for it, so that they need not go and seek it from the heretics, is not only of a spiritual order but also of an intellectual order. The distinction between the intellectual and the spiritual, between the conceptual-discursive and the intuitive, is not very clear in Christian antiquity: you get to God one way or the other, using all the powers of the mind. At the end of the *Treatise on First Principles*[22] Origen defines those for whom the book is intended as 'those who, sharing our faith, are accustomed to look for reasons for believing' and 'those who raise controversies against us in the name of the heresies'. These educated Christians to whom the book is addressed have problems, problems posed by introducing their Christian faith into the thought world that surrounds them and into the culture which they share, and also the problems that Greek philosophy claims to solve and to which they want to give a reply consonant with their faith. They are concerned, following the apostle's precept,[23] to be able to give to any one who asks, a reason for the hope that is in them. They must also be protected from the attraction of the great gnōstic heresies which attract them the more, the greater their intellectual needs.

Philosophy and the moral sciences have their part to play in this enterprise. Origen cannot be considered in the strict sense a philosopher: his explicit judgements on philosophy show this, as do those that Gregory Thaumaturgus gets from him.[24] He knows it well, but uses it as a theologian, convinced of his right to dig his wells in the land of the Philistines in spite of their recriminations.[25] It enables him in part to formulate his problems and his expressions, as well as providing some solutions. However, we must not lose sight of the fact that some of his positions, for example, about the body of flesh, flow as much from his personal experience of asceticism as they do from Platonism. Besides this he possesses a sound training in philology and dialectic and is acquainted with all the subjects studied in his day: he uses these in the explanation of the literal meaning of Scripture, in his teaching, say Gregory[26] and

[20] *ComJn* XX, 1.
[21] *PArch* III, 5, 8; IV, 1, 7; IV, 3, 14; cf. II, 9, 4.
[22] *PArch* IV, 4, 5.
[23] 1 Pet 3, 15.
[24] *RemOrig* XIII–XIV, 150–173.
[25] *HomGn* XIII, 3.
[26] *RemOrig* VII–VIII, 93–114.

Eusebius,[27] and in his controversy with Celsus. Alone the rhetoric of the schools finds no favour in his eyes[28] and that distinguishes him sharply from Tertullian, Cyprian and many of the later Fathers, Greek and Latin.

Origen does not attach much importance to considerations of style and he justifies that, as Clement did, by pointing to the scant literary merit of the letter of Scripture, a vessel of clay that holds the treasure of the Word: the poverty of the human means brings out the divine origin of the message. Thus his style is unaffected and this is made worse by the fact that all his works were dictated and most of his homilies taken down in shorthand by his stenographers at the time of delivery. However, if Origen's style has been subjected to criticism, it also has its admirers, for example the great Erasmus in the preface to his edition of Origen's works.[29] Erasmus praises the absence of contrived effects, of artificial rhetoric, of formalism, the evident concern for the idea alone, the clarity of the diction – a clarity that is not always so evident! He considers meritorious the absence of numbers and sub-clauses in his sentences and contrasts his simplicity with the grandiloquence and affectation of many of the Latin Fathers. He lauds the natural way in which Scriptural quotations are introduced, sometimes by simple allusion; the alacrity and vigour of his phraseology; the familiarity, moderation and gentleness of his homilies. A. Miura-Stange[30] emphasises that it is a work without pretension, where style counts for nothing, thought for everything. Origen is not after creating art: there is no pathos, never a word of wit or irony – that is not quite fair – but an enthusiasm that brings it all alive. A. Miura-Stange exaggerates however when she says that it is impossible to find a well-minted phrase that could pass into a proverb: what about, in the *Commentary on Matthew*[31] the expression *'peponthen ho apathēs'* –He suffered, the Impassible'. It is not that Origen cannot, continues the writer, whose judgement we are stating, but that he will not: he is sensitive to the beauty of the Greek language, he praises it in others, but care about style is inconsistent with the serious nature of his apostolic task.

Few works have been devoted to the study of Origen's style and language, but there are some, for example that of J. Borst.[32] For him Origen's vocabulary bears witness to the universality of his culture: pedagogy, medicine, natural sciences, grammar and philology, the language of law, not forgetting, of course, the words of biblical and

---

[27] HE XVII, 2–4.
[28] *RemOrig* VII, 107.
[29] Basle, 1536.
[30] *Celsus und Origenes*, Giessen 1926, pp. 163–164.
[31] ComMt X, 23.
[32] *Beitrage zur sprächlich-stylistischen und rhetorischen Würdigung des Origenes*, Freising, 1913.

philosophical origin. Atticisms far exceed popular turns of speech, and poetic diction is not uncommon. J. Borst has patiently noted the figures of style in the *Homilies on Jeremiah* and the *Commentary on John* and he reveals a rhetoric in no way contrived but arising naturally from Origen's culture and his innate eloquence. The effect is not sought for its own sake but the tropes and figures 'flow very often mechanically from his pen, almost involuntarily' and they give his writings 'their beauty and their power of attraction'.

More recently G. Lomiento has devoted several essays to the same subject, studying in this way the *Exhortation to Martyrdom*,[33] the Greek fragments of the *Homilies on Luke*,[34] the *Dialogue with Heraclides*,[35] a passage from the *Commentary on Matthew*,[36] Jerome's translation of the *Homilies on Jeremiah*[37] compared with the Greek text. He pays particular attention to the way in which the movement of thought corresponds to that of the sentence in the light of the knowledge of the Greek grammarians and of the spiritual life of Origen, who is trying to communicate with his hearers, more exactly he is examining the *proprietas verborum*. The study of the *Dialogue with Heraclides* is the more interesting in that we have here an oral style and that of Jerome's translation of the *Homilies on Jeremiah* shows that, if the substance is faithful, the movement of Origen's thought is not preserved by the translator, his ardour is chilled by Jerome's rhetoric. From the various works of Lomiento it emerges that, contrary to many current evaluations, Origen is a writer of worth, without useless ornamentation, but with a great power of expression. Certainly he should have watched his phraseology more carefully, have avoided the careless expressions and sometimes obscurities; but he presents us, when all is said and done, with a fine style for an intellectual, always paying attention to the fulness of the idea, those 'abundant and, so to speak, piled up ideas', those 'thoughts which have nothing empty about them', which in the dedication of Book XX of the *Commentary on John* he prays to receive 'from the fulness of the Son of God, in whom it has pleased all the fulness to dwell'.[38]

[33] *Vetera Christianorum* 1, 1964, 91–111; 2, 1965, 25–66.
[34] *L'esegesi origeniana del Vangelo di Luca*, Bari, 1966.
[35] *Il dialogo du Origene con Eraclido*, Bari, 1971.
[36] ComMt X, 1–12; GCS X: in *Vetera Christianorum* 9, 1972, 25–54.
[37] *Vetera Christianorum* 10, 1973, 243–262 or H. Crouzel et alii, *Origeniana*, Bari, 1975, pp. 139–162.
[38] ComJn XX,1,1: author's translation into French.

Part 2

EXEGESIS

4
The Interpretation of Scripture[1]

Origen is best known for his spiritual or allegorical exegesis – we use those two words in the same sense —, but it must not be forgotten that he is also, with Jerome, the greatest critical exegete and the greatest literal exegete of Christian antiquity. In our quick sketch of the *Hexapla* we have given some idea of his critical exegesis. We need only add that he constantly paid attention in his commentaries and often also in his homilies to the different readings that he found in the manuscripts. But we must pause a moment to look at his literal exegesis before going on to the spiritual exegesis, of which he is not the inventor but the great theorist.[2]

Literal exegesis
The room that Origen finds in his homilies for the literal sense, which he also calls the historical or the corporeal, varies considerably: some homilies are almost entirely built around it, in others it occupies a minimal space. Normally the literal sense is the source of the spiritual sense: if that were not so there would only be an arbitrary sense whose relation with what the Scripture says would be merely extrinsic. It is Origen's practice to explain the literal meaning, however briefly, as he does for every verse of the Song of Songs, before going on to the spiritual meaning.

All the resources of the scholarship of the time and the philological training that Origen received in his native city contribute to the interpretation of the literal meaning: explanations drawn from history, geography, philosophy, medicine, grammar, or even facts about natural history, whether true or alleged. We see him listing the literary genres

[1] The fundamental book is H. de Lubac, *Histoire et Esprit*, Paris, 1950; and also *Exégèse Médiévale*, I/1, Paris, 1959, pp. 198–304. A rather different position is found in R. P. C. Hanson, *Allegory and Event*, London, 1959. We deal with many questions of exegesis in *Origène et la 'connaissance mystique'*, Bruges/Paris, 1961.
[2] Origen stated the theory of spiritual exegesis in the *Treatise on Principles* and several times in his homilies; the texts gathered in the first twenty chapters of the *Philocalia* also deal with this subject. His practice is even richer than his theory. We shall not expound in this chapter the exeplarist vision of the world which underlies this exegesis but shall do so in connection with his spiritual doctrine in the chapter on knowledge.

used in Scripture, discussing the meaning of a preposition, travelling to verify on the spot whether there is a Bethany beyond Jordan,[3] expressing surprise at the mention of a 'Sidon the Great', when he has not come across any 'Sidon the Little',[4] testifying to the shape of the cave of Machpelah at Hebron where the tombs of the patriarchs were to be found,[5] relying on medical ideas coming down from Hippocrates and Galen or appealing to information about natural history that he found in the Greek naturalists. He also has friends among the rabbis and consults them about Jewish interpretations, customs and traditions, of which he has a good knowledge.

However, there is a statement in the *Treatise on First Principles*[6] which has given rise to much scandal and which is still constantly a subject of reproach to Origen as showing that he despised history: it is the assertion that passages can be found in the Old Testament that have no valid literal meaning and are thus only true on the spiritual plane: that the Holy Spirit wished by these stumbling-blocks to force us to rise to the spiritual level on which alone these texts turn out to be coherent. The difficulty arises from the fact that the literal or corporeal meaning is not defined in the same way by Origen and by modern critics. While we usually employ this expression to mean what the sacred writer was seeking to express, Origen means by it the raw matter of what is said, before, if it were possible, any attempt at interpretation is made. The difference is particularly felt when the Bible speaks, as it frequently does, in a figurative or parabolic language: the modern exegete will call 'literal' what the sacred writer meant to express by this figure or parable, but for Origen that would be the 'spiritual' meaning. Take, for example, the parable of the Prodigal Son: the material story will be for Origen the literal sense but the drama of the Gentiles (the prodigal son) and the Jews (the elder brother), with the affirmation of the divine mercy, which was what Jesus wanted to express, will be the literal sense for the moderns but the spiritual sense for Origen. As this narrative in its material content, does not relate a real story, it has no historicity, and so Origen can affirm that the literal sense is in this case inconsistent with history, all the more so when the figure used lacks consistency in itself. Origen cites in this connection Prov. 26, 4; 'Thorns grow in the hand of a drunkard.'[7]

To confirm what we have just said from Origen's own practice we have picked out from the homilies on the Hexateuch all the cases of this kind and have examined the reasons that led him to find the literal meaning

[3] *ComJn* VI, 40 (24), 204.
[4] The adjective implies admiration, not size, Sidon, the great city, Jos. 11, 8: in *HomJos* XIV, 2.
[5] *PArch* IV, 3, 4.
[6] IV, 2, 3, to IV 3, 3.
[7] *HomGn* II, 6.

inconsequent. In many cases the problem arises from a defective translation in the Septuagint: now for all the Fathers before Jerome it is that version that is held to be reliable, for it is the one the apostles gave to the Church and even where comparison with the Hebrew or with Aquila's version belies it, it is the one that Origen follows. Sometimes he declares rather hastily that the literal sense is incoherent because he does not place himself in the literal context, literary, psychological or moral: but that is relatively rare. Or else he considers that the literal sense does exist but is unsatisfactory to the Christian because it is useless, contrary to Christ's precepts, scandalous or impossible. It may well be thought that these judgements are partly due to an inadequate knowledge of the Hebrew language and civilisation: it does not seem that Origen was aware that there was in the Old Testament evolution and progress in respect of moral and religious standards.[8] But it must also be realised that his homilies are not aimed at producing history. It is for us Christians, as Paul says in 1 Cor. 10, 11, that Scripture has been composed: it must bring us a teaching that will enable us to live better. This pastoral aim always underlies all Origen's exegesis, all the more so when he is preaching.

Furthermore the enquiry we have carried out shows that Origen's objection to the literal meaning bears only on unimportant details which often represent only manners of speech arising from a certain rhetoric. It is surprising to find modern critics making a point of these, when Origen in fact believed in the historicity of the Bible much more than the most traditionalist of our exegetes do today. Who among these would bother to defend the historicity of Noah's ark with over subtle replies to the objections of the Marcionite Apelles, when he declared that the dimensions given would not permit the loading of so many animals?[9]

Furthermore, in spite of the spontaneous reactions of many modern scholars it must not be concluded from the fact that Origen allegorises a story that he does not believe in the historicity of the literal account, which is perfectly compatible with the quest for a spiritual meaning. As we shall see when we come to study his doctrine of knowledge, the beings and events of the perceptible world, while possessing a reality of their own, are images of those of the supernatural world of the mysteries, and that way of looking at things happily harmonises Platonism and Christian sacramentalism. When Paul in Gal. 4, 23–31 allegorises Abraham's two wives as the two covenants he does not thereby cast doubt on their historical existence.

Some of the words of Christ in the gospels are expressed, Origen

---

[8] H. Crouzel 'Pourquoi Origene refuse-t-il le sens littéral dans ses homélies sur l'Hexateuch?' *Bulletin de Littérature Ecclésiastique* 70, 1969, 241–263.

[9] *HomGn* II, 2; *CCels* IV, 41.

thinks, in a striking and radical fashion that is not to be taken too literally. The theophany at Jesus's baptism or the scene of the Temptation are to be regarded as inner visions: where is the mountain from which all the kingdoms of the earth can be seen? The discrepancies between the gospels are explained by their profound intention which corresponds for Origen to the spiritual meaning. In spite of expressions which may sometimes be thought clumsy, his insights often enough coincide with those of modern critics.

The accusation of literalism due to ignorance of the spiritual meaning is quite frequently levelled by Origen against the Jews – whether always fairly this is not the time to consider – as it is against the Marcionites and the gnostics, and we shall see why. But it could well be turned sometimes against Origen himself, when without taking sufficient account of the literary context of the passage he points out the absurdity of the literal sense as he understands it and takes it in the most absurd way possible in order to show how indispensable it is that the allegory should spring out of it. Thus it is possible to be at the same time literalist and allegorist.

The scriptural basis of the spiritual exegesis

Varied as they are, there is regularly to be found a common basis for the spiritual exegeses: that the Old Testament in its entirety is a prophecy of Christ, who is the key to it. Such is the fundamental principle which radically differentiates Christian allegory from Greek allegory, the latter originating from the desire to cover the immorality of certain myths of Homer and Hesiod by giving them a philosophical meaning. Christian exegesis has, however, been affected in its procedures by the influence of Hellenic exegesis. The spiritual exegesis of the New Testament answers to other concerns which we shall expound later.

Certain polemical intentions are present in the practice of spiritual exegesis. It says in 2 Cor. 3, 4–18, a fundamental passage for Origen, that the Jews who did not accept Christ have always before their faces a veil which hides from them the true meaning of the Bible, for they get no further than 'the letter that kills'. It is only when Jesus reads to his Church the old Scriptures, showing as He did to the disciples at Emmaus that they speak of Him, that the 'letter which kills' loses its deadly power. So allegorical exegesis gives the Old Testament its true meaning. Thus this exegesis affirms its value against the criticisms offered by the gnostics and Marcionites who devalue or even suppress it, as the work of an inferior god, distinct from the supreme God or even opposed to Him. By displaying a relationship between the two parts of the Christian Bible which is that of portrait to subject, of the signifying to the signified, Origen affirms their correspondence, their unity, the unity of the God of which they speak and of the Spirit that inspires them. And the heretics mentioned above separate the two Testaments by treating them unequally:

they refuse to allegorise the scenes of cruelty in the Old Testament and that allows them to cast the responsibility for these onto the cruel God of whom they speak; but they hasten to interpret favourably the analogous passages of the New Testament when they find any.

The spiritual exegesis of the Old Testament finds its main justification in the New Testament itself, for the latter practises it. But before demonstrating that, it is important to emphasise the indirect sources, both remote and near at hand, that are to be found for this method in Scripture taken as a whole. The first lies in the symbolic language which the Bible often uses: it is in fact impossible to speak of God otherwise than in symbols. Symbols abound in the wisdom and prophetic writings, in the apocalypses with their massing of imagery, more or less coherent, in the early chapters of Genesis whose literary genre is close to parable and whose cosmological scenery is akin to the Bablylonian cosmology: likewise in the New Testament with its apocalyptic passages and parables. Mention must also be made of a problem which was important for the early Church, that of the anthropomorphic treatment of God in the Bible. Whatever we do we cannot speak of God without representing Him as a man, even when we use the most discarnate concepts of metaphysics and theodicy. The Bible often represents God with human parts, hands, feet, eyes, ears, mouth, etc. and it also tells of Him having human feelings, anger or repentance. Among the early Christians were some, the anthropomorphites, who took the anthropomorphisms literally, while others, millenarians or chiliasts, conceived the promised beatitude in carnal terms. They were not heretics, but Christians belonging to the Great Church. In more refined terms the same views are to be found in some theologians. Justin and Irenaeus are millenarians. Under stoic influence Tertullian conceives God and the soul as more subtle bodies, without being anthropomorphist in the strict sense. Clement and Origen were later to interpret the divine anthropomorphisms as symbols of the deeds and powers of God.

Furthermore, in many passages of both Testaments, especially in John and often also in the synoptics, the reason for the narrative lies in a didactic intention on the part of the sacred author: for the modern exegete that will be part of the literal meaning, but for Origen it constitutes, we repeat, the spiritual meaning. Thus the miracles recorded in the Fourth Gospel illustrate its great theological themes: the wedding at Cana and the feeding of the five thousand have a eucharistic sense; the healing of the man born blind fits into the theme of the conflict between light and darkness. It seems possible to say the same about many of the miracles recorded by the synoptics.

The symbolic etymologies which consist in seeking the spiritual significance of a person or a place in terms of its true or alleged etymology and the symbolic arithmetic which consists in giving a symbolic value to numbers, are among the methods of patristic exegesis which surprise, and sometimes grate upon most of today's readers. But it would be wrong to hold the Greeks solely responsible for these procedures. For the Bible itself often does the same. Thus the false etymology given to Babel in Gen. 11, 9, 'confusion', when the word actually means 'gateway of God': but by it is expressed the meaning that attaches to Babylon throughout the Bible, from Genesis to Revelation, or the *Prima Petri*. As for numbers, think of the three-and-a-half which, disguised as forty-two months or 1260 days,[10] becomes in the Apocalypse the number denoting persecution. For Origen, if two-and-a-half tribes remained in Transjordania when the Holy Land was shared out, that means that the Old Testament, of which the land beyond the Jordan is the symbol, has arrived at a certain but incomplete knowledge of the Trinity.[11]

Nearer to the kind of spiritual exegesis that the New Testament will inaugurate is the continual mention in the Old of certain events in the history of God's Chosen people, for example the Exodus, which is the subject of ever-renewed reflection in the prophetic and wisdom literature in the light of the misfortunes that befall God's people: in this way the events become ever more profoundly spiritual, being seen as the pledge of the future liberation and the final glory in the expectation of the Messiah. The Exodus is then considered as God's greatest gift to His people and throughout their history the Hebrew people read and re-read at an even deeper level of spiritualisation certain elements of this story. This is not yet Christian spiritual exegesis, for only with the advent of Christ would the key of the old Scriptures be revealed, but it is certainly getting near it.[12]

We shall examine the essential passages of the New Testament quoted by Origen[13] to justify the spiritual exegesis of the Old: first those which provide examples, then those which were useful to Origen in working out the theory of it. In the first category the most important are 1 Cor. 10, 1–11, and Gal. 4, 21–31. According 1 Cor. 10, 1–11 the pillar of cloud which guided the Hebrews in the wilderness, the crossing of the Red Sea, the manna, the water spouting from the rock, the death in the wilderness of the first generation of Hebrews, represent baptism, the eucharist, divine punishment for sin. The word *typos*, type or figure, will become one of the master-words used in the exegesis and verse 11 enunciates one of its fundamental principles: 'that happened to them to serve as a figure (*typikos*) but it was written as a warning to us, who live at the end of the age.' It is for us Christians that the Old Testament was written and that

---

[10] Apoc. 11, 2; 11, 3; 12, 6.
[11] *HomJos* III, 2.
[12] See J. Guillet, *Thèmes bibliques*, Collection Théologie 18, Paris, 1951.
[13] *PArch* IV, 2, 6.

affirmation necessarily implies a spiritual interpretation, for a good many of its precepts, those concerned with ceremonies and the law, are no longer binding on us in their literal sense: however, they were written for us too, so they must have a meaning for us. The narratives have now only a historical interest and yet they must carry a meaning of concern to us.

Next Gal. 4, 21–31: Sarah and Hagar, the wife and the concubine of Abraham, symbolise the two covenants, or rather the Christians are prefigured by Isaac, son of Sarah, the free wife, and the Jews by Ishmael, the son of Hagar the slave. The word allegory, another master-word of this exegesis, occurs in this passage, meaning a manner of speech in which what is said conceals a meaning other than the one appearing on the surface.

Several other passages also furnish examples of spiritual exegesis. Deut. 25, 4 'Thou shalt not muzzle the ox that treadeth out the corn', is twice applied by Paul[14] to the labouring apostle who must normally be supported by his apostolic work. Christ is the posterity of Abraham[15] and will fulfil the promises made to the patriarchs. The ceremonies of the old covenant are 'shadows of heavenly realities'.[16] The Temple symbolises the Body of Christ,[17] the three days spent by Jonah in the great fish symbolise the three days that Jesus will spend in the 'heart of the earth',[18] whether the grave or Hades, the abode of the dead; the preaching of Jonah at Nineveh represents that of Christ to the Gentiles.[19] The appearance of Jesus to the disciples on the road to Emmaus is for Him an opportunity for a lesson in spiritual exegesis. He explains to them 'that it was necessary that the Christ should suffer and enter into his glory. And beginning with Moses and all the prophets he explained from all the Scriptures the things concerning Himself'.[20] The brazen serpent represents Christ lifted up on the cross;[21] the manna the Bread of Life which is Jesus, Word, the Eucharist.[22] Over and over again the Church is called the New Israel, the Christian 'a Jew who is Jew in the secret'[23] bearing the spiritual circumcision. The Epistle to the Hebrews is dominated throughout by the idea of Christ, the High Priest of the new covenant, of which the old covenant is the figure.

The principle elements of Origen's theory of exegesis can be found in the Pauline letters. First in 1 Cor. 10, 11, already mentioned. Then in

[14] 1 Cor. 9, 9; 1 Tim 5, 18.
[15] Gal. 3, 15.
[16] Col. 2, 16–17. Heb. 8, 5.
[17] Matt. 26, 61; John 2, 19–21.
[18] Matt. 12, 39–40.
[19] Matt. 12, 41.
[20] Luke 24, 26–27.
[21] John 3, 14.
[22] John 6, 22–59.
[23] Rom. 2, 29.

2 Cor. 3, 6–18 which gives a spiritual interpretation of Exodus 34, 20–35. The veil with which Moses covered his face when he came down from Mount Sinai where he had contemplated God, because the Hebrews would not have been able to stand the glory that shone on his countenance, is a figure of the veil which still hides from the Jews the true meaning of the Scriptures. It is Jesus who takes the veil away. To read the Bible without seeing that Jesus shows its meaning, is to remain in the 'letter which kills' without going on to the 'spirit that gives life'. For the veil to be taken away, one must turn to the Lord. 'We all who, with unveiled face, reflect (Origen reads "contemplate") as in a mirror the glory of the Lord, are transformed in that same image from glory to glory, as under the action of the Lord who is Spirit.' This last verse[24] is for the Alexandrian the origin of the theme of transforming contemplation, that is the shaping of the contemplator to the image of the contemplated by a kind of spiritual mimesis. So before Jesus the true significance of the old Scriptures could not be seen, and the same goes for the Jews of today who have not accepted Him. The true meaning is not in the letter, but in the spirit when the veil is taken away by Christ.

According to Hebrews 10, 1 the Law has 'the shadow of future good things, not the image of realities'. Origen, followed by Ambrose of Milan and the mediaeval tradition, will draw out of this text three levels of meaning. The 'realities', *pragmata*, are, giving them a meaning derived from Platonism, the divine realities, the mysteries, which will be contemplated in what Origen calls, according to Rev. 14, 6, 'the eternal Gospel', that is the perfect knowledge that belongs to the state of blessedness. But the Law offers of these realities no more than 'the shadow', the hope, the desire, the presentiment. Now the gospel preached here below, the 'temporal' gospel, gives much more, the 'image', a word which expresses for Origen a real, though imperfect, participation in the 'realities'. For the eternal Gospel and the temporal Gospel are a single Gospel: they do not differ in their *hypostasis*, their substance, but only in the *epinoia*, the human way in which they are conceived, 'face to face' in the eternal Gospel, 'through a glass darkly' in the temporal Gospel. This last expression is never applied by Origen to the Old Testament. Applied to the temporal Gospel, it expresses the essence of sacramentalism: here below we possess the true realities, but we perceive them hidden under the veil of an image. This subject will be more fully treated later in connection with Origen's doctrine of knowledge.

Note also Rom. 7, 14: 'We know that the law is spiritual'. The use which Origen habitualy makes of this text transposes into an exegetical plane what the apostle was saying with a moral or ascetic bearing: the epistle was contrasting the carnal man, delivered up to the law of sin, and

---

[24] 2 Cor. 3, 18.

the law which is spiritual for it aims to make a man live according to the Spirit. Except in the commentary on this epistle, where he is bound to respect the context, Origen often quotes this sentence giving it the same meaning as 2 Cor. 3, 6–18.

Origen often quotes 1 Cor. 2, 13: 'comparing the spiritual to the spiritual'. The coherence or consistency of biblical teaching is not always clear on the literal level, but must be sought on the spiritual level by bringing together different passages of Scripture which thus suggest analogous meanings. We shall shortly see that that method carries with it a certain weakness, that of not paying enough attention to the human writer.

The theological justification of spiritual exegesis

The main theological justification proceeds from the fact that for us Christians the revelation is identified with Christ. In the strict sense of the term Christianity is not a religion of the Book, the book is secondary. The revelation is in the first place a person, Christ. He is, as the Johannine writings say, the Logos, the Word of God. He is God Himself speaking to men, God revealing himself. He is the creative Word by whom all things were made, in whom is life and light, the Word who came to teach men and, to that end, was made flesh. Again He is the Word of Life whom the apostles saw with their eyes, heard with their ears, touched with their hands, the same that the seer of the Revelation saw leaping from heaven on the white horse, a victorious knight, king of kings and lord of lords, to crush the army of the minions of Satan.[25]

The Word became man in order to translate his message into a human person, into human acts and deeds: it is in fact the whole life of the incarnate Logos that is the Word.

The patristic doctrine of the Logos has a double origin, Hebrew and Greek. In it have come together from the one side the biblical theme of the Word (Dabar) of God which expresses the divine action in the world and recurs in the Johannine Word, and from the other side the Heraclitean and later stoic theme of the Logos – reason, the Greek word logos having both meanings, word and reason, and many others besides. In Origen the Logos is not only the Word, but also the eternal Reason of the Father, an expression which ought not to be understood in the 'natural' sense that scholastic theology gives to the word 'reason'.

Through the anthropomorphisms of the Bible, Origen explains, God has already manifested Himself to men after the fashion of a man: we cannot understand Him otherwise, we cannot escape from our human experience. Conscious, however, that God is infinitely beyond it, we can only express ourselves from that starting point. The creation of man in

[25] John 1, 1–14; 1 John 1, 1–3; Apoc. 19, 11–16.

the image of God, a truth which, dominating Origen's spiritual anthropology, is the basis of his mysticism, gives a certain validity to the anthropomorphic knowledge of God. So God has had Himself represented as man to be known of men. For the same reason the Christ was made man, thus imitating his Father in reality, no longer in image, to make known to us the Divine in a form that we could receive.

If the Revelation is the Christ, the Scripture is only revelation indirectly, making possible the mediation of the Christ, to the extent that it expresses and shows Him. That is clear in the case of the New Testament, which reports the life and teaching of Christ. But the Old Testament also will only be revelation to the extent that it speaks *entirely* of Christ.

There is another point to be added to this one. The Fathers of the early centuries present the Bible as the work both of the Son and of the Spirit and make no clear distinction between their roles. It is the Word of God, but the Son is also the Word of God. Could it be that God has two Words? Such an assertion would have had at that time, as in ours, a pejorative sense: the *dilogos* or the *diglossos* is a swindle. In fact Scripture and the Logos constitute a single Word. Scripture is, in a way, an incarnation of the Word into the letter analogous to the other incarnation into the flesh: not, however, a second incarnation for it relates entirely to the Unique Incarnation, preparing it in the Old Testament or expressing it in the New. For all the ante-Nicene Fathers the thephanies or appearances of God in the Old Testament, sometimes in the form of an angel or a man, are regarded as appearances of the Son, since He is, for Origen in his Divinity even before the incarnation, the mediator between God and man, the One in whom the Trinity acts externally. Thus He appears to Abraham at the oak of Mamre, prevents him from sacrificing Isaac, wrestles with Jacob, shows Himself to Moses in the burning bush.[26] The fact that He manifests Himself either in the form of an angel or in the form of a man is explained by Origen in terms of his favourite hypothesis of the pre-existence of souls, including the soul of Christ: he appears through the medium of his soul which, being without sin, has kept the primitive humano-angelic form. And when we read at the beginning of the prophetic books: 'The word of God came to Hosea, son of Beeri', to 'Jeremiah', to 'Ezekiel', to 'Joel', etc. this Word is none other than his Son, for God has only one Word.[27]

Thus the Word speaks in the Old Testament and that is revelation only because it speaks of Him, prophesies about Him, in its entirety and not simply in the few passages considered to be direct prophecies. It is a kind of indirect prophecy, in which the exegete, following in the footsteps of the New Testament itself, will find types of the Christ, the Church, the

[26] Gen. 18, 1–15; 22, 11–12; 32, 25–33; Exod. 3, 1–6.
[27] Hos. 1, 1; Jer. 1, 2; Ezek. 1, 3; Joel 1, 1.

sacraments, etc. The principal types of Christ are Isaac, son of Abraham, who symbolises the old covenant, Joshua, whose name in Greek is Jesus, the successor of Moses who represents the law, and several others like Solomon, who receives the queen of Sheba, the Church gathered from the Gentiles, or again the High Priest, Joshua or Jesus, son of Josedec.

Spiritual exegesis is in a kind of way the reverse process of prophecy: the latter looks to the future, but the former looks back from the future to the past. Prophecy follows the course of time forwards and in a historical or contemporary event sees darkly the messianic or eschatological fact that is prefigured. Spiritual exegesis follows the course of time backwards and, starting from the Messiah already given to the People of God, recognises in the old Scriptures the preparations and the seeds of what is now accomplished. But this accomplishment is in part prophetic in relation to what will take place in the end time.

But at this point a grave problem is posed by Origen's exegesis and that of other Fathers. To be sure, the whole Old Testament must be considered as prophecy of Christ, but do we have to conclude from that that every event under the old covenant prefigures some specific reality in the new and thus extend to other facts the prophetic and prefigurative character that the New Testament acknowledges in some? That is what Origen is constantly doing. Thus in the *Homilies on Leviticus* he gives a spiritual meaning to every detail of ceremonial worship, distinguishing for example the cases in which the sacrificial meat must be cooked in the oven, on the stove, or on the grill.[28] Although some of the explanations given possess a beauty of their own, is not this to fall into the artificial and the arbitrary? Origen, like many of the ancient Fathers, had an inadequate idea of the inspiration of Scripture: he thought of it rather like a dictation. The Holy Spirit is the author of the Bible, the human author is of little account. Now it would be unbecoming for the Spirit to dictate a useless word: every detail must have meaning and meaning worthy of the Holy Spirit, making known an infinite number of mysteries. Every term in a pleonasm must make its own point. The Bible is not to be treated as one would a human book, but as the work of the Spirit. To find the meaning of a word or the symbolism of an object Origen searches the whole Bible for the other cases in which the word is used or the object mentioned: it seems that for him the Bible has only one author, the Holy Spirit, and that the human writer is of very little importance.

To be sure, this conception of inspiration reminds us of something that we are at times liable to forget, that the the Bible is a book through which God speaks to us. But divine inspiration is not a dictation: the inspired authors express themselves as men, even if the action of the Holy Spirit confers on their writings a meaning that surpasses theirs. It can be said

[28] *HomLv* V, 5.

that just as Christ is perfectly God and perfectly man, so the Bible is in its
entirety a human book and in its entirety a divine book. The figures of
style, pleonasms and others, are no more than figures of style. And the
Bible can only be understood by first putting oneself in the context of the
human writer, whether literal, literary, psychological or historical.
Origen indeed generally does this, although in this respect some shortcomings will be found from time to time in those cases where he dismisses
too hastily the literal sense as non-existent, because the Holy Spirit put as
it were a stumbling block at that point to stimulate us to rise to the
spiritual meaning.

This inadequate notion of the part played by the human author in the
compilation of Scripture is the more astonishing in that it seems to
contradict an argument on prophetic inspiration which holds a considerable
place in his teaching on spirituality. It is directed against the Montanists.[29]
In prophetic inspiration, they thought, the Holy Spirit suspends the
consciousness and the freedom of the prophet and puts him in a state of
trance, of sacred derangement: he is used as an instrument to utter words
which the Spirit puts in his mouth, a passive instrument, operated by the
Spirit as the lyre is plucked by the plectrum, to use the classic image
recorded by Epiphanius.[30] That was a conception often debated in Greek
philosophy with reference to poetic or mantic inspiration; some passages
supporting it were even to be found in the great Jewish theologian, Philo.
In spite of his admiration for Philo, Origen does not follow him on this
point. He holds on the contrary that the Holy Spirit puts the prophet into
what might be called a state of super-consciousness and super-freedom
and that the prophet collaborates consciously and freely with the Spirit
who inspires him. God does not cloud the consciousness or override the
liberty of the being whom He created conscious and free. Only the devil
does that to the demoniacs he possesses.[31] It is astonishing that Origen
did not draw from his conception of prophetic inspiration the conclusion
that more attention should be paid to the role of the human author in the
compilation of the Scriptures.

If his search for a spiritual meaning in all the details of the Old
Testament stories had been criticised, he would not have lacked
arguments in its defence. The instructions on law and ceremonial, as we
have seen, were abolished by Christ in their literal application: if they
have no spiritual meaning, then they have no meaning at all for us, yet it
was for us Christians, says I Cor. 10, 11, that the books which contain

[29] Montanism arose in Phrygia about 170 from the preaching of the shepherd Montanus
and the prophetesses Priscilla and Maximilla. It spread rapidly in the empire and a little after
200 it began to seduce by its moral rigorism the great theologian at Carthage Tertullian and
in the end brought him to break with the Great Church.
[30] *Panarion* 48, 4, 1: GCS Epiphanius II.
[31] See our book *Origène et la 'connaissance mystique'* pp. 197–207.

them were written. There is sometimes mention in Origen's homilies of Christians who keep some of these laws, who do not take baths on the Sabbath or who eat unleavened bread at Easter time: the preacher reproaches them with nothing more nor less than refusing Christ's salvation by sticking to these 'Jewish fables'.[32] Likewise with the narratives: they belong to the past and Origen's point of view was nothing in common with that of the historian or the archaeologist, he is in his preaching before all else a pastor watchful of the spiritual benefit that his hearers will be able to receive. The past is only of importance because of the meaning it has for the present: otherwise we are stuck with 'Jewish fables', that is with a story that lacks Christian meaning and practical application. So if the Bible, with all that it contains, was compiled for us, what instructs us and is useful to us is not the literal sense of the rules laid down nor of the stories, but the meaning that spiritual exegesis seeks to express. Certainly the objection we formulated above is not without foundation: it seems artificial to look for a spiritual meaning in all the passages and in every detail of the holy books. But the reply that Origen would make to it has also a certain force.

Spiritual exegesis is spiritual in the strictest sense of the term
We have already drawn attention to this at the end of the previous chapter. In Origen's exegesis the spiritual and the speculative interact. A modern scholar might sometimes criticise him for not distinguishing between the intellectual factor based on conceptual and discursive reason and the spiritual factor derived from intuition: but the same is true of most of the Fathers. If Origen makes use of all the scholarship of his time to explain the literal meaning he does not by that imply that the word addressed by God to man comes wholly within the competence of that scholarship. Nor does it belong exclusively to the theologian who develops its doctrinal lessons, draws from them a Christian vision of the world, shows the coherence of the work of salvation. If the Bible is not to remain the 'closed book' of Isaiah or of the Revelation,[33] an intimate word of God must be heard by the soul when it is read. The charism of the interpreter is the same as that of the inspired author. To understand Isaiah or Daniel one must have in oneself the same Holy Spirit[34] and one can only interpret the Gospel if one has in oneself the *nous*, the mind of Christ, which the Spirit gives;[35]; this is a frequent assertion of Origen's repeated by Gregory Thaumaturgus in these terms:

> There is need of the same power for those who prophesy and for those who hear the prophets; and no-one can rightly hear a prophet, unless the same

[32] Tit. 1, 14; *HomJr* XII, 13.
[33] Isa. 29, 11; Apoc. 5, 1.
[34] *Fragm.* 1 Cor. XI: *JThS* IX p. 240, l. 22; *SerMt* 40: GCS XI.
[35] *ComJn* X, 28 (18), 172; *ComMt* XIV, 11; XV 30 (GCS X).

Spirit who prophesies bestows on him the capacity of apprehending His words.[36,a]

Indeed, the divine inspiration of Scripture is in some way mystically perceptible to the reader:

> And he who approaches the prophetic words with care and attention will feel from his very reading a trace of their divine inspiration (une trace d'enthousiasme) and will be convinced by his own feelings that the words which are believed by us to be from God are not the compositions of men.[37,b]

This 'enthusiasm' is not to be understood in its modern colourless and secularised sense: in accordance with its etymology (en, in theos, God) it is the feeling experienced that God is there.

This feeling shows that the Three Persons constantly intervene to enable us to understand the sacred words. The grace of the Logos and the Spirit which made the hearts of the disciples burn within them on the road to Emmaus[38] acts in us and shows us the meaning of Scripture. But this grace falls upon a nature ready to receive it. The doctrine of the image of God in man, which we shall study in relation to Origen's spiritual anthropology, occupies an essential place in his mystical theology, following an old Platonist adage, which is simply a matter of common sense: only like can know like; it is necessary to be similar to anything to know it. It is our kinship with all the beings of this world which enables us to know them, and we find them, as it were, repeated in ourselves, whether we are dealing with inanimate matter, living creatures or other men: because he is a microcosm, a little world, a man can understand everything in the macrocosm, the great world. In the same way, created in the image of God, encountering God in this image that is within him, he can have a certain knowledge of God. The more he develops this resemblance by living a life in conformity with what God is what God wills, the more he is fit to receive from God the grace of knowledge.[39]

Consequently the spiritual interpretation is only to be understood in a context of contemplation and prayer. Failure to understand and to be aware of this truth is the cause of many depreciatory and false judgements passed on this interpretation. The criticism is often made that it does not observe the rigour and objectivity which the scientific exegesis of our time sets out to attain: to say that is to place side by side on the same footing two forms of interpretation which do not have the same aim. The spiritual exegesis has its basis in the literal and situates what the literal says in the history of salvation. To appreciate the spiritual exegesis

---

[36] RemOrig XV, 179;   [a] Tr. Salmond, op. cit., p. 74.

[37] PArch IV, 1, 6;   [b] Tr. Butterworth, op. cit., p. 275.

[38] Luke 24, 32: several texts in Origen, see Origène et la 'connaissance mystique', p. 193, note 4.

[39] This subject will be more completely expounded in Chapter VI on knowledge.

outside the content of prayer in which it works would be to condemn oneself to understand nothing in it. To be sure it is normally based on the literal meaning and is not to be confused with making the text mean what the interpreter wishes. But the voice which God causes the soul to hear is not tied to words and their objective meaning.

This reply may well alarm many theologians who will see in it a danger of private judgement such as arose at the time of the Reformation: one might then take one's own lucubrations for the voice of God. But it does not seem that the Fathers had the slightest sympathy with private judgement and Origen less than any of them, in spite of the errors for which he has been blamed. Sometimes he begs his hearers to judge, according to the Scripture and the sense of God which is in the Christian people, whether he has spoken 'with the heart of the Holy Spirit' or 'with his own heart', whether he is orthodox – a 'churchman', he says – or a heretic, a true or a false prophet.[40]

To be sure, these interpretations are usually in accordance with the rule of faith, especially if we remember that at that time the rule was much more succinct than ours and even than the one that was to follow the Arian crisis at the time of the first quarrel about Origen. But they can be called subjective, taking the word in its original sense which does not mean fanciful, imaginary or purely individual but indicates that they are addressed to a subject, a person. The preacher enriches his sermons with them, for they are not so personal that he cannot communicate them to others, but they are not presented as the only interpretations possible. Rather are they pointed out as 'opportunities for understanding',[41] to use an expression frequently employed by Origen; he means by it a starting point for understanding and prayer. Distinction must obviously be made of those cases where the interpretation is found in the New Testament and so possesses the authority conferred by Scriptural inspiration: in other cases we have personal, hypothetical suggestions to help us see the meaning of a passage with the help of the grace of God and to provide the hearer with something that will help him in his prayers.

Origen's conception of the role of the preacher, when he suggests a spiritual meaning, must be understood in terms of the one assigned in Christian tradition to the spiritual director. It is very well expressed in a short fragment on the first epistle to the Corinthians: 'The human master suggests some ideas. Take for example Paul teaching Timothy: Timothy receives suggestions from Paul and goes himself to the source from which Paul came; he delves there and becomes Paul's equal.'[42] The Christian

---

[40] *HomEz* II, 2: GCS VIII.

[41] The expression is found in *HomNb* XIV, 1 and the idea which it expresses is developed frequently: *PArch*, II, 6, 2; IV, 2, 2; *ComJn* XXXII, 22 (14) 291 (GCS IV); *ComMt* XIV, 22 (GCS X).

[42] XI: *JThS* p. 240, 1. 5.

master is an intermediary who helps his disciple to enter into contact with
God in prayer. When he is no longer needed, he withdraws. Many
students of Origen have emphasised the modesty with which he puts
forward his interpretations and it frequently happens that he says, in
effect: 'If anyone finds a better answer I am ready to accept it and to
support his opinion'. He does not claim that his interpretation expresses a
final and universally valid meaning, but a personal attempt, open to
debate but available to others, to reach the profound sense of the passage.
We shall see likewise that his theology is explicitly presented in the
preface to the *Treatise on First Principles* as a quest starting from the rule
of faith and he does not give it the status of dogma.

The subject of these interpretations is very often the conduct of the
Christian in the time separating the two advents of Christ. If we have
spoken so far mostly of the spiritual exegesis of the Old Testament which
sees in Christ the one who reveals its meaning, we come here to one of the
essential aspects of the spiritual exegesis of the New Testament. Of course
the new Scriptures are also prophetic since the Incarnation prefigures the
glorious Advent at the end of time and helps us to guess at the 'true'
realities which will then be revealed to us. But there is not a strict
parallelism between the relationship of the Old Testament and the Gospel
lived here below, the temporal Gospel, and the other relationship
between the temporal Gospel and the eternal Gospel of the ultimate
blessedness, for there is in reality only one Gospel and we are already in
possession of the ultimate good, although we only see it 'in a glass darkly'
and not 'face to face'.[43] The new Scriptures already bring to reality what
they prophesy. So the exegesis of the New Testament will be in great
measure the application to each Christian of what is said of Christ, an
interiorisation in each Christian of the facts, of the deeds and virtues of
Christ. 'What does it profit me to say that Christ has come to earth only
in the flesh He received from Mary, if I do not show that He has also
come in my flesh?'[44] This sentence recurs several times in Origen's works,
in different forms. For the birth of Jesus at Bethlehem to produce in me
and in others the salvation that it should, it must be reproduced in each of
us by a personal adherence to the Redemption. God respects the freedom
of men: his promptings are aimed at producing a personal attachment to
Him. We have seen this already over Origen's opposition to the
Montanist conception of the prophetic trance: the devil possesses, God
respects freedom. Most of the great themes initiated or at least advocated
by Origen in the Christian tradition express the interiorisation of the
Christ in the Christian, the appropriation by the Christian of what is said
of Christ.

---

[43] See below pp. [149–156].
[44] *HomGn* III, 7: author's translation.

Several basic convictions underpin Origen's exegesis of the New Testament and its mystical themes. First that of man's freedom willed by God: of this we have already spoken.[45] God does not rule man as a Master, as He does the rest of creation, but as a Father: He asks him to adhere freely to the union to which the Father's prevenient love destines him. Second, a balanced position between the individual and the collective: redemption is not simply a collective matter nor simply an individual one, but indissolubly both: salvation is both personal and ecclesial. The *Commentary on the Song of Songs* find no problem in passing, sometimes without the transition even being noted, from the Church as Bride to the soul as bride: Origen seems to think that these ideas, far from exhibiting a contrast, are complementary: the faithful soul is bride of Christ because she forms part of the Church which is the Bride; and the more she behaves as a bride in the perfection of her Christian life, the more the Church is the Bride.

What has been said with reference to Heb. 10, 1, about the distinction between the temporal Gospel and the eternal Gospel, identical in their *hypostasis*, their substance, differing only in the *epinoia*, the human way of looking at them,[46] applies also to the sacraments. Baptism, followed by a Christian life that is in conformity with it, constitutes the 'first resurrection',[47] which remains partial, 'through a glass darkly', to distinguish it from the second, the final resurrection, which will be 'face to face'.[48] It is the same with the purification performed here below and the eschatological purification of which Origen is the first great theological exponent.[49] The same distinction can apply to all the sacraments here below and to their perfect realisation in the blessed state.

Origen defends, sometimes protesting too much, the old covenant against the contempt in which the Marcionites held it: he seems anxious to equate the knowledge its saints enjoyed with that of the apostles for example in the Book VI of the *Commentary on John*, though Book XIII restores the balance.[50] If the Old Testament is shadow, if it does not possess the 'true' realities, if it only sees 'in a glass, darkly', it has been changed into a New Testament by the advent of Christ and the new exegesis that that inaugurates, as the water became wine at the wedding in Cana:[51] It is sufficient for that that Jesus should read to his Church the old Scriptures showing that they speak of Him. To the saints who came

---

[45] For example p. 85. But the idea will constantly recur in the course of this work.
[46] See below pp. 107–112.
[47] Rom. 6, 3ff.; Apoc. 20, 5–6. Origen strives to suppress the meaning that the millenarians gave to this text.
[48] 1 Cor. 13, 9–11: *Fragm* 1. Cor. XXIX, *JThS* XIII, 363.
[49] *ComMt* XV, 23 (GCS X), suppressing the unintelligent correction of the translator into Latin which E. Klostermann introduced into the Greek text. See below p. [315–317].
[50] VI. 3–6, 15–31; XIII, 48, 314–319.
[51] *ComJn* XIII, 63 (60), 438.

before it the Incarnation has revealed the 'Day of the Lord': that Day was
manifest to Moses and Elijah on the mount of the Transfiguration and to
the others when Christ went down after his death to Hades to free them
and bring them with Him into his glorious Ascension.[52]

Multiplicity of meanings and attempts at classification
So far we have restricted ourselves to the main lines of spiritual exegesis,
whether of the Old or of the New Testament. In fact we have here a very
complex reality which has been affected by numerous cultural influences.
For Alexandria, the city of Origen's birth, was the principal cultural
centre of the Roman Empire and the cross-roads of all the wisdoms of the
East: capital of living Hellenism confronting Athens, city of the past,
capital of the Hellenistic Judaism of the diaspora, capital of a Hellenised
Egypt. In all these cultures symbolism and allegory had their place.

The most important influences are clearly Hebraic and Hellenic. We
have spoken of the figurative language of the Old Testament, of the
anthropomorphisms for which an evolved religious consciousness had
necessarily to find some interpretation, of its great themes which the
wisdom and prophetic literatures developed and spiritualised. But there
are also the rabbinic exegeses which had already influenced the New
Testament through Paul and which were to affect Origen too, who shows
a very advanced knowledge of them,[53] acquired from friends among the
rabbis. The influence of various Jewish trends like the one revealed in the
Qumran writings is perhaps also perceptible. More certain is that of the
apocalypses, canonical or not, and of the apocryphal literature of the Old
Testament.

The cultural environment is Greek. The allegorical exegesis of the
pagan myths, those told by Homer and Hesiod, originated from a desire
to answer criticisms of immorality that were made against them by seeing
in them symbols of philosophical truths in comformity with the school to
which the interpreter belonged: several of their procedures are to be
found in the spiritual exegesis of the Fathers, notably the principle that
the exegesis must be *worthy of God*. In addition to the elements which
Platonism, with stoicism and to a lesser degree other philosophical
schools, contribute to his theology, the context of Origen's exegesis is a
vision of the world dominated by the relation of the model and the image,
which makes it akin to the exemplarism of Plato. The divine world of the
mysteries, analogous to Plato's ideas, possesses perfect existence and
intelligibility; the perceptible world, image of the mysteries, has a reality
of participation and intention.[54] Plato also sometimes uses a language of

---

[52] *Hom I Kings*, i.e. I *Sam*, 28 (GCS III) on Saul with the witch of Endor.
[53] N. de Lange, *Origen and the Jews*, Cambridge, 1976.
[54] See below pp. 116–119 on knowledge.

imagery and myth when he cannot express himself more concretely: the explanation given to these myths is not unrelated to the exegesis of Origen.

Philo, who was the first to attempt a synthesis of Judaism and Hellenism, uses the Greek philosophical disciplines in his psychological and moral exegesis and allegories of the Philonian kind are not rare in Origen's works. The latter was also inevitably influenced by his principal adversaries, the gnōstics, especially the disciples of Valentinus, whose theology is dominated by the events of a world on three planes, the 'pleroma', place of fulness, where are to be found the divine entities known as the Aeons, the intermediate plane (*mesotes*) where the Demiurge reigns, the creator God, and the *kenōma*, place of the void, dominated by the Prince of this world, the Devil. Finally Origen is acquainted with the apocryphal literature of the New Testament. Perhaps there ought also to be added the Egyptian traditions preserved in the pagan gnōsis known as hermetism, as well as Mesopotamian, Iranian, Indian traditions. On minds as encyclopedic as those of Clement and Origen a great many influences have had an effect.

Several attempts have been made to reduce all this to some order. Origen himself in the *Treatise on First Principles*[55] and in several passages of the homilies formulated the theory of the triple meaning starting from his anthropology which sees man as a trichotomy of body, soul and spirit: so the literal sense corresponds to the body, the moral sense, which is concerned with life in this world, to the soul, and the mystical sense which already glimpses the mysteries, to the spirit. This classification does little to clarify Origen's exegesis: developed by starting from a different reality, anthropology, it gives the impression that it is imposed from without. It is difficult to see whether the psychic or moral sense is about a natural morality, independent of the advent of Christ, or about the life of the Christian after that advent. In fact Origen hardly ever expounds all three meanings but goes on from the literal to either the moral or the mystical. His vocabulary, which expresses before all else the exemplarist vision of the world, does not permit a simple distinction between the second and third meanings. On the one hand there is the symbol, the type, the image, the enigma, as well as the adjectives perceptible, corporeal, visible, etc.; on the other hand the mystery, the truth, the realities, as well as the adjectives mystical, true, intelligible (as opposed to perceptible), spiritual (as opposed to corporeal), reasonable, invisible (as opposed to visible). There is scarcely any difference to be seen between these words when they are applied to spiritual exegesis. Such is also the case with the three essential words which express the allegorical method, in spite of divergent and even contrasting images

55 IV, 2, 4–6.

suggested by their etymology: *allegoria,* the fact of saying something other than what one says, *anagoge,* that of rising above the literal, *hyponoia* that of grasping the underlying sense.

In *Exégèse Médiévale*[56] H. de Lubac points to Origen as the true author of another classification, one which corresponds more closely to his practice but which he never expressed as a theory, the doctrine of the quadruple meaning. Formulated for the first time by Cassian, expressed in the famous distich of the Dominican Augustine of Dacia, it was to be current throughout the Middle Ages. After the literal meaning the allegorical meaning is the affirmation of Christ as the key to the Old Testament and the centre of history. Then come two corollaries, the moral or tropological meaning which governs the moral life of the Christian in the interval between the two advents of Christ, and the anagogical meaning which gives a foretaste of the eschatological realities. The allegorical meaning brings us from the Old Testament to the New, it corresponds to the spiritual exegesis of the old Scriptures. The tropological meaning concerns the temporal Gospel: it applies to the Christian what is said of Christ and that is an important aspect of the spiritual exegesis of the New Testament. The other aspect of this same exegesis, the prophetic role which the new Scriptures possess in relation to the eschatological good, by a prophecy that makes already present what is prophesied, is the anagogic meaning, placed at the meeting point of the temporal Gospel with the eternal Gospel. But these last two meanings can also be found in the Old Testament, after the allegorical meaning has transformed it into a New Testament.

A third distinction has attracted a certain degree of attention recently, that between 'typology' and 'allegory'. We put these two words in quotation marks to avoid confusion between the 'allegory' that is in question here and the allegorical meaning that forms part of the doctrine of the quadruple meaning: in fact the latter corresponds more closely to the 'typology' than to the 'allegory' of the new distinction. The 'allegory' is so called by analogy with the allegorical exegesis of the Greeks to which it is related by the authors of the distinction, but to call it so is unfortunate for it alters a traditional meaning and leads to a regrettable confusion of terms. The starting point is to be found in a Christian theory of time. The ideas of those Greek philosophers who hold a cyclical theory of time can be represented graphically by a series of closed circles in which events repeat themselves Inversely Christian time can be represented by a straight line going in one direction, with an irreversible event, the first advent of Christ, and moving towards a second advent and the end of time. Every exegesis answering to this scheme is called 'typological' and would belong to the essence of the Christian revelation.

[56] 1/1 Paris, 1959, pp. 198–219.

But, starting from the Christian Alexandrians, there would be a second scheme cutting across this first one: it would be linked to symbolism and to an exemplarism, no longer horizontal but vertical, assuming there to be above the perceptible world another world, divine and angelic, with constant relations between the two. This 'allegorical' exegesis would not be of Christian origin, but Platonist or apocalyptic: This wherever the relation between the Old Testament and the New is emphasised, we remain within the Christian tradition. Wherever, on the contrary, there is assumed to be a world of supernatural beings whose doings have their reflection in our terrestrial universe, we are outside the Christian tradition, confronted with a Hellenisation, or, at best, with an influence drawn from apocalyptic. Some consider that this kind of 'allegory' distorts Christianity, others that it is a fact of culture, not illegitimate, but none the less alien.

To distinguish different literary forms can be justified, although ancient and mediaeval scholars do not seem to have noticed the differences. It is quite another thing to pass on each of these forms a judgement of value and especially to consider 'allegory' as lacking in Christian authenticity. This verdict arises from too narrow a conception of Christian time, reducing it to the single horizontal line, when the vertical is the expression of sacramentalism, of the anticipated presence of the eschatological blessings in the temporal Gospel. Christian time has both dimensions, the vertical as well as the horizontal: it can only be expressed in antitheses, like that of the Kingdom of God, which the Gospel declares to be at once present and future.

The New Testament itself affords examples of 'allegory' in the sense in which the word is used in this distinction. The fourth Gospel, not to speak of the Revelation of John, refers several times to a higher, divine world, the one where the Word is from the beginning with God, the one whence Christ comes and of which the Jews are ignorant, the one to which Christ will return and where the apostles cannot yet follow Him, the Father's house in which there are many mansions and where Jesus goes to prepare a place for his disciples.[57] Some will perhaps reply that in the Gospel of John these expressions are a sign of Hellenism. But the presence of this Gospel in the New Testament suffices to prevent us saying that 'allegory' is not in the Christian tradition. Moreover, the dependance of this Gospel on Hellenism is strongly contested by many exegetes. So it is impossible to affirm without reservation the influence of Hellenism on the 'allegory' of the Alexandrian Fathers, for in Origen it is seen as its clearest in his *Commentary on John*. More than in Plato should we not look for its source in this Gospel itself, of which Origen is the first 'ecclesiastical' commentator?

[57] John 1, 1; 8, 21–23; 8, 42; 14, 2–5.

Paul also provides examples of 'allegory'. Is not Sarah in Gal. 4, 22–31 the figure of 'Jerusalem above', who is 'Free and our mother',[58] an expression which evokes the New Jerusalem at the end of the Revelation, 'coming down out heaven from God, prepared as a bride adorned for her husband'?[59]

The horizontal dimension is not then sufficient to characterise Christian exegesis and the vertical is none the less necessary. In the period that separates the Incarnation from the Advent in glory of Christ the believer naturally relates in his faith to the celestial blessings which are already sacramentally at his disposal, he places himself in that divine and angelic world where he has his citizenship, his *politeuma*,[60] another Pauline expression which conveys the vertically of 'allegory'. In its judgement of value the distinction between 'allegory' and 'typology' is too systematised and for that reason it sacrifices an essential aspect of Christian reality.[61]

The results, past and present, of spiritual exegesis
Spiritual exegesis has greatly helped the Church to become aware of its tradition, that is of the way in which the thought of Christ has come down to us, as the source of faith and theology. We are not thinking here of the numerous traditions which are not sources of the faith and in any case not everything in the tradition is of equal value; we must distinguish the fundamental affirmations from the explanations that are given of them, and that calls for discernment. In the strong sense, let us make it clear, tradition is not a process of literal repetition: it is living. It is a current, both one and diverse.

The fact is that Christ, the Word of God, spoke and lived with his apostles and his teaching was transmitted both by his life and his words. He expounded the Old Testament showing, as He did to the disciples of Emmaus, that the old Scriptures had spoken of Him. The Holy Spirit, Whom He promised them was to teach them all things and put them in mind of his teaching, bear witness of Him, guide them into all the truth.[62] This message did not come to the apostles simply in the form of a body of propositions that they could have expressed. They had received it, to be sure, but only the Spirit could lead them to a more perfect awareness. There is thus in the history of the Church a progressive getting to know the message of Christ and all that it implies, and this begins in the apostolic Church through its teaching, its catechesis, its liturgy, even

[58] Gal. 4, 26.
[59] Apoc. 21, 22.
[60] Phil. 3, 20.
[61] On this question: H. de Lubac, 'Typologie' and 'Allégorisme', *Recherches de science religieuse* 34, 1947, 180–226; H. Crouzel, 'La distinction de la 'typologie' et de l' 'allégorie', *Bulletin de Littérature Ecclésiastique* 65, 1964, 161–174.
[62] John 14, 26; 15, 26; 16, 13.

before the compiling of the New Testament which, because of its inspiration, was to bear a privileged witness to it.

The growth of the Church is comparable to that of a child, who as he grows older becomes more and more clearly aware of what, in a way, he has had within him from the start. The Holy Spirit is in a way the inner agent of this development, but the development also takes place as a result of external opportunities which with the passage of time bring an increase in the Church's experience; the encounter with new civiliations, the new problems that arise in each period, the heresies which force the Church to envisage more clearly points of doctrine that were previously left vague, the thought of theologians, the example of the saints: all these contribute to this development. Among these factors, in antiquity and in a great part of the Middle Ages, the spiritual exegesis which Origen expressed with all his might has taken its place. It has proved one of the privileged means of this developing awareness and in large measure theology has emerged from it.

To explain this, let us begin with the reaction often felt by the modern reader when, without being previously warned about it, he starts on the homilies of Origen or of other Fathers. He is tempted to accuse them of arbitrary interpretations, finding too great a distance between what the literal meaning says and what the exegete gets out of it. He can admire the explanations given, but all the time he suspects the commentator of taking advantage of a passage to set out his own ideas rather than settling down to listen to the word of God. This reproach would certainly have been considered unjust by the Fathers, at least in most cases. Certainly there are cases where it would be justified, for the 'rule of faith' in these early centuries, that is the points of doctrine that had entered clearly into the consciousness of the Church and which one could not be dispensed from believing, was much less developed than at a later time. It was possible for a theologian of the early centuries to put forward personal ideas which he believed to be compatible with the faith of the Church: this was the case with Origen over the pre-existence of souls. The incompatibility only became clear later, as progress was made in the formulation of dogma. When exegeses have been constantly repeated by later generations and have become incorporated into the common teaching, they cease to derive from personal opinions but rather from the mental climate of faith that the interpreter carries within himself as a member of the Church. Even if to our modern eyes his interpretation seems more or less distant from the letter of the dogma, it is linked to the tradition in a relationship that is not arbitrary. These are not individual opinions then substituted for those of the Saviour, but they flow from the message confided by Christ to his Church. In this way is best understood the revealing, one might also say catalysing, role played by spiritual exegesis in the unfolding of the faith in antiquity and the high Middle Ages.

But must we nowadays consider this kind of exegesis as a fact of culture that had its importance in the past, or does it remain to a certain degree valid for us, although contemporary exegesis seems quite different? It is, however, worthy of note that not so very long since, after three centuries of incomprehension, the meaning and value of this kind of interpretation was rediscovered. It is also true that the Bible now plays a much greater part in the piety of ordinary Christians than was the case in times gone by and one may wonder whether we are not sometimes performing spiritual exegesis without knowing it, as Monsieur Jourdain spoke prose.[c]

It is not a Christian way of meditating on the Old Testament to fail to see in it the pre-figuration of Christ. However valuable the lessons that can be drawn from many passages of the Old Testament, to do no more than this is to remain a man of the old covenant which was not yet Christian, incapable of seeing how Jesus gives its meaning to the whole story that precedes Him. Likewise the New Testament asks of me a personal adherence to this Jesus of which it speaks and because of that its story is not comparable with any other. A great man's life may interest me intellectually, even emotionally, but whether it is true or false does not change anything fundamentally in my life. Even an unbeliever cannot read about Jesus as about any other character, for the Gospel shows that He claims to affect his life, even if that claim is rejected. Prayer that starts from the New Testament must express both this assimilation to Christ for free participation in the work of salvation and the prophetic aspect of the new covenant, already realising what it prophesies. And if present-day preaching cannot take the same liberties as the old orators did, the expounding of both Testaments in accordance with the fundamental ideas of spiritual exegesis remains one of its essential aims.

The scientific exegesis of our times has sometimes been contrasted with spiritual exegesis as if they were incompatible. But the contrast is not as sharp as that. Origen and Jerome practised both kinds without running into problems. Literal exegesis, by its modern definition, aims to recover what the sacred author meant. When that is established, spiritual exegesis gives the passage its place in the mystery of Christ. To explain the Bible as one would any secular book is only the first stage. The second is the one that gives the Christian his spiritual food. There is no need to contrast things which are complementary.

[c] Main personage in Molière's 'Bourgeois Gnetilhomme'.

Part 3

SPIRITUALITY

5

The Doctrine of Man as a Spiritual Being

In the fourth part, when we shall be considering Origen's speculative theology, we shall expound what he had to say about the origin of humanity, that is the hypothesis of the pre-existence of souls and of their fall, as well as about the end time. For the moment we shall confine ourselves to the strictly spiritual aspect: what is it in the very structure of humanity that permits man's contact and dialogue with God? Two main doctrines of Origen's give the answer to this: his doctrine of man as a trichotomy and of man's sharing in the image of God.

Man as a trichotomy[1]

The trichotomic conception of man derives from the list given by Paul in the final greeting of the first epistle to the Thessalonians:[2] 'May your spirit, soul and body be kept sound and blameless at the coming of our Lord Jesus Christ.' It is found in a rather disorganised and variable fashion in most of the authors before Origen, and it begins to be systematised in Irenaeus on the one hand and in the Valentinian gnōstics on the other. Origen makes of it a coherent synthesis which is found virtually unchanged at all stages of his career. It is curious to note that it disappears rapidly after his time, even among his principal disciples, Didymus the Blind who puts forward several formulas, and Evagrius of Ponticus, who distorts it, suppressing the delicate dialectic that is characteristic of it, by confusing the *pneuma* with the *nous*.

In defiance of stubborn assertions to the contrary it is not possible to assimilate Origen's trichotomy to Plato's: the latter is about the soul alone, the former about the whole man. And the terms are different in each case: in Plato – *nous*, intelligence, *thymos*, anger, *epithymia*, covetousness; in Origen – *pneuma*, the spirit, *psyche*, the soul, *soma*, the body. Although Greek ideas are grafted onto Origen's trichotomy, as we

---

[1] We have expounded this subject in much greater detail in 'L'anthropologie d'Origène dans la perspective du combat spirituel', *Revue d'ascétique et de mystique* 31, 1955, 364–385, and this has been subsequently taken further by J. Dupuis, 'L'esprit de l'homme': *Étude sur l'anthropologie religieuse d'Origène*. Bruges, 1967.

[2] 5, 23.

shall see, its origin is essentially biblical, for the dominant concept that gives it form is the *pneuma*, the spirit, which comes through Paul from the Hebrew *ruach*, expressing the action of God. The *pneuma* in Origen is absolutely immaterial, while in the Greeks it always has a subtle form of material existence.

So there are three elements: the *pneuma* or *spiritus*, which we translate by 'spirit' in order not to confuse it with the *nous*; then the soul (*psyche, anima*) and the body (*soma, corpus*). But the soul itself contains a higher and a lower element: the term element or part is inadequate, it would be better to speak of a tendency, for Origen's trichotomic doctrine is of a dynamic or tendential order rather an ontological one, although it has an ontological basis. The higher element is called, either by a Platonist term, the *nous* or the *mens* which we shall call the 'intellect' to avoid using for this concept the word 'spirit':[a] or by a Stoic term, the *hegemonikon*, translated into latin by *principale cordis* or *mentis* or *animae*, the 'governing or principal faculty'; or by a biblical term *kardia* or *cor*, the 'heart'. The lower element has several names which we shall discuss later.

The spirit is the divine element present in man and thus it has real continuity with the Hebrew *ruach*. Being a gift of God, it is not strictly speaking a part of the human personality, for it takes no responsibility for a man's sins; nevertheless these reduce it to a state of torpor, preventing it from acting on the soul. It is the pedagogue of the soul, or rather of the intellect, training the latter in the practice of the virtues, for it is in the spirit that the moral consciousness is found;[3] and training it also in the knowledge of God and in prayer. Distinguished from the Holy Spirit, it is nonetheless a kind of created participation in the latter and the latter's seat when He is present in a man. It is one of the many expressions used by Origen approximating to what would later be called sanctifying grace; but it differs from the scholastic conception, first in that it is found in every man and not simply in the baptised, second in that it does not quit a man when he sins here below: it stays with him in a state of inertia, but as a possibility of conversion.

The soul is the seat of the free will, of the power of choice and so of the personality. If it submits to the guidance of the spirit, it is assimilated to the spirit, becomes wholly spiritual, even in its lower element. But if it rejects the spirit and turns towards the flesh, the lower element takes over from the higher its governing role and renders the soul entirely carnal.

[a] Fr. *esprit*, which can, of course, be used in the sense of 'mind', a natural translation of *nous* and *mens*; but here it is necessary to distinguish *nous* from *pneuma*, as defined in the next paragraph.
[3] The duality of the *pneuma* and the *nous* expresses what underlies the experience of remorse, a rupture between the moral conscience which reproaches and the man who refuses to accept these reproaches. Repentance, which is the acceptance of these reproaches, restores unity and inner peace.

This higher element, intellect, heart or governing faculty, constituted the whole of the soul in the pre-existence, according to the theory favoured by Origen. Created in the Image of God which is his Word, being therefore the locus of man's participation in the image of God, it is akin to the divine, which it comes to resemble more and more through living the Christian life. It is the *pneuma*'s best pupil: the spirit represents the active aspect of grace, it is a divine gift, while the intellect is the passive and receptive aspect, the one that receives and accepts this gift. It is the organ of the moral and virtuous life, of contemplation and prayer, all under the guidance of the spirit. It bears the 'divine senses', spiritual sight, hearing, touch, smell and taste.[4] Between the spirit and the intellect, notions clearly distinct, yet inseparable here below, a delicate dialectic expresses the two fundamental aspects of grace, the gift of God and its reception by man.

The lower element of the soul was added to it after the primitive fall: it corresponds to the soul's standing temptation to turn aside from the spirit and yield to the attraction of the body. It is the source of the instincts and the passions, and it is sometimes treated as equivalent to the two lower elements in Plato's trichotomy, the *thymos* and the *epithymia*, without Origen distinguishing between the noble and the evil tendencies in these. It is also called, following Rom. 8, 6, *to phronèma tès sarkos*, 'setting the mind on the flesh', a phrase rendered by the Latin translators as *sensus carnis* or *sensus carnalis*. This is often what is meant by the expression *sarx* or *caro*, 'flesh', which unlike 'body' has always a pejorative sense: the 'flesh' is the force that attracts the soul towards the body. All that corresponds more or less to what later theology would call concupiscence, but only to a certain degree, for 'the thought of the flesh' means more than the attraction to sin. It contains natural functions, which are not evil in themselves, and can be spiritualised without being destroyed, when the intellect adheres to the spirit. All that is clearly shown by Origen's reflections on the humanity of Christ. The soul joined to the Word in the pre-existence is absolutely incapable of sin, for it is united to Him by the intensity of its charity to the extent that it is in a measure transformed into the Word, as iron plunged into fire becomes fire, and to the extent of becoming like Him 'in the form of God',[5] possessing the Good as a matter of substance, as the Deity does, and not in the contingent way known to creatures. However, in his incarnation, his soul has that lower part without which He would not be a man like unto us: for He shared in our human weaknesses with the exception of sin. So the lower part of the soul could not be for Him a source of temptation, but it was a source of distress, sadness and suffering, as the Gospel testifies.

[4] The theme of the five spiritual senses will be studied in Chapter VII.
[5] Phil. 2, 6: *PArch* II, 6, 6.

Origen's notion of the body (*sōma, corpus*) is not easy to pin down and shows many ambiguities. The *Treatise on First Principles* asserts three times over that the Trinity alone is absolutely incorporeal: so the body is what characterises the creature. That does not mean for Origen, as it does for Tertullian, that the soul is corporeal:[6] its incorporeality is clearly affirmed but it is always joined to a body. The body, sign of the creaturely condition, expresses the creature's contingency, contrasted with the substantiality of the Three persons,[7] that is to say the fact that the creature has received all that it possesses, and that it holds it all in a precarious fashion, dependent on the movements of the free will. On the other hand the end of the preface of the *Treatise on First Principles*[8] notes that the word incorporeality can have two different meanings: that of absolute incorporeality which is of a philosophical order and that of a relative incorporeality, corresponding to a more subtle kind of corporeality, as when one says in current usage that air is incorporeal. In fact, Origen applies the word body both to the terrestrial body and to the more subtle bodies which he distinguishes in his speculations on the history of rational beings: 'ethereal' bodies or 'dazzling' bodies, belonging to the pre-existent intelligences; the angels; those raised from the dead to eternal blessedness; the 'dark' bodies of the demons and of those raised from the dead to damnation. But the word incorporeality which can express either the absence of any body, however subtle, or simply the absence of the earthly body, has yet a third sense, that of a way of life without regard to the unlawful desires of the body, a meaning that is thus of a moral order: applied to the blessed in eternity, it is also applied fairly often, though obviously in a relative degree, to the righteous still living on earth.

We have seen that we must not confuse the meaning of the word body with the almost always pejorative meaning of the word flesh, which expresses an undue attachment to the body and thus refers rather to the lower part of the soul. Of course, as we shall see, the ethereal body of pre-existent state took on after the fall an earthly 'quality'. Because of man's selfishness the body then becomes, like everything else that is perceptible, a standing temptation to stick at the level of the perceptible and frustrate the ascent of the soul to the contemplation of the mystery, of which the perceptible is the mere image. But the earthly body, like everything perceptible, is good in itself: created by God, it is among those realities of which the Bible says that when He looked at them in their profound being: 'God saw that they were good.'[9] In terms of the exemplarism that

[6] *PArch* I, 6, 4; II, 2, 2; IV, 3, 15.
[7] On the contrast between the 'accidentality' of the creature and the 'substantiality' of the Trinity, in the Aristotelian terms used by Rufinus (in Greek *ousiōdōs kata symbebēkos*), see the beginning of Chapter X, 'Trinity and Incarnation'.
[8] §§8–9; and in the same book IV, 3, 15.
[9] Gen. 1, verses 10, 12, 18, 21, 25, 31; *ComJn* XIII, 42, 280.

underlies Origen's vision of the world the body, like all the beings in this world, is the image of divine realities. If the point of man's contact with the image of God lies in the soul and not in the body, the worth of this nonetheless redounds on the body which is as it were the shrine containing this image: and that is why in accordance with 1 Cor. 6, 13–20, the sins of the flesh are a profanation of this body which is holy. The ethereal body of the pre-existence survives in the earthly body after the fall in the form of *logos spermatikos*, seminal reason. Whence it will sprout to form the body of glory: or, in other words, the 'substance' of the body remains the same, only the quality changes, heavenly, then earthly, then again heavenly. For the righteous man still living on earth, the body of clay has itself also entered the radiance of the spirit which makes itself known through it, as Origen notes in connection with the action of the Holy Spirit on the prophets.[10]

The trichotomic make-up is confirmed at every stage in the existence of humanity. In the pre-existence, where the rational beings, all created equal, were absorbed in the contemplation of the Deity, before the fall differentiated them into angels, men and demons, the intellects, which will be reduced to souls as their ardour cools, were guided by their spirits and clothed in ethereal bodies. This last point is scarcely affirmed directly in what survives of Origen's work. It is assumed, partly because he says that absolute incorporeality is the privilege of the Trinity alone, partly because he mentions the ethereal bodies of the angels and the dark bodies of the demons, as well as speculating on the bodies of those resurrected. Finally, Procopius of Gaza, in his *Commentary on Genesis*, which refers to Origen's, mentions and contests the interpretation that Origen gives of the second chapter of Genesis where he saw the creation of the 'glittering' body (*augoeides*) which 'conveyed' the pre-existant intellect created in the first chapter. The 'conveyed' is borrowed from the Middle and Neo-Platonist doctrine of the 'vehicle of the soul', of which Origen, as we shall see, several times makes use. And Procopius goes on to show that after the fall this same body, while remaining the same, hid its brilliance under the 'tunics of skin',[11] which symbolise the earthly quality that it is putting on. Later on in this chapter we shall look at the problems posed by those passages in Origen which seem to find in the second chapter of Genesis the creation of the earthly body, while presenting it as following the fall, which occurred in chapter three of the same book.

After death, even before the resurrection, the soul retains a certain bodily dress which Origen infers from the parable of the evil rich man and Lazarus and from the appearance of Samuel to Saul, if we rely on a text quoted by Methodius of Olympus in his *Aglaophon or On the*

[10] CCels VII, 4.
[11] Gen. 3, 21: see M. Simonetti, 'Alcune osservazioni sull' interpretazione origeniana di Gen. 2, 7 and 3, 21', *Aevum* 36, 1962, 370–381.

Resurrection:[12] he assimilates it expressly to the 'vehicle of the soul' and it is of course a logical consequence of the affirmation that the Trinity alone is absolutely incorporeal. Origen's doctrine of the risen body, severely criticised following a misunderstanding of this same Methodius, will be studied below:[13] here let us just say that it aims at maintaining, following Paul's comparison of the seed and the plant,[14] at once an identity of substance and a difference of quality between the earthly body and the body of glory, which is assimilated to the ethereal bodies of the angels. An essential difference between those who are raised to glory and those who are raised to damnation is that the latter no longer have any *pneuma*: God has taken back the gift He gave them. Origen explains this three times over[15] when interpreting Matt. 24, 51 or Luke 12, 46: if the master finds the bad servant busy beating his fellow servants and drinking with drunkards, he will 'cut him in two' (*dichotomesei*) as both the evangelists put it, that is, according to Origen. He will take back the *pneuma*, while the soul and body will go to Gehenna, the soul keeping nonetheless its indelible participation in the image of God, which now becomes the source of its torment.

The dominant context of this trichotomic anthropology is more moral and ascetic than mystical: it is the spiritual battle. The soul is torn between the spirit and the attraction of the earthly body, the flesh: of this struggle the soul is both the scene and the stake, and it is the soul, with its free will, that has to decide for one or the other. In itself, by reason of the two elements or tendencies that divide it, the soul is in league with both sides.

Man's participation in the Image of God[16]

The theme of the creation of man in the image of God flows from three passages in Genesis: 1, 26–27 which links the image of God with man's domination over the animals; 5, 1–3 where the image expresses a certain filiation; 9, 6 where the image makes man a sacred being whose blood may not be spilt. But the Septuagint version by translating *selem*, image, and *demut*, likeness, by *eikon* and *homoiosis* has injected into the biblical text the philosophical speculations of which those terms are the expression. *Eikon* brings in the Platonist exemplarism which makes perceptible being the image of the divine and supreme realities that Plato calls the ideas: it is true that Plato does not use *eikon* to express the

---

[12] III, XVII, 2–5, in the Greek preserved by Photius, Bibl. 234 (CUFn V), 300b–301a, and the Old Slav version: all in GCS Methodius.

[13] See pp. 248–250.

[14] 1 Cor. 15, 35–38.

[15] *PArch* II, 10, 7 which also shows two other interpretations, but this one is the only one mentioned in *SerMt* 62 (GCS XI) and in *ComRm* II, 9 (PG 14).

[16] On the whole of this section see our book *Théologie de l'image de Dieu chez Origène*. Paris, 1956 (cited below as *Image*).

kinship of the soul with the divine beings, for with him the word always relates to the senses: he uses *syngeneia*, kinship, or else *oikeiosis*, familiarity. But *homoiosis*, likeness, to God, is already considered by the presocratic philosophers and by Plato in the celebrated passage of the Theaetetus[17] to be the aim of human life. So it is not surprising that a doctrine of the image of God in man should be present in the work of, first, Philo the Jew, and then of a great many of the Fathers before and after Origen.

For the Christian the testimony of Genesis must be reconciled with several Pauline texts, especially Col. 1, 15 which calls Christ the 'image of the invisible God'. For Origen this reconciliation is easy. Only the Christ is in the strict sense the image of God, the perfect image: He is this by his divinity alone, 'invisible image of the invisible God', for God, invisible and incorporeal, can only have one image, invisible and incorporeal. Irenaeus reasoned quite differently and saw the Image of God in the Incarnate Word with his double nature, present from all eternity in the divine designs, for the image of God cannot be for him anything other than a translation into the visible. But the relationship of the Word with man under the aspect of the image is the same in both theologians: 'God said: Let us make man after our image and our likeness.' Leaving aside for the moment the word 'likeness', which we shall take up again shortly, we can explain the sentence as follows. First, the famous plural 'Let us make'; this is regularly interpreted by Origen, as by most of the ante-Nicene Fathers, as a conversation between the Father and the Son, his collaborator in the creation. So man is created after the Image of God who is the Word, at once agent and model for the creation of man, as elsewhere, in a different way, for that of the world. Thus – and this is one of the few points on which Origen's terminology never varies – only the Son will be called the Image of God, man will simply be 'after the image' or 'image of the image' and the expression 'the after-the-image'[b] (*to kat'eikona*) is frequently used by Origen to denote man's participation in the image of God.

If the humanity of Christ is not included by Origen in the Image of God, it is, like that of all men 'after the image' or 'image of the image'. However, it plays a special part in the transmission of the image, it is like a second, intermediate image, the Word being the first, between God and us, for it is the most immediate model offered to us to imitate, and, according to Origen's interpretation of *Lamentations* 4, 20 which we shall explain below, the Shadow of the Lord Christ under which 'we live among the nations'. Contrariwise, we know of no passage in Origen which brings in the Holy Spirit in connection with the image. Although

[17] 176–177.

[b] I have taken the word 'after' from Gen. 1, 26 EVV and use it for the author's frequently repeated 'selon l'image'.

Origen makes the spirit of the Father come through the medium of the
Son who communicates to the Spirit all his *epinoiai*, in other words his
attributes,[18] he never calls the Spirit the image of the Son. The first to
draw that conclusion would be his dearest disciple, Gregory Thaumaturgus,
in the *Exposition of the Faith* which is preserved in the *Life* of him written
by Gregory of Nyssa.[19]

Origen understands the first two chapters of Genesis, not as two
accounts of the creation, but as two distinct creations. Of these the first
relates to the soul, which alone is created after the image, the soul which is
the incorporeal and invisible image of the incorporeal and invisible Word,
and the second relates to the body, which is simply the vessel containing
the image. We have seen, when dealing with the trichotomic anthropology
that, according to the testimony of Procopius of Gaza, Origen in his
Commentary on Genesis saw the second chapter as an account of the
creation of the ethereal body of the pre-existent: since only the Trinity is
without a body, these two creations, though logically distinct, must have
been chronologically simultaneous. We must not, however, conceal the
fact that in the texts that have come down to us it is not made clear
whether the ethereal or the terrestrial body is meant; out of the eight
passages in which Origen speaks in this way of the double creation, only
one mentions sin in connection with the second one, and the seven others
do not say which body is meant. If the earthly body was meant, that
would raise a grave problem of interpretation. Since the earthly 'quality'
was given to this body, according to Origen's theory of pre-existence,
after the fall which took place in the pre-existence and is represented by
chapter three of Genesis, it is difficult to understand how the creation of
the earthly body could be recorded in chapter two, that is prior to the fall.
That is why Procopius of Gaza's point solves the puzzle when it moves
the body's change of quality from heavenly to earthly to the episode of
the tunics of skin.[20] Can we suppose that, if Origen paid attention to this
difficulty in his *Commentary on Genesis*, because he was there explaining
the text itself, he was more careless elsewhere? Besides, several of the
passages in which he is not precise about the nature of the body meant are
taken from homilies intended for a popular audience: Origen does not
want to embarrass his hearers by going into his hypothesis of pre-existence.

So Origen places the 'after-the-image' not in the body – in that case
God would be corporeal as the Anthropomorphites claimed – but in the
soul, or rather in the soul's higher element, the intellect or governing
faculty, sometimes also in the *logos*, the reason which is in man,

---

[18] *ComJn* II, 10 (6), 75–76.

[19] PG 46. 912 D.

[20] Gen. 3, 21: Procopius of Gaza in PG 87/1, 221. See Simonetti's article mentioned in
note 11.

participating in the divine Logos: but this logos represents the same reality as the intellect.

The 'after-the-image' is participation in the Father and the Son. It is participation in the Father, 'the One who is', according to the word heard by Moses at the Burning Bush:[21] all those who *are* participate in the Father, the source of being. But the notion of being is often taken by Origen in a sense more supernatural than natural, though that is to bring in a distinction recognised by the Alexandrian incidentally, but in general foreign to his way of thinking: thus evil is a 'non-being', that 'nothing' which according to John 1, 3 was made without the Word.[22] The demons which at the beginning were 'beings', created by God, renounced their relation with God and became 'non-beings'. But the 'after-the-image' is also participation in God as God: rational creatures, even in the 'accidentality' of their creaturely being, that is their contingence, receive divinisation and progress in it: by the action of the Son they become those 'gods' of which Psalm 81 (82) speaks, gods-in-the-making, so to speak, whose divinisation will only be complete in the eternal blessedness, when the 'after-the-image' will have progressed to complete 'likeness'. For the participation in God which it expresses is a dynamic concept: the image tends to rejoin the model and to reproduce it. Like the spirit that is in the man, the 'after-the-image' is one of Origen's numerous approximations to sanctifying grace.

The 'after-the-image' is also participation in the Son, and that goes for all the titles (*epinoiai*) of the Son which play a primary role in Origen's christology: these are the titles given to Christ in the New Testament, but also in the Old if it read according to the spiritual exegesis; they correspond to the diverse attributes of the Son, in Himself and in relation to us. In the first place it is by the 'after-the-image' that He communicates to us the quality of sons: adopted sons of the Father, who have become such through the action of the Only Son. Likewise, with his quality as the Christ, the Anointed. He gives us what He is, Wisdom, Truth, Life, Light, etc. Finally, as Logos, He makes of us beings who are *logika*, a word, the meaning of which, being above all supernatural, is not well rendered by 'rational'. only the saint is *logikos*, he declares. The demons, having once been *logika*, have become, through their rejection of God, *aloga*, beings without reason: thus they are assimilated to the animals, becoming as it were spiritual beasts.

The 'after-the-image' is, Origen expressly says, 'our principal substance',[23] the very basis of our nature: man is defined, at the deepest level of his being, by his relation to God and by the movement that leads to his becoming more like his model, thanks to the divine action which is

[21] Exod. 3, 14.
[22] ComJn II, 13 (7), 91–99; PArch I, 3, 6.
[23] ComJn XX, 22 (20), 182.

manifest at the beginning and at each of the stages of this development, and thanks also to the freedom that God has given man when creating him. This freedom, in which free will, the power of choice, holds an important place, is not, however, limited to free will, but exhibits, through our author's spiritual doctrine, all the shades of meaning of Paul's *eleutheria*. The truth is that adherence to God liberates, rejection of God enslaves. The 'after-the-image' is, in addition, a 'source of knowledge': of course, all knowledge of God is revelation, but the first of these revelations is the one God gave us when he created us in his image: in this 'after-the-image', which is the most profound element of our being, we find God. Here, Origen reproduces a principle of Greek philosophy which is a common-sense affirmation: only the like knows the like. We have already drawn attention to this when studying Origen's exegesis.

But since man is free, it can happen and does happen, that instead of choosing God, he chooses against God. What then becomes of the 'after-the-image' at grips with sin? Sin wraps it up in adverse images, hides it under a pile of them. These images are of various kinds. The image of the Earthly is superimposed on that of the Heavenly: but in most of the texts the earthly is not Adam, as in 1 Cor. 15, 49, but the devil, cause of the fall of the pre-existent intellects. Men are now in the image of, and have become children of, the devil, a relationship that is not natural, for God alone is their father naturally, and the devil is stealing his children. The image of Caesar, which adorns the tribute money,[24] represents the prince of this world, the devil: a rather negative insight, but there are more positive ones in Origen's political theory. Finally, sin imposes bestial images which Origen lists according to the main characteristics of each species, thus creating a whole theological menagerie. This assimilation to the beasts, which is on the moral plane, is probably the explanation of Jerome's strange accusation that Origen believed in metempsychosis, in spite of frequent undisputed texts, taken from the works preserved in Greek, in which the Alexandrian calls this doctrine stupid and shows it to be contradictory to the teaching of the Church.[25]

However, these diabolical and bestial images cannot destroy the image of God. The latter endures beneath the former like the water in Abraham's well which the Philistines filled with mire.[26] A picture painted by the Son of God, it is indelible.[27] But, just as Isaac had to come to clear out the wells his father had dug, only Christ, our Isaac, can clear the wells of our soul of the filth that our sins have accumulated, so that the living water can flow again. The permanence of the 'after-the-image' in man

[24] Matt. 22, 15–22.
[25] See *Image* 181–215.
[26] *HomGn* XIII, 3–4.
[27] Ibid.

despite his faults assures, through the grace of Christ, the possibility of conversion: it is the same with the permanence of the spirit, an element of the trichotomic anthropology.

The 'after-the-image' is, as we have said, a dynamic reality and it tends to rejoin its model and to assimilate itself to it. It is a point of departure, a kind of seed which must germinate and grow. The goal of this growth, which will only attain perfection in the final beatitude, is the 'likeness'. Origen notes that when in Gen. 1, 26, God announces his intention to create man He mentions both the image and the likeness, but when in Gen. 1, 27, the holy book shows that creation accomplished, there is no longer any question of the likeness, only of the image: the likeness is reserved for the end, it will be the fulfilment of the image. Likewise – and here the Scriptural support is firmer, for it no longer depends on an interpretation – John writes in his first epistle:[28] 'we know that when He appears (the Christ at his parousia), we shall be like (*homoioi*) Him, for we shall see Him as He is'.[29] The likeness (*homoiōsis*) will coincide with the knowledge of Christ and of God face to face just as the 'after-the-image' coincided with the beginning of knowledge. This notion of likeness, we repeat, is linked with those of the pre-socratics and of Plato who regarded it as the goal of human life. It is already to be found in Clement, though Irenaeus gives to the distinction image/likeness another meaning which suggests rather that between the natural and the supernatural.

The way from the 'after-the-image' to the likeness is the road of spiritual progress. The themes which express it in relation to the theology of the image bring out, without Origen attempting a synthesis or posing a problem, now man's own action, now that of God's grace. In man's action is seen above all the imitation of God and of Christ.[30]

But other themes put the emphasis more on the divine action. The Word *forms* (verb *morphoun*) its believer as Jesus went, still carried in his mother's womb, to form John who was still in Elizabeth's womb.[31] Better still, the Word forms itself in the Christian: we have already pointed this out when studying the spiritual exegesis of the New Testament and we shall speak of it again more fully in connection with

---

[28] 3, 2.

[29] *PArch* III, 6, 1.

[30] The imitation and 'following' of God are already found in Greek philosophy, in Plato, in the Stoics of various periods, in Middle and Neo-Platonism. Almost absent from the Hebrew Old Testament, but abundantly present in Philo, the imitation and 'following' of God, to which are joined the imitation and 'following' of Christ, can be found in the pages of the Gospels, of Paul, of the Epistle to the Hebrews and the Catholic Epistles. Thence they pass to the Fathers of the 2nd century and become a commonplace in the literature of martyrdom. In Origen they hold a considerable place. See our article 'L'imitation et la "suite" de Dieu et du Christ dans les premiers siecles chretienas ainsi que leurs sources gréco-romaines et hébraiques'. *Jahrbuch für Antike und Christentum*. 21, 1978, 7–41.

[31] *ComJn* VI, 49 (30), 252–256.

the great mystical theme of the birth and growth of Jesus in each one of us. The Word forms itself in the Christian through the practice of the virtues. Indeed, among the titles of Christ (*epinoiai*) are to be found the virtues: He is virtue and He is each virtue, the virtues are Christ. In a striking formula He is 'Virtue entire, animated and alive',[32] the last two adjectives meaning that Virtue in general and each virtue in particular are the divine Person of the Son. Thus the practice of virtue – but you cannot practice one without practising them all, the Greeks had already said that – is a participation of an existential order in the very Person of Christ. Finally, as we have already pointed out in connection with the spiritual exegesis, the contemplation of Christ's glory transforms (2 Cor. 3, 18) the contemplator into the very image of what is contemplated: this contemplator is the intellect, the governing faculty or the heart, the higher element of the soul, when, turning to the Lord, it has put off the veil that hides the true meaning of the old law, the veil of attachment to the perceptible, the veil of sin, of a coarse understanding of Scripture. Thus some passages point also to the action of the Holy Spirit as the power which brings the seed to fruition, which makes the 'after-the-image' grow into the perfect likeness.[33]

The likeness will be achieved, then, with perfect knowledge, in the resurrection and the beatitude. We do not press the point here, for it will be studied more completely in connection with Origen's eschatology. Let us simply say that the likeness will end in unity with Christ, a unity which is not understood in a pantheistic manner, for it respects the 'hypostases' of the angels and of men as Origen makes clear in contradiction of the Stoic 'conflagration'. But all, having become sons, somehow within the Only Son, will see the Father in the same way that the Son sees Him. All having become one Sun in the Sun of Righteousness, the Word, will shine with the same glory. It would not do to conclude, as has sometimes too hastily been done, that there will not then be any further mediation by the Word. That will always exist, but its mode will have changed: it is in becoming within the Son that the saints will see the Father as Himself and will shine with his glory.[34]

*   *   *

Even before expounding Origen's theological speculations about anthropology, the doctrines of the first and last things, we are in a position to estimate the spiritual riches of his conceptions. The trichotomic scheme, through the theme of spiritual struggle, controls his ascetic and moral teaching. The theology of the image of God, at the root of the possibility of knowing God, is the foundation of the whole of Origen's mysticism.

[32] *ComJn* XXXII, 11 (7), 127.
[33] *SchLc* 13, 27 (PG 17, 357 C); *FragmEp* IIIon Ep. 1, 5 (*JThS* III, p. 237, 1, 21).
[34] *ComJn* I, 16, 92; *ComMt* X, 2; *ComJn* XX, 7, 47.

6
The Doctrine of Knowledge[1]

The only kind of knowledge that really interests Origen is the kind that
he calls 'mystical': *mystikos* being the adjective that corresponds to
mysterion, mystery. The meaning of the expressions 'mystical knowledge
(*gnōsis*)' or 'mystical contemplation (*theōria*)' is essentially that of
knowledge or contemplation of the mystery. Only at the end of this
chapter shall we raise questions about the mystical nature, in the modern
sense, of this notion of knowledge. We use the word 'knowledge' to
translate *gnōsis*, which is the common term corresponding to that word.
When dealing with Origen, as with Clement, French scholars often use
the word 'gnose'. We shall not do so. For one thing we see no reason thus
to distinguish by a special term knowledge in Origen from the knowledge
that is in question in the whole Christian spiritual tradition and in doing
this to associate it willy nilly with the dangerous notion of what Paul[2] and
Irenaeus call the 'knowledge falsely so called', that of the heterodox
gnōstics. For another thing, if this term could seem in some measure
legitimate in the case of Clement, because he constantly uses the word
gnōstikos to mean spiritual, it is all the more inadequate for Origen in that
the latter never denotes by this term the Christian 'spiritual', being
undoubtedly anxious, in reaction against Clement, to separate clearly the
ideal that he is presenting from the one offered by the heretics in
question; he uses the Pauline terms *teleios*, perfect, or *pneumatikos*,
spiritual.

Nor must we lose sight of the fact that Origen's theology always
remains synthetic in this sense, as we shall see, that knowledge is for him
the same thing as union and love. To ask Origen the question whether
blessedness is knowledge or love would be for him a nonsense, for
knowledge is love. People have often spoken of Origen's 'intellectual
mysticism': the adjective is acceptable if it means that he normally
approaches the problem of the spiritual life from the angle of knowledge;
but not if a distinction is being made between the intellectual and the
spiritual which Origen does not make, or again if there is an attempt

[1] The justification for all that we say in this chapter and all the references can be found in
our book *Origène et la 'connaissance mystique'*, Bruges/Paris, 1961 (cited below as
Connaissance). See also M. Harl, *Origène et la fonction révélatrice du Verbe incarné*, Paris,
1958.
[2] 1 Tim. 6, 20.

thereby to attribute to him a 'mysticism' of lower value, a suggestion that
will be refuted, we think, in the pages that follow.

Of this 'mysticism' the setting is an exemplarist view of the world,
dominated, as Platonism is, because of the doctrine of the ideas, by the
relation between the image and its mode: the same view is also to be
found in his exegesis. For if man was created after the Image of God, the
Logos, all the perceptible beings that surround Him are also images of the
divine realities, the mysteries which are the supreme object of knowledge.[3]
And Origen's notion of sin also fits into this perspective.

The knowing subject

In expounding Origen's anthropology and in particular his view of
creation after the image of God, we have seen what is essential about the
knowing subject. Since only like can know like, man's participation in the
image of God, which is already grace in itself, allows man to receive the
further graces of knowledge of God and of the divine realities. And the
more the 'after-the-image' progresses in the direction of the 'likeness', the
more man becomes capable of knowing. The goal is knowledge 'face to
face', coinciding with the perfect 'likeness'.

Knowledge is the meeting of two freedoms, that of God and that of
man. That of God on the one hand, for a divine or angelic being is only
seen if he is willing to make himself visible.[4] The Contra Celsum[5] clearly
asserts, dealing with passages from Plato that Celsus brings up, the whole
distance that separates Christian grace from the approximations known to
Plato and the Platonists. Of course, for the latter, the divine realities can
only be seen in the light of God,[6] but this light will necessarily come to
anyone who places himself in certain conditions of ascesis. Now, Origen
recalls, the grace of knowledge is a free gift of the divine love. It must be
received freely by man and ascesis is the witness to this will on man's part.
Origen criticised the conception held by the Montanists of trance as
unconsciousness and that shows that God does not take possession of a
soul without its consent.

So a man must prepare himself to receive grace: first by reading and
meditating on Scripture, in an attitude of prayer, enlightened by divine
grace: this is what the later monasticism was to call lectio divina. At the
same time the obstacles must be removed which hinder the reception of
the divine light: attachment to the body and to the perceptible, as well as
sin. For it is impossible to know the divine realities if one is living an evil
life. That is why the demons cannot understand anything that relates to
the work of salvation. Sin is incompatible with the prophetic gift and the

[3] ComCt III (GCS VIII, 208, 1, 14).
[4] HomLc III, 1.
[5] VII, 42.
[6] CCels VII, 45 referring to Plato, Republic VI, 508b.

Holy Spirit only rests on the prophet transitorilly, for every man, except Jesus, is a sinner: on Christ alone the Spirit rested permanently because there was no sin in Him. The virtue most closely linked with knowledge is purity of heart, of the heart that is to say of the intellect or principal faculty: this virtue, also, is grace and drives from the soul attachment to sin. Humility and charity necessarily go with it. Action and contemplation are inseparable, and Origen is the first to identify this with the story of Martha and Mary. The apostolic life of the preacher and teacher only has value if its aim is contemplation; and contemplation blossoms into apostolic action. To see Jesus transfigured on the mountain, and thus to contemplate the divinity of the Word seen through his humanity – the Transfiguration is the symbol of the highest knowledge of God in his Son which is possible here below – one must, with the three apostles, make the ascent of the mountain, symbolising the spiritual ascent. Those who remain in the plain see Jesus 'with no form nor comeliness',[7] even if they believe in his divinity: for these spiritual invalids He is simply the Doctor who cares for them. Or to use another image from the Gospels Jesus speaks to the people in parables out of doors; He explains them to the disciples indoors: so one must go into the house in order to begin to understand.[8]

The object of knowledge

The object of knowledge is the Mystery. Denoted by *mysterion* and its adjective *mystikos*, it can also be spoken of as Truth, *alētheia* and its adjectives *alēthēs* and *alēthinos* – using a Platonist vocabulary in which Truth is normally the opposite of image, not of error or falsehood – and by other words as well, both nouns and adjectives. There are some pairs of adjective, opposite and relative to each other, which express Origen's exemplarism, in each case one relating to the perceptible reality, which is image, the other to the mystery of which it is the image. Thus *aisthetos*, perceptible, is the opposite of *noētos*, intelligible; *somatikos*, corporeal, that of *pneumatikos*, spiritual; *oratos*, visible, that of *aoratos*, invisible. Perceptible or corporeal or visible bread becomes the image of intelligible or spiritual or invisible bread, the Word which nourishes souls.[9]

So Origen sees in perceptible beings, especially in those to which the Scripture bears witness, images of the divine mysteries, and he relates them to the mysteries in much the same way that Plato related them to the ideas. To a certain extent the mysteries correspond to the Platonic ideas and include them. For the ideas in Plato's sense, as well as the 'reasons' in the Stoic sense which are more or less confused with them, in spite of the fact that originally the former were general and the latter particular, all

[7] Isa. 53, 2.
[8] See *Connaissance* 399–442.
[9] Ibid. 24–46.

these fall for Origen into the category of the mysteries: they constitute, as
it were, the plans and the seeds of the future creation and, just as the
Middle Platonist philosophers did with the ideas of God, Origen makes
of them an 'intelligible world' which the Son holds in Himself in that He
is Wisdom, his first title, logically prior to that of Logos. Thus organised
knowledge of the world can only be religious, as Origen's own work
attests, and also the panegyric of Gregory Thaumaturgus. 'Physics' or
'physiology' consists in recovering the divine idea which corresponds to
each thing in order to use that thing in accordance with the will of the
Creator: it shows indeed the insufficiency of the perceptible, the vanity of
the man who puts his trust in it, but also its value as image of the divine,
the value which is given it by the divine will that is in it. It is true that the
perceptible world was created, as we shall see, after the fall of the pre-
existent intellects, but its purpose is to show man the way to those
mysteries of which it is the image, to give man by its beauty the desire for
those mysteries, and also to guide him towards the One who holds all
those mysteries in Himself, the Son, Image of the Father. In Origen's
exegesis one sometimes comes across short dissertations on natural
history taken from the Greek naturalists, but what matters to him is the
spiritual or moral lesson that can be drawn from them. In this Origen was
inaugurating a tradition which would not only be found in later Fathers –
think of the *Homilies on the Hexahemeron* of Basil, but even in spiritual
writers of more recent times – as in the *Treatise on the Love of God* of
François de Sales.

Alongside the perceptible world there are the spiritual beings. The
human soul has its mysteries: so have the angelology and demonology
that are so well developed in our author. The world above has its
symbolical geography of which that of the Holy Land, with Jerusalem at
the centre and the other towns of Judea and the other countries
surrounding it, represents the image.[10] Such are also the mysteries of the
Kingdom of Heaven, those of the Word in his divinity and in his
incarnation, or in each event of his earthly life, and finally the mysteries
of the Father. As with the knowledge of the visible world, that of the
celestial world is also contained in the Son, Image of the Father. In the last
analysis the Mystery is not an idea, but a Person, the Son, and in spite of
the multiplicity of 'theorems', that is of objects of contemplation, which
it provides, the Intelligible World finds its perfection in the unity of the
Person of the Son, one and multiple, as we shall see when we study
Origen's Christology.[11]

But to see in the mystery the supreme object of knowledge is surely
paradoxical to the point of absurdity. Is not mystery, by definition, the
unknowable? Origen is aware of the paradox. He would reply that the

[10] Thus PArch IV, 3, 6–9.
[11] See *Connaissance* 47–84.

mystery is not unknowable in itself. The Father knows Himself and knows the Son and the Son knows the Father.[12] On this last point there are enough texts to bring out the absurdity of the accusation put forward by Epiphanius and by Jerome in which they blame Origen for saying that the Son cannot see the Father; the passage in the *Treatise on First Principles*[13] on which they rely is in fact directed against the Anthropo- morphites who attribute both to the Father and to the Son in his divinity bodies and corporeal senses. Epiphanius and Jerome understand it as if Origen meant that the Son does not know the Father and see in it a proof of the inferiority of the Son to the Father. As for the Holy Spirit He too knows the Father and the Son, but as He proceeds from the Father through the Son, He knows the Father through the medium of the Son. The Father and the Son know each other by the very act, both eternal and continual, by which the Father begets the Son.

As far as angels and men are concerned – angels have knowledge greatly surpassing that of men – there are different degrees in their knowledge of the mysteries, depending both on their nature and on the spiritual level reached by each knowing subject. Although Origen sees God more as Light than as Darkness, he sometimes alludes to the Darkness in which God hides Himself.[14] But this relates to our ignorance: in Himself God is Light. Our ignorance belongs to our carnal condition: in the resurrection we shall have a knowledge like that of the angels, though Origen does not say clearly how perfect that knowledge is. At the moment we are ascending towards God. Our starting point is the creation: the Word, in that He is Wisdom, holds within Himself the ideas and reasons that are the basis of creation. Our ascent continues through the Incarnate Word, the normal intermediary through whom God, as the Scriptures present Him, is known.

But grace is necessary for all knowledge of God: the divine Being is only known if He freely makes Himself known.[15] Thus the three Persons have each a role in the imparting of this knowledge. All wisdom comes from God: this Word is sometimes understood even of technical skill. Through the two other Persons it is always the Father, source of the Trinity, who teaches: He does it through human masters. It is He who gives deep understanding to those who receive that particular grace. But to a certain degree the human master is no longer necessary and the man who has reached the spiritual level is taught directly by God. To understand the Gospels we need the *nous* that is the mind of Christ[16] and to have in ourselves the spring of living water which the word of Jesus

[12] Among other texts *FragmJn* XIII (GCS IV, 495).
[13] I, 1, 8.
[14] Ps. 17 (18), 12 and Exod. 20, 21; thus *ComJn* II, 28 (23), 172–174.
[15] *HomLc* III, 1.
[16] 1 Cor. 2, 6.

pours into the soul. The son is not only the physician who cures the blindness or deafness of the soul so that it can see and hear, he is the Revealer in person who communicates to men the knowledge He has of the Father. The Spirit unveils the spiritual meaning of the Scriptures which He inspired and He acts within the soul. The role of each of the divine Persons in this teaching is not always clearly distinguished. It can be said, however, that the Father is the origin, the Son the minister, the Spirit the medium in which the teaching is produced. This teaching role is also very often expressed in the theme of light meaning the grace of knowledge: we shall study this among the great spiritual themes.[17]

There is one further point to be emphasised: it is dangerous for the spiritual master to reveal the mystery prematurely or wantonly to someone who is not ready to receive it. 'Do not throw what is holy to the dogs, or cast pearls before swine, lest they trample them underfoot and then turn and rend you.'[18] Indeed, to anyone that is not ready, this revelation can do harm, like over-rich food given to one with fever; and, worse still, it has happened that a wrong understanding of these mysteries, spread abroad, has turned against the faith: reading the apologists of the second century is enough to show the calumnies spread among the pagans because of a mistaken understanding of the eucharistic mystery and this explains the reluctance of the primitive Church to talk about it. But this advice of Origen's has often been wrongly interpreted as implying that there were in his teaching secret traditions, like those to which the Gnōstics appealed, traditions that were only passed on to the initiated. This was because people understood the mysteries to be in Origen's view doctrines of an intellectual order and not insights of a spiritual order. Now there is no question in the work of Origen of secret traditions circulating in the Great Church: he knows of them among the Jews and the Gnōstics, but not in orthodox Christianity. Nor is there any question of philosophical esotericism, of something like that which Ammonius Saccas, according to Porphyry's *Life of Plotinus*, kept for his three favourite disciples. It is simply a counsel of prudence that any spiritual director is capable of understanding.[19]

Other features of the mystery will be studied with the spiritual themes: the mystery is light; the mystery is food; the mystery is wine that rejoices the soul.

The starting point of knowledge
Since perceptible beings are images of the mysteries they constitute the starting point of knowledge. The main terms which express this relationship are *eikon*, image, *skia*, shadow, *typos*, type, figure, *symbolon*,

[17] See *Connaissance* 85–154.
[18] Matt. 7, 6: *HomJos* XXI, 2.
[19] See *Connaissance* 155–166.

symbol, *ainigma*, enigma, as well as the pairs of adjectives that have been noted in connection with the vocabulary of the mystery.[20] So these words are applied to the perceptible beings of the world around us, and specially to those of which the Scripture speaks. As far as the former are concerned we shall only draw attention to a long fragment of Book III of the *Commentary on Genesis* preserved in the *Philocalia*[21] which deals with the heavenly bodies. There Origen refutes the astrological beliefs which make the stars the agents of human destiny, and thus entail a determinism destructive of all free will. But if they are not agents, they are, in Origen's view, signs, which only the angels can read and not men. It is through the stars that God communicates to the angels what He wants them to make known; the starry heaven is thus the Bible of the angels. Fallen angels communicated to men the knowledge they thus acquired before the fall and in this way they gave birth to astrology, a science that is deceptive and diabolical even in the cases where it speaks the truth, because it is used to do men harm.

The Scripture is symbolic: that emerges from all that has been said about Origen as an exegete. The Old Testament is a figure of the New and through it and like it a figure of the eternal Gospel of the beatitude. The ultimate truth of Scripture cannot belong to the historical order but must belong to the spiritual, and when Origen attaches, which is not often, a historical fact of the old covenant to a historical fact of the new, he has in mind the unique mysterious reality figured by them both, having regard to the different relations of each Testament with the mystery.

Two problems are rooted in the fact that not only is Scripture as a whole symbolic, but that the very word of Scripture itself is so: we have discussed the procedure by which mysteries are sought in the smallest detail of the sacred text. The first problem is the one that was fiercely debated in Greek philosophy – think of Plato's *Cratylus* – that of the origin of words. For Origen the relationship between a word and its meaning is not a matter of convention, it is part of the nature of things. That is why Origen looks into the etymology of the names of persons and places to find the mystery which the person or place symbolises. Magic, to which he accords a certain reality, while condemning it as diabolical and harmful, shows him that names really have a power and he explains in analogous fashion the power of the divine names in exorcism. In a rather surprising passage[22] he encourages a man to go on reading the Bible if he is tempted to give it up because he does not seem to be understanding anything: reading the Scripture will still have an effect on him, destroying the asps and vipers that lurk in his soul. In spite of appearances this is not really magic, in that magic tries to get power over things, without regard

[20] Ibid. 216–235.
[21] *Philoc.* 23.
[22] *HomJos* XX, 1–2 or *Philoc.* 12.

to doing God's will. The reading of Scripture is in this case an act inspired by a *bona fide* wish to understand: it is effective, even if one does not get an impression of understanding, but not if it is not desired, because the act is fundamentally a prayer. Reading the Bible is a sacramental act in which God answers man's prayer.

The second problem is that of the anthropomorphisms attributed either to God or to that spiritual reality that we call the human soul. We explained above how this problem arose in the primitive Church. Of course the corporeal organs and passions attributed to God in the Bible cannot be taken literally, but that does not mean that they are devoid of meaning: they correspond to certain divine activities or faculties. The mention of God's eyes expresses his universal knowledge, that of his feet his presence everywhere on earth, etc. But there is one passion that the Father really experiences, as does the Son before the incarnation, that of love which gives the two Testaments and the whole work of Redemption their meaning. For, in contradiction to what the philosophers say, 'the Father Himself is not impassible'.[23] The anthropomorphisms attributed to God and the soul are images of the mysterious realities. There is a 'law of homonymy' which applies the same terms to the inner and the outer man: the highest point of this conception is found in the theme of the five spiritual senses which we shall expound below.

But why has God spoken to men in symbols and why has He only given them the truth in this obscure form? First, because man is a body, rivetted to a corporeal world which is a world of images. There is a close connection between literality and corporeality: the same reason lay behind the divine anthropomorphisms in the Bible and the Incarnation of the Son. Now corporeality on earth, and thus the necessity for symbolism, is a consequence of the fall: that will be explained with Origen's thought on the beginnings of humanity, the pre-existence, the original fault as a cooling of fervour and a surfeit of contemplation. And that is why, in the course of the spiritual ascent, the symbols become less opaque, and yield up ever more clearly the mysteries that they contain. And so the symbol takes its place in the long road followed by God in the education of man. To man imprisoned in his body, incapable of understanding anything that is not made known to him through his physical organs, God could only reveal Himself through perceptible figures which would bring man little by little to the discovery of God's true nature. To the multitude Jesus speaks in parables, but indoors he explains these parables to his apostles who are somewhat more advanced and at least want to understand them. The parables themselves let through a certain amount of light which can give them that desire. Education through the image is a law of our present condition: it leads fallen man to

[23] *HomEz* VI, 6: GCS VIII.

a kind of contemplation and gets him progressively used to the divine by means of the subdued light that filters through the symbol.[24]

Therefore the symbol has in the divine strategy a transitory function: we have to get beyond it. To stay with the symbol as if it were the truth – in Origen's Platonist sense – as if it were the end of the journey, when in fact it is only an instrument, that in Origen's view is essentially what sin is. It is of the nature of created things that they must be left behind: the soul in its soaring must aim far beyond them. So it is insofar as we will to get beyond them that the created things show the Creator and arouse in us a desire for Him. Let it not be said that this attitude shows a contempt for created things: on the contrary it gives them their true value, an eternal value since they show the way to true eternity, instead of conferring on them, by taking them for something that they are not, an absolute and eternal status which they do not have. Such is the sin of the idolaters who take the creature, which is the means by which we know, for the absolute which we are seeking to know, thus turning it into an idol. In a way all sin is idolatry. Thus Origen casts the stigma of idolatry on the 'wisdom of this world', the materialism of Epicurean ethics or Stoic physics, astral devotion, which however he credits with a particular nobility, and the Aristotelian theory of the three kinds of good which considers good not only the virtues which are good for the soul, but also whatever is good for the body and good 'outside'. He recognises the value of the Platonist dialectic which takes the creatures up to God, but he blames Plato, and Socrates, for practising idolatry, in spite of their lofty thoughts on God.[25]

What is true of created things applies also to Scripture, but in a different way to each Testament. As far as the Old Testament is concerned, its literal message is out of date, its letter 'kills'. The ceremonial and legal precepts have been abolished. The sack of Jerusalem by Titus marked the end. The old cult was a pattern that lost its usefulness when the new cult was instituted. Jerusalem and its temple, the pattern, were destroyed so that nothing should distract from what they prefigured, the Church. There are, however, some precepts which persist in their literal meaning, the Decalogue. In the case of the others we must look for the Holy Spirit's will, the 'meaning' willed by God, which is the spiritual meaning: only the man of God, with divine help, will know how to draw out of the well of the Scriptures this spiritual meaning and communicate it to others as Rebecca gave drink to Abraham's servant.[26] Such is the 'spiritual law' of which Paul speaks, the law considered in its spiritual sense. However, we are to get beyond even this spiritual law itself. The glory of Moses and Elijah at the Transfiguration is not equal to

---

[24] See *Connaissance* 236–272.
[25] *CCels* VI, 4, referring to Plato, *Republic* I, 327a and *Phaedo* 118a.
[26] Gen. 24, 15–27; *HomGn* X.

that of the God-Man who, on the contrary, illuminates them. The
presents brought by the prophets and the angels to the Bride, the Church
of the old covenant, are only 'imitations of gold':[27] only the Bridegroom
at his coming will bring the true gold. Even when it is understood
spiritually the Law is only a rudiment which Christ will in one sense
destroy, in another bring to perfection: it is like a child who must become
adult. It is symbolised by John the Baptist, its culmination. Like him it is
a preparation for the revelation of Christ. Like him too, it must be left
behind: 'He must increase, and I must decrease.'[28]

This spiritual meaning of the Old Testament, this 'spiritual Law', was
known to the great men of the old covenant, patriarchs and prophets.
They knew that the Incarnation was going to happen, but they had to
wait for it to be accomplished before they could see 'the Day of the
Lord'.[29] Faithless Israel became blind, deaf and dumb: for her the Bible is
Isaiah's 'closed book',[30] for she no longer sees its meaning and God has
caused all wisdom and all prophecy to cease in her. In fact she is held up
at the letter, at the image. The Pharisees are those Philistines who filled
with earth the wells dug by Abraham. They did not know how to listen
'after the fashion of a mystery'. Therefore they have been abandoned by
the Lord, a punishment that could fall on us also if we imitate their
infidelity; it would not fall on the Church but on such and such a
particular church. They were unable to profit from the teaching of Jesus
because they did not question Him to find things out but to catch him
out. In the end they put Him to death and that means: 'the figure, for its
self-preservation, prevents the manifestation of the Truth it prefigures'.[31]
Like the rebellious husbandmen of the parable of the Vineyard they
thought 'they would become masters of the realities[32] (*pragmatōn*)'. In
these two expressions we again find what is for Origen the essential
nature of sin: to stop at the image as if it were the mystery, to put the
image in the place of the mystery.

Henceforth the literal meaning of the law, detached by them from the
Truth that it prophesied, has lost for them its link with the mysteries, and
so has lost its truth and its intelligibility: it has become a fable, a myth, it
no longer has what gave it coherence and reality. That is the meaning that
Origen attaches to the Pauline expression 'the Jewish fables'.[33] He does
not mean to dispute the historical value of the biblical narratives, which
he defends repeatedly in the *Contra Celsum*, but their value as revelation

[27] Cant. 1, 11: *ComCt* II: GCS VIII, pp. 156–165.
[28] John 3, 30.
[29] We have mentioned above the different views in Book VI and Book XIII of the
Commentary on John about the comparison between the knowledge of the pre-Christian
saints and that of the apostles: see p. 111.
[30] 29, 9–13.
[31] *ComJn* XXVIII, 12 (11), 95.
[32] *ComMt* XVII, 11 (GCS X).
[33] Tit. 1, 14.

when they are not read in the light of the New Testament: the myth is the interpretation of the Jews when they stop at the letter. This meaning is not without analogy with that which contrasts Truth with symbol instead of with falsehood. The symbol does not lie, so long as it participates in its model. But if one stops at the symbol, without following the natural movement which leads on to the truth, if one makes of the symbol an end in itself, an autonomous entity, grasping the reverence due to the mystery for which it stands, then one takes up a position of error and the symbol becomes a lie. In that case the literal meaning, although historically true, is myth, because it does not follow the will of the Spirit, because it refuses to efface itself before that which it represents. The sin of the Jews becomes identical with that of the pagans, they put fables in the place of Truth.[34]

The problem posed by the temporal Gospel, the one by which we live here below, in relation to the mysteries vouchsafed by the eternal Gospel[35] of the blessed state, is much more complex. Three series of texts are to be distinguished, and they can be classified under the formula: thesis, antithesis, synthesis. Thesis: the New Testament brought the Truth, put an end to the images of the old Scriptures. Antithesis: the temporal Gospel is still an image when compared with the eternal Gospel. The synthesis is achieved in a few texts which expressly envisage the three periods and state exactly the relation of the temporal Gospel to the eternal Gospel.

On the one hand the incarnation has taken away the veil that lay over the law: it has thus abolished the figures, the Christian already lives in spirit and in truth, he is already in the knowledge of the Last Things. The moment of this change is either the Incarnation in general, or the Passion, or the Resurrection added to the Passion, or the coming of the Holy Spirit, or even the Transfiguration which reveals to Moses and Elijah the Day of the Lord, turning the spiritual law into the New Testament. Comparisons illustrate this change over and over again in different ways.

But on the other hand the temporal Gospel is still image and we must get beyond it. It has also a literal meaning, a letter which does not kill like that of the Old Testament and which saves the more simple minded, but which, nonetheless, we must get beyond. Of course Origen does draw attention to some cases in the Gospel of the 'letter which kills'; in reality these represent false interpretations or ways of speaking that pay no attention to Christ's intention. The Gospel itself expresses mysteries under its literal meaning. The temporal Gospel is still a shadow, but this shadow is that of Christ, his humanity, 'under which we live among the nations',[36] guided and protected by his human soul, image and shadow of

[34] See *Connaissance* 273-323.
[35] Apoc. 14, 6.
[36] Lam. 4, 20; see below [p. 257].

the Word. The virtues, titles (*epinoiai*) of the Son we receive through this
shadow which is his soul. The temporal Gospel brings us a personal
knowledge of Christ, but it remains indirect: his divinity is perceived so
far as we can see it through the humanity that holds it but also hides it
from those who are incapable of seeing it. We must get used to perceiving
more and more through the man Jesus the light of God, to the point of
climbing the Mountain like the three apostles to contemplate the
humanity glorified and transfigured by it. The new Scriptures do not
reveal the divinity of Christ to everybody, any more than seeing the man
Jesus does. If seeing Him had been enough to lead anyone to contemplate
the Word and through Him the Father, then Pilate, Judas, Herod, the
Jews who clamoured for his death, would have seen God, which is absurd
for they were not in the necessary state of mind. A divine Person is only
seen when He desires to make Himself known and that assumes that the
percipient is prepared for this. It is in this way that the humanity of
Christ takes its place in the strategy of the divine education and Origen
sees in the kenosis of the Incarnation the 'foolishness of God, which is
wiser than the wisdom of all men'.[37]

That the temporal Gospel is still image and must be left behind is also
shown by the innumerable passages in which the Pauline antitheses are
found 'the imperfect/perfect' and above all 'through a glass darkly/face to
face', applied to knowledge in the temporal Gospel and in the eternal
Gospel. Never does he refer 'in a glass, darkly' to knowledge in the Old
Testament, still inferior to that of the temporal Gospel. In the majority of
instances this distinction is applied to knowledge, in accordance with the
Pauline passage, but Origen also extends it to other realities of the
Christian life such as faith, the way of life, the virtues, adoration,
freedom, the presence of the Lord, etc., and he even comes to distinguish
the sacrament of baptism which is 'through a glass, darkly' from the
eschatological baptism of fire and spirit, corresponding to what we call
Purgatory, which is 'face to face'. Another distinction means the same to
him. God says of Moses:[38] 'I will speak to him mouth to mouth, *en eidei*,
and not in riddles.' And Paul in the same way[39] contrasts being guided by
faith and being guided *dia eidous*. Origen does not interpret this word
eidos in its popular sense of appearance, but in accordance with the
metaphysical sense attested by Plato and Aristotle of the direct vision of
the 'realities' such as they are, that is of the mysteries. So the contrast is
normally established by these words between the temporal and the
eternal Gospels, but sometimes, when the expression *en eidei* is used,
between the Old Testament and the New.

37 1 Cor. 1, 25; *HomJr* VIII, 7–8.

[37] 1 Cor. 1, 25; *HomJr* VIII, 7–8.
[38] Num. 12, 8.
[39] 2 Cor. 5, 7.

The synthesis between these two series of texts is made by the few passages that expressly envisage all three periods, illustrating the distinction shadow/image/reality,[40] or refer to the interpretation of the tents and houses[41] which contrasts either the law and the Gospel or the temporal and eternal Gospels. Adoration is either in the figures (Old Testament) or in spirit and in truth, but the latter is also in two ways: 'through a glass, darkly', relying on the earnest of the Spirit, at the present time (Temporal Gospel) or 'face to face', according to the Spirit at a future time (eternal Gospel).[42] In the Old Testament the friends of the Bridegroom only bring to the Bride imitations of gold: it is only those who have been conformed to the Resurrection of Christ who will receive pure gold;[43] but this 'being conformed' can take place in two ways, 'through a glass, darkly' by the first 'resurrection' obtained by baptism and a life in conformity with it, 'face to face' by the second and final resurrection.[44] Unlike the 'shadow of the law', the 'shadow of Christ', his humanity, brings Life, puts us on the Way, guides us to the Truth, already confers the realities which are Christ and protects from the evil sun, the devil:[45] so we have a possession of the mysteries, here below, where we are still exposed to the attacks of the Evil one. At the Passion of Christ the first curtain of the Temple, that of the Holy Place, was torn down, and the mysteries were revealed, but not perfectly: for the second curtain, that of the Holy of Holies, will only be taken away at the end of the world.[46] Other texts can be adduced. According to the *Commentary on John*[47] the perceptible Gospel on the one hand and the intelligible and spiritual Gospel on the other, in other words the temporal and the eternal, are distinguished by the *epinoia*, a word which always expresses in Origen a human view of things and is normally contrasted with *hypostasis*, substance, and sometimes with *pragma*, reality. If it is the *epinoia* that distinguishes the two gospels, they are one in substance and reality: so there is really only one Gospel and so we are already here below in possession of the 'true' realities. But we still perceive them hidden under a veil of 'image', we shall see them face to face only in the future world. On the other hand the Old Testament only had the presentiment, the hope of them: it did not possess them. This doctrine of the temporal Gospel and the eternal Gospel expresses, let there be no doubt about it, Christian sacramentalism, the sacrament being at once, according to its classic definition, *sacramentum et res*, that is sign and

---

[40] Heb. 10, 1; *HomPs* 38, II, 2 (PG 12, 1402 C).
[41] *HomGn* XIV, 1–2; *HomNb* XVII, 4.
[42] *ComJn* XIII, 18, 109–113.
[43] *ComCt* II, (GCS VIII, pp. 161–162).
[44] *FragmRm* XXIV: *JThS* XIII, p. 363, 1, 12.
[45] *ComCt* III, (GCS VIII, p. 182).
[46] *SerMt* 138 (GCS XI).
[47] I, 8 (10), 44.

reality, *res* translating *pragma* which represents the eschatological mystery.

It must be repeated that, according to the measure of spiritual progress made, the veil of 'image' which still covers the mystery in the temporal Gospel becomes more and more transparent, revealing the truth that it holds. When one turns to the Lord, the veil is taken away,[48] gradually no doubt, and the divinity of Christ shows more and more through his humanity, the flesh no longer forming a screen for those who have 'spirit. : eyes' capable of perceiving the divinity.[49]

The way of knowledge

A passage in Plato's Letter VII, quoted by Celsus,[50] distinguished five elements on which knowledge depends: the name (*onoma*), the definition (*logos*), the image (*eidolon*), the science (*episteme*), finally the object which is both knowable and true, that is the idea in the Platonist sense. Origen gives an exegesis of this text, truth to tell one which is fairly far from Plato's meaning, but one which sums up admirably his own conception of knowledge.

To the name corresponds 'the voice of him who cries in the wilderness, John', symbolising the Old Testament, precursor of Christ. To the *logos*, the One John shows, Jesus, the Logos made flesh, the historical Jesus. As for the image, 'since we use this word (*eidolon*) in another sense (=idol),' it means 'the print of the wounds that form in each soul after the Word (the Logos), that is the Christ who is in each of us, issuing from the Logos-Christ'. The Christ enters into the soul and in that sentence are brought together two of the great mystical themes which we shall study soon, that of the birth and growth of Christ in the soul, and that of the dart and wound of love. As for the fourth stage, science, it is still 'the Christ, Wisdom, who is found in those whom we consider to be perfect':[51] this represents, as in the Transfiguration, the highest knowledge of God in his Son that a man can have while still on earth. It is not possible to say why Origen did not finish his interpretation and show something equivalent to the fifth element: the object 'which is knowable and true' still corresponds in fact to Christ, the intelligible World of the mysteries, of the ideas in the Platonist sense and of the 'reasons' in the Stoic sense, contemplated in the 'face to face' of the beatific vision.

Such are the five stages of knowledge: they refer to five successive aspects of the Christ, the first being John the Baptist, the Harbinger, the Voice of the Word, with the Old Testament which he represents. There is no difficulty in showing the way that leads from one to the other; from

[48] 2 Cor. 3, 16.
[49] See *Connaissance* 324–370.
[50] *CCels* VI, 9 quoting Letter VII 342 ab.
[51] 1 Cor. 2, 6.

the Old Testament to the historical Christ the spiritual exegesis of the
Old Testament: from the historical Christ to Christ present in the soul
the spiritual interpretation of the New Testament, with that interiorisation
of the Christ in each Christian which characterises it; from Christ present
in the soul to the Wisdom Christ of whom there is speech among the
perfect, to the transfigured Christ, the spiritual ascent symbolised by that
of the three apostles climbing the Mountain; from the Wisdom Christ of
whom there is speech among the perfect to the Wisdom Christ who is
tantamount to the Intelligible World, the beatific vision.[52]

Origen is very fond of underlining the gradations which he draws from
scriptural texts, but he does not always interpret them with perfect
consistency; he has taken note of three spiritual gifts distinguished by
Paul,[53] the utterance of wisdom, the utterance of knowledge, and faith, all
three coming from the Spirit. Faith is belief as confidence, and it is
sufficient for salvation: it is not a purely intellectual activity, but is
expressed in its works. Progress in faith is possible: to believe in the name
of Jesus is less perfect than to believe in Jesus. But the perfection of faith
is knowledge, which in its turn depends on faith as its foundation and its
starting-point. Faith retains an indirect character, but knowledge, the
fulfilment of faith, is in a certain manner a direct contact with Christ and
the mysteries contained in Him. You can believe without seeing; you
cannot see without believing. Knowledge is an improvement on faith in
that it affords a greater evidence, a direct perception through the five
spiritual senses of the realities of the mystery: it is a true experience of
God present in the intellect. Obviously it would not do to contrast
knowledge as Origen understands it, which is of a mystical order, with
the reply of the Risen Christ to Thomas: 'Because you have seen me, you
have believed; blessed are those who have not seen yet have believed.'[54]
The vision which Thomas demanded in order to believe was of a physical
nature and it became the cause of his faith; knowledge as Origen
understands it starts from faith of which it is in a sense the perfecting.

It is more difficult to see the distinction, in his view, between the
charism of knowledge and the supreme charism of Wisdom. Wisdom is
the first title of the Son, ontologically and logically but not chronologically,
anterior to all the others, and it by this that the Son is the Intelligible
World, the Mystery par excellence, the Model of the creation. Wisdom,
the most perfect of human virtues, is a participation in the Wisdom which
is the Son. It seems above all to be a *habitus* in the scholastic sense, a state
of the soul, bringing with it a certain community of nature with the divine
realities which makes it possible to know, while the word knowledge
refers rather to the action. So it seems that for Origen knowledge and

[52] See *Connaissance* 213–215.
[53] 1 Cor. 12, 8–9.
[54] John 20, 29.

wisdom are really not to be distinguished as two different degrees, but as two aspects of the same degree, superior to faith.

But within faith on the one hand, and knowledge-wisdom on the other, there are many degress. The starting point is always the knowledge given by the Incarnation: One must start from the incarnate Logos to reach the Logos-God and there is no stage, even in the final state of blessedness, when the humanity of Christ can be lost from sight; even if the attention is directed more and more to his divinity the latter is still contemplated through his transfigured humanity. The progress of the soul in knowledge is unending: the more it advances, the more it sees that it must go on advancing. The 'epectasis' of Gregory of Nyssa is already present in Origen: to be convinced of that one need only read the magnificent text of the Homily on Numbers XVII, 4. Origen also applies to the development of the soul images taken from the growth of the child and he shows in a passage of the *Treatise on First Principles*[55] this progress continuing after death under the guidance of angel-tutors in different 'mansions'[56] situated in the planetary spheres, and then in that of the fixed stars: it is then pursued under the guidance of Christ before the Father is reached. Each one knows God through his Son in the degree of growth that he has attained and to the extent that he is capable of knowing Him: this explains the statement, at first sight surprising, that Christ is seen in different forms, according to the spiritual level each one has reached, an assertion that we shall come across again when we get to the mystical theme of the foods. These different forms have nothing to do with what He looked like as a man, for anyone who met Him saw Him, but relate to the perception of the divinity through the humanity. Let us not forget, indeed, what we said at the beginning of this chapter about knowledge as an encounter of two freedoms: the freedom of God who wills to reveal Himself, the freedom of man preparing himself for that revelation. Some have sensed in this a vague trace of docetism, but they are wrong: it is in fact a view of spiritual theology which must not be judged as if it related to cosmology or natural anthropology. It is a very profound statement, which is verified by experience of spiritual life and missionary work: the more trust one has in the spiritual dimension, the more one takes it seriously and lives it, the greater one's perception of spiritual things.

So there are different levels of Christian life. By saying this Origen laid himself open to an undeserved accusation of elitism, because he distinguishes the 'more simple' from the spiritual or perfect, two Pauline terms. If he had really been the spiritual aristocrat he is accused of being there would not have been in his homilies, preached to all comers among the Christians at Caesarea, so many exhortations to the moral progress that would fit them to receive illumination from on high. The vigour of

[55] II, 11, 5–7.
[56] John 14, 1.

his polemic against the 'friends of the letter' shows that he was not resigned to seeing the mass of Christians stopping half-way in this preparation and in this knowledge: a more elitist attitude would have brought him more serenity and a real disdain would have brought him more rest.

There is, moreover, as several of his declarations show, only a short distance separating the simple Christian from the spiritual one, if one compares both with the spirituality of the beatitude. A man whom we find admirable here below is not, when all is said and done, any more in the sight of those above than a child compared to an adult or even an animal compared to a man.[57] When Origen paints his portrait of the spiritual man made perfect, he is in fact looking at his ideal, one which is never really fulfilled in this life.

Not only intellectual reasons, but moral and spiritual reasons, cause the majority of Christians to stop at simple faith, without progressing in any way towards knowledge: nor is it a question of great sinners but of tepid Christians whose victory is not complete over the sin that still has a hold on them. Thus their spiritual comprehension is very limited, for a lot of neglect and laziness characterises their response to God. Even among those who lack humane culture, true 'spirituals' are to be found, who show it by their life and by the steadfastness of their faith to the point of martyrdom, although they are not capable of giving an account of their faith in words.[58] In any case the Christian who believes and commits no grave sin will be saved. The letter of the Gospel does not kill even the one who gets no further than the letter: faith is the necessary and sufficient condition of salvation.

As we have already said, the terms spiritual and perfect only apply in a very relative way to men living on earth and these ideals will only be completely achieved in the beatitude. Origen describes their characteristics and their charisms using Pauline texts. They have 'their citizenship in Heaven',[59] even while they still live on earth, that is to say all their desires bear them on high and that is why, given the purity of their lives, the mysteries are to a certain extent disclosed in them. Portraits of such people are not lacking, men and women: from the Old Testament such as Abraham, Moses and John the Baptist in whom that Testament culminated: from the New Testament the apostles, especially Paul; finally and supremely Mary whose virtues and spiritual gifts Origen emphasises, although, for essentially theological reasons, the universality of Redemption, he does not believe her to be absolutely free of sin. Among the spiritual gifts Origen emphasises the discernment of the spirits and the doctrines, a

[57] HomIs VII, 1 (GCS VIII); HomEx III, 1; ComMt XVI, 16 (GCS X); SelPs 22, 5 (PG 12, 1264 A).
[58] ComMt XVI, 25 (GCS X).
[59] Phil. 3, 20.

participation in the divine mystery which has the result that its subject
cannot be truly judged by anyone, the presence of the Holy Spirit which
raises a man above the human condition, a purity of life without which
the Spirit could not dwell in him, and finally the apostolic urge which
drives him to offer to others what he has received.[60]

The act of knowing

Contemplation is denoted by *thea* and *theōria* and the words of the same
root. Spiritual understanding by *noein* which, with the words of the same
root, is almost confined to this meaning: also by *chōrein* which means
both contain and comprehend, or, followed by a verb in the infinitive, 'be
capable of'; the expression *chōretikos theou* was to be rendered by the
Latin translators as *capax Dei*, 'capable of God'. Finally, knowledge by
gnōsis and the words of the same root with a meaning almost always
spiritual: *gnōstikos* is very rare and is only found once applied to the
spiritual, in a fragment, with a clearly ironical intention about those who
hold to the 'supposed gnōsis'.[61]

The analysis of the act of knowing shows it to consist of an activity of
an order decidedly mystical: knowledge is a vision or a direct contact, it is
participation in its object, better still it is union, 'mingling' with its object,
and love. In the state of blessedness, we repeat, the saved will have been
taken, as it were, into the Son, yet without pantheism, for they will see
God with the very eyes of the Son.

Knowledge is, then, vision or direct contact, dispensing with the
mediation of the sign, the image, the word, which are rendered necessary
here below by our corporeal condition. This is often brought out, in
Origen as in his fellow student Plotinus, by the word *prosbolē* which
expresses the leap of vision or thought towards its object. The supreme
branch of the 'divine philosphy' following the prologue to the *Commentary
on the Song of Songs*, is the 'enoptic', or perhaps better, for the word is
not the same in different manuscripts, the 'epoptic', a word translated by
Rufinus as 'inspective', that is the science of vision, of contemplation.
Not only is the wisdom of the blessed characterised by the *prosbolē*,
'stripped of sounds, words, symbols and types',[62] but there can exist on
earth too a prayer directed to God which is troubled by no phantasm of
the imagination.[63] In that way the contemplator becomes a direct
spectator (*autoptēs*) of the Word. All that is summed up in the famous
theme of Origen's of the five spiritual senses, spiritual sight, spiritual
hearing, spiritual touch, spiritual taste, and spiritual smell, which among
other things, attributes to the 'intellect' of the man described in these

[60] See *Connaissance* 443–495.
[61] Ibid. 375–398.
[62] *ExhMart* XIII (GCS I).
[63] *HomNb* XI, 8.

terms the same direct relationship between the subject and the object that one normally believes to exist between the sense organ and what it apprehends.

But the theme of the five spiritual senses is built on the duality of the subject and the object. Origen's ideal is more demanding: this duality has to be overcome. First, it will be overcome in part by the fact that knowledge is participation, and presupposes a community or communion of nature between the parties. The same point is made by the theme of the five spiritual senses which affirms, in Origen's view, that the sense organ in order to perceive its object must have some analogy, some similarity with it: the eye is akin to light, to colour etc., the ear to sounds and so on. Here we find again the principle that only the like knows the like: it is the same with the presence in man of the 'after-the-image' which makes him akin to God and causes him to know God whom he finds in a way in himself, more and more intensely as he assimilates himself to the mysteries, and progresses towards the eschatological likeness. The sign of this kinship with God is 'the desire of piety and of communion with Him which, even among the lost, preserves some traces of the divine will', or again that 'ineffable desire to know the reason of the works of God which we see', a desire which without any doubt has been 'placed within us by God'.[64] The two texts from which we draw these quotations contain the foretaste of an argument of Blondel's philosophy. To progress towards the likeness, is to progress in sonship of God and so to know God as Father, to know this in experience: he who sees in God only the Master, because he retains towards God the feelings of a slave, cannot experience God as Father. But if becoming a son allows us to know Him, there is a reciprocal relation between the two terms: knowledge develops both the filiation and the glorification.

The duality of the subject and the object will be still further overcome, for knowledge is union, or, to use a very realistic term that he uses several times, a mingling. Commenting on certain passages from both Testaments and fully aware of the divine omniscience, of God's role as teacher and his infinite patience with the sinner, Origen several times over states that God and Christ do not know the sinner: they know him of course as a creature, by the very act of having created him, by the 'after-the-image' that he can never lose, but they do not know him insofar as he is a sinner, because they did not create sin, this 'nothing' which according to the prologue of John's Gospel[65] was made without the Word, and above all because they cannot 'mingle' with him. All that is in keeping with a supernatural conception of what it is to exist which we have already stressed. Knowledge leads to union and better, is union. And therefore knowledge is love. To demonstrate this Origen relies on the Hebrew

[64] *ExhMart* XLVII (GCS I); *PArch* II,11, 4.
[65] John 1, 3: *ComJn* II, 13 (7), 91–99.

meaning of the verb to know, used to express the human act of love: 'Adam knew his wife Eve.'[66] Such is the ultimate definition of knowing, compounded with love in union. This last quotation excludes all pantheism: just as the man and the woman are 'two in one flesh'[67] so God and the believer become two in 'one and the same spirit'.[68]

This conception of knowledge is of a mystical kind in the strongest present-day sense of the word: it is indisputable that a mystical desire powerfully inspires and directs this work, gives form to this thought, and explains this life.[69]

Origen as a mystic

Can one, however, see in Origen a mystic in the strict sense of the term? One could of course in theory suppose that all his life he desired such knowledge without ever attaining it. That is why among those who know him there are such divergent views on the point.

One of the difficulties in answering this question arises from the fact that Origen in his works, like most of the Fathers, hardly ever speaks of himself. A few rare testimonies allow us to glimpse a personal mystical experience. We will only quote one of them, the clearest, often mentioned in this connection: it comes from the first *Homily on the Song of Songs*,[70] relating to what might be called 'the game of hide-and-seek' between the Bride and Bridegroom:

> Next the Bride looks for the Bridegroom who, after showing himself, has disappeared. That often happens throughout this song, and only he can understand it who has himself experienced it. Often, God is my witness, I have felt that the Bridegroom was approaching, and that he was as near as possible to me; then he has suddenly gone away, and I have not been able to find what I was seeking. Again I set myself to desire his coming, and sometimes he comes back, amd when he has appeared to me, so that I hold him in my hands, once more he escapes me and once more vanishes, and I start again to look for him. He does that often, until I hold him truly and rise leaning on my well-beloved.

Attempts have been made to weaken this text and many other passages of the *Commentary on the Song of Songs*, by speaking of the 'literary genre' as if Origen had here employed conventional language that did not correspond to his experience. The same thing has been said about the strongly emotional devotion that he shows towards the incarnate Word, of a kind scarcely found elsewhere before the Middle Ages. But a literary genre presupposes one or more pre-existent models and what models could Origen have been following? There were of course before him

---

[66] Gen. 4, 1: *ComJn* XIX, 4 (1), 22–23.
[67] Gen. 2, 24.
[68] 1 Cor. 6, 16–17.
[69] See *Connaissance* 496–523.
[70] §7: Fr. translation by O. Rousseau, SC 37.

mystical writers in the Christian tradition, the apostles Paul and John, Ignatius of Antioch or Clement of Alexandria, but nothing in these is exactly like what we hear in numerous passages of Origen, notably in the *Commentary on the Song of Songs* with its burning emotion, yet different from that of his predecessors like Ignatius. As for the Philonian, gnostic or middle Platonist mystics, it is difficult to see what they could have done to prepare Origen on this point; there is lacking in them a fundamental aspect, the personal relation of love between the believer and Christ. If there is no model to be found before Origen, how can we speak of a 'literary genre'? Would that not be to evade the issue, to find too easy a way of shutting our eyes to what the texts are quite simply saying.

In fact the enormous influence that Origen had on later spirituality makes it unlikely that he was without experience of his own. On the one hand Origen is, after Clement but on a much greater scale, the first in the Christian tradition to express in its full extent an ideal of knowledge of a mystical nature: where did he get this from, if not from his own experience? In the next chapter we shall study some of the great mystical themes of which he is either the inventor or the propogator. He drew all that from the Bible, but he gave to isolated sentences a vast spiritual orchestration, taking some texts in an allegorical sense, and discovering in the hurried sentences of Paul a depth of spiritual life that is not apparent at first sight. Is it likely that, without being familiar in his own life with these mysteries of which he is ceaselessly speaking, his intuition would have been so correct that he would have invented for himself the expressions that later came to be used by men authentically inspired? How could he have been so sensitive, when developing his spiritual themes, to all the mystical nuances of Scripture, inventing a language which so many spiritually minded people would later use, if he had not experienced these things himself? Only the spiritual can know the spiritual, he often wrote, following Paul. Must we not deduce from this that the language in which a mystic recovers his own experience and which he uses to express it is also the work of a mystic?

So we conclude with some words of H. de Lubac:

> As for the question whether he was himself a mystic, it seems to us that only those can seriously doubt it who begin by postulating a certain dichotomy between doctrine and experience, such as has been current for some centuries. But is this dichotomy absolutely justified? Does it not constitute in any case an anachronism? By the very stuff and movement of his thought, which cannot be separated from the most intimate aspects of his life, it seems to us that Origen was one of the greatest mystics in the Christian tradition.[71]

---

[71] Preface to H. Crouzel, *Origène et la 'connaissance mystique'*, p. 11.

7
The Mystical Themes

Origen is one of the creators of the language of mysticism. He created some of these themes by starting from Scripture and also using philosophic data and Hellenistic imagery. He found other themes in earlier Christian tradition, but while they had hitherto been used in a fairly limited way, he enriched the expression of them very considerably. After him these themes were repeated by generations of mystics who used them to express their own experience.

That raises the problem of the transmission and the expression of mystical experience. The knowledge which the mystic receives is in its essence inexpressible: it is a direct contact between the divine Spirit and the human spirit, by-passing, to a certain extent at least, every mediating factor, whether concept, sign or word. And yet the beneficiary tries to describe it in order to communicate it. In doing this, he cannot avoid distorting it more or less, for he is trying to translate into words what is by definition ineffable. And he expresses it in terms of his culture, using the words and images which that culture provides. Sometimes polemical considerations intrude. For example, Origen and Gregory of Nyssa have often been contrasted by attributing to the former a mysticism of light and to the latter a mysticism of darkness: that can be defended provided that nothing is made absolute. Now it is not impossible that Origen's mysticism of light is influenced by his polemic against the Montanist conception of trance as unconsciousness, while the mysticism of darkness favoured at Nyssa perhaps arises in part from Gregory's reaction, following his brother Basil, against the neo-Arianism of Eunomius who maintained that the divine nature was strictly defined by the fact that the Father was unbegotten. Behind the different forms of expression it is by no means certain that the experience of the one was all that different from the experience of the other. Besides, mystics read mystics and the themes are thus transmitted from one generation to another, each enriching them with his own experience and his own culture.

The nuptial themes
After Hosea the prophets often represented the covenant between Jahveh and Israel as a marriage:[1] Israel is Jahveh's wife. Whatever be the origin,

[1] See our article: 'Le thème du mariage mystique chez Origène et ses sources.' *Studia Missionalia* 26, 1977, 37–57.

secular or sacred, of the love poem called the *Song of Songs* – it cannot be said that contemporary exegetes have reached agreement on this point – it was understood by the Jews themselves as being about the mutual love of God and Israel. The New Testament inherits this idea and applies it to Christ and the Church. The first Christian commentary on the *Song of Songs*, that of Hippolytus, retains the collective meaning of the Bride.

But an individual application of the same theme, in which the Bride would also represent the faithful soul, is suggested by two passages in the first epistle to the Corinthians.[2] Three texts from Tertullian, which remain isolated in his work, present virgins and widows as brides of Christ.[3] In Origen both meanings of Bride, the collective one, the Church, and the individual one, the faithful soul, are frequently to be found. They occur mainly, as might be expected, in the *Commentary* and the two Homilies on the *Song of Songs*, but they are frequently met throughout the rest of his works. Far from being opposed to each other, these two applications are linked and complementary. The faithful soul is bride because she forms part of the Church which is Bride. If the progress of the soul in the likeness of Christ makes it more and more perfectly bride, the Church, the community of believers, also becomes more and more perfectly bride.

In the *Commentary on the Song*, as he explains each verse, Origen begins with a short literal explanation, in the setting of the love drama which, in his view, the poem is. Then, in the majority of cases, taking first the Church as Bride and then the soul as bride, or vice versa, he explains the verse in an orderly way under both heads. There are few exceptions to that: some verses are interpreted in only one of the two ways; in others the two are more or less mingled and he passes imperceptibly from the one to the other, although generally the transition is well marked.

There is quite a long story behind the marriage of Christ with the Church as there is behind that of Christ with the soul. It begins in the pre-existence, when the soul joined to the Word, or in other words the pre-existent humanity of Christ, is the Bridegroom of the Church of the pre-existence, consisting of all the 'intellects', those which the original fall was to turn into angels, men and demons. This fall separates the Bride and Bridegroom. In the Old Testament the Bride is represented by ancient Israel: it is a time of betrothal, when the betrothed woman is visited by the 'Bridegroom's friends', patriarchs and prophets, who prepare her; sometimes she is even visited by the Bridegroom Himself, for it is He who appears in the theophanies in human or angelic form. At the Incarnation the Bridegroom assumes a body of flesh, although He has committed no sin, in order that He may rejoin out of love his Bride who

---

[2] 6, 15–17; 7, 32–34.
[3] *Ad Uxorem* I, 4, 4; *De Resurrectione* 61, 6; *De Virginibus velandis* 16, 4 (CChr 1–2).

has fallen into the flesh through her fault. But the union will only be perfect in the final blessed state, when the parable of the Wedding Guests[4] will be fulfilled and when the Father will unite for ever his Son to glorified humanity.

But the opposite to the mystic marriage can happen, both on the individual and on the collective plane. If union with Christ is a marriage, every sin is an infidelity to the lawful Husband, and an adultery with Satan. Hosea wrote about the idolatry of Israel as adultery against Jahveh, her Husband. Origen applies that to the soul which recants under persecution or is defiled by carnal thoughts; but he also applies it to the tragedy of the Synagogue which fornicated with the demon, plotted against her lawful Husband and put Him to death. Spiritual fornication with the demons is the antitype of the mystical marriage in both its forms. Every sin is both adultery and idolatry: adultery because it is infidelity to the sole lawful Husband; idolatry because it takes the perceptible creature, image of the heavenly realities, as being those realities themselves.[5]

The mystical marriage lays the stress before all else on the union of Christ with the Church and the soul and on the mutual love which is the bond between them. Closely linked with it is another theme centred on love, that of the dart and wound of love.[6] There is no trace of this before Origen. So he it was, in all probability, who first brought together the two verses of the Old Testament which are the source of this theme. The first is the Septuagint reading of Isaiah 49, 2, which makes the Servant of Jahveh, who is for all Christian tradition Christ prophesied, say: 'He set me as a chosen arrow, in his quiver He hid me away'. The second text is Song of Songs 2, 5 which, also in the Septuagint, puts in the Bride's mouth the words: 'I am wounded with love (*agape*)'. It is not impossible that the Hellenistic image of little Eros with his bow and arrows, mentioned at the beginning of the *Commentary on the Song of Songs* in the context of carnal love,[7] played some part in the building-up of this theme, the image being projected onto the heavenly 'Eros of Plato's *Symposium*[8] which is recalled in this same prologue and also upon Christ who, according to Origen, is said to have been called Eros by Ignatius of Antioch.[9]

The theme that we are studying is attested in works belonging to all periods of Origen's life, from Book I of the *Commentary on John* or the

---

[4] Matt. 22, 2–14.
[5] See H. Crouzel, *Virginité et Mariage selon Origène*. 1963, pp. 17–24, 39–44.
[6] Same author: 'Origines patristiques d'un thème mystique: le trait et la blessure d'amour chez Origène', in *Kyriakon: Festschrift Johannes Quasten*, Münster i, W. 1970. vol. 1, 309–319.
[7] Prol. (GCS VIII, p. 67, 1, 1).
[8] Ibid. p. 63, 1, 12.
[9] Ibid. p. 71, 1, 26, quoting Ignatius, *Rom*. 7, 2 (SC 10).

Commentary on Lamentations, works composed at Alexandria, through to the homilies preached in his last years. It is echoed in the *Address of Thanks* of Gregory Thaumaturgus. The finest passages, elevated by a burning eloquence which comes through in the translations of Rufinus and Jerome, are the notes on *Cant.* 2, 5 in the Commentary (Rufinus's version) and in the second homily (Jerome's version) on that poem.[10] The archer is either the Father or the Son; the arrow is obviously the Son; but the latter also becomes the wound which the arrow inflicts on the soul according to a passage of the *Contra Celsum* to which we have already made reference,[11] 'the impress of the wounds that are marked on each soul after the Word, that is the Christ in each individual, derived from Christ the Word'[a] The Bride whom the arrow wounds is never, in the texts that have come down to us, the Church, but only the faithful soul. But Christ is not the only one to be a chosen arrow, for He communicates this quality to all who bear his word, Moses, the prophets, the apostles, the preachers of the Gospel: these various arrows are not, however, to be counted with the unique chosen Arrow, for in all of them it is the Christ who speaks. So this arrow represents above all love: sometimes it is also question of darts that arouse in the hearer penitence and contrition. Sometimes, on the contrary, the talk is of the flaming darts of the Evil One which produce, if they are accepted by the one who receives them, the sins and the vices: but on this point Origen is less original, for the idea is already found in Paul[12] and several times in Philo.

So far, we have only been concerned in dealing with these nuptial themes with union and love, not yet with begetting. That is the subject of a third theme already glimpsed when we were speaking of the spiritual exegesis of the New Testament, that of the birth and growth of Christ in the soul: the soul conceives by the Word and conceives the Word, the Word present in the soul. This theme is not a creation of Origen's for it is found in Paul[13] and it is close to that of the indwelling of Christ and of the Trinity in the soul to which there is several times testimony in Paul and in John. It was also used in the *Writing to Diognetus*[14] and several times by Hippolytus. But Origen extended it considerably.[15]

If the soul is to give birth to the Word, then Mary is its model: 'And every soul, virgin and uncorrupted, which conceives by the Holy Spirit, so as to give birth to the Will of the Father, is the Mother of Jesus.'[16] This

[10] *ComCt* III (GCS VIII, p. 194, 1, 6); *HomCt* II, 8.
[11] VI, 9: cf. pp. 112–113.
[a] Chadwick 323.
[12] Eph. 6, 16.
[13] Gal. 4, 19.
[14] XI, 4; XII, 7 (SC 23).
[15] See G. Aeby, *Les missions divines de Saint Justin a Origène*, Fribourg (Switzerland) 1958, pp. 164ff.
[16] *FragmMt* 281; GCS XII/1.

brief fragment is a comment on Matt. 12, 46–50. The Will of the Father is the Son, Power of the Father, begotten as the Will that proceeds from the intelligence.[17] This birth of Christ in the soul is essentially bound up with the reception of the Word and in a certain way Jesus is thus being continually born in souls. The Father originates this generation. It first becomes apparent in the virtues, for Christ is all virtue and every virtue, the virtues are identified with Him as it were in an existential way. But if the Christ is not born in me, I am shut out from salvation: Origen states that several times in different but equivalent ways. The birth of Jesus at Bethlehem is only effective in the order of Redemption if Jesus is also born in every man, if each adheres personally to this advent of Jesus into the world, and thereby in him.[18] Such is 'the Christ in each individual, derived from Christ the Word'.[19]

When Jesus from the Cross said to Mary, indicating John: 'Behold your son,' He did not mean that He was in this way making John another son of his mother, for Mary never had more than one son, but that John was in this way becoming Jesus Himself, so much so that it is impossible to understand the Gospel of John unless one has the mind, the *nous*, of Christ.[20] Just as the Son is begotten of the Father, not only from all eternity – 'There was not a time when he was not' – but continuously, so the righteous man is begotten by God, begotten in his Son, in each of his good deeds.[21] And the result will be the condition of blessedness in which all men, having become in a way inferior to the Only Begotten Son, will see the Father as the Son sees Him.[22]

But this Jesus who is born in us is killed by sin: He cannot be contained in souls which sin renders too narrow and He is barely alive like an anaemic baby in lukewarm souls: in the others He grows.[23] It can even happen that some accord Him such a place within them that He walks in them, lies down in them, eats in them, with the whole Trinity.[24] It is in our hearts that we must prepare a way for the Lord, both by the purity of our moral life and by the development of contemplation.[25] In each of us Jesus can grow in wisdom and stature and in grace.

There is one conclusion to be drawn from these three nuptial themes. First, in the presence of God and his Christ, every human soul is feminine, Wife and Mother. Its role is to receive in order to procreate. In spite of certain expressions which later theologians were to find awkward,

---

[17] *PArch* I, 2, 6.
[18] *HomGn* III, 7; *HomJr* IX, 1; *HomLc* XXII, 3.
[19] *CCels* VI, 9.
[20] *ComJn* I, 4 (6), 23.
[21] *HomJr* IX, 4.
[22] *ComJn* X, 16, 92.
[23] *ComJn* XX, 6, 40–45.
[24] *ComCt* II (GCS VIII, p. 164, 1, 20).
[25] *HomLc* XXI, 5 and 7.

counterbalanced by others which respect all the delicacy of the relationship between grace and freedom, Origen is a long way from Pelagianism or even semi-Pelagianism. As for the 'synergism' of which there is sometimes talk in his case as with other Greek Fathers, the word scarcely seems appropriate to Origen's doctrine of grace. It gives the impression that divine grace and man work together like two men pulling a cart together. As the themes that we have been studying and the ones we are about to study show, it is God and his Christ who are working: man's role is to let God act in him or to stop Him doing so.

The symbols of grace

Origen's doctrine of grace goes a lot further than the various uses he makes of the word *charis* or *gratia*. It is also expressed through a whole series of symbolical expressions. When we were looking at Origen's doctrine of man we studied two of them, the 'spirit (*pneuma*) which is in man' and the participation of man in the image of God of which the meaning is mainly supernatural.

Light[26] symbolises the graces of knowledge: it is the most natural analogy for this and is found in the Bible[27] as well as in Plato. Book VI of the *Republic*[28] develops the ideas that Celsus was summarising in his *True Doctrine*:[29] just as the sun by lighting up objects enables the eye to see them, so God is the Light that makes it possible to know the intelligible realities. Origen approves and he does not on this occasion show – as he does in the case of other passages of Plato quoted by Celsus – how great is the distance separating Christian grace from Plato's approximation to it, a distance depending on the free and voluntary nature of the divine gift.

Each of the divine Persons has his part to play in the giving of this light. The Father is the Light of which the Son is the reflection: this light acts through the medium of the Light which is the Son. 'In thy light do we see light':[30] for Origen that means: 'we shall see the Light that is the Father through the Light that is the Son.' But it is to the latter that are especially attributed the tiles or *epinoiai* relating to Light attested by the Bible: Light of the World, True Light, Light of men, Light of the Nations, Sun of Righteousness, Rising Sun. Evening and morning, night and day, stand for the periods at which this Sun either disappears or shines, whether here below, 'through a glass, darkly', whether in the Beyond, 'face to face'.[31] The Holy Spirit is hardly ever called Light, but illumination is also attributed to Him. The Church has also been called, in the persons of the

---

[26] See M. Msartinez Pastor. *Teologia de la Luz en Origenes.* Comillas 1963, and our *Origène et la 'connaissance mystique'*, pp. 130–153.

[27] Hos. 10, 12.

[28] 18–19, 506–509.

[29] *CCels* VII, 45.

[30] Ps. 35 (36), 10; *PArch* I, 1, 1.

[31] *ComJn* VI, 52 (33–34), 270–272; *HomLv* XIII, 2.

apostles, the Light of the World. She is the moon passing on to men by her teaching the brightness given her by the Sun. For the light of Christ becomes inward in the one who receives it: the latter himself becomes light as he conforms to Christ. In the Beatitude all the saints will become one single solar light in the Sun of Righteousness.

But Satan, Prince of Darkness, apes the Light. To deceive the souls he turns into an angel of light.[32] Thus he becomes an evil sun, with his moon, the congregation of the wicked. In reality he is darkness. Unlike the praiseworthy darkness in which God conceals Himself, blameworthy darkness is voluntary ignorance and refusal of the light which the darkness persecutes and tries to destroy; but cannot, for the darkness scatters when the light appears.

The theme of Life[33] overflows that of Light in that it encompasses the whole supernatural life of the soul and connects with what was later to be called sanctifying grace. With the three kinds of death which Origen distinguishes, death to sin, which is good, death in sin, which is bad, and physical death which is morally neutral – in this Origen is following a fundamental moral distinction made by the Stoics – with these, then, he contrasts three kinds of life, natural life, neutral, the life of sin and 'true life', as well as two immortalities, a natural immortality which prevents the soul dying a physical death, and an immortality of grace which prolongs the 'true life'. We shall come back to these three deaths and two immortalities when we study Origen's eschatology.[34] Here we are mainly concerned with the 'true life', distinguished from the natural and perceptible life which we have in common with the animals.

Now the 'true life' is not only as in Middle Platonism a life turned towards the world of intelligible, as distinct from perceptible, realities. Without excluding philosophical influences it must be said that Origen's source for this expression is the constant use of the word life in almost all the writings of the New Testament to denote the blessed life, 'eternal life': a glance at a concordance will clearly show that the expression is used in the sense of supernatural life much more often than in the sense of natural life. 'Eternal' life is not for the sacred authors the exclusive privilege of the Beatitude, where it will receive its fulfilment: we can already share in it here below in an imperfect but progressive way. Like the Kingdom of God or of heaven it is a reality both present and future. Origen speaks almost often of 'true life' when he is commenting on texts from the New Testament, especially from the Gospel of John.

Man receives true life from his participation in Christ who is Life who transmits to man the life that He eternally and unceasingly receives from

[32] 2 Cor. 11, 14; ComCt III (GCS VIII p. 183, l. 17).
[33] See G. Gruber, Z Q H Wesen, Stufen und Mitteilung des Wahren Lebens bei Origenes. Munich 1962.
[34] See pp. 235–241.

the Father. In the hierarchy of the *epinioai* or titles of Christ, drawn from the beginning of the Johannine prologue, Life occupies the third place after Wisdom which is the 'principle' and after the Logos, but before Light. It is Jesus who brings the living water, the water that gives life: this water brings death to sin, detaches the recipient from the flesh and from the perceptible, gives him virtue and knowledge: in this last acceptation Life becomes indistinguishable from Light. Christ's gift of Life is in this world progressive and brings with it the benefits of Life. The action of the Holy Spirit is also marked in the gift of the living water.[35]

The theme of spiritual food[36] is not unrelated to those we have so far studied and Christ plays the central part in it also. Origen often recalls the threats God made through Amos[37] that He would send on earth a hunger and thirst to hear the Word of God. This is a matter of punishment: the hunger and thirst are not a desire for the Word, but famine and drought, God having deprived his people of all the ministers of his word. This punishment has already fallen on the Jews and it could very well fall also not on the Church in general, but on this or that section of the Church because of its faults.

This spiritual food consists in the revelation of the mysteries and also in that of the divine nature itself: the angels are fed with it by Christ and the latter is constantly fed by his Father in his begetting which Origen represents as eternal and continuous, conveying to Him his divinity. In the same way the Son distributes to men the food He receives from the Father, for 'the sole food of the whole creation is the nature of God'.[38]

But there is a great diversity in the spiritual foods that are available in the framework of moral or mystical teaching. The same diet does not suit all: they vary in spiritual age and in spiritual health. And yet the Christ is all the food and every kind of food: the fact is that He takes on different forms to suit the needs of each. For the soul still at the animal level, the sheep that needs a shepherd to guide him and to bring him into green pastures.[39] He becomes grass. For the childlike soul He turns into milk: Origen alludes to three texts in the New Testament taken in their strict sense, for milk is there presented as the food of spiritual babes.[40] For spiritual invalids he is vegetables: Origen relies on Rom. 14, 1–2, not interpreted according to the apostle's meaning in the previous texts, but given an allegorical sense; Paul had in mind 'those who are weak in the faith', Christians who stay faithful through superstition to Jewish dietary observances. But the soul that is spiritually strong can receive 'the solid

[35] *ComJn* II, 16–19 (10–13), 112–132.
[36] See C. Blanc, 'Les nourritures spirituelles d'après Origen', *Didaskalia* (Lisbon) 6, 1976, 3–19; and *Origène et la 'connaissance mystique'* pp. 166–184.
[37] 8, 11.
[38] *Hom Is* III, 3 (GCS VIII).
[39] Ps. 22 (23).
[40] 1 Cor. 3, 2; Heb. 5, 12–13; 1 Pet. 2, 2.

food of the perfect, of those who have exercised their senses by practice in the discernment of good and evil'.[41] This food is the flesh of the Lamb, Christ figured as the paschal lamb,[42] or the true bread that comes down from heaven, the living Bread.[43]

The theme of food thus expresses both knowledge and grace, in a realistic manner, with a background that is eucharistic. As the foodstuffs become our substance, this divine food which is the Person of the Word is turned into us and we are turned into it. It operates the progressive divinisation which is the goal of the spiritual ascent by communicating to us the very life of the Word. That is how the mysteries are nourishing, and how knowledge leads to divinisation. Another thing taught by the theme is the educational function of the Word. It alone is the food of the soul. But the same food does not suit all: too rich for some, it is not enough for others. Thus the Logos takes on all the forms necessary to meet the need of each. His humanity – the Scripture that predicts it and relates it – is the diet adapted to this earthly life and through it his divinity is absorbed in doses that vary in accordance with our capacities.

So the mystery is food; it is also a wine, rejoicing the soul.[44] The origin of this theme is found in the Jewish theologian Philo. It constitutes for that author the 'oxymoron'[45] of 'sober drunkenness'. However, between Philo's 'sober drunkenness' and Origen's, there is one capital difference, already explained in connection with his exegesis. Origen is opposed to the Montanist conception of the prophetic ecstasy as unconsciousness or sacred madness, a conception that is not absent from certain texts of Philo. If, for Origen, the drunkenness occasioned by the wine of the True Vine 'takes one out of the human',[46] only the bad wine of false doctrine 'takes one out of the intellect'.[47] An ecstasy that would be unconscious is for Origen the sign that the demon is present, manifest in the evil passions that warp, cloud and enslave the intellect.

The True Vine which produces this Wine is clearly the Christ.[48] This theme insists on the emotional effects of knowledge which are scarcely covered by the bare term 'knowledge'. Although the word drunkenness is sometimes used by Origen, he more often describes the experience in more moderate terms: 'this drunkenness is not irrational but divine.'[49] It is joy, delight, consolation, the pleasure felt by the five spiritual senses, a participation here below in the Beatitude. Knowledge of the mysteries

[41] Heb. 5, 14.
[42] Exod. 12, 1.
[43] John 6, 26ff.
[44] *Origène et la 'connaissance mystique'*, pp. 184–197.
[45] An 'oxymoron' is an apparently contradictory affirmation, which seems stupid or foolish (*moros*) but is really acute (*oxys*).
[46] *ComJn* I, 30 (33), 206.
[47] *HomJr* (Latin) II, 8 (GCS VIII).
[48] John 15, 5.
[49] *ComJn* I, 30 (33), 206.

causes our hearts to burn within us, like the hearts of the two disciples on the road to Emmaus. It brings rest and peace, but an active rest impelled by the fire that it lights in the soul. It is also sweetness. But the most characteristic quality attributed to it is 'enthusiasm', that is to say the feeling that God is present by which the inspiration of the sacred author becomes in a way perceptible to the reader: *enthousiasmos* is in fact the perception of the *entheos* character of the divine Scriptures (*en*, in, *theos*, God): the reader feels that God is in them.

If Light essentially expresses the grace of knowledge and Life what would later be called sanctifying grace, the two kinds of grace are not distinguished when it comes to the theme of food which denotes both the knowledge of the mysteries and the communication of the divine life; likewise with the wine. In Origen's synthetic way of looking at things, everything is in one way or another united: we saw above how knowledge is mingled with love in union; we see now how knowledge and divine life overlap.

The spiritual ascent and its results

For Origen every 'going up' mentioned in the holy books, for example from Egypt to Palestine or from Galilee to Judaea, symbolises a spiritual ascent, and every 'going down' a decline. Thus Mary, after the Annunciation, goes into the hill country to meet Elizabeth and in her presence to give vent to an outburst of joy: in this she is fulfilling an apostolic mission, in that she is allowing the Jesus she carries in her womb to 'form' (*morphoun*) the John that is in Elizabeth's.[50] There is a whole symbolism in this of the mountain as the place for the spiritual ones and the plain as the whereabouts of Christians who stay at the level of simple faith.

Above all it is the scene of the Transfiguration[51] which is the favourite subject of this theme: comment on this is found in the works of Origen's old age, *Commentary on Matthew, Contra Celsum* and homilies. It is placed in the context of the 'wisdom of which one speaks among the perfect'.[52] The three apostles whom Jesus took with Him, Peter, James and John, have climbed the Mountain:[53] it is the symbol of the effort at asceticism that they have made. The ascent took place 'after six days':[54] now six is, because of the creation, related in Gen. 1, the figure for the world. Their ascetic effort has thus been a detachment from the world. On the top of the mountain they see Jesus transfigured, his divinity showing through his humanity. It has sometimes been said that for

[50] *ComJn* VI, 49 (30), 252ff.
[51] *Origène et la 'connaissance mystique'*, passim, e.g. 438–441, 470–474.
[52] 1 Cor. 2, 6; *CCels* VI, 9.
[53] Origen does not say, and probably does not know, which mountain.
[54] Matt. 17, 1: *ComMt* XII, 36–37 (GCS X).

Origen the humanity of Jesus was like a screen hiding his divinity from the eyes of men. Many shades of meaning can be given to this statement. What hides the divinity of Jesus from the eyes of men is first the will of Jesus not to reveal it so, since a divine Person is only seen when He reveals Himself: and second, man's unpreparedness in ascetic terms to perceive it, the lack of 'spiritual eyes', as we shall put it. It is, however, true that elsewhere the humanity of Jesus takes its place in the divine scheme of education, so that in a way it lets the radiance of divinity filter through. But only those can see this radiance through it who have climbed the Mountain. A similar explanation is given of the fact that the risen Jesus, manifesting Himself in his divinity through his glorified body, only showed Himself to his apostles and not to Pilate, to Herod, to the chief priests, who had had Him crucified, for they were incapable of perceiving his divinity.[55]

Origen's interpretation of the transfiguration is double: in the first place the divinity showed through the physical body of Jesus; in the second place the divinity showed through that other body of Christ which is the letter of Scripture. We have indeed seen that Scripture is itself another incarnation of the Word, in the letter which is analogous to the flesh, preparing or relating the unique Incarnation, both presenting the unique Word of God. Thus for the man who has climbed the mountain, Scripture is transfigured, the divinity of the Word shows through the letter. Such is already the 'trace of enthusiasm' which reveals to the reader the inspired character of the Scripture.[56]

The Scripture in question is the Old Testament as well as the New. Such is the meaning of the appearance of Moses and Elijah, symbolising the law and the prophets, with the transfigured Jesus. They are illuminated by the light that shines from Him and thus perceived by the three apostles. Not only do they at this moment see for themselves the 'Day of the Lord', but the transfiguration of Jesus has transfigured for them the Old Testament, turning it into a New Testament, of which the apostles thus receive the highest knowledge that a man can have while still on earth. In fact, the Transfiguration does not normally represent the beatific vision, except as a kind of foretaste, it still belongs to the temporal Gospel.

Origen's famous theme of the five spiritual senses,[57] drawn from figured or allegorised Scriptural expressions – and perhaps also from Platonist images – expresses the state of the spiritual man who has attained the supreme virtue, wisdom, and who thus knows by an intimate community of nature the supernatural realities: this community of nature

[55] CCels II, 63–64; VII, 43.
[56] CCels VI, 77; PArch IV, 1, 6.
[57] See K. Rahner, 'Le début d'une doctrine des cinq sens spirituels chez Origène', Revue d'Ascétique et de Mystique 13, 1932, 113–145.

evidently has its source in the development within him of the 'after-the-image'. Before Origen, Theophilus of Antioch[58] spoke of the 'eyes of the soul' and the 'ears of the heart', but Origen was to use this theme on a great scale. It constitutes a chapter of the 'law of homonymy' which applies the same terms to the inward as to the outward man in the explanation of the bodily anthropomorphisms applied to the human soul. Several passages of Origen set out the theory of this relying on some scriptural texts, notably the beginning of the first Epistle of John understood in a spiritual sense. If the most representative senses are sight and hearing, and more rarely touch, the most moving senses, taste and smell, add the idea of the delights of knowledge, associated, as we have seen, with the wine that rejoices the soul. What these senses apprehend is the divine realities, the mysteries.

Two essential affirmations are brought out by this theme. First there is kinship between a sense organ and what it senses: there is an analogy between the eye and what is visible, between the ear and what is audible, etc.[59] And correlatively there is an analogy between all the eyes that perceive the same objects, although their powers of perception vary. At the end of *Treatise on First Principles*[60] he was to rely on this double line of argument to demonstrate the immortality of the soul and the kinship of all the souls which perceive the spiritual realities. Then again we spontaneously get the impression that perception is an immediate, intuitive knowledge of objects. In fact, the study and analysis of perception show that this impression is not justified, for many habits acquired in early childhood, habits of which we are no longer aware, intervene to link the sensations together and to identify what is perceived with beings distinct from us and exterior to us. But Origen's conception is based on that spontaneous impression. The spiritual senses give of the spiritual realities a knowledge which is more and more, at least in tendency, of an immediate, intuitive order, taking account, however, of the fact that the perfect 'face to face' is reserved for the eternal Gospel.

Those who are made perfect 'have their senses skilled by habitual practice in the discernment of good and evil'.[61] Or according to an *agraphon*[62] Christians are exhorted thus: 'Become experienced money changers', who can distinguish false from genuine coins. Or again, according to 1 Thess. 5, 21: 'Prove all things, hold to the good.' This discernment applies to many kinds of reality: to the meaning of Scripture and of the mysteries that are hidden in it; to the doctrines, to find out

[58] *To Autolycos* I, 2 (SC 20).
[59] *EXhMart* XLVII (GCS I).
[60] IV, 4, 9–10.
[61] Heb. 5, 14. See Fr. Marty, 'Le discernement des esprits dans le Peri Archon d'Origène', *Revue d'Ascétique et de Mystique* 34, 1958, 147–164.
[62] An *agraphon* is a saying attributed to Christ in the primitive Church but not found in the New Testament.

whether they are or are not in accordance with the divine intention, whether they belong to the teaching of the Church or to that of the heresies which interpret Scripture in their own way, expounding under cover of it their own ideas; to the extraordinary facts, miracles or particular revelations. Finally, we come to the 'discerning of the spirits', a Pauline expression[63] to which Origen, founding a tradition that would long continue, gives the following meaning: since Satan can disguise himself as an angel of light and deceive souls under a semblance of good, it is necessary to distinguish the inspirations that come from him from those which come from God. Thus Gideon demands proof from the angel who visits him[64] and Joshua does the same.[65] The fundamental rule for discerning the spirits derives for Origen from his polemic against the unconscious ecstasy of the Montanists which we have already described: God respects the consciousness and freedom of men, only the devil clouds it and 'possesses' it.[66] Consequently, peace and clear-mindedness will be the sign that an inspiration truly comes from God. The discernment of spirits is a charism, that is a divine gift communicated by the Holy Spirit. But the gift cannot be received unless the life is virtuous.

✻   ✻   ✻

There, then, are some of the principal mystical themes of which Origen was the inventor, or at any rate the propagator. And they were to be constantly repeated by those who came after. This exposition is no more than a sample of some of the most important, and there are many others that could be found in his work and made the subject of study.

---

[63] 1 Cor. 12, 10.
[64] Judges 6, 17.
[65] Jos. 5, 13–14; *HomJg* VIII, 4 (GCS VII).
[66] *PArch* III, 3, 4.

8

Questions of Ascesis and Ethics

Although several valuable works have been written, though unfortunately not all published, Origen's ascetical and ethical doctrine is one of the most neglected areas of his thought: the same can be said of many other Fathers. This is regrettable, for even if his work was not as systematic as the ascetical and ethical theology of recent centuries, it is not without interest. It is to be found scattered haphazard through his exegeses. Its sources are in the first place biblical, but philosophical influences are discernible, first Stoic, then Platonist, and to a lesser degree Aristotelian; Origen is indeed very critical of Aristotle. The doctrine of virginity which we shall expound is very complete and very explicit about the spiritual value of this state. It is not always noticed, for, unlike some of his successors in the 4th century, for example Gregory of Nyssa or John Chrysostom, Origen did not write a treatise on virginity: his teaching about it is scattered through his works and contained especially in the fragments that survive of his exegesis of the first Epistle to the Corinthians. But before coming to this subject we must consider the spirituality of martyrdom which played so great a part in his life.

Martyrdom[1]

Origen often speaks of this in his homilies, but he also devoted a writing to it, the *Exhortation to Martyrdom*.[2] Martyrdom is the witness borne to Christ in physical suffering and death. It thus consists of two elements, a faith without reservation and a manifestation of that faith in the refusal of all idolatry, that is worshipping as God what is not God. If God is the jealous God, who will share with none, it is in our interests that He is jealous: to confess Him is to be united with Him, to deny Him is to be separated from Him. The martyr remains faithful in all circumstances to the undertaking given in baptism, to belong to God in Christ. He offers himself to God as a sacrifice, as a priest, in union with the sacrifice of Christ: he offers, with himself, all that he has on earth, fortune, family, children.

[1] See P. Hartmann, 'Origène et la théologie du martyre', *Ephemerides Theologiae Lovanienses* 34, 1958, 773–824.
[2] GCS 1: in the bibliographical notice at the beginning of this book there is mention of the Fr. translation by G. Bardy.

A martyr is a wrestler, an athlete, and his martyrdom is a fight, in an arena, at grips with the diabolical powers which want to make him sacrifice to idols in order to recover their strength in his defeat: he is encompassed with heavenly witnesses who await his triumph, for his victory defeats the principalities and powers of the demonic world. This fight is a test, showing whether the Christian has built his house on the rock or on the sand, whether the seed of the word has in him fallen upon good ground or on stony ground where it cannot take root.

The martyr does not fight alone, divine succour comes to his aid, the Spirit whispers to him what he should reply. But above all the martyr is the most perfect imitator of Jesus in his passion: that is a commonplace of the martyrological literature of the 2nd century, the Letters of Ignatius of Antioch, the Letter recounting the martyrdom of Polycarp, the Letter on the martyrs of Lyons and Vienne. He carries his cross with Christ, renouncing his own life that Christ may live in him. He follows Christ in his sufferings, and then in his glory, seated at the right hand of the Father, for communion in the passion leads to communion in the triumph.

The martyr participates in Christ's work of redemption. His confession is a baptism which completely purifies him of sin, the supreme baptism, the mystery of which baptism in water is the sacramental image, for it accomplishes in a deed the conformation to the death and resurrection of Christ of which baptism in water is the efficacious sign. The sufferings of the martyr work together with those of Christ in the great task of redeeming and purifying the world. Added to that of Christ the sacrifice of the martyrs brings about the rout of the diabolical powers.

The martyr's reward is glorification with Christ and eternal union with Him: the present sufferings are not to be compared with the future glory and that is why the Christian must not be troubled by ordeals which pass. He will live with the Lord, will enjoy perfect knowledge and blessedness in peace and unity, will receive again a hundredfold what he lost here below, and will take his place with Christ at the eternal banquet.

What we have said about Origen's life, about his father's martyrdom and those of several of his students, and finally about his own sufferings under Decius, shows that this subject was not for him a matter of pure intellectual speculation: at certain periods of his life martyrdom was a daily possibility. All his life Origen desired martyrdom: one of his finest passages on this subject is found in the *Dialogue with Heraclides*.[3] He desires it in order to be with Christ, out of the earthly body. But, as we said above, he condemns all seeking of martyrdom and requires the Christian to escape if possible confrontation with the authorities, out of charity for the persecutor who in putting him to death would commit a crime. On this point, as on most others, Origen's teaching is in a continual state of tension.

[3] §24.

Virginity and marriage: prolegomena[4]

Origen's teaching on virginity cannot be separated from what he says about marriage with which it is very closely linked. The spiritual value of both derives from their connection with the theme of the mystic marriage. Virginity, lived under the conditions that will be set out, is a specially close participation in this; it makes the union of Christ and the soul more possible. It is thus a witness both to the first and the last things because it evokes the perfect marriage of Christ and Church which was present in the pre-existence and will be again at the Resurrection. The Church, Bride and Virgin, holds her virginity from the chastity of her members leading a life either of virginity or of chastity according to the state in which they find themselves. So chastity appropriate to the state of marriage is an element in the virginity of the Church. So the husband must love his wife as Christ loves the Church and vice versa. Virginity is superior to marriage because it already makes real what marriage imitates and the latter finds itself, like all the realities here below, in an ambiguous position. It is spiritual if it imitates the union of Christ with the Church, but at the same time it has a place in the darkness of the flesh. It must overcome that darkness and then it is chaste. But the body is dangerous, like everything perceptible: image of divine mysteries, there is the risk that, instead of guiding the intellect towards those mysteries, it will hold it back at the bodily level. That is to substitute idolatry for adoration of the One God. As an image of the union of Christ and the Church, marriage is limited to the flesh and to time: it only makes sense in this lower world. Virginity, on the other hand, would have no point in a life limited to the here below. He who is a virgin behaves in this world as if he did not belong to it: in the midst of men he is the prophet of, and the witness to, a future in which the desires of the flesh will no longer have reality, where only the link that binds us to Christ will count. We must add, extending Origen's thought a little, that a marriage lived chastely – and we shall see what he means by that – while remaining a temporal reality, in some way partakes of eternity.

When dealing with his trichotomic anthropology we emphasised some of the difficulties presented by Origen's notion of the body. We shall find another which matches them. Many passages affirm, of course, the essential goodness of the body of flesh, work of the Creator. It also, when the soul turns towards the 'spirit', and still more when the Holy Spirit is in the man, shares in the transfiguration of the whole man. The chaste body is the temple of the Trinity in which the soul made in the image of God officiates as the priest of the Holy Spirit. Directed by the soul the Saint's body becomes Christ's instrument. Elsewhere Origen is always affirming that impurity does not reside in beings or substances but in

[4] H. Crouzel, *Virginité et Mariage chez Origène*, Bruges/Paris, 1963: referred to below as *Virginité*.

thoughts and actions that do not conform to the divine will: he confirms the lawfulness of marriage against the rigorists who deny it, Marcionites or Montanists. And yet a whole series of texts sees an impurity in sexual relations even when they are legitimated by marriage, an impurity which is transmitted to the child born of them. It is thus that a triangular relationship exists in Jesus between his divinity, his virginal conception and his freedom from concupiscence. While clearly excluding a docetic interpretation of his words, for he never ceases to say the body of Jesus was a body of flesh like ours and not an appearance, he uses in this way Rom. 8, 3: God has sent his Son in 'a likeness of sinful flesh', not in a sinful flesh, the word likeness applying not simply to the word flesh but to the total expression 'sinful flesh'. This absence of concupiscence is of course due principally to the infinite love which joins the soul of Jesus to the Word as Origen explains in one of the finest passages of the *Treatise on First Principles*.[5] But it also derives from the fact that Jesus was born of a virgin.

The impurity of even lawful sexual relations also emerges from Origen's interpretation of 1 Cor. 7, 5: that which is in Paul a piece of advice or a permission aimed at the withdrawal of the married couple for prayer becomes for Origen an obligation, temporary, to be sure, and agreed between them, but extended to religious fasts and to the reception of the eucharist. On this point Origen was to be followed by a great part of subsequent tradition.

However, he is careful to distinguish this kind of impurity from sin, which some of his successors would not bother to do: it only exists 'in some way' and it is only 'a certain' impurity.[6] While sin adheres to the soul so long as it is not expiated and forgiven, this impurity does not prevent married people from offering their bodies to God as 'a living sacrifice, holy and pleasing to God' outside their conjugal relations.[7] How are we to explain this notion of a stain? That Platonist influences have played a part, we do not deny. But we do not think that that is the essential explanation: it is not Origen's habit to repeat without a personal motive what others have said. This sense of stain has in his thought a justification both metaphysical and theological linked to his inner experience as an ascetic. But to understand it we must associate it with a wider impurity of which it forms part, that of the carnal condition.

In the divine thought, as we have said, the aim of the perceptible is to point the soul in the direction of the true realities and by its beauty to inspire in the soul the desire for these. There is, however, the risk, because of the weakness and selfishness of man, that it will take the place of its Model and arrogate to itself the adoration due to the Truth which it

---

[5] II, 6, 4–6.
[6] *ComMt* XVII, 35 (GCS X).
[7] *ComRM* IX, 1 (PG 14): *HomNb* XXIII, 3: on Rom. 12, 1.

figures. Such is, in its deepest and most original aspect, Origen's doctrine of sin, following his symbolic Platonist view of the world. The flesh is impure because it is ambiguous and dangerous. So this impurity does not attach to the perceptible as such but to the selfish passion of man. Used in accordance with the divine plans, the flesh is good. Its ambiguity is subjective, depending on man, not objective, depending on itself. Jesus assumed – Origen says this several times – the carnal condition which is impure, but that could not be for Him the source of sin because of the total union in which his soul is joined to the Word. The flame of divinity and love sets wholly alight the human nature of Jesus, leaving no room for selfishness: the saint escapes impurity in so far as he abandons himself to Jesus, but he cannot do this entirely because his union with the Word is contingent, always subject here below to progress or to backsliding. Whatever victories the saints win over sin, they never entirely escape, even in their triumphs, from the impurity of selfishness or the contagion of the demon. Origen expresses this in a homily on Numbers,[8] interpreting allegorically the purifications which the Israelites had to undergo on their return from a triumph over the Midianites. He emphasises here the imperfection of every human act performed by a being whom selfishness and concupiscence never entirely leave, a being for whom throughout time until the Last Judgement the trace of past deeds is engraved on the heart – Origen points this out frequently – and even the trace of passing thoughts which the will rejected from the first moment. The theme of the purifications, in this life and in the Last Things, is frequent in Origen's work and he is the first great theologian of Purgatory.

Between this impurity of the carnal condition and the impurity of sexual relations the only difference is one of intensity. His outlook as an ascetic and mystic makes Origen very sensitive to the increased danger of idolatrous enjoyment to which sexual relations can give rise. If the deeds of the saints never escape the radical impurity of the human condition, what can be said of conjugal relations, even when they are inspired by Christian love. The stain which Origen finds in them seems to have no other meaning.

A third prolegomenon on virginity and marriage concerns the nature of the love that should inspire these two states of life. In the first homily on the Song of Songs and in the prologue of the Commentary on the same book, Origen contrasts spiritual and carnal love essentially in respect of the object to which they are directed and consequently in respect of their origin, God or Satan. Love for the perceptible is bad, since it is the property of the perceptible to be left behind, to show the way to the spiritual, and not to arrogate to itself the homage of men. In fact, the only love worthy of the name is the charity which has the divine Father as its

[8] XXV, 6.

source, begets the Son and produces the Spirit and spreads from Them over mankind: carnal love is only an abuse of the love which God has put in our hearts so that we should love Him.[9] To be sure, Origen scarcely distinguishes in that love the movement of the gift from the movement of the desire, the distinction that our contemporaries denote by the Greek words *agape* and *eros*. Following A. von Harnack, A. Nygren reproached Origen with this in a book that had considerable success.[10] But if the ideal of Christian love offered to God was a pure *agape* without any contamination from *eros*, in other words a pure gift of oneself without desire, it would be in contradiction, not only with the desire for union which is characteristic of love, not only with hope, a theological virtue, but even with the act of adoration in so far as the latter also emphasises our state of poverty towards God: to think ourselves capable of giving everything to God without desiring anything from Him, as if everything that we give to God did not come first from Him, beginning with this love itself, would betray an inconceivable *hybris*. One might perhaps have wished that Origen had made a clearer distinction between these two aspects, but not that he had separated them, for they are not separable, and the most perfect love that we can imagine will always be both gift of oneself and desire. That Origen conceived spiritual love as a gift derives from the fact that he saw it as in some way overflowing from God and from the two other divine persons onto the creatures, giving them the power to love; that Origen elsewhere conceived love as the desire for the divine realities, that is to say for God Himself, that is the mainspring of all his mysticism which tends continually towards union.

But love must be ordered: this theme is developed in the *Commentary on the Song of Songs* at Cant. 2, 4 (Septuagint) 'Order the love that is in me',[11] and likewise in the *Homily on Luke XXV* and is the beginning of a whole tradition. Only God and his Christ, who are subjects and objects of the same love, must be loved 'with all our heart, with all our soul, and with all our strength':[12] to love a creature like that is to confer on it what must only be given to God, it is idolatry. God alone is to be loved without limit. The neighbour must be loved 'as ourselves'.[13] First among neighbours is the wife whom the husband must love as his own body, just as Christ loves the Church: this love 'is of a particular nature and is separate from all other'.[14] Next come the other affections in the family. But none of these loves are to be preferred to the love of God, when the

---

[9] *ComCt* Prol. (GCS VIII, pp. 66–74).
[10] See the Fr. translation *Eros et Agapé: La notion chrétienne de l'amour*. Paris, 3 volumes 1944–1952: in volume II/1, pp. 153–178.
[11] III (GCS VIII, pp. 186–191).
[12] Mt 22, 37.
[13] Mt 22, 39.
[14] *ComCt* III (GCS VIII, p. 189, 1, 2).

choice must be made, for example by the martyr: to put those one loves before God would not be truly to love them.

While preserving its carnal aspects, conjugal love must tend more and more toward the spiritual: by the harmony between the spouses which would be disturbed by passion, the sign of a selfish love which seeks the satisfaction of enjoyment, not the good of the partner. The conjugal act should be performed with reverent calm, 'in good order and at the right time' with the self-control and renunciation implied by it. The accord between the two spouses is the sign of a *charisma*, of a grace, coming from the Holy Spirit. In the fragments that remain of his exegeses on the first epistle to the Corinthians, Origen insists on the concord, the accord, the harmony which are the signs of the divine presence in the marriage.

Procreation is, as in the Stoic philosophy, the essential justification of the carnal aspects of marriage. There is also the fact that it is a 'remedy against concupiscence' according to 1 Cor. 7, 9. But Origen scarcely thinks, any more than Augustine and the other Fathers, that sexual relations can have any effect on conjugal love itself.[15]

Virginity

After these three prolegomena we shall treat virginity and marriage successively. First, let us note that Origen was the first theologian clearly to teach the perpetual virginity of Mary, for the writers of the 2nd century, like Justin and Irenaeus, only did so implicitly by calling her Mary the Virgin. For Origen this is by no means, as has been suggested, an open question, with no obligation on the Christian to believe it: it is the only 'healthy' view of the matter and that word is used to express a close connection with the faith; those who uphold the contrary are treated as heretics; Mary among women is the first fruits of virginity as Jesus is among men.[16]

But virginity, and chastity in all its forms, presupposes moral conditions. Virginity of practice must be lived in the virginity of faith. Origen is very critical of the virginity imposed by certain heretical sects, notably the Marcionites, that 'first draft' of Manichaeism. He indeed judges its motives to be blasphemous: because they think the Creator God, whom they distinguish from the Father of Jesus Christ, to be evil and the body to be his work, they condemn marriage. But Origen is equally critical of the chastity practised by other heretics, for less valid reasons than the Marcionites, because it is for them a way of seducing souls. Virginity of faith is more important than virginity of morals, which has no value if the doctrine is false. The same can be said of the virgin priestesses of paganism. Nowadays, we should think Origen's judgements

[15] Cf. *Virginité* 15–83.
[16] *ComJn* I, 4 (6), 23; *HomLc* VII, 4, from the Latin, and a Greek fragment (GCS IXbis); *ComMt* X, 17: on marian theology see the preface to SC 87.

too severe, and rightly so, for he does not take account of the heretic's *bona fide* intention, which gives his deeds their moral value.

We should more readily agree with three other affirmations. First, virginity to be worthwhile must be accompanied by the other virtues, or at least by effort to attain them, and Origen does not hesitate to declare the virtuous married person superior to the proud single one, guilty of vanity or love of money: indeed – and this point is found earlier in the Greek philosophers – all the virtues hang together and one cannot really practise one of them if one deliberately rejects the others: the Foolish Virgins were not admitted to the wedding because they had not put into their lamps the oil of charity. Next, the aim of bodily chastity is chastity of the heart, that is of the intellect. Thoughts are more important than deeds, for they lead to deeds. He who remains chaste in body but gives himself up to impure thoughts and desires is not chaste. On the other hand the virgin raped in the wilderness, Deut. 22, 25ff., did not lose her chastity of heart which was essential. Origen did not, at least in the writings that have come down to us, face the question which preoccupied later Fathers in connection with persecution at Antioch, that of the suicide of a virgin threatened with rape. If Ambrose of Milan or Chrysostom approved that action, Augustine took a position which would probably have been that of Origen. No one should put himself to death to prevent the sins of others. Virginity of body only has meaning where there is virginity of heart: violation of the first is important when there is also violation of the second.[17] Finally, Christian virginity is a voluntary decision: it must not be confused with the factual virginity of a woman who has not found a husband or a man incapable of marriage, unless that factual virginity has been freely undertaken from a religious motive. Christian virginity is a deliberate decision to preserve celibacy for the service of God.

Just as marriage involves a mutual giving of the spouses to one another, so celibacy takes its place in the theme of mystical marriage because there is a mutual self-giving between God and his creature. Chaste celibacy bears a charism, as does marriage: both states imply grace. We should not expect Origen, seeing that the notion of sacrament only became precise in the high Middle Ages, to distinguish between the sacramental grace of marriage and the non-sacramental grace of virginity. In both cases grace is the Holy Spirit that is given, it is He who constitutes the 'nature' and the 'matter' of the charisms. It is also a divine vocation, God preserves virginity in the soul, which is identified with Christ who is not only the model for each virtue, but in his divine nature is each virtue and all the

---

[17] The facts are reported without critical comment by Eusebius HE VIII, XII, 3–4. In John Chrysostom two homilies on Pelagia, one on Berenice and Prosdoce in PG 50, 585 and 629. Ambrose speaks of Pelagia in *De Virginibus* III, 7 (PL 16, 229–232). Augustine gives his opinion in *De civitate Dei* I, 36; PL 41, 39–40.

QUESTIONS OF ASCESIS AND ETHICS

virtues. Virginity is then a gift of God to the soul which must receive it in faith and prayer. But virginity is also a gift that the soul makes to God, the most perfect after martyrdom, a gift made in response to the first gift which comes from God. In the sacrifice of virginity the man is at once by his intellect the priest who immolates, and in his flesh the victim which is immolated: thus he imitates Christ on the Cross, at once priest and victim. A fragment of Origen's exegeses of the first Epistle to the Corinthians[18] clearly distinguishes two kinds of commandments, the kind imposed on all and necessary to salvation, and the kind, including virginity and poverty, which go beyond what is imposed and necessary for salvation. Such was the celibacy lived by Paul out of devotion to the Church. If chastity appropriate to one's state of life is a commandment imposed on all, celibacy goes beyond what is imposed on all. We do not find in Origen any clear statement about obligatory celibacy or continence for bishops, priests and deacons: the first canonical rules with that effect date from the 4th century. To be sure, Tertullian says that celibacy was widely spread among the clergy,[19] but he says nothing about an obligation.

Virginity imposes a sacrifice, a mortification of the flesh which does not consist in refusing it what is needful, but in not serving its evil desires. The measure and the manner of this mortification are not the same for all, for all do not have the same difficulties. Some are naturally chaste and have little difficulty in keeping themselves free of evil imaginations; with others this is not so, and they have to struggle constantly. The means vary, but in no way can one attain here below a chastity which would take away all danger of falling and make precautions unnecessary. The actions of the saint, even the best of them, are not exempt from stain. Closely linked with chastity are the keeping of the heart and the senses, consisting in the avoidance of dangerous thoughts and sensations, flight from occasions where that could happen, fasting with abstinence from certain kinds of food and drink considered particularly rousing, prayer in the storm of temptation with the effort to keep calm and confident. However, temptation is normal for man in this lower world: it takes many forms and spares no age or state of life, the healthy no more than the sick. It is for the Christian yet another opportunity to offer to God his chastity.

In fact, virginity is the source of fecundity and freedom. The fecundity of the chaste is like that of Mary, Virgin and Mother, it begets Jesus in the soul. Jesus is born only in the one who is chaste and He grows all the more if the individual is a virgin. With Jesus, all the virtues that are identified with Him grow in the soul. Unlike the married person, who is in a sense, the slave of his partner, for he has surrendered rights over his

18 XXXIX (*JThS* XX, p. 508).
19 *De Exhortatione Castitatis* XIII 4 (CChr II).

own body, the celibate is free, not with a freedom to give rein to selfishness, but with a freedom that finds its justification in a more complete service of God. We saw above that we must distinguish in Origen free will, that is the power of choice, from freedom. The former occupies a major place in his work because it was one of the points most endangered at the time on account of gnōsis, astrology and the determinism of certain philosophical schools. But free will is not the whole of freedom, only one of its essential characteristics. Through Origen's spiritual doctrine there appears a more complete conception of freedom which reproduces the *eleutheria* of Paul: giving oneself to God liberates, sin enslaves, causing a man to relapse into the bondage of animal determinisms. Thus it can be understood how the freedom of celibacy undertaken for God's sake is identified with the service of God.[20]

Marriage

Several times Origen defends the state of marriage against heretics who attack it, Encratites, to whom he refers in the words of Paul in 1 Tim. 4, 3. These are mostly the Marcionites whose reasons we have noted and the Montanists whose position is made clear in the works written by Tertullian after he had joined the sect. Origen's exegeses often reveal a fairly strong misogyny, for they apply favourable significance to the masculine unfavourable to the feminine, while asserting that there are before God many virile women and effeminate men. However, he follows Paul in affirming the absolute equality of the spouses in the fundamental rights of marriage. This is a point on which the Apostle's position is nowadays often unfairly criticised, because we judge it by our present-day conceptions, without historical perspective and consequently without appreciation of the considerable revolution that Paul brought about. In Hebrew legislation and in Roman law there was no equality of the spouses in the matter of adultery. A married man who allowed himself extramarital relations with an unmarried girl was not an adulterer; he in no way wronged his wife, who had no rights over him. On the contrary, the married woman who did the same was an adulteress and was punished severely by the law as was her accomplice, for she was her husband's property. While in Roman circles the wife could take the initiative to end the marriage, in Jewish circles she could not. When Paul writes:[21] 'For the wife does not rule over her own body, but the husband does; likewise, also, the husband does not rule over his own body, but the wife does', he is re-establishing equality, giving the wife a right over her husband's body similar to the one he has over hers. Paul was to be followed in this by the Fathers generally, with two regrettable exceptions, Basil of Caesarea in his Canonical Letters and the unknown writer known as Ambrosiaster.

[20] See *Virginité* 105–131.
[21] 1 Cor. 7, 4.

Several Latin Fathers were to repeat in equivalent words: 'What is not permitted to the wife is not permitted to the husband either'; and Augustine was to draw from that one of the fundamental principles of his doctrine of marriage.

This equality in respect of the fundamental rights which is to be found fairly clearly in the works of Origen does not prevent the man from remaining the head of the family nor from being likewise within the family the one who leads prayer. Paul's rule 'That the women should keep silent in the churches'[22] is used by Origen against the Montanists, by reason of their prophetesses, Priscilla and Maximilla, to show that their Church was not the Bride of Christ.

On the subject of the grace, the *charisma* of marriage, the fruit of which, as we have seen, is the accord and harmony between the spouses, there is a problem about the participation of the Holy Spirit in this charism: two fragments express contradictory positions on this matter. A fragment on the Epistle to the Romans, confirmed by Rufinus's translation of the *Commentary*[23] says that the Holy Spirit is not present, because here he is looking at the matter in its carnal aspect. On the contrary, another, on the first Epistle to the Corinthians,[24] shows that this charism truly comes from God 'when moderation is observed ... when there is no inconstancy, when all is peace and accord'. And we find in this last fragment in words concerning a marriage between a believer and an unbeliever a theology several centuries before its time: there cannot be in that marriage a charism coming from God, but if the unbeliever begins to believe, he will receive the charism.

Origen is strongly opposed to unions between believers and unbelievers. They are 'unequally yoked' to use a Pauline term, *heterozygountes*,[25] and Origen cannot see in that a true marriage of which God is the author: the accord that comes from the Lord is lacking. Some Christians consider themselves authorised to marry pagans by what Paul says in 1 Cor. 7, 14: they will sanctify their partners. But for one thing the case envisaged by the apostle is not the same: it is that of a marriage between two unbelievers, one of whom is converted subsequently, and not that of an inter-faith marriage contracted between a Christian and a non-Christian. For another thing, when he said that the believer would sanctify his partner, Paul only mentioned the more favourable solution, for the other possibility also exists: that the Christian is soiled by the pagan partner and that there ensues a struggle starting from the 'abundance of the heart',[26] that is to say from the strength of the convictions of each; it is

---

[22] 1 Cor. 14, 35; *Fragm* 1 Cor. LXXIV, *JThS* X, pp. 41–42.
[23] *FragmRm* III, *JThS* XIII, p. 213; *ComRm* I, 12 (PG 14).
[24] XXXIV, *JThS* IX, p. 503, 1.40.
[25] 2 Cor. 6, 14; *Fragm 1 Cor.* XXXV, *JThS* IX, pp. 504–505.
[26] Matt. 12, 34; *Fragm 1 Cor.* XXXVI, *JThS* IX, p. 505.

not certain that the Christian will win and keep his faith. As Paul requires of the widows,[27] marriage must be 'in the Lord', which Origen, in common with most but not all the Fathers, interprets to mean with a Christian partner.

Concerning remarriage after divorce the comments made by Origen on Matt. 19, 3–11 have often been interpreted in ways that pay little attention to the general run of his thought. The most complete exposition that we have made of this is to be found in our book *L'Eglise primitive face au divorce*.[28] Here we can only summarise its argument briefly. First, Origen is unaware – as are all the Fathers before Nicaea and the Greek Fathers until the 5th century – of the text of Matt. 19, 9 as we have it today. This is a *crux interpretum* because it speaks in the same sentence of the exception 'save in the case of *porneia*', which the Fathers in general understand to mean adultery, and at the same time of remarriage. Origen quotes this text three times[29] in the same passage, but in the form of Matt. 5, 32, where the exception is mentioned but not remarriage. Evidence from the Fathers shows that this latter reading is almost certainly the original one, not only for Matt. 5, 32, but also for Matt. 19, 9 and that our present reading of Matt. 19, 9 is due to contamination by Mark 10, 11.[30]

In allegorical developments that are not always very consistent, Origen shows Christ repudiating the Synagogue for its crime against Him and espousing the Church drawn from the nations. The conclusion of some scholars is that if He acted thus, Christians can do the same. Unfortunately, on the one hand this conclusion hardly fits other passages in the same chapter about the indissoluble union of Christ with the Church in the pre-existence, in the Old Testament (the Synagogue) and after the Incarnation right through to the glory;[31] on the other hand it betrays a total ignorance of Origen's allegorical method of exegesis. It refers in fact to an interpretation of Deut. 24, 1–4, the passage in which Moses, yielding, says Jesus, to the hardness of heart of his fellow-countrymen,[32] authorised them to dismiss their wives by giving them a certificate of repudiation. According to Origen's allegorical exegesis this precept is fulfilled spiritually by Christ, but like everything juridical or ceremonial in the Old Testament it is no longer valid on the literal plane for Christians.

[27] 1 Cor. 7, 39; *Fragm 1 Cor.* XXXVI, *JThS* IX, p. 505.
[28] Paris, 1971, pp. 74–89.
[29] *ComMt* XIV, 24 (GCS X).
[30] See on this subject our two articles 'Le texte patristique de Matthieu V, 32 et XIX, 9' in *New Testament Studies* 19, 1972/1973, pp. 98–119 and 'Quelques remarques concernant le texte patristique de Mt 19, 9' in *Bulletin de Littérature exxlésiastique* 82, 1981, 83–92. The two articles were republished in *Mariage et Divorce, Célibat et caractère sacerdotaux dans l'Eglise ancienne*, Turin, 1982, pp. 92–113, 233–242.
[31] *ComMt* XIV, 19–20 (GCS X).
[32] Matt. 19, 8.

Finally, Origen testifies[33] that bishops, probably in the neighbourhood of Caesarea of Palestine where he was then living, had permitted the remarriage of a woman while her husband was still alive. He reckons that they did not do it without good reason, but emphasises three times that in doing so they acted contrary to Scripture, which is in fact the harshest censure that he could have inflicted upon them. And in a short passage not often noticed at the end of the next chapter[34] he goes back to the case in point to say that in spite of the authorisation of the bishops, this woman is an adulteress, her second marriage a sham, and that her husband has not truly married her. So Origen does not accept remarriage after divorce and he expresses so the invalidity of a marriage contracted in those circumstances.

What about second marriages after widowhood? Origen does not forbid them absolutely,[35] for the apostle permitted them. He even harshly blames the rigorists who exclude the remarried from the assemblies as if they were open sinners. But he is far from encouraging second marriages, seeing no better reason for them than inability to live continently and to control one's instincts: it is astonishing that Origen, like many other Fathers, never mentions any other motives for remarriage such as economic factors or the requirements of children's education. Second marriages are presented only as an extreme concession to weakness: it is better to marry than to live in sin because one cannot put up with continence. To take a second wife is not in conformity with the primitive law of Gen. 2, 24: one cannot be one flesh with a second woman. But what about the multiple unions of the patriarchs, which were even simultaneous? They symbolise 'mystical economies'. In this connection Origen affirms the only law of which there is evidence at this period about the matrimonial situation of the clergy: according to Paul,[36] bishops, priests and deacons should be 'the husband of one wife'; they cannot remarry if they are widowed and remarried men must not be ordained. Such was the only interpretation of these texts which was given in the 3rd century.[37]

With the freedom of the celibate is contrasted the bondage of the married man, consisting above all in the rights that each partner has given the other over his body. But the married Christian who lives his marriage as a Christian should is in a way the freedman of the Lord, not because he can free himself from the bondage of marriage but because he lives it in prayer, imitating the union of Christ with the Church: married life is for him the opportunity for the only liberation that counts, the one that leads

[33] *ComMt* XIV, 23 (GCS X).
[34] *ComMt* XIV, 24 (GCS X).
[35] 1 Cor. 7, 39–40.
[36] 1 Tim. 3, 1–2 and 12; Tit. 1, 5–6.
[37] *HomLc* XVII, 10–11; *ComMt* XIV, 22 (GCS X).

to Christian freedom. So it is not by getting rid of his conjugal obligations that the married Christian becomes the freedman of the Lord, it is by a life of virtue. As for abstention from conjugal duties, Origen only admits what Paul recognises, temporary abstention by agreement that they may betake themselves to prayer and meet the need for meditation. Origen seems very reticent about any abstention for a longer period and he would hardly have accepted, as Basil was to do, that a couple should separate so that one of them could lead a monastic life, nor even it seems, that married people should live together in complete continence, which is something to be constantly allowed in the 4th and 5th centuries and at that time to be imposed on clergy who had been married before ordination. He is too much afraid that in such a case the desire of the one for continence should endanger the chastity of the other, unable to put up with the life imposed on him or her.

A fine passage on the first Epistle to the Corinthians[38] affirms that charity, being the main component of conjugal love and the dominant virtue of marriage, takes precedence over all desire for chastity that is incompatible with the good of the partner. How could one spouse seek salvation by causing the fall of the other? 'It is better that both be saved by the works of marriage than to see one fall, on account of the other, from the hope he has in Christ. How could the husband be saved if he were responsible for the death of his wife?' However, he alludes, without really taking it into account, to Clement's opinion that the 'true companion' (*gnesie syzyge*=*germane compar*) whom Paul addresses in Phil. 4, 3 must be the wife whom Paul with her agreement had left for the sake of his ministry:[39] in fact, *syzygos* like the Latin *conjux* to which it exactly corresponds etymologically – yoke-fellow – can mean marriage partner, but it also has a wider sense than its Latin equivalent, parent, friend, companion. Elsewhere, Origen strongly censures, as does Clement, the heretics who dissolve marriages for religious reasons and that would assuredly apply to some of the decisions of the Fathers of the following century. Besides, conjugal duties are not simply required by charity, they are imposed by justice. Since there is absolute equality between the partners on this point, each one is, in relation to the other, in the position both of master and of slave. Of course, it is not forbidden for the spouses by common agreement to renounce the exercise of their rights: but Origen fears that such renunciation would often be to the detriment of one of the partners. Such is the bondage which the state of marriage entails and because of it this condition can often seem more difficult than that of the celibate. To live in marriage as a perfect Christian, with the reserve and self-control which conjugal love demands, in self-giving to the partner and the children and not in the desire to enjoy

[38] *Fragm 1 Cor.* XXXIII, *JThS* IX, p. 500.
[39] Clement *Stromateis* III, 6, 53, 1 (GCS Clement II); Origen *ComRm* I, 1 PG 14.

the other, is difficult for one who, like every other man, has to overcome the trend of a nature marked by selfishness. Marriage is a way of perfection that is far from easy and the grace of the sacrament is very necessary for that.[40]

* * *

There are many other points that could be studied, and we have come across some of them incidentally. For example, there is the spiritual combat that determines the trichotomic anthropology and also the angelology-demonology; the relations of free-will and freedom; the virtues, titles (*epinoiai*) of Christ and participation in his nature; sin, which consists in stopping at the image when the soul should soar to the mystery; apathy and metriopathy, eradication of the passions or the limit to be imposed on them. The moral and ascetic teaching of Origen offers ample material to anyone wishing to study it.

---

[40] See *Virginité* 132–169.

Part 4

THEOLOGY

9
Characteristics
of Origen's Theology

When telling the story of Origen's life we emphasised the fact which started his career as a writer, his encounter with and conversion of Ambrose. Encouraged by the latter and helped by the considerable resources that he placed at his disposal. Origen sought to provide for Christians who raised problems of an intellectual order, usually arising from Greek philosophy, the principal cultural influence in the Roman Empire, answers in accordance with the Scriptures, so that they would not go and seek these in the gnostic sects. In the same way he compiled the *Treatise on First Principles* 'for those who, sharing our faith, are accustomed to look for reasons for their belief and for those who stir up conflicts against us in the name of the heresies'.[1] To understand Origen's thought it is therefore necessary to know what these heresies were and also to know his attitude to philosophy and the use that he made of it. Next we must ask how he conceived theological research. It is most important to retain a strict historical perspective, and to be sufficiently aware of the development of dogma, not to condemn him as his detractors of the 4th and 5th centuries did; for they took no account of the progress that had clearly been made since his time in understanding and expression of the deposit of faith and likewise in theological method.

Heresies and errors controverted by Origen
This account can amount to little more than a list of the doctrines and some indication of the principal objections raised to them by Origen. The major heresies of the time, the gnostic sects, have been the subject of a considerable literature, especially since the discovery during the Second World War of the gnostic library at Nag Hammadi or Chenoboskion in Egypt.[2]

Origen aims his polemic mainly at the trio Basilides-Valentinus-Marcion. The objections he makes to them and the ideas that he attributes to them are somewhat stereotyped and do not reflect a very deep first-

[1] IV, 4, 5.
[2] For a general account of the different sects and of the discoveries at Nag Hammadi, see J. Doresse, *Les livres secrets des gnostiques d'Egypte*, Paris, 1958.

hand knowledge of them.[3] The main points of the controversy are as
follows: the three heresiarchs contrast the two Testaments and the
allegorical exegesis which Origen uses shows that, on the contrary,
they belong together. In the same way they contrast the Gods that inspire
the respective Testaments, while Origen insists on the identity of the
Creator God and the Father of Jesus Christ. He particularly objects
to Valentinus's doctrine of the three natures of souls and to the
predestinarianism which underlies it: on the one hand, Valentinus held,
there were the pneumatics or spiritual souls, consubstantial (*homoousioi*)
with the divine beings, the Aeons whom the Pleroma comprises: these are
necessarily saved; at the other extreme were the hylics (material souls) or
choics (terrestrial souls), who belong to the Cosmocrator, the Prince of
this world, the devil, and are necessarily damned; between these two were
the psychics, the 'animal' men of 1 Cor. 2, 14, who, according to their
conduct, can obtain either a second-class salvation in the 'intermediate
state', the realm of the Creator God, or damnation with the hylics. It was
by reason of this doctrine that Origen drew up his chapter on free will in
the *Treatise on First Principles* and constantly spoke of the original
equality of rational beings, an equality only to be broken by the free
choice of their will: the cosmology described in that book is explained by
the dialectic between divine action and human freedom which can accept
or reject the divine.

Valentinus pictures the generation of divine beings in the manner of
human or animal generation with division of substance, a *probolé* or
prolatio: for Origen this generation is purely spiritual, the Son remains in
the bosom of the Father, even when He is present in the Incarnation with
his human soul while still having a personality different from that of the
Father. Marcion makes of the Creator God of the Old Testament a just
but not a good God and even one positively cruel and malicious: he
argues from the scenes of cruelty in the Old Testament which Origen
explains by his allegorical exegesis, and also from the inequality of human
conditions at birth.[4] It is to save the Creator God's reputation of
goodness from these objections that Origen erects his favourite hypothesis,
certainly too easy a solution of the problem of evil, that based on the pre-
existence of souls: the different conditions in which men are born derive
from faults anterior to their birth on earth.

The gnöstic sects and the Marcionites – the latter did not completely
adhere to the gnösis – were, in Origen's day, religious communities
separated from the Great Church. It was the same with the Montanists.

[3] For Origen and the gnöstics see especially A. Le Boulluec, 'La place de la polémique
antignöstique dans le *Peri Archon*' in *Origeniana* (ed. H. Crouzel et al.), Bari, 1975,
pp. 47–61.
[4] See J. Rius-Camps, 'Origenes y Marcion', in *Origeniana* (see note 3) pp. 297–312.

Origen alludes to their doctrine of the Holy Spirit[5] and opposes their conception of prophetic inspiration, rejecting, as we have seen,[6] an unconscious trance. The other errors that he fought were not characteristic of constituted sects but rather of various trends within the Great Church. They are, to begin with, two opposite tendencies in Trinitarian theology of which we spoke in connection with Beryllus of Bostra and Heraclides.[7] The Modalists are also called Monarchians because they were trying to safeguard the divine 'monarchy', the unity of the Deity, or else Noetians and later Sabellians, from the names of the main leaders, Noetus of Smyrna and the Libyan Sabellius; in the West they were called Patripassians, because it followed from their doctrine that the Father suffered the Passion: they made of the Father, the Son and the Holy Spirit three modes of being of a single divine Person. The Adoptianists also safeguard the 'monarchy' by seeing in Christ a man whom God adopted. In fact it could happen that modalism and adoptianism were mixed up. That seems to have been the case with Beryllus of Bostra, as it was to be after Origen's death with Paul of Samosata, bishop of Antioch, who was to be condemned by several synods in which pupils and friends of Origen's would play a prominent part: Firmilian of Caesarea in Cappoedocia, Dionysius of Alexandria, Theotecnus of Caesarea in Palestine, Gregory Thaumaturgus and his brother Athenodorus.[8] Against these heretics Origen insists on the distinction of the three hypostases, the generation of the Word, the rejection of all *probolé* or generation by division.

Finally, Origen opposes again, within the bosom of the Great Church, those whom he calls the 'simpler' and whom we might call by three names: Anthropomorphites, because they take literally the anthropomorphisms that the Bible attributes to God and to the soul and consequently picture God as corporeal: against these Origen clearly affirms the absolute incorporeality of the three Persons and of the soul; Millenarians or Chiliasts, because they take literally the thousand years of Apoc. 20, 1–10, and believe, as did Papias, Justin and Irenaeus, that Christ and the martyrs will reign for that time in the earthly Jerusalem, before the final resurrection, of which, like Athenagoras, they hold an absurdly materialistic conception. It was in opposition to them, successfully 'safeguarding the tradition of the ancients' that Origen formulated his doctrine of the risen body, affirming between the earthly body and the body of glory both their identity and the difference that there is between the seed and the plant (1 Cor. 15, 35–44): although slanderously criticised, following the misunderstanding about the corporeal *eidos*, for

[5] *PArch* II, 7, 3; *ComMt* XV, 30 (GCS X).
[6] See pp. 71–72.
[7] See pp. 15–33.
[8] Eusebius, HE VII, 27–30.

which Methodius of Olympus was responsible, it was none the less one of his most successful ideas. Finally we may call them Literalists, because they preserve the literal meaning of the Scriptures, even to the absurd lengths of which anthropomorphism and millenarianism are examples: Origen's doctrine of Scriptural allegory is also directed against these.

Origen and philosophy

On this subject there are two questions to ask. First, what is Origen's judgement of pagan philosophy and its utility to Christians? Second, what use did Origen himself make of it?

The encounter of Jewish Christian revelation with Greek philosophy is a favourite theme for Origen's two predecessors at Alexandria. Philo devotes to it *De congressu eruditionis gratia,* the exegesis of Gen. 16, 1–6, Sarah advising Abraham to take Hagar as a concubine: he returns to the subject frequently in other works and that shows it was for the Jewish theologian no passing side issue but a constant preoccupation. After Philo, whose words he sometimes repeats to the letter, developing and adapting them to the new situation created by the advent of Christ, Clement deals with the subject in the first of his *Stromateis* and in a part of the sixth.[9] So Origen takes his place in a tradition mainly centered in his native city. But he is less enthusiastic than Clement for Hellenic philosophy: he does not, like his predecessor, regard it as a Testament given to the Greeks as the Bible to the Jews and he was more reticent about the salvation it brings; many of his judgements on it are harsh. But he was very learned in philosophy and used it widely as is evident not only from the *Treatise on First Principles* and the *Contra Celsum,* but also from the *Commentaries.* That he taught it is clear from Eusebius[10] and from the curriculum described by Gregory Thaumaturgus. Of course Tertullian himself, despite his expressed hostility, had a good philosophical training and did not disdain to use it. But unlike his contemporaries at Alexandria he offers no positive reflections on the use of philosophy by Christians.

Origen, like Clement, frequently emphasises the insufficiency of philosophy, although on certain issues it is in agreement with Christianity.[11] He criticises the philosophers, even Plato, from the standpoint of his Christian faith. However, he does not treat all the schools alike and passes a different judgement on each; at the bottom of the order of merit is Epicureanism, 'philosophy's shame' with its morality of pleasure which is the opposite of the Cross of Christ, its negation of Providence which makes it a veritable atheism, its atomic physics, its refusal to recognise

---

[9] SC 30. For the *Stromateis* 6 (GCS Clement II).

[10] HE VI, XVIII, 2–3; VI, XIX, 1–14.

[11] On what follows see our book *Origène et la philosophie* (Paris, 1962) with appendix 'Origène est-il un systématique?'

man's spiritual privileges. Aristotle is not much more highly esteemed, although Origen does sometimes use elements of his doctrine and vocabulary. With the Platonists and Stoics he is against Aristotle's doctrine of three kinds of good. This doctrine counted as goods not only those of the soul, the virtues, but also those of the body, like health and beauty, and those external to a man such as riches and honours. Aristotle does not believe that the action of Providence extends to our sublunary world and that is why he also is dubbed an atheist: but this denial of Providence comes in fact from the pseudo-Aristotelian *De mundo* which dates from the beginning of the Christian era. Rejected also is Aristotle's theory of the ether as a fifth element – the ether only survives in Origen's work as a 'quality', – the intellectual essence of the stars as gods and of the human intelligences, a theory which Aristotle expounded in his early treatise *On Philosophy*. As for the Stoics, their morality is accepted, but their cosmology and their theology are regarded as materialist and Origen pokes fun at their cyclical view of time. The Pythagoreans, some of whom like Numenius, are also called Platonists, are respected but also blamed for the cyclical theory and also for their metempsychosis – Origen says 'metensomatosis'. Plato is certainly for Origen the high point of Greek thought, of human thought apart from revelation, and he constantly draws inspiration from him, at least in the form in which Middle Platonism presented him. In the controversy with Celsus over knowledge of God many texts of Plato are called to witness by Celsus and sometimes admired and sometimes contradicted by Origen on the basis of the Christian revelation. The exemplarist view of the world underlying Origen's theology comes to him from Platonism, although he gives it a different content. However, he rejects metempsychosis, Plato's tripartite view of the soul, etc. In spite of his great admiration for Plato, Origen retains his independence of him and is able to criticise him.

Origen holds in high esteem the moral ideal of the philosopher characterised by the love of truth and the quest for it: negatively expressed, this is seen in his constant reproach of Celsus for behaving in a way unworthy of a philosopher. Origen does not contradict Celsus when the latter claims that Christian morality is no different in content from that of the philosophers: he explains this by the notion of natural law, inscribed by God in the hearts of men, a Stoic notion taken over by Paul:[12] this is confirmed by a series of parallels between the lives of the philosophers and the life of Jesus and his apostles, brought forward either by Celsus or by Origen. All the same Origen puts his finger on a fundamental difference: unlike the Christian the philosopher does not relate his actions to God by thanksgiving. This criticism is already found in Philo and in Clement, who both see that *philautia*, the love of self, can

[12] Rom. 2, 14–16; *CCels* I, 4.

endanger all the philosopher's virtues. Origen's criticism is not so much directed against their objective morality, the actions themselves, as against their subjective morality, the intention that informs it. Of course the intention of the Stoic, motivated by the sense of the common good and the just respect shown to others, is part of an authentic morality. But it is not enough for the Christian whose love of God must inspire his whole life. It must be solely to the Lord that his actions are directed, love of neighbour and all the other loves, the sense of the common good, all being integrated into the love of God. The moral inferiority of the philosopher derives from his religious inferiority: in spite of certain lofty intuitions, he has no full appreciation of grace, for God has not revealed Himself to him as a personal being, and his relations with God are not personal relations. He neither gets his virtue from God nor offers it to Him. His religious life has not transfigured his moral life.

Elsewhere Origen denounces the philosopher's attachment to his system as a veritable idolatry[13] and the *Address of Thanks* gives a remarkable illustration of this aspect of the master's teaching: philosophy is incapable of opening itself to another system of thought; its system is compared to a bog in which one is engulfed, or a wood out of which there is no path, or a maze that one cannot get out of.[14] Philosophy is incapable of providing a true saving knowledge of God; it cannot cure the one ill that matters, sin; in it the false is inextricably mingled with the true. From the Homilies or the *Contra Celsum* one does not get the impression of peaceful relations between Christianity and philosophy: the scorn poured by the philosophers on his faith pricks Origen at the deepest point of his religious sensitivity. Relations of the Christians with philosophy are symbolised in the Homilies by the sieges of fortresses, Hebron, Hesebon and Jericho.

Origen's teaching on the use that the Christian can make of philosophy is mainly expressed in allegorical exegeses, some of which became famous and were repeated throughout the Middle Ages. Joshua is one of the principal figures for Christ, especially because their names are the same: in Greek Joshua is expressed as *Iēsous*, Jesus. When 'Jesus son of Navē', that is Joshua, arrives with the Hebrews before Jericho, it is 'my' Jesus appearing before the city of the philosophers, preceded by the priests, his apostles, sounding their trumpets, the writings of the New Testament, and the walls of the philosophers' city fall down.[15] But the comparison stops there: the anathema with which the Canaanite city is stricken by Jahveh, requiring the conquerors to destroy everything and preserve nothing, would compel Origen to a course which, in spite of his warlike formulae, would be opposed to his way of thinking. The ingot of gold

[13] *HomJr* XVI, 9.
[14] XIV, 158–173.
[15] *HomJos* VII, 1.

which Achan withheld from destruction only represents perverse doctrines hidden under fine language or the idolatry that lurks in the verses of the poets,[16] but not philosophy in general. So it is permitted for the disciples of Jesus to look for booty in the Jericho of the philosophers, provided that they do it discreetly and prudently.

It might have been expected that Origen, as he wished to show that something can be saved from the city of the philosophers, would have interpreted on these lines the character of Rahab, the Canaanite courtesan, the only one spared with her family because she had received Joshua's spies. But Rahab is given a wider meaning which implicitly contains our suggestion: she is the Gentile world, given over to debauchery until the day when, receiving the apostles of Jesus, it becomes the Church of the Nations.[17] But if Abraham cannot give Sarah, virtue, to Abimelech the Philistine petty king, who represents honest philosophy, and seeks it, Jesus will do so and Virtue, which is, as in Philo, the same thing as Wisdom, will pass to the Church of the Nations. Then all that is positive in the heritage of philosophy will be transmitted to Christianity. The wife and the handmaidens of Abimelech, that is natural philosophy and the 'reasonings of dialectic varying according to the schools', will be cured by Jesus of their sterility and will 'bring forth sons for the Church: it is indeed the day when the barren gives birth'.[18]

Two exegeses are especially famous. First that of the 'fair captive' which had a long Mediaeval posterity:[19] Deut. 21, 10–13, orders a warrior who wants to marry his prisoner to shave her head and cut her nails: that is to say, explains Origen, that before using what he has gleaned from the philosophers the Christian must detach from it what is dead and useless.[20] The second is that of the 'spoils of the Egyptians', developed in his *Letter to Gregory*.[21] Origen has exhorted his pupil to use philosophy and the encyclic studies as auxiliary to Christian learning and he explains this advice as follows: before leaving Egypt the Hebrews had taken from their neighbours all kinds of items to build the tabernacle of Jahveh:[22] in the same way the Christian will use all that he can of philosophy to build the 'divine philosophy' of Christianity. Irenaeus had already given a wider interpretation[23] of this text which he said he got from a presbyter, an immediate disciple of the apostles: the spoils of the Egyptians represent for him everything the Christian receives from the surrounding civilisation.

Origen does not object to young Christians taking lessons from pagan

[16] *HomJos* VII, 7.
[17] *HomJos* VII, 5.
[18] *HomGn* VI, 2–3.
[19] H. de Lubac, *Exégèse Médiévale* I/1, Paris, 1959, pp. 290–304.
[20] *HomLv* VII, 6.
[21] §§2–3.
[22] Exod. 11, 2; 12, 35.
[23] *Adversus Haereses* V, 30: SC 153.

masters provided that they have the resources to go beyond this teaching and to integrate it into a Christian view. Intellectual training can produce good as well as evil. The study of philosophy and the academic subjects shows to souls in doubt about it that Christianity is superior and allows students to defend it against pagan attacks: a deep knowledge of philosophy is necessary to the educated Christian, so that he can give reasons for his faith when asked to account for it, and competently judge in terms of it doctrines that are strange to him. He must be capable of refuting the philosopher on his own ground, which is that of philosophy, and of destroying one by one the arguments of his adversaries: but the role of the secular subjects must be simply that of servants: his knowledge of God comes to the Christian from a much higher source.

When he lacks the necessary discernment the study of pagan philosophy entails a grave danger to the Christian, that of heresy, which is the application of philosophic method to Scripture without safeguarding the primacy of the word of God. The basic project of the heretic is the same as that of the philosopher, an idolatrous project: they both worship what their minds construct: but as the heretic tries to maintain an outward fidelity to the Scriptures, he soils the whole Church of God. Like the false prophet of the Old Testament the heretic does not express the words of God, but speaks out of his own heart and then presents his thoughts as God's. The *Letter of Gregory* judges in the same way the story of the Idumaean Hadad, called in the Septuagint Ader and confused with Jeroboam, the instigator of the schism of the ten tribes. Hadad deserted the land of Israel and the wise Solomon, symbolising the Wisdom of God, and went off to Egypt, the land of paganism: he came back to Israel only to provoke the schism among the people and to erect golden calves at Bethel, the 'house of God', symbol of the Scriptures, and at Dan, near the pagan frontiers. Such is the tragedy of many Christians thrown into the study of Hellenic sciences, for 'numerous were the brothers of the Idumaean Ader', those for whom philosophy has become the mother of heresies,[24] an idea frequently repeated in the 2nd and 3rd centuries, and especially illustrated by the Elenchos attributed to Hippolytus.[25]

Origen's caution about the use of philosophy by Christians is not of a kind to forbid its use, for his correspondent Gregory received from him a lengthy introduction to Greek studies, but rather to warn that it be used prudently and that meanwhile the exclusive love of the only Wisdom of God, his Son, be kept bright in the student's heart. After describing the readings of philosophical texts that Origen gave to his students and praising the care he took to separate the true from the false. Thaumaturgus

[24] *Letter to Gregory* §3.
[25] GCS Hippolytus III: this book is an attempt to relate the heresies studied to philosophical schools.

adds: 'On this subject he advised us not to become attached to any philosophy, not even to one that enjoyed among men a great reputation for wisdom, but to be attached to God alone and his prophets.'[26] And that is why Origen had passages read from all the authors so that his hearers would not become attached to a single school or to a single system.[27] King Solomon, in spite of his wisdom, was led astray by his many wives, who represent many philosophies and drew him into their respective idolatries. He (Solomon) could not say, as does Cant. 6, 8–9: 'There are sixty queens and eighty concubines and girls without number, but one alone is my dove, my perfect one, the only daughter of her mother, the sole offspring of her who gave her birth.'[28] To remain faithful to the unique teaching of Christ amid secular learning of all kinds one needs the support of divine grace. One must also be careful not to cause the weak to stumble, not to draw into these studies by one's example brothers whose faith could not stand up to them.

The main aim in studying philosophy is to build up a Christian philosophy, that is to say theology. After destroying Hesebon, the 'city of thoughts', the Christian does not leave it in ruins but rebuilds it in his way, using the materials that suit him in what remains of the demolished town.[29] Misunderstanding Pauline texts, Celsus accuses the Christians of banishing all wisdom. Origen establishes the existence of a true Christian wisdom which has its source and finds its supreme criterion of judgement in the Scriptures, in their most profound meaning, their 'will', and not in their use as a protection for personal opinions. The Hellenic disciplines and methods will help in this, but the intellectual aspects of this new wisdom take second place to the spiritual and mystical aspects, for its purpose is the understanding of the divine mysteries contained in the Scriptures. Such is the 'divine philosophy' which in the prologue to the *Commentary on the Song of Songs* is described according to the divisions of secular philosophy;[30] and such is the Christianity, constructed with the help of philosophy and the encyclical subjects which, in his *Letter to Gregory*,[31] Origen would like to see his pupil embrace.

So the 'divine philosophy' is a theology in the broadest sense of the term, with exegetical and spiritual content as well as speculative. On the other hand Origen seems to have no idea of a permanent rational philosophy in Christianity alongside theology. For that he would have needed to distinguish more fully between Reason and Revelation and between Natural and Supernatural. Reason is for him participation in the

---

[26] *RemOrig* XV, 173.
[27] Ibid. XIII–XIV, 150–173.
[28] *HomNb* XX, 3, quoting Cant 6. 8–9.
[29] *HomNb* XIII, 2.
[30] GCS VIII, pp. 75–79.
[31] §1.

supernatural Reason of God, his Son, who is also the Revelation. If there are two passages[32] in which a correct distinction is found between natural and supernatural, this distinction is offered in a way that does not seem familiar to him. Origen holds above all to a supernatural in which the natural is implicity contained. Why have recourse to an imperfect source when perfect learning is given? When God speaks must not every human voice keep silence? The Fleshpots of Egypt would be of little value, seeing that we have the manna of Scripture. The philosophy Origen wants is not the work of reason, it flows directly from Scripture: or rather, if there is nevertheless, especially in the *Treatise on First Principles,* appeal to reason, that is simply to unfold, starting from Scripture, what the latter does not clearly say. Indeed it seems that for him philosophy of a purely rational order ceased to exist with the appearance of Christianity, not of course as reflection but as an independent discipline. Philosophy belongs to the past, a productive past, which the present uses for the building up of Christian theology, but does not sustain. The inheritance is accepted, with reservations.

Taken mainly from the Bible, Origen's theological vocabulary also comes to him in part from philosophy: different schools have provided him with terms and expressions. One thing must be noted, however, in connection with the use by the Fathers of a *technical* vocabulary drawn from philosophy or in the case of the Latins from law. This use is not to be restricted by our modern canons of criticism. Faithful to the general meaning of the term, the Fathers adapt it to the Christian content that they had to express. Thus it can never be argued from the use of a 'technical' term that it must be understood in accordance with the meaning given to it by the philosophers, but in contradiction or opposition to the Christian thought of the period. Besides, to require such rigour in the use of the technical vocabulary even by the philosophers would perhaps be an anachronism.

The *Address of Thanks,* in its chapter on the study of the philosophers, is very critical of the breadth of system that he attributes to them and shows the will to eclecticism which characterised the philosophical training given by Origen to his students. This eclecticism is common with philosophers of the first centuries of the Christian era, but Origen has another motive for using it: only the Word of God deserves the unconditional involvement of Christians. Middle Platonism – it was this after the teaching of Ammonius Saccas and the wide reading of which Porphyry drew up a list,[33] which provided Origen with the essential basis of his philosophical knowledge and the current interpretation of Plato – was not exempt from this eclecticism. The dominant Platonist core was joined by numerous Stoic elements and by some data from Aristotle. If

[32] CCels V, 23; ComJn I, 37 (42), 273.
[33] Quoted by Eusebius HE VI, XIX, 8, from Porphyry.

Plato's successors, the Academy, for centuries put more emphasis on Plato the nationalist than on Plato the mystic, going as far as the semi-scepticism of the New Academy, a revival of Plato the mystic was the work of the Middle Stoicism of Poseidonius of Apamea, who was one of Cicero's teachers in the 2nd century before Christ, for Middle Stoicism was strongly impregnated with Platonism. It is reasonable to think that Middle Platonism emerged from this Middle Stoicism about the first century of our era, by an increase in the Platonic as compared with the Stoic elements. We say no more about Middle Platonism for the question has been studied in depth several times with reference to Origen.[34]

A research theology[35]

When relating Origen's life we drew attention to the influence of Ambrose's conversion on the beginning of Origen's career as a writer and we quoted the passage from the *Commentary on John* which indicates one of the main objects of his work: to provide Christians who raise problems of an intellectual order with answers in conformity with Scripture so that they do not go and look for these in the great gnostic sects. So he is guided by missionary considerations relating to the intelligentsia of Alexandria in his day. Origen has in mind educated Christians who have received a philosophical training, and face the problems of contemporary philosophy, who desire to search the Scriptures deeply with a method that meets the requirements of demonstration and proof. The case of Ambrose shows him the need for intellectual reflection about Christianity, using means that are in part rational and philosophical, in order to meet the propaganda of the gnostics and to present Christianity to the intellectuals.

One of the texts that throws the most light on Origen's intentions, not only in the *Treatise on First Principles*, but in his great commentaries as well, is the remarkable preface that he placed at the beginning of that book. The essential criterion of the truth of Christianity is conformity with 'the ecclesiastical and apostolic tradition'. But that does not solve all the problems. There are to begin with truths which the apostles stated and which the Church transmits – it is the duty of Christians to believe in them and lack of faith produces the diversity of the heresies. But the apostles did not say everything: they affirmed the existence of certain realities but said nothing of their manner of existence nor of their origin.

[34] E. de Faye, *Origène, sa vie, son oeuvre, sa pensée.* Vol. II: *L'ambiance philosophique*, Paris, 1927; Hal Koch, *Pronoia und Paideusis: Studien über Origenes und sein Verhältnis zum Platonismus*, Berlin/Leipzig, 1932: Second Part: *Origenes und die griechische Philosophie*, pp. 163–304; J. Daniélou, *Origène*, Paris, 1948, pp. 85–108.
[35] See the second part of our article 'Qu'a voulu faire Origène en composant le *Traité des Principes?' Bulletin de Littérature Ecclésiastique* 76, 1975, 241–260. It is summarised in the introduction to SC 252, pp. 46–52.

Thus they left to those most zealous for religious knowledge 'something on which to exercise' their intelligence, an intelligence that is not understood in a purely intellectual sense, since these enquiries can only be made by those who receive from the Holy Spirit the gifts enumerated by Paul in 1 Cor. 12, 8–9.[36]

This passage is quoted with comment by the martyr Pamphilus of Caesarea in his *Apology for Origen*.[37] About what is not preached by the Church in a clear manner Origen says what he thinks he can say, but makes no firm statements. Sometimes he gives several interpretations of the same passage, and they clearly remain hypothetical: they are statements *by way of exercise, gymnastikōs*. Athanasius also expresses approval of this way of proceeding, when he is writing about Origen.[38] Most of the time Origen expresses himself thus when neither Scripture nor reason allows him to affirm more strongly, that is *dogmatikōs*. The same can be said of the exegeses that do not originate from the New Testament: they are also put forward by way of research.

The researcher who merely suggests his solutions to the reader and leaves the latter free to adopt others if he finds them preferable cannot be other than modest. The Alexandrian's modesty is noted by a considerable number of critics. The same goes for the Scriptural interpretations of which we have just spoken; they are suggested as something to reflect on and to contemplate and Origen declares himself ready to abandon them if anyone finds anything better. The numerous expressions of modesty in Rufinus's version of the *Treatise on First Principles*, which are mostly missing from the fragments by Jerome and Justinian, are not therefore an addition by the translator, as has somtimes been said, but correspond to what is found abundantly in the Greek works.

Pamphilus of Caesarea, a writer who shows the most intelligent appreciation of Origen's manner, also emphasises this aspect in the preface to his *Apology for Origen:*[39]

> We frequently find, however, that he speaks with a great fear of God and in all humility when he excuses himself from expounding what comes to his mind in the course of very advanced discussions and a full examination of the Scriptures: and when he is expounding he is often wont to add and to avow that he is not uttering a final pronouncement nor expressing an established doctrine, but that he is researching to the limit of his ability, that he is discussing the meaning of the Scriptures and that he does not claim to have understood that meaning wholly or perfectly: he says that on many points he has a preliminary idea but that he is not sure that he has reached in every respect perfection or a complete solution. Sometimes we see him recognising that he is hesitating about a number of points on which he

---

[36] *PArch* Preface §§1–3.
[37] PG 17, 549ff.
[38] *De decretis Nicaenae Synodi* 27, 1–2 (ed. Opitz III/2, p. 23).
[39] PG 17, 543 Cff.

raises questions that come to his mind; he does not give a solution to them, but in all humility and sincerity he does not blush to admit that all is not clear to him. We often hear him inserting into his addresses words which today even the most ignorant of his detractors would be too proud to utter, namely that if anyone speaks or expresses himself on these subjects better than he, then it is preferable to listen to that teacher rather than to him. In addition to this we sometimes find him giving more than one answer to the same question: and quite reverently, as someone who knows he is speaking of the Holy Scriptures, after setting out the numerous ideas that come to his mind, he asks those who are listening to test each of his statements and to retain what a prudent reader would find most correct; that assuredly because not all the questions that he has raised and discussed must be held worthy of approval or be considered finally settled, the fact being that, according to our faith, there are in Scripture many things that are mysterious and wrapped in secrecy. If we pay careful attention to the sincerity and catholic spirit with which he describes all his writing in the preface to the Commentary on Genesis, we shall easily get from this text an insight into all his thought.

Here is the passage from the Commentary on Genesis which Pamphilus goes on to quote:[40]

If we were in every way too lazy and negligent to set about research, even though our Lord and Saviour invites us to undertake it, we should certainly recoil (from such work), considering how far we fall short of the spiritual understanding with which the intellect needs to be endowed if it is to devote itself to research into such great matters ... If in the course of discussion a profound thought occurs to one, it must be stated but not categorically affirmed: to do the latter would be the act of a rash man who had forgotten himself and lost the sense of human weakness: or, alternatively, the act of perfect men who knew in complete confidence that they had been taught by the Lord Himself, that is to say that they get what they assert from the Word of Truth and from the very Wisdom by which everything was made; or again it would be the act of men who have received from heaven divine answers, having gone into the tempest and the darkness where God is to be found, where the great Moses found it so difficult to go, and having there been enabled to understand and to express such great matters. But we, by the simple fact that we believe, however poorly, in Christ Jesus, and that we boast of being his disciples, nevertheless do not dare to say that we have perceived face to face the meaning that He has passed on to us of what is contained in the divine books; for I am certain that the world itself could not hold that in a manner proportionate to the force and majesty of its meanings. That is why we do not dare to affirm what we say in the way that Apostles did and we give thanks that, while so many are unaware of their own ignorance and affirm, in all conscience as it seems to them, to be veridical every passing thought that occurs to them, without rule or order, sometimes even in a stupid or a mythological way, we, in relation to these great realities and to everything that is beyond us, are not ignorant of our ignorance.

[40] PG 17, 544 BCff.

Several features of Origen's theological method can be traced to this conception of theology as research. First there are the discussions between two or three alternatives, often without reaching a conclusion, leaving the question open and the reader free to choose. Such are the discussions in the *Treatise on First Principles* about an embodied or a disembodied final state:[41] each side of the alternative is developed to its full extent and supported by all the arguments on which it is based, philosophical arguments for the disembodied state, Scriptural ones for the embodied. In this book Origen does not decide between the two solutions, but in his other works we only find the embodied state, in conformity with the dogma of the resurrection, and of a resurrection which is a definitive state. Another example, from the same book, is the discussion of the unity or duality of the soul in each man, which ends without a solution: but Origen's opinion, such as we find it elsewhere, draws on both answers. In the commentaries also many questions remain open.[42] Origen's procedure can be compared to that of a professor of philosophy who tries to present to his students different doctrines with all their implications and in all their force even if he personally holds yet another view or has not decided on any. Origen was acting in this way when he read before his students, as Thaumaturgus[43] tells us, passages from all the philosophers except the atheists. This was no mere intellectual game, but very often an exploration in depth, and even if it had an apologetic aim, it was a more profound apologetic, for it is not possible to make a serious evaluation of a doctrine if one has not made a sincere effort to understand it. Thus it can happen that Origen puts himself in the place of the philosopher who holds such and such a theory and puts forward the arguments for it without holding the view himself and then makes that clear at the end of the exposition. Pamphilus notes this in connection with metempsychosis and reports Origen's concluding denial in a form analogous to that which Jerome reproduces. But Jerome was scandalised that Origen dared to speak of so impious a subject, and, without taking account of his concluding statement or of the numerous passages in the commentaries on John and Matthew and in the *Contra Celsum*[44] which criticise metempsychosis, sees in this a hypocritical way of giving currency to erroneous opinions. In fact in a book like the *Treatise on First Principles* Origen could not avoid mentioning this

[41] *PArch* I, 6, 4; II, 3, 2–3; III, 6, 1–4; IV, 4, 8. On these texts see J. Rius-Camps, 'La suerte final de la naturaleza corpórea según el *Peri Archon* de Origenes' which appeared in both *Vetera Christianorum* 10, 1973, 291–304 and in *Studia Patristica* XIV (*Texte und Untersuchungen* 117) 1976, 167–179.

[42] H. J. Vogt, 'Wie Origenes in seinem Matthäuskommentar Fragen offen lässt' in *Origiana Secunda* (ed. H. Crouzel and A. Quacquarelli), Rome, 1980, 191–198.

[43] *RemOrig* XIII, 151–157.

[44] *ComJn* VI, 10–14 (7), 62–87; *ComMt* X, 20; XI, 17; XIII, 1–2 (GCS X); *CCels* III, 75; IV, 17; V, 49; VIII, 30 and other texts in other works.

doctrine which was professed by several schools of philosophy and was the cause of disquiet among Christians.[45]

One deficiency of Origen's had grave consequences and caused him to be accused of multiple heresies, often for that matter mutually contradictory: he never took enough trouble to define what he had to say, that is to give an opinion on a point that was complete and balanced, bringing together in the same passage the antithetical tensions which characterise Christian doctrine, in such a way as to leave the least possible opportunity for false interpretations. In his exegeses Origen is often very dependent on the scriptural text that he is commenting on: he does not worry much about balancing it with the complementary proposition that is to be found elsewhere, in another text. That is why to find out his opinion on any subject it is no good relying on an isolated text, for in that case his opinion will seem one-sided: the text of all his works, which deal with the same point or at last those which are still extant, must be studied, for they complement and correct each other. When this has been done it will be realised that the supposed heresies for which he is blamed have practically no valid foundation. We come here to one of the main difficulties in studying Origen, the necessity of examining all the works that we possess before asserting anything at all about him.

According to Rufinus's version the preface to Book 1 of the *Treatise on First Principles* concludes with these words:

> Everyone therefore who is desirous of constructing out of the foregoing a connected body of doctrine must use points like these as elementary and foundation principles, in accordance with the commandment which says, 'Enlighten yourselves with the light of knowledge'.[46] Thus by clear and cogent arguments he will discover the truth about each particular point and so will produce, as we have said, a single body of doctrine, with the aid of such illustrations and declarations as he shall find in the holy scriptures and of such conclusions as he shall ascertain to follow logically from them when rightly understood.[a]

Many historians have translated the expression 'body of doctrine' by 'system' and this word has been used over and over again of the *Treatise on First Principles*. If reference is made to the definition in the *Larousse Encyclopedia*,[47] 'a gathering of principles co-ordinated in such a way as to form a scientific whole or a body of doctrine', it has to be admitted that Origen is not at all systematic. His research theology, the antithetical

---

[45] See in SC 253 pp. 119–125 (notes 28 and 29) the commentary of *PArch* I, 8, 4, with the fragments of Pamphilus, Jerome and Justinian. In like manner Pamphilus's explanations in PG 17, 607 C–608 A. And again on Origen and metempsychosis G. Dorival, 'Origène a-t-il enseigné la transmigration des âmes dans les corps d'animaux?' in *Origeniana Secunda*, Rome, 1980, pp. 11–32.

[46] Hos. 10, 12.

[a] Trans. Butterworth, p. 6.

[47] 1964, X, p. 123.

tensions that he does not bother to balance on the spot, his statements
made in an inconclusive form, would constitute too many cracks in such
an edifice. Anyhow, can a theologian be systematic? How could you
confine God in a rational principle and draw logical conclusions from
Him, when in his absolute simplicity. He is far beyond the grasp of man,
who can only glimpse Him in a multiplicity of ways, some antithetical to
others. Let us not forget that Thaumaturgus tells us how sharply Origen
criticised the broad systems of the philosophers[48] and also how he often
accused them of idolatry because they worshipped the work of their
minds. So Origen's expositions are rarely systematic even in the *Treatise
on First Principles*.

Nevertheless, the idea of a systematic Origen dominated thinking
about him in the first half of the 20th century. The explanations of
Pamphilus, well versed in the subject matter, were held to be suspect
because he was an apologist; and so, in spite of them, Origen's work was
seen as a 'system', arrived at by absolutising certain ideas in the *Treatise
on First Principles*, without seeing that they come from a 'theology' by
way of exercise'. No notice was taken of contrasting features in the same
book and in his work as a whole. Less importance was attached to the
works preserved in Greek than to the *Treatise on First Principles* which
has mainly come down to us in translation, but which was considered the
work in which Origen had systematised his thought. In the evaluation of
this book Rufinus was put out of court, to an extent far exceeding the
modifications he admitted making, and that made it possible to substitute
arbitrarily for his statements the ideas that must have been held by the
Origen of the critic's imagination:[49] on the other hand there was no
attempt to criticise the fragments of Jerome and Justinian in spite of, or
perhaps because of, their animosity towards the Alexandrian and our
ignorance of the context of these fragments which were often part of a
discussion: as if hate were easier to believe than love. Besides, before
A. Guillaumont's book, *Les 'Kephalaia Gnōstioa d'Evagre le Pontique et
l'histoire de l'origénisme chez les Grecs et chez les Syriens*[50] there was little
idea of the gap separating Origen's own doctrine and the later Origenism,
that of Evagrius of Pontus and the Egyptian and Palestinian monks of the
4th century, that of Stephen bar Sudaili and the Palestinian monks of the
6th century: this 'scholastic' of Origen was treated as if it were at every
point in conformity with the thought of the master whom it was
systematising, suppressing his hesitations and antitheses, forming a
system out of a small part of his doctrine which it preserved. In this way
P. Koetschau in his edition of the *Treatise on First Principles* thought it

[48] *RemOrig* XIV, 158–173.
[49] The best illustration is volume III of *Origenè* by E. de Faye mentioned in note 34.
[50] Paris, 1962.

right to insert into the Rufinian text itself, as if Rufinus had left them out, not only the fragments of Jerome and Justinian which at least had the advantage of referring to this book, but other fragments too that were drawn from later Origenism or emanated from anti-Origenists, including the *De Sectis* of the pseudo-Leontius of Byzantium and the ananthemata of 553 attributed to the Fifth Ecumenical Council, but directed specifically against the Origenists of the time.[51]

The causes of the misunderstandings between Origen and posterity.[52]

The misunderstanding which led to Origen being accused of multiple, often contradictory, heresies were caused in large measure by his detractors' ignorance of the historical evolution and development of dogma, that is to say of the process by which Christian thought acquires in the course of the centuries a more acute awareness of what its faith and tradition involve. Perhaps the reader will retort: the historical sense and a doctrine of the development of dogma are relatively recent notions. Therefore you are guilty of an anachronism when you blame Origen's accusers of neglecting them. We are not concerned to blame his accusers, but to decide whether their victim's memory should still suffer the consequences of their misconceptions or their faulty methods.

We have just seen that Origen did not bother to 'define' what he said: his vocabulary was rarely fixed and to perceive the balance of the antitheses which express his teaching, it is necessary to study it in all the surviving texts on each point, so as not to accuse him of contradictory heresies. But, except for Tertullian with his lawyer's training, the Ante-Nicene Fathers were rarely concerned to define. Two principal reasons would make this necessary in later times. First the accord between Church and State after Constantine would entail a more and more formal assimilation of the rule of faith and the civil law. Thus it is striking to note that the first councils of which we possess canons belong to the beginning of the 4th century: only the very first, that of Elvira of which we do not have the exact date, seems prior to what is called the Edict of Milan. The second reason was the reaction to the Arian crisis which lasted in the Roman Empire until the end of the 4th century. The skill with which Arians or Arianisers could find their doctrine in the confessions of faith of their adversaries forced the latter to pay careful attention to the terms they used. Origen never had worries like that. But he was to be judged in the light of those requirements, notably in the controversy that raged at the end of the 4th century and the beginning of the 5th. Here is one example among others: Theophilus of Alexandria would judge to be scandalous and mutually contradictory two sentences which are to be

---

[51] See in the introduction to SC 252 (*PArch* I–II) p. 33.
[52] See the first part of the article cited in note 35, pp. 161–186. In SC 252, pp. 33–46.

found half a page apart in the *Treatise on First Principles*,[53] without having the wit to explain one by the other. The shocked Theophilus betrays the lack of a method of elementary interpretation which consists in using the different elements of a text to throw light on each other, rather than in contrasting them as if each was an absolute.

Between the first half of the 3rd century, when Origen was alive, and the end of the 4th when the first Origenist crisis broke out the situation of the Church as well as that of the pagan world and the Roman Empire had greatly changed, so that it was scarcely possible for the triumphant Church of the 4th century to have a fair understanding of the minority Church under persecution in the 3rd. Having become the dominant religion Christianity is now organising itself: questions of ecclesiastical structure and authority take a larger and larger place. The rule of faith, as a result of the Arian crisis, has been made considerably more precise and is tending to be imposed on the model of the civil law. Consequently people will apply to Origen standards which are required by Christian society in the 4th century – or later in the 6th – and will be shocked that he meets them so inadequately.

This change of outlook was mainly seen in the attitude to philosophy. The great effort to convert the intelligentsia undertaken in the 2nd and 3rd centuries by Clement and Origen must be interested in Greek philosophy which represented the essential core of the culture. So they had to speak the language of the philosophers in order to be understood and they had to try and show the light which the Christian faith could throw on their problems. Of course, in the 4th and 5th centuries also eminent theologians were interested in philosophy, like the Cappadocians, Ambrose or Augustine, but these were not the ones which got cross about Origen. One gets the impression that if Jerome sometimes shows a certain philosophic learning, he scarcely thinks of pagan philosophy as a contemporary force still worth converting. For Theophilus force, if not violence, must be used with paganism. As for the 'pentaglot' Epiphanius

---

[53] IV, 4, 4. In the *Paschal Letter* of 402, known by Jerome's translation, Letter 98 of his correspondence §16 (CUFr V): this passage is quoted in Greek by Theodoret of Cyrrhus, *Eranistes*, Florilege II, §58 (ed. G. H. Ettlinger, Oxford, 1975). The first text is the following: 'In fact the soul which was in trouble and distress was not the Only Son and the First-born of all production (Col. 1, 15), nor the Logos-God who is higher than the soul: the Son himself says "I have the power to lay it down and the power to take it up again"' (John 10, 18). And the second: 'As the Son and the Father are one, so the soul which the Son has assumed and the Son Himself are one,' We translate in the first text the word *ktisis* by 'production', for Origen is not giving it the sense of 'creation'. In SC 268 (see SC 269 notes 31, p. 251 and 34 p. 253) these two passages are only half a page apart. The first, which aims to show that is was not the divinity of Christ but his humanity that suffered seems to separate the natures too much; on the contrary the second uses an unfortunate comparison to affirm their unity. After Nicaea and Constantinople it would be said that the unity of the Father and the Son is a unity of nature, that of the Son with his humanity a unity of person. But taken together, as their proximity requires, they do not deserve the scandal aroused by Theophilus.

his intelligence does not rise to these speculations. As early as the beginning of the 4th century Methodius, who is far from being a dunce in philosophy, founds on two philosophical blunders his two main attacks on Origen, *Aglaophon or On the Resurrection, Xenon or On the Creatures*.[54] Origen's detractors do not understand the Platonist language which makes Truth the opposite of image and not of falsehood and talking of the Father who is the Truth of the Son, his Image, Theophilus attributes to Origen a blasphemy that arises from his own mistake: 'The Son campared with us is Truth, compared with the Father is a falsehood.'[55]

Numerous problems raised in the *Treatise on First Principles* are questions of a philosophical order which were of interest to contemporaries. In the 4th century they were of less interest. Origen's desire to reconcile fidelity to the tradition with a certain freedom of research which makes room, alongside firm dogmatic assertions on points which are sure, for hypotheses and opinions in a manner more or less open to question, was hardly compatible with the outlook of his accusers. Nor was it any more acceptable that Origen should expound the doctrines held by the adversaries of Christianity which ought to be honestly set out. It is also true, as we have seen, that the rule of faith had been made much more precise after the Arian crisis and that many questions which could be regarded as open in Origen's day were no longer so at the time of Jerome.

We have listed the heresies of Origen's day to which his theology tried to reply. The 4th and 5th centuries would have their heresies too and the mind of an Epiphanius and of a Jerome were in a way obsessed with them. But these heresies were different. Origen would be read in the light of these new errors, instead of being considered in relation to the ones he had to confront. People would roundly reproach him with not having foreseen the heresies to come and with not having replied to them in advance and with having naively used expressions to which these would give a heretical sense.

Origen would then be read in the context of heresies other than the ones he had in mind: as he had not foreseen these, some of his expressions or speculations could, with a bit of a push, be made to look as if he embraced those heresies, especially when no trouble was taken to look in other parts of his work for the key to his assertions. The main one was Arianism. Origen, whose trinitarian vocabulary was not yet sufficiently precise, might seem opposed to the unity of nature defined at Nicaea, although he held its equivalent in a dynamic rather than an ontological mode. Some expressions could draw his subordinationism, which is in terms of origin and 'economy', towards the Arian subordinationism of

---

[54] For the *Aglaophon* see pp. 256–257 and for Xenon p. 189–190.
[55] *PArch* I, 2, 6: see SC 253, note 41, pp. 42–44.

inequality using texts which assert nothing more than a hierarchy of
origin. Besides, he is constantly accused, for reasons of vocabulary which
we shall explain, of making the Son and the Holy Spirit creatures of the
Father. In this his detractors take no account of his speculations on the
enternal generation of the Word in the *Treatise on First Principles* itself
and of the celebrated formula attested as being in Origen by Athanasius
himself: *'ouk ēn hote ouk ēn* – there was not a moment when He (the
Word) was not'.[56]

When all the texts are studied in which Origen deals with the relations
of divine grace and human freedom, it will be seen, with some of them
complementing others, than he is orthodox on this point. But this
question had not yet clearly impinged on the Christian consciousness as it
would when the Pelagian controversy arose: that is why some passages
can easily be understood in a Pelagian or semi-Pelagian sense while others
express the subtleties of the Christian faith with as much precision as the
Council of Orange.[57] But the existence of the former will allow Jerome to
describe Origen as the ancestor of Pelagius.

Justinian saw Nestorianism in Origen's doctrine of the soul of Christ
when he wrote the following introduction to one of Origen's fragments:
'He says that the Lord is a mere man'.[58] This judgement takes no account
of the fact that the chapter of the *Treatise on First Principles* in question is
developing a doctrine of the *'communicatio idiomatum'*, that is of the
communication to the man Jesus of the qualities of the Word and to the
Word of the qualities of the man, a doctrine incompatible with
Nestorianism, and that certain features of the same chapter, notably the
image of the iron which, plunged in the fire, becomes fire, can be attacked
as monophysite. To call someone at the same time Nestorian and
monophysite, on the basis of the same text, when these heresies are
mutually contradictory, shows on the one hand that he is orthodox on
this point – for orthodoxy consists in respect for the antitheses that
heresy cannot accept – and further that these terms cannot fairly be
applied to a theologian living before they were current. To accuse a
theologian of a heresy subsequent to himself, relying on expressions that
will only subsequently take on the sense in question, without having
made the effort to gather together all that he said on the subject to see
whether that is really his opinion, when he could not have had his
attention drawn, as ours has been, to the danger of that kind of
formulation, is clearly a major betrayal of history by a historian: even if

[56] I, 2, 9 (Rufinus): IV, 4, 1 (Rufinus and the Greek of Athanasius); *ComRm* I, 5 (PG 14)
(Rufinus).

[57] Thus it is possible to contrast *FragmJn* XI (GCS IV) which has a semi-pelagian flavour
with a text of indisputable authenticity, *ComJn* VI, 36 (20), 181: the Council of Orange did
not express itself better than the latter passage.

[58] Fragment corresponding to *PArch* II, 6, 4: SC 253, note 25, pp. 178–179.

the ancients had some excuse for this, we cannot leave the matter to their judgement.

So Origen was read in the 4th and 5th centuries by theologians preoccupied with heresies other than the ones he had known and his accusers took little account of the ones with which he had himself fought. Such is the reason for the absurd reproach made by Epiphanius, which Jerome was weak enough to echo: that Origen had said that the Son could not see the Father. Now that is said in a chapter dealing with the divine incorporeality[59] and attacking the Anthropormorphites who thought God had a body: that is why Origen insists on his invisibility. But if the Son does not *see* the Father, because to see is a bodily act and presupposes a body, the Son *knows* the Father. Even if it is true, as Jerome suggests, that the clarity of this passage in Rufinus's version comes from the fact that Rufinus inserted an explanation which Didymus the Blind gave in his scholia on the *Treatise on First Principles*,[60] there are plenty of speculations in Origen's other works, preserved in Greek, about the knowledge the Son has of the Father, and these suffice to render Jerome's accusation unacceptable: he means it – and so does Epiphanius – as if Origen said the Son does not know the Father and this assertion is linked in their thought with the idea that the Son is a creature, in the Arian way of thinking.

The misunderstanding that led to the crises over Origen were thus caused by the considerable progress, as we have said, of the doctrine of the Trinity and of Christology at that time. The accusation of Nestorianism made by Justinian could not be explained without the development of the notion of person. Origen has no precise term for that. The Latin word *persona*, whether of Etruscan origin (*phersu* = mask) or related to the Latin *personare*, to resound, meant the theatrical mask which served as a megaphone: thence it passed to the actor who wore the mask, to the character whom the actor portrayed, and then came into legal parlane to denote the subject of rights and duties; Tertullian brought it into theological discourse. The corresponding Greek word *prosōpon* which also originally meant the theatrical mask placed in front of the face (*pros ops*), the actor, the character he plays, and then the face itself, passed with Hippolytus into theological language, perhaps under the influence of the Latin *persona*. Origen is ignorant of this use of *prosopon* and his nearest equivalents are *hypostasis* and *ousia* which do not clearly give the idea of an intellectual substance. He has, however, like his predecessors and Philo the Jew, a sense of the divine personality, as his concept of grace notably shows, and of the human personality, given the place that free will holds in his thought and also his rejection of unconscious trance.

---

[59] *PArch* I, 1, 8: SC 253, note 36, pp. 27–29.
[60] *Contra Rufinum* II, 11.

It he had had a precise concept of the person, his doctrine of the pre-existent soul of Christ would scarcely have avoided Nestorianism, for he would then have seemed to give to the Word become Flesh a double personality, that of the Word and that of the soul. So it is the progress of theology that made Origen look like a heretic.

When we come to study Origen's teaching about the beginnings of humanity,[61] we shall see, as Pamphilus did, for what reasons he adopted, as a favourite hypothesis, the strangests thing in his theology, the pre-existence of souls. Let us simply say for the moment that the Church had then no doctrine about the origin of souls except that they were created by God and that the two opinions about which Christians were divided, traducianism – the soul comes like the body from the paternal seed – and creationism – God directly creates the soul of each man when the embryo is formed – were both open to grave criticism, especially from the Marcionites. Origen thought to escape from these difficulties by the hypothesis of pre-existence. Although his solution was, from the beginning of the 4th century – since Pamphilus tries to explain it without defending it – subject to strong attack, the question of the origin of the soul continued to torment Augustine to the end of his life, to the time of *Retractationes:* so the Church in the 5th century still had no firm position on the subject.

In the accusations brought against Origen questions of vocabulary still have their part: through their lack of historical sense and knowledge his detractors read into the expressions he used the meaning that they had in their day, which was not Origen's. Thus in the preface of the *Treatise on First Principles* he declares, according to Rufinus's version, that the Christ 'was born (*natus*) of the Father before all creation' and then asks whether the Holy Spirit 'is born or not born'. In Letter 124 to Avitus Jerome thus transposes the first sentence: 'The Christ, Son of God, is not born but made (*factum*)' and the second about the Holy Spirit 'whether he is made or not made'.[62] Thus Origen is drawn towards Arianism. This discrepancy is easily explained: the text of Origen must comprise *genētos* and *agenētos* with a single n. For him, as for most before the Arian crisis, *genētos* and *gennētos*, *agenētos* and *agennētos*, with a single n or with two, are equivalent and interchangeable. In the 3rd century indeed the double consonants are no longer pronounced and Origen frequently in the *Contra Celsum* uses *genēsis* with a single n and not *gennēsis* with two for the generation of Jesus by Mary. The need to distinguish generation from creation to answer Arianism would bring back the specialisation of forms with one n to signify creation (*gignomai*) and double n to indicate generation (*gennao*). Jerome, taking no account of what Origen says

---

[61] Chapter XI.
[62] See SC 253, note 14, p. 13 and note 21, pp. 14–16.

elsewhere, and in the *Treatise on First Principles* itself, about the generation of the Son, translates *genētos* and *agenētos* according to the theological usage of his time by *factus* and *infectus*. Origen would in that case make the Son and the Holy Spirit creatures. Rufinus was probably no more aware than Jerome of the difference of vocabulary, but he takes account of other texts and his good will helps him to avoid too serious a mistake.

The same remark can be made about the use by Origen and the Ante-Nicenes of the verb *ktizein* and its derivatives *ktisis* and *ktisma*. Prov. 8, 22 puts into the mouth of Wisdom, who for most of the early Fathers represents the Son, the words '*ho kyrios ektisen me*' and a little further on it is a question of the generation (*gennao*) of Wisdom. Likewise Col. 1, 15 calls Christ the first-born of all *ktisis*, thus including Him in the *ktisis*. That is why these words do not have for Origen the strict meaning of creating: from Gen. 1–2, following the Septuagint, *poiein* denotes the creation of spiritual natures and *plassein* that of material ones. So *ktizein* applies to all God's production, by generation or by creation. The series *ktisma/poiēma/plasma* is found expressly with this sense in the *Commentary on John*.[63] This usage of Origen's is also found in the letter of Pope Dionysius about Dionysius of Alexandria, in 'the affair of the two Dionysii': 'The expression *ektisen*, as you well know, does not have a single sense'.[64] The Arian quarrel will necessitate a stricter terminology. Because of this Ante-Nicene vocabulary, not suited to the more rigid theology to which the reaction to Arianism would give rise, Origen would be accused by Epiphanius and by Jerome of making creatures of the Son and the Holy Spirit, in spite of many clear and indisputable texts.

Another cause of misunderstanding was the projection onto Origen of the doctrines of the various Origenist schools. At the time of each of the great Origenist crises there existed self-styled Origenists who had some responsibility for their outbreak. In the second half of the 4th century speculation and a spirituality inspired by Origen were thriving in the Egyptian deserts, where they encountered the hostility of other monks, heirs of Origen's *simpliciores* and holding like them anthropormorphite opinions. We know particularly about the victims of Theophilus's proscriptions, Isidore and four others who were blood brothers – two of them had been raised to the episcopate – who were known because of their stature as the 'tall brothers': exiled by the 'ecclesiastical Pharaoh' they were charitably received at Constantinople by John Chrysostom and this fact unleashed against John the persecutions of Theophilus. The principal representative of Origenism at that time was Evagrius Ponticus.

[63] XX, 22 (20), 182: cited below p. [276–277].
[64] In Denzinger-Schönmetzer, *Enchiridion symbolorum, defitionum et declarationum* §114 (50).

The relationship of this Origenism to Origen can be expressed in an image: '*Origenes aqua de mare* – Origen is the water of the sea', said a 9th-century Latin letter.[65] But the Origen ocean has its ebb and flow, its currents and counter-currents. The Alexandrian is more a mystic than a logician and is making for an unknowable reality toward which he pioneers various routes. Hence comes the antithetical structure of his mind: we have antitheses of which the terms are not always rationally expressed in relation to each other, the complementary aspect being found elsewhere in another passage. This theology which boils over in all directions the later Origenism will try to set in order: it will leave out one side of the antithesis and build a system on the other. That is the best way to turn a doctrine into a heresy: the heresy in effect suppresses the tension of the antitheses that express Christian doctrine, it rejects one aspect and makes the other absolute.

Origen's detractors in the 4th century challenged the Origenism of their time rather than Origen himself, dead for a century and a half, and they read the Alexandrian through spectacles provided by contemporary Origenism. Let us take a precise example. Four times in the *Treatise on First Principles* Origen discusses the question of the ultimate corporeality or incorporeality of rational creatures.[66] If Rufinus gives the advantage to corporeality, he does not conceal incorporeality. Reading Jerome we find practically nothing but incorporeality; he only gives extracts and, suppressing in this way their context, which is discussion, he distorts them profoundly. In Jerome's exposition the glorious bodies appear as a transitional stage before complete incorporeality. If Origen does not take a clear position between these alternatives in the *Treatise on First Principles,* there is not to be found in his other works either the hypothesis of incorporeality. Now the solution favoured by Jerome is that of Evagrius in his *Kephalaia Gnōstica.*[67] We may well think that, if not Evagrius, then at least the Origenist circles in Egypt which he represents, are the principal source of the opinion that Jerome imposes on Origen.

In the first half of the 4th century a strongly Evagrian trend developed in the laurae of the rule of St Sabbas between Jerusalem and the Dead Sea. About 514 Agapetus, ruler of the New Laura, expelled four monks who 'were whispering in secret the doctrines of Origen'.[68] Among them was Nonnos who was later to emerge as the leader of the Origenist trend. This event was connected, it seems with the presence near Jerusalem from 512

[65] Quoted by H. de Lubac, *Exégèse Médiévale* I/1, p. 241, note 8.

[66] See above note 41.

[67] See the sentences quoted by A. Guillaumont, *Les Kephalaia Gnōstica . . .* (see note 50 and corresponding text p. 116).

[68] Cyril of Scythopolis, Life of *Saint Sabas* XXXVI, 124–125: Fr. trans. by A. J. Festugiere in *Les moines d'Orient* III/2, pp. 50–51.

of a Syriac monk who had been forced to leave Edessa in a hurry on account of opinions dubbed Origenist: he was Stephen bar Sudaili, author of the Book of St Hierotheus, the principle surviving source for the Origenism of this period. Re-admitted to the New Laura on the death of Agapetus, Nonnos and his companions kept quiet until 532, the date of the death of Sabbas. Then, supported by several former Palestinian monks now in favour at the court of Justinian, Leontius of Byzantium – probably the well-known theologian – Domitian, Theodore Askidas, they dominated the monasteries of the region. The death of Nonnos in 547 broke up the group: on the one hand there were the extremists, the Isochristes, because for them all men will be equal with Christ in the apocatastasis, on the other hand the moderates, called Protochrists, because they saw in Christ as man the first created, or Tetradites because their adversaries accused them of introducing the Man-Christ as a fourth hypostasis in the Trinity which was thus tranformed into a Tetrad. Agreement was reached between the Anti-Origenists and the moderates and this brought about the condemnation of the Isochristes in 553.

The *Book of St Hierotheus*,[69] written in Syriac, but supposedly written in Greek by the legendary master of the pseudo-Dionysius the Areopagite, is a kind of epic history of the intellects from their creation as indistinguishable equals, through their fall which entailed their inequality and distinguishability, and an ascension that reproduces some of the moments of the life of Christ, notably the crucifixion and the resurrection, to the final state in which the intellects, having become the equals of the Great Intellect, the Christ, in an absolutely universal apocatastasis, go beyond the Christ and every name, even the divine name, and are absorbed in God in complete unity. According to this extreme isochrism all distinction of persons is called upon to disappear into a unique essence, called to melt into unity. There is not in Christ a divine nature consubstantial with God and a human nature: his nature is that of all the intellects, with the sole difference that He did not take part in the fall which entailed their differentiation and that He had thus become provisionally their chief and their guide. This strange and powerful epic ends in a pantheism which Evagrius, whose doctrine underlies it together with that of the pseudo-Dionysius, had managed to avoid. As for the relationship of such a doctrine with Origen's, one can well recognise that it is founded on ideas and hypotheses of his, but its general shape has not much to do with his thought.

Two series of documents condemning Origen and Origenism were issued by Justinian in 543 and 553. The first series was the work of the permanent domestic synod which met at the Emperor's court, and it was signed by the Pope and the four eastern Patriarchs: they comprise a *Liber*

---

[69] Ed Marsh, Oxford, 1927, in Syriac and Eng. trans.

adversus Origenem or *Letter to Menas,* patriarch of Constantinople, some extracts from the *Treatise on First Principles* and some anathemata.[70] These documents are aimed at Origen himself, but it is the Palestinian Origenism of the time that worries the anti-Origenist monks who are the authors of this anthology of extracts and of the pamphlet which was the origin of the letter. The anathemata condemn through Origen points brought out by contemporary Origenists and freeze in dogmatic assertions hypotheses already hardened by his disciples. There is, however, little foundation in Origen for some of the statements: that the body of Christ was formed before the Word and the soul were united (anathema 3); that the glorious bodies will be spherical (anathema 5). As for anathema 7 declaring that Christ will be crucified again for the demons, it seems to be based on a failure of understanding, if not by the Origenists, then by Jerome and Justinian. The *Letter to Menas* itself claims that Origen sited in the body the locus of participation by man in the image of God: it thus attributes to him an opinion which he always resisted in his anthropomorphite adversaries.

As for the texts of 553, attributed to the 5th Ecumenical Council,[71] the Second of Constantinople, they do not appear in the official minutes of that Council: so they are not canonically the work of an ecumenical council. According to the hypothesis of Fr. Diekamp,[72] they may have been discussed and voted on before the official opening of the council, when Justinian was trying unsuccessfully to convince Pope Vigilius, whom he had brought by force to Constantinople and who was opposing him. On the other hand these anathemata are aimed specifically at the Isochristes, not at Origen, who is only mentioned as their forerunner: it is the same with Justinian's letter which contains a sketch of the anathemata. Finally, as A. Guillaumont[73] has shown, some of them are copied from the *Kephalaia Gnōstica* of Evagrius. In the official minutes of Constantinople II, that is in the anathemata against the Three Chapters, Origen is mentioned in the list of heretics in anathema 11.[74] Now he does not appear in the *Homologia* of Justinian,[75] an outline of these anathemata, which gives at no. 10 the same list without his name. He has been added afterwards, which is confirmed by the fact that his name is last, although he is the earliest and the other names are in chronological order. It is probably that his name appears there because of the discussion

[70] PG 86/1, col. 943–994: to be found also in the collections of Council documents by Mansi or more recently by Schwarz. The anathemata of 543 (but not those of 553) are quoted by Denzinger-Schönmetzer (see note 64), 403–411 (203–211).

[71] They are reproduced by Fr. Diekamp, *Die origenistischen Streitigkeiten im sechsten Jahrhundert und das fünfte allgemeine Concil Münster,* 1899, pp. 90–97 and studied in detail by A. Guillaumont (see note 50 and corresponding text).

[72] See note 71.

[73] See note 28 and corresponding text.

[74] Denzinger-Schönmetzer (see note 64), 433 (233).

[75] PG 86/1, col. 993ff.

on the Origenists which preceded the opening of the Council and that he is thus named as the supposed symbol or inspirer of the Isochristes. The documents of Pope Vigilius, approving afterwards the decisions of a council held without his agreement, make no mention of Origen.

So Origenism had quite a history and it is wrong to attribute to Origen without further enquiry the systems of Evagrius or the pantheism of Stephen bar Sudaili, on the pretext that they were Origenists. Before attributing to Origen himself the interpretations of his detractors one must ask whether the latter have not projected onto him the lucubrations of his supposed disciples.

* * *

To recover with certainty the doctrines of Origen one must look for them in his own work, studied not in some particular text or other, but in his work as a whole. As what remains of this immense work is still substantial, this research is neither simple nor easy. In addition it is necessary to have historical sense and knowledge of his times so as not to project onto him frames of reference that belong to a later period. Neither the doctrines of the Origenists nor the imputations of the anti-Origenists are any substitute for the direct reading of the works of the Alexandrian, for their assertions must always be treated with reserve. For example, Origen's doctrine of the resurrection of the body has often been studied, without looking for it in his own works where it is widely scattered, but by taking it from the exposition which Methodius of Olympus made of it in his *Aglaophon* without noticing the considerable misconception on which the latter's criticisms are based.

10

Trinity and Incarnation

Origen scholars sometimes say that with him the fundamental distinction is not, as in the biblical tradition, between the Creator and the creature but, following the Platonist schemes, between the intelligible or spiritual world and the perceptible or material world. The second statement is not false but the first is. There is indeed, as several passages of the *Treatise on First Principles* show, a radical contrast between the deity and the rational creatures, the difference between 'substantiality' in the former and 'accidentality' in the latter. Although the Son and the Spirit have received all that they are from the Father, who is the origin of the deity and of the universe, they possess it as their own and perfectly, without possibility of increase or decrease. The rational creature on the other hand always partakes of the good things of the deity in an imperfect manner, and his share in them can increase or decrease in accordance with the movements of his own free will; it is thus precarious although progress in charity brings about progress towards immutability.[1] This substantiality in all that the three Persons possess, which extends even to the human soul which the Word took on himself – although endowed like the other souls with free will, it is by its participation in the Word absolutely impeccable – distinguishes them clearly from the creatures and establishes an equality between Them which is not incompatible with there being a hierarchy within the Trinity.

In a passage of the *Commentary on John*[2] which has given rise to scandal, Origen remarks that in John 1, 1 'the God – *Ho Theos*' stands for the Father, while the Son is called '*Theos* – God' without the article. 'The God' is in a way the proper name of the Father, source and origin of the Deity. In the case of the son, '*Theos*' is adjectival, it denotes the divinity that the Son receives from the Father. Karl Rahner[3] has shown that these explanations are strictly in accordance with the New Testament: 'There are in all six passages in which the predicate "*Theos*" is used to express the

---

[1] *PArch* I, 2, 10; I, 2, 13; I, 5, 3–5; IV, 4, 8. See in SC 253, note 69, pp. 51–52.
[2] II, 1–2, 12–18.
[3] *Écrits théologiques*, vol 1, Paris, 1959, pp. 81–111, especially 93–96.

fact that the Christ has the divine nature. It is not without interest to note that in all these passages the word "Theos" taken absolutely, without any adjective, is never used with the article when it stands for Christ.'[4] But a considerable number of texts in the New Testament affirm the divinity of Christ by recourse to other expressions. In any case in Origen the term 'Ho Theos' without any qualification is normally applied to the Father.

The God and Father

The kind of doctrines which are believed in plain terms through the apostolic teaching are the following:

> First, that God is one, who created and set in order all things, and who, when nothing existed, caused the universe to be. He is God from the first creation and foundation of the world, the God of all righteous men, of Adam, Abel, Seth, Enos, Enoch, Noah, Shem, Abraham, Isaac, Jacob, of the twelve patriarchs, of Moses and the prophets. This God in these last days, according to the previous announcements made through his prophets, sent the Lord Jesus Christ, first for the purpose of calling Israel, and secondly, after the unbelief of the people of Israel . . . of calling the Gentiles also. This just and good God, the Father of our Lord Jesus Christ, himself gave the law, the prophets and the gospels, and he is the God both of the apostles and of the Old and New Testaments.[a]

The essential concern of this statement which opens the list of propositions of the rule of faith in the preface of the Treatise on First Principles[5] is to oppose the Marcionite and gnostic doctrines which separated the Creator God of the Old Testament from the Father of Jesus Christ, making the former a just God, the latter a good God. There is only one God, who created everything out of nothing, who was the God of all the holy men of the old covenant, who promised by his prophets the coming of his Son and subsequently sent Him. There is only one God for the law, the prophets and the apostles, for the Old Testament and the New.

In the Treatise on First Principles there are two passages which cover what it has to say about God. We have explained above the plan of this work.[6] The first part opens with a study of the Trinity, first the Father, then the Son, then the Spirit; then the activity proper to each of them. The second part does the same, Father, Son, Spirit. The exposition of the first part[7] is mainly concerned with the conceptions that Origen held in

---

[4] p. 94.

[a] Trans. Butterworth, p. 2.

[5] §4. See J. Ruis-Camps, El dinamismo trinitario en la divinización de los seres racionales según Orígenes, Rome, 1970. Same author 'Communicabilidad de la naturaleza de Dios según Origenes', Orientalia Chrsitiana Periodica, 34, 1968, 5–37; 36, 1970, 201–247; 38, 1972, 430–453; 40, 1974, 344–363. M. Simonetti, 'Note sull teologia trinitaria di Origene', Vetera Christianorum 8, 1971, 273–307.

[6] p. 75.

[7] I, 1.

common with Middle Platonism. The incorporeal character of the Father has an important place in this: the same incorporeality is true also of the other two Persons, with the exception, of course, of the Incarnation of the Son: in several places the *Treatise on First Principles*[8] affirms that only the Trinity is absolutely incorporeal, the rational creatures, though incorporeal as souls, being always united to a body, terrestrial or ethereal, even the angels and demons. The basic problem is that of the divine anthropomorphisms, since it is impossible for man, and this goes for Scripture itself, to speak of God in any other way. The adversaries he has in mind are both the Christian anthropomorphites and the Stoics. Anthropomorphisms like fire, breath, etc., are explained as referring to divine realities. God is likewise incomprehensible, known only through his works. God is an absolutely simple intellectual nature, whose simplicity is expressed by Greek terms in Rufinus's Latin, 'monad' from *monos*, alone, and 'henad' from *heis*, one. As a purely intellectual nature God is not in a place and, strictly speaking, terms which only apply to a body, such as 'size', cannot be applied to Him. Finally, He is invisible and cannot therefore be seen by the eyes of the body. When Origen comes to the activity proper to each Person, he attributes to the Father the gift of being: He is 'the One who is'[9] and the source of being. He does not hold his existence from anything else, and everything else holds its existence from Him. Sometimes He is called *nous*, intelligence, and *ousia*, being, and sometimes with the Platonists, beyond *nous* and beyond *ousca*[10]

But many of these divine characteristics borrowed from Middle Platonism are frequently found counterbalanced by statements pointing in another direction, so true is it that everything that is affirmed about God must also at the same time be denied. Of course, God is not subject to the passions, and the anthropomorphisms in the Bible which attribute to Him anger or change of mind are not meaningless, but must be understood of certain divine realities. However, from a celebrated text in a homily on Ezekiel[11] we learn that the Father Himself is not impassible, that He feels the passion of love and that that is the origin of the Redemption. God weeps over sinners, and rejoices at the salvation of men. He is, of course, the origin and creator of everything, even of matter, but not of sin and evil. This last point is explained in a way that does not conflict with philosophy: sin and evil are not positive realities, but negative; sin is that 'nothing' which, according to John 1, 3 was made without the Word.[12]

[8] I, 6, 4; II, 2, 2; IV, 3, 15 (27).
[9] Exod. 3, 13.
[10] *ComJn* XIII, 21, 123; XIX, 6, 37; *CCels* VII, 38: Origen there takes up a formula of Celsus.
[11] VI, 6.
[12] *ComJn* II, 13-15 (7-9), 92-111.

The second passage in the *Treatise on First Principles*[13] is directed against the heretics, gnōstics of course, but especially Marcionites. Origen reacts against the separation that they make between the creator God of the Old Testament and the Father of Jesus Christ: he shows that Jesus in the Gospels always calls the Creator God his Father and that Paul does the same; he takes up again the question of the anthropomorphisms and finally he rejects the Marcionite separation of the just God and the good God. The heretics have a wrong conception of justice and goodness. Besides, certain passages of the Old Testament, if they are not allegorised, would not allow us to say that the Creator God was just and some in the New Testament, taken literally, would not show the God of which they speak as good. There cannot be justice without goodness nor goodness without justice. Even when God punishes, He does it out of goodness. And God is called good in the Old Testament and just in the New.

This defence of the goodness of the Creator God against the attacks of the Marcionites is one of the essential points of Origen's way of thinking. It was for that purpose that he built up his hypothesis of the pre-existence, in order to transfer from God to the free will of man the responsibility for the unequal conditions in which human beings are born. It was for that reason also that he tended to consider all punishments as remedial, while still recognising the possibility that the free will could become hardened in evil. God is the source of all charity which overflows from Him onto the Son and onto the Spirit and thence onto men. In that He is good, the source of charity, the origin of all that is, God is Father, father of the Only Son, father of the adopted sons, and then more generally father of all the creatures.

Of course, God acts in the world, as we shall see, through the intermediary agency of his Son and his Spirit. But Origen is very far from the idea of a 'lazy God'[14] towards which certain tendencies in Greek philosophy were moving as they exaggerated God's impassibility. For through the Son, his minister, and through the Spirit, it is He who acts. From Him in some way emerge the decisions about the Trinity's actions, He is the centre of that unity of will which guides the activity of the three Persons. His role is primordial, as much in the internal operations of the Trinity, the generation of the Son and the procession of the Spirit, as in the creation, Providence, the divinisation of the rational creatures, and the last things. All that will be studied in connection with the Son, the Father's minister and collaborator. Here we simply say this. In the matter of the generation of the Son it is necessary to guard against a dilemma

[13] II, 4–5.
[14] It is this doctrine of the 'lazy' God which Origen's pupil Gregory Thaumaturgus opposes in a writing preserved in Syriac *To Theopompus: On God passible and impassible*, published by P. Martin in J. B. Pitra, *Analecta Sacra*, vol. IV, 100–120 (Syriac), 360–376 (Latin).

arising from our anthropomorphisms. If the divine freedom is imagined after the pattern of human freedom, then either one must say that the Father begets his Son freely, from which the conclusion is that the Son might not have been, or one must deny that He begets his Son freely and that is no more and no less than to take away his divinity by imposing on Him a necessity that governs Him. Origen did not fall into that trap. On the one hand he writes of the Son 'born of Him (=the Father) as a will of his, proceeding from his intelligence' thus: 'I think that the will of the Father must suffice to make what the Father wills come to pass.'[15] 'It is the goodness of the Father which is the source from which the Son is born and from which the Spirit proceeds.'[16] The generation of the Son is thus on the Father's part a free act. But this free act can also be said to be necessary, for with God freedom and necessity coincide. God is Father from all eternity, for there is no change in Him: therefore He begets the Son from all eternity.[17]

When we come to Providence, the continual care that God takes of his creatures, Origen joins with the Platonists and the Stoics against the Epicureans and the pseudo-Aristotelian *De Mundo*. But Origen's debate with Celsus, a Middle Platonist tinctured with Epicureanism, shows a difference between the two conceptions: for Origen divine Providence extends, of course, to the whole world, as Celsus would have it, but it extends in particular to men in their individual personalities.[18] In his *Address of Thanks* Gregory Thaumaturgus shows the divine Providence concerned with him individually in all the vicissitudes of his existence, through the medium of his guardian angel or of his master.

Finally the statements that the creation was made by God out of nothing, that matter is not co-eternal with God, that the souls are not unbegotten, are found in two passages of the *Treatise on First Principles*,[19] not to mention the development of the same subject that occurs at the end of that book.[20] What we find there are certainly Origen's opinions and not Rufinus's additions: they can indeed be found in Greek in volume I of the *Commentary on John*.[21] written in the same period as the *Treatise on First Principles*, with the same two Scripture references, 2 Macc. 7, 28, and the *Shepherd* of Hermas,[22] the latter quoted by Origen as Scripture.

[15] *PArch* I, 2, 6.
[16] *PArch* I, 2, 13.
[17] *PArch* I, 2, 9; IV, 4, 1 according to Rufinus and to the Greek of Athanasius.
[18] *CCels* IV, 23ff.
[19] I, 3, 3 and II, 1, 5.
[20] IV, 4, 6–8.
[21] I, 17 (18), 103.
[22] *Precept* I (26), 1.

The Son of God in his divinity

'Then again Christ Jesus, he who came to earth, was begotten of the Father before every created thing. And after he had ministered to the Father in the foundation of all things, for "all things were made through him",[23] in these last times he emptied himself and was made man, was made flesh, although he has God. And being made man, he still remained what he was, namely God. He took to himself a body like our body, differing in this alone, that it was born of a virgin and of the Holy Spirit. And this Jesus Christ was born and suffered in truth and not merely in appearance, and truly died our common death. Moreover he truly rose from the dead, and after the resurrection companied with his disciples and was then taken up into heaven.'[b]

These are the words of Origen reproducing in the Preface to the *Treatise on First Principles*[24] the rule of faith of his time about Christ. We have seen above the reasons why Jerome substituted *factus* for the *natus* of Rufinus.[25] This exposition is aimed at several contemporary heresies: at modalism and adoptianism and also, by the statement that his body is like our body, that he was born and suffered in truth and not in appearance, at docetism which at that time was mostly found among the gnōstics. Note also his insistence on the fact that 'having become man, he remained what he was, God'. His kenosis did not put an end to his divine character. To what contemporary heresy is that addressed? It is difficult to say.

Many times over Origen, starting from Scripture, meditated on the ineffable mystery of the generation of the Son by the Father. Because of the Stoic materialism that was infiltrating the 'simple' of the Great Church and affecting even so important a theologian as Tertullian, he wanted to rule out any bodily connotation. The Son is begotten by the Father as the reflection is by the light, as the will proceeds from the intellect, or as the word is emitted by the intellect. Origen applies to this generation the titles given to Wisdom in the *Book of Wisdom*,[26] 'a breath of the power of God, a very pure emanation of the glory of the Almighty, the radiance of his eternal light, the stainless mirror of the activity of God and the image of his goodness'. Likewise those of Col. 1, 15: 'The image of the invisible God, the first-born of all *ktisis*', a term which does not express for him, as we have said, creation only, but is applied to everything that comes from God. Or indeed in Heb. 1, 3, 'the effulgence of his glory and the very image of his substance'.[27] Contrary to what Arianism was to say, the eternity of this generation is clearly affirmed, for

[23] John 1, 3.
[b] Translated Butterworth p. 3.
[24] §4. See H. Crouzel, 'Le Christ Sauveur selon Origène', *Studia Missionalia* 30, 1981, 63–87.
[25] See p. 174.
[26] 7, 25–26.
[27] *PArch* I, 2.

it is inconceivable that the Father ever existed without his wisdom, his Reason, his Word, all expressions which, as we have seen, denote the Son. Nor did the Father begin to be Father, as if He had not been so before, since all change in God is inconceivable. Twice in the *Treatise on First Principles*[28] and once in the *Commentary on the Epistle to the Romans*[29] we find the famous sentence that was to be used against the Arians: 'ouk en hoti ouk en – There was not when He (the Son) was not'. These are not, as has sometimes been thought, additions by the translator Rufinus, for the second text from the *Treatise on First Principles* is quoted in Greek by Athanasius and explicitly attributed by him to Origen with the formulation that we have reproduced.

Eternal generation but also continual generation: the Father is begetting the Son at each instant, just as light is always emitting its radiance.[30] By eternity and continuity Origen expresses eternity conceived as a unique instant of which he has not a very clear notion. The words *aiōn* and *aiōnios* denote for him sometimes a very long time, sometimes a duration without beginning or end. The generation of the Son is identified with 'the uninterrupted contemplation of the profundities of the Father' who is making the Son of God[31] or in other words, the Son is constantly 'fed' by the Father[32] who communicates to Him at every instant his own divinity. Numerous texts, using all kinds of images, in forms that are dynamic rather than ontological, compel recognition that Origen is expressing the equivalent of the Nicene *homoousios*. His attacks on the Valentinian *probolē* or *prolatio*, which he tells us, made the divine generation like human or animal generation, involving separation of the begotten from the begetter, were not simply occasioned by the fact that that would implicitly imply a bodily process, but also by the fact that these ways of looking at the matter mean that the begotten *comes out of* the begetter, becomes external to him. Now the Son does not *come out of* the Father: he dwells in the Father and the Father in the Son, even in the Incarnation when the Son is at the same time on earth with his human soul.[33] Everything that belongs to the Father belongs also to the Son, and everything that belongs to the Son belongs to the Father:[34] Father and Son are subjects and objects of the some love.[35] The Son is an effulgence of *all* the glory of God[36], the only one who can fulfil *all* the Father's will.[37] As He is the Image of God, He is 'of the same dimensions' as

---

[28] I, 2, 9 and IV, 4, 1.
[29] I, 5 (PG 14).
[30] *HomJr* IX, 4.
[31] *ComJn* II, 2, 18.
[32] *ComJn* XIII, 34, 219.
[33] *ComJn* XX, 18 (16), 153–159.
[34] John, 17, 10.
[35] *ComCt* Prol. (GCS VIII, 21ff) and *HomLc* XXV, 7–8.
[36] *ComJn* XXXII, 28 (18), 353 (GCS IV).
[37] *ComJn* XIII, 36, 231.

Him.[38] Father and Son are a single and identical almightiness.[39] That is confirmed with the greatest clarity in the *Address of Thanks* of Thaumaturgus, reproducing the teaching he received: the Father 'made the Son one with Him' and 'so to speak wraps Himself up in Him by the power of his Son which is quite equal to his own'.[40]

Of course, Origen cannot express himself in the very terms of Nicaea, for *ousia* and *hypostasis* have not sufficiently precise meanings for him and he does not present the problem in an ontological way. Some texts seem clumsy to us because the question of the equality of the Father and the Son does not arise for him with the clarity shown in the anti-Arian reaction after Nicaea and still more after Constantinople, and also because we read these texts and project a later theology onto them, without understanding the precise point that he was trying to make. The 'subordination' of the Son to the Father does not bring into question either identity of nature or equality of power. The Son is both subordinate and equal to the Father, a double affirmation that can be found again after Nicaea in Athanasius and Hilary themselves. The subordination arises in the first place from the fact that the Father is Father, origin of the two other Persons and initiator of the Trinity. The latter role concerns the 'economy': the word *oikonomia*, the Latin equivalent of which is generally *dispensatio* denotes the activity of the Trinity externally, in the Creation and in the Incarnation-Redemption. The Father gives the orders, the Son and the Spirit receive them and are the envoys, the agents *ad extra* of the Trinity, each for his own part. If the Father is the centre of decision, the Son and the Spirit are not mere executants of the paternal will, for while the Father's initiative is often emphasised, so is the unity of will and of action[41] on the part of the Three Persons. Thus the subordination of the Son and the Spirit is closely linked to their 'divine missions'. The mediating role of the Son in his divinity even rebounds in some measure onto his inner being, for if the Father is absolutely One, the Son, One in his hypostasis, is multiple in his titles, his *epinoiai*. That is the third reason for the 'subordinationism' and if on this point the relationship of Origen with Plotinus, probably through their common master, Ammonius Saccas, is clear, Origen's equivalences based on the unity of their nature must not be forgotten. When one speaks of Origen's 'subordinationism' it is easy to forget that it is a quite equivocal notion: as Marcus's book has shown,[42] it is wrong to confuse the subordinationism of the Ante-Nicenes with that of the Arians.

---

[38] *CCels* VI, 69.
[39] *PArch* I, 2, 10.
[40] IV, 37.
[41] *PArch* I, 3, 7.
[42] W. Marcus, *Der Subordinatianismus als historisches Phänomenen*, Munich, 1963.

With the titles of Christ[43] we approach one of the central points of Origen's christology which, as we have just said, is not devoid of analogies with the middle and Neo-Platonists,[44] nor even with the gnōstics. It is, in fact, a theology of the titles of the Christ, of the names that are given Him by the New Testament and also by the Old when read according to the allegorical exegesis: they represent the different functions or attributes that the Christ takes on in his role as Mediator in relation to us. The Valentinians had hypostatised the biblical titles of the Christ and the Church into separate entities to denote some of the Aeons which populated their Pleroma. For Origen it is simply a matter of the different aspects under which the Christ appears to us: the word *epinoia* expresses a human way of looking at these things, with or without foundation in the real, without this distinction of concepts corresponding to different beings; he is opposed to *hypostasis* or *pragma*, meaning reality. The doctrine of the *epinoiai* of the Christ, to be found throughout Origen's work, is especially given theoretical form in Book I of the *Commentary on John* and in chapter 2 of Book I of the *Treatise on First Principles*.

We shall not enumerate here all these *epinoia* – Book I of the *Commentary on John* alone studies about fifty of them and in Origen's work as a whole about a hundred can be found – but simply to point out the most important of them and to see their mediating role, which is double: the rational creature on the one hand is the beneficiary of the activity of Christ denoted by the *epinoiai* and on the other hand can participate in it directly and thus become the collaborator of Christ for the service of other rational creatures; thus the mediating role of Christ can be shared by the angels and by men. The principle *epinoia*, the 'most ancient', by a priority of logic not of time, is Wisdom: according to Prov. 8, 22, she is the 'beginning' in which according to John 1, 1 the Logos is found: 'In the beginning was the Logos.' Wisdom contains in herself the Intelligible World in which are the 'ideas' in the Platonic and the general sense, as well as the Stoic 'reasons', taken in an individual sense, that is for Origen the plans of the creation and the seeds of the beings: 'ideas' and 'reasons' have been confused since the Middle Stoicism of Poseidonius. The Intelligible World, present in the Son in that He is Wisdom, was created by the Father in the eternal generation of the Son: it constitutes that creation co-eternal with God[45] which Origen affirmed and which caused so much scandal after the *De Creatis* of Methodius.[46]

[43] See our article: 'Le contenu spirituel des dénominations du Christ selon le livre I du Commentaire sur Jean d'Origène' in *Origeniana Secunda* (ed. H. Crouzel, A. Quacquarelli), Rome, 1980, pp. 131–150.

[44] In the system of Plotinus the Intelligence contains the multiplicity of the 'ideas' in contrast with the absolute unity of the One.

[45] *PArch* I, 2, 10.

[46] After Photius, *Bibl* 235, 302a (CUFr V).

The Alexandrian's essential argument for it, is that God could not begin
to be a creator as if He had not been one before, since no change in Him
can be conceived: it is parallel to the argument for the eternal generation
of the Son. Methodius was scandalised by this because he thought that
this creation co-eternal with God was that of the 'pre-existent intellects',
while in fact Origen clearly asserts that the latter had a beginning which
was the cause of their 'accidental' status.[47] But that he was really talking
about the Intelligible World of the 'ideas' and the 'reasons' contained in
Wisdom, is made clear in the *Treatise on First Principles* by an appendix[48]
added at the end of the discussion of the Trinity.[49] This explanation given
in terms of the Platonic and Stoic philosophies contains nothing contrary
to the faith and is found again in many later Fathers, including Methodius
himself and Augustine. Wisdom which is the Son can be shared by
rational creatures: the virtue of wisdom is in fact the highest of all, the
mystical virtue par excellence which enables its possessor to see as by an
intimate connaturality the divine realities.

The second *epinoia* of the Son, in order of importance, is that of Logos,
in both senses of the Greek word: Word, brought out by the biblical and
Johannine tradition, and Reason, flowing from the philosophical tradition
of Heraclitus and the Stoics, but meaning in Origen the eternal and
supernatural Reason of God. The role of the Son-Logos is a double one:
He reveals to beings that are *logika*, 'rational' in a sense more
supernatural than natural, the mysteries contained in Wisdom: and the
logika are *logika* by reason of their participation in the Logos. The other
epinoiai are named, either from abstract notions, Life, Light, Resurrection,
Truth, Power, Justice, etc. or from human titles, First-Born from the
dead, First-Born of all creatures, etc., or from beings inferior to man,
Lamb, chosen Arrow, Vine, Bread of Life, etc. All relate to the mediating
and saving role of Christ. The virtues are also included in the *epinoiai*.
The Christ in his divine reality is all the virtues and each virtue, virtue
'whole, animated, and living'.[50] that is Virtue turned into a Person. A
certain parallelism may be noted between Origen's teaching on this point
and that of Plotinus:[51] in the Father and in the One, the first origin; in the
World and in the Intelligence the virtues as a paradigm: in the human soul
of the Christ and in the Soul of the World the source of the virtues that
are present in men.

Creation, like Providence, is the work of the whole Trinity. Origen

[47] *PArch* II, 9, 2.
[48] *PArch* I, 4, 3–5.
[49] *PArch* I, 1–4. This appendix cannot be an addition by Rufinus, for a Greek fragment
preserved by Justinian is translated here. Unfortunately the fragment is missing in one of the
two collections of manuscripts and consequently in all printed editions prior to that of
P. Koetschau in GCS V.
[50] *ComJn* XXXII, 11 (7), 126 (GCS IV).
[51] Plotinus, *Enneads* I, 2 (CUFr).

reads this in Col. 1, 15: 'For in him all things were created, in heaven and on earth, visible and invisible, whether thrones or dominions or principalities or authorities – all things were created through (*dia*) him and for (*eis*) him.' Likewise in Psalm 32 (33), 6, rendered thus by the Septuagint: 'By the Word (*logō*) of the Lord the heavens have been established and by the breath (or the Spirit, *pneumati*) of his mouth all their power.' The Son thus assumes two of the roles distinguished by Plato in the *Timaeus*: as Wisdom, as the Intelligible World of the 'ideas' and the 'reasons'. He is the model in conformity with which the world was created; as Logos He is the intelligent instrument, the Father's collaborator in the Creation, for He expresses the 'ideas' and the 'reasons' which are in Wisdom to make individual beings. But for Origen there is not one part of the creation that is the work of the Father and another part which is the work of the Son: 'The Gospel does not say that the Son made similar works, but that He made the same works similarly.'[52]

This double role, of model and agent, is seen again in the creation of man 'after the image'. Strictly speaking, the Son alone is the Image of God,[53] man was created 'after the image', that is to say 'after' the Son. The famous plural of Gen. 1, 26: 'Let us make man after our image and likeness' is explained, as in many ancient Fathers, as a conversation between the Father and the Son and the Father says to the Son something like: 'Let us both make man after my image which Thou art.' In the creation of man 'after the image' the Son is both the model, in that He is the Image of the Father, and the agent with the Father.

An important section of the study of the Trinity which opens the *Treatise on First Principles*[54] is concerned with distinguishing the proper role of each Person in the government of the beings created (the trinitarian appropriations), while still affirming that their action is common: the role of the Father is to give being, that of the Son to make the being *logikos*, this representing as we have seen a mainly supernatural rationality, and that of the Spirit to confer sanctity. From this essay in appropriation Jerome and Justinian reached the conclusion that there was a hierarchy of power, based quantitatively on the number of their respective subjects, while, according to Rufinus, Origen was afraid that it would comprise an inverse hierarchy based on the nobility of the respective functions. The testimony of Pamphilus and even more that of Athanasius on this text shows that Jerome, followed by Justinian, projected conclusions onto it which were personal to them and which Origen did not draw.[55] The same section of the *Treatise on First Principles*

---

[52] *PArch* I, 2, 12.
[53] Col. 1, 15.
[54] I, 3, 5 to I, 4, 2.
[55] See H. Crouzel, 'Les personnes de la Trinité sont-elles de puissance inégale selon Origène *Peri Archon* I, 3, 5–8?', *Gregorianum* 57, 1976, 109–125.

see the Father as the origin of the gifts of the Spirit, the Son as the minister who distributes them, and the Spirit as the 'matter' of those gifts, the Trinity acting together in each of its acts, even in those which are referred more precisely to a particular Person.

The Son of God in his humanity

We have several times mentioned the hypothesis of the pre-existence of souls which will be studied more fully in the following chapter on the origins of humanity. The 'intellect' that was joined to the Word was created with the others and was united at its creation with the Son of God. A fragment of Justinian corresponding to the *Treatise on First Principles*[56] affirms that it 'was never separate from the Only Son' and a passage in the *Commentary on John*[57] that it was then 'in God and in his fulness'. This union, then, gives it the 'form of God'[58] which is proper to the Word, establishing between God and man a perfect '*communicatio idiomatum*',[59] that is to say everything attributed to the Word can be said of the man and vice versa. This union confers on the soul, which is nevertheless endowed with free will like the others, a 'substantial' impeccability, like that of the Deity, because of its immeasurable charity, for it is like the iron which when plunged in the fire becomes fire.[60] In the Pauline notion of freedom which underlies Origen's spiritual doctrine, there is no contradiction between it and this impeccability. All this is worked out in one of the finest chapters of the *Treatise on First Principles*[61].

So the Christ-man exists in the pre-existence, long before the Incarnation, and has quite a history before that event. He is the Bridegroom of the pre-existent Church formed of the totality of rational creatures. Thus it is He rather than the Holy Spirit, of which Origen says the pagans have not even the idea,[62] who corresponds to the third hypostasis of Plotinus's triad, the Soul of the World: the latter in fact contains within itself the individual souls, which are both distinct from each other and not distinct. Origen expresses a relationahip between the Christ-man as Bridegroom of the Church and the rational creatures that constitute the Church analogous to that of Plotinus, but in a form that pays greater respect to the person. But the reproach was unjustified which the extreme Origenists, the Isochristes, made against the moderate Origenists of Palestine in the 6th century, calling them Tetradites because they were held to be turning the Trinity into a Tetrad by introducing into

---

[56] II, 6, 4. See SC 253, note 25, pp. 178–179.
[57] XX, 19 (17), 162.
[58] Phil. 2, 6: *ComMt* XIV 17 (GCS X).
[59] *PArch* II, 6, 3.
[60] *PArch* II, 6, 5–6.
[61] II, 6.
[62] *PArch* I, 3, 1.

it the soul of Christ; for the latter never occurs in the work of Origen, in spite of appearances, as a Person distinct from the Word: it is part of Trinity by virtue of its union with the second Person who gives it the 'form of God'.

The impeccability of substance belonging to this 'intellect' protected it from the original fall, which occurred, as we shall see, in the pre-existence; the same was true of certain others who would become the angels. But the greater part of the members of the pre-existent Church at that point turned away from the contemplation of God and from the unity of beings. However, the Christ did not abandon his fallen Bride. In the days of the Old Testament, when the Church is indistinguishable from ancient Israel, He sends her patriarchs and prophets to prepare for his coming and these are, with the angels, the 'friends of the Bridegroom' so frequently mentioned in the *Commentary on the Song of Songs*. He himself visits the Church from time to time, since, in accordance with the doctrine generally held by the ante-Nicenes, the theophanies described in the old Scriptures are appearances of the Son, agent of the Trinity *ad extra*. In some of these appearances, for example the one to Abraham at the Oak of Mamre and the other one when He prevents the sacrifice of Isaac, the wrestling with Jacob, the appearance to Moses in the Burning Bush,[63] it is a man or an angel who is seen and subsequently revealed as being God. It is in this context that Origen declares that the Christ made Himself man among men, angel among the angels.[64] The explanation seems to be as follows: He then shows Himself in his humanity, both angelic and human, since, not having sinned, He is not affected by the distinction resulting from the fall.

When the moment fixed by the Father for Him to rejoin his fallen Bride arrives, the soul of the Christ gives up 'the form of God' to take on 'the form of a servant',[65] our coarse earthly corporeality, taking flesh in the womb of Mary. The fact is that for Origen the subject of the 'kenosis' of Phil. 2, 6–7, is sometimes said to be the Word and sometimes the soul.[66] Given the hypothesis of the pre-existence of the souls and in particular of that of the Christ, it is logical that the subject of the kenosis should be directly this soul, and only indirectly the Word, by virtue of the '*communicatio idiomatum*'. The word of the angel to Mary: 'a Holy Spirit shall come upon thee and a power of the Most High shall overshadow thee'[67] has for Origen the following meaning: the Power of the Most High is the Word, Power (*dynamis*) being one of his *epinoiai*.

[63] Gen. 18; 22, 12; 32, 22–33; Exod. 3–4.
[64] *HomGn* VIII, 8; *ComJn* I, 31 (34), 216–218.
[65] Phil. 2, 6–7.
[66] See J. L. Papagno, 'Flp 2, 6–11 em la cristologia y soteriologia de Origenes', *Burgense* 17, 1976, 395–409.
[67] Luke 1, 35.

ORIGEN

Several times over, and we shall see why, Origen calls the soul assumed by the Word the 'shadow' of the Lord Christ. So it is the Word, Power of God, who casts his shadow, his soul, over Mary, so that she conceives flesh within her.[68] In other words the soul of the Christ, which has not sinned, accomplished through love for his sinful Bride the descent into the earthly and corruptible corporeality to which God has condemned the latter because of her fault. Origen relates his explanation of this to the River Jordan, symbol of the Christ, of the Incarnation and of baptism, the name of which according to him means 'their descent' (*katabasis autōn*): 'Some – probably Philo – have supposed that this descent indicated in a veiled way that of the souls into bodies . . . If so, what would this river be, 'their descent', to which they must come to purify themselves and which does not descend of its own descent, but because of men's descent if it is not our Saviour . . .'[69] The Christ does not descend of his own descent for He has not sinned, but because the descent of men who have sinned, and the only object of his descent in their redemption.

A study that appeared some years ago[70] expounds the various schemes by which the Alexandrian expresses the work of Redemption accomplished by the Passion and the Resurrection. It concerns directly the humanity of the Christ since it is the latter which undergoes death and rises again, the divine Word not being liable to death. The author finds in Origen's explanations of the Redemption five principal schemes which are not to be considered separately, but which are interdependent: no one of them exactly corresponds to what it expresses – that is true of every image of the supernatural which always in large measure eludes our grasp – and each fails to express something which another expresses better. Each of them starts from Scriptural expressions or images.

The first set of ideas can be called the *mercantile* scheme. It is based on 1 Peter 1, 18–19: 'it is not with perishable things such as silver and gold that you were ransomed from the futile ways inherited from your fathers, but with the precious blood of Christ, like that of a lamb without blemish or spot'. Likewise 1 Cor. 7, 23: 'You have been bought with a great price' and Apoc. 5, 9; 'Thou hast ransomed for God by thy blood men from every tribe and tongue and people and nation.' The image of a contract of purchase and sale is here joined to that of sacrifice and the victim which belongs to a different scheme. For Origen the seller is the devil, which the New Testament quotations do not say, the buyer is Christ, we are the merchandise and the price paid is Christ's humanity: we have here a slave market. Belonging to God, we have been delivered up to the devil by our sins and Christ buys us back. But a slave is bought so that he can serve his purchaser: here Christ buys us to set us free. The image of the prisoner of

[68] See especially *ComCt* III, GCS VIII, p. 182.
[69] *ComJn* VI, 42 (25), 217–218.
[70] J. A. Alcain, *Cautiverio y rendención del hombre en Orígenes*, Bilbao, 1973.

war is mingled with that of the slave. So the devil takes in payment the humanity of Christ, or more precisely his soul, and takes it away into Hades, the abode of the dead, the Sheol of the Old Testament: the descent of Christ into Hades after his death is in fact an important article of faith in the primitive Church. But the devil is mistaken if he thinks he will retain control of this soul: he does not know that it is united with the Word and therefore strong with the very strength of God. This ignorance on the part of the devil which makes him the dupe in this transaction fits in with one of the major ideas in Origen's doctrine of knowledge: only a pure soul can know God and the divine realities and consequently the devil is ignorant of everything that concerns the order of salvation: that cannot be revealed to him for he is incapable of understanding it. Thus the soul of Christ remains 'free among the dead'.[71] And we are freed both by the price paid by Christ and because Christ, our head, although He was delivered up, has remained free.[72]

The *warrior* scheme interpenetrates the mercantile scheme: the victory of Christ over the diabolical powers whose prisoners we are gives us our freedom. That the Passion was conceived as a victory of Christ over the demonic forces we already read in Paul. Thus Col. 2, 15: 'He disarmed the principalities and powers and made a public example of them, triumphing over them in his cross.' The battles of Joshua – of Jesus the son of Navē – represent those of 'my' Jesus over these powers. The descent into Hades figures in this scheme too, as does the deception of the devil caused by his ignorance of the true identity of his opponent: the latter, having in this way got into the devil's lair, frees the captive souls and takes them with Him in his glorious Ascension. Then the cross becomes the instrument of Christ's triumph and it is the devil himself who is finally nailed.[73] But this victory does not automatically ensure our freedom and that is a point that must always be kept in mind, especially when reading Origen, the theologian *par excellence* of free will: each one must freely associate himself with this triumph. The victory of Christ will thus only produce its results progressively in the time separating the two advents, depending upon the adherence that each man gives to him personally.

The *juridical* scheme aims at paying the debt inscribed on the 'bond' of which Col. 2, 14 speaks: 'he has cancelled the bond that stood against us with its legal demands; this he set aside nailing it to the cross.' Of course, God punishes sin, but he does it to convert: for the Alexandrian the chastisement has, we repeat, a remedial aspect; however he perceives that

---

[71] Ps. 87 (88), 6.

[72] The texts studied by Alcain are innumerable: *ComRm* II, 13 (PG 14); *ComJn* VI, 63 (35), 274; *HomEx* VI, 9; VIII, 5, *HomLv* XV, 2; *ComMt* XVI 8 (GCS X); etc.

[73] Among other texts: *HomJos* I, 1; *HomCt* II, 11; *HomJr* IX, 1; *HomNb* III, 3; XVIII, 4; *HomEx* XI, 4; *ComRm* V, 10 (PG 14).

our actions affect our personality by force of habit to the point of
becoming our nature and at the Day of Judgement our hearts will be
opened and all will see the actions inscribed on them.[74] This debt seems
indeed to be a debt owed to the devil, 'the accuser of our brethren' as
Apoc. 12, 10 calls him, echoing the opening of the Book of Job, and he it
is whom Origen sees in the adversary of the little parable in Luke 12, 58–59,
who is to be agreed with while we are in the way with him, lest he
denounce us to the Judge.[75]. By Christ the debt is suppressed and the
devil's action against us is dismissed: but the pardon obtained by Christ is
only received in faith which is the acceptance of this pardon by each one.

The *ritual* scheme is based on the Epistle to the Hebrews: Christ is in
his Passion priest and victim, a double role that corresponds to his
divinity and his humanity. Of Himself he delivers up his humanity, body
and soul, in sacrifice, not by a purely passive acceptance, but by a positive
act of immolation. All the sacrifices of the old covenant are the figure of
his, for He is the true Paschal Lamb, the one of whom the paschal lamb
was the figure. Abraham sacrificing Isaac represents the Father sacrificing
the Son: but in the last analysis the victim is not Isaac who prefigures the
Word in his divinity but the ram symbolising his humanity.[76] And his
sacrifice has the effect of purifying everything in heaven and on earth.
One of the functions of the high priest who is Christ is intercession near
the Father, the reconciliation of the creature with Him: he makes God
propitious towards men, purifying them of sin, stripping the devil of his
power. And the martyrs, victims too in union with Christ, are co-
redeemers with Him, sharing in his double function as priest and victim.

The scheme based on *mystery* is founded on the death and resurrection
of Christ in which a man shares by his baptism.[77] Origen distinguishes
two stages of resurrection of a man, according to the image of Christ's
resurrection, first, a partial one, 'through a glass, darkly', which begins
with baptism followed by a life in conformity with it, and a second one,
perfect, 'face to face',[78] the final resurrection. Redemption is then
conceived as a death to sin with Christ and a regeneration by conformity
with the risen Christ. In this He is not simply a model, but the agent of
this new birth in which a man acquiesces by faith. Origen's whole
doctrine of the resurrection emphasises the mediating and redemptive
action of Christ.

In connection with the ritual scheme the cosmic and hypercosmic effect
of the sacrifice of the Cross: as several texts show, He has purified

[74] *HomJr* XVI, 10; *ComRm* II, 10 (PG 14); *PArch* II, 10, 4.
[75] *HomLc* XXXV.
[76] Such is the spiritual exegesis that runs right through *HomGn* VIII. See *ComJn* VI, 53
(35), 273; XIX, 15 (4), 91ff; *HomLv* I, 3; IX, 5.
[77] Rom. 6, 3ff.
[78] 1 Cor. 13, 12: H. Crouzel, 'La "première" et la "seconde" résurrection des hommes
d'après Origène', *Didaskalia* 3, 1973, 3–19.

everything, on earth as in heaven. That is why Origen speaks sometimes of a double efficacity of the one sacrifice. A similar affirmation in the *Treatise on First Principles*[79] was understood in a wrong sense by Jerome: 'although Origen does not say so', Jerome nevertheless understands the matter as if Origen was affirming a duality of sacrifices, Christ having to be crucified again for the demons. But Book I of the *Commentary on John*[80] of similar date to the *Treatise on First Principles*, clearly affirms the uniqueness of the sacrifice – 'the victim once offered – *ten hapax thysian'* – and at the same time its double efficacy. The uniqueness of the sacrifice is also affirmed in the *Treatise on First Principles* itself.[81] Jerome must have misunderstood. He sees a confirmation of his point of view in the idea that Christ was made man among men, angel among angels, whence, as Jerome extends Origen's thought in his own way, we get demon among demons. But that Christ became a man among men and an angel among angels is only said in a very precise context, that of the theophanies,[82] not that of Christ's sacrifice, and nothing justifies us in extending it to that.

These explanations of Redemption show the value of the role played by Christ's humanity. Origen constantly applies to it this verse of the *Book of Lamentations*[83] in the Septuagint version: 'The breath (*pneuma*, the spirit) of our face, the Lord Christ (has been taken in their destructions), He of whom we said: In his shadow we shall live among the nations.' The literal sense concerns the last king of Judah of the Davidic dynasty. Zedekiah, the Anointed (Christ) of the Lord, made prisoner and carried away into captivity in Babylon when Jerusalem was destroyed. For Origen this is about Christ and his shadow is his human soul, because, just as our shadow reproduces all the movements of our body, so the humanity of Christ accomplishes in all things the will of the Word. Here below in the present life that we lead among the nations, it is through the humanity that He has assumed that the Son manifests Himself to us: that humanity shares fully in his mediatorial work and offers itself as the most immediate model for our imitation.

If we were now to run through the chapters that we have devoted to Origen's spirituality, about the image of God, knowledge, spiritual themes, virginity and marriage, and likewise the doctrine of the virtues, titles of the Son, we should see that the central place in all this is held by the Christ in his divinity and in his humanity. And Origen's deeply emotional devotion to the humanity of the Word, such as it is expressed

---

[79] IV, 3, 13: see SC 269, note 80, pp. 226–231; lists the different opinions of contemporary authors on Jerome's allegation.

[80] I, 35 (40), 255.

[81] II, 3, 5.

[82] See pp. 251–252.

[83] 4, 20; *PArch* II, 6, 7; IV, 3, 13 (25); see SC 253, note 39, p. 184.

in the *Commentary on the Song of Songs* and elsewhere, demonstrates that his Christology is the central point of his teaching and of his life.

The Holy Spirit

In the case of the third Person of the Trinity the history of patristic theology centres on the date 360. That is, in fact, the year in which arose the first important heresy relating to the Holy Spirit, that of the Pneumatomachoi, 'those who fight against the Spirit', also called Macedonians, from the name of Macedonius, bishop of Constantinople. These were theologians belonging to the homoiousian tendency, supporters of the Nicene *homoiousios* (of similar essence) instead of *homoousios* (of the same essence). Although in the matter of the Son they were opposed to the Arians and to Arianisers of all kinds, the Macedonians were like these in contesting the divinity of the Holy Spirit. They were to provoke a reaction in which a considerable literature was to be devoted to the defence of the Spirit's divinity: the *Letters to Serapion* in which Athanasius attacked heretics of a similar outlook called Tropicoi, the treatises *On the Spirit* of Basil of Caesarea and of Didymus the Blind, to mention only the most important.

Before that date the doctrine of the Holy Spirit, not having been called in question, had not taken up much space in patristic literature and questions about the Trinity seemed to be limited to the dual relationship of Father and Son rather than to extend to the triple one of the three Persons. Some would be tempted to say that reflection on the Holy Spirit was at that time non-existent: but that would certainly be a mistake, the same mistake that a historian of the 21st century would make if he attempted to write the history of a period in the 20th century relying solely and uncritically on newspapers that favoured the sensational at the expense of the ordinary facts of everyday life. What the Church holds as an undisputed possession takes up much less space in theological literature than that which is attacked and must be defended: the doctrine of the Holy Spirit before 360 is a good illustration of this. In spite of problems arising from certain passages in the Apostolic Fathers and the Apologists the personality of the Holy Spirit and his Divinity are demonstrated by the numerous instances in which the three Persons are named one after the other: the Spirit's roles as inspirer of Scripture and of the Church, and as sanctifier of souls, are likewise emphasised. Irenaeus offers in a few words a fairly complete doctrine. The personality and the divinity of the Spirit are presupposed there also in the trinitarian formulae and in those which place Him in parallel with the Son. The Spirit and the Son shared in the creation as the two hands of the Father. Both are inspirers of Scripture without their functions being clearly distinguished. The Spirit also played a part in the incarnation of the Son and follows up that incarnation in the Church; before all else He is the One who sanctifies, gives life, confers the spiritual gifts, effects our adoption as sons; that is the proper task of the Spirit. But Irenaeus says nothing of the way in which the Spirit proceeds from the Father.

In the preface to the *Treatise on First Principles*[84] Origen expounds the points that were clear in the rule of faith of his time:

> (The Apostles) delivered that the Holy Spirit is associated with the Father and with the Son in honour and dignity. As far as He is concerned, it is not clear whether He is born or not born, whether He is to be considered as Son of God or not. But all that is to be enquired into, using the best of our power from holy scripture, inquiring with wisdom and diligence. It is, however, certainly taught with the utmost clearness in the Church, that the Spirit inspired each one of the saints, both the prophets and the apostles, and that there was not one spirit in the men of old and another in those who were inspired at the coming of Christ.'[c]

That the Holy Spirit is associated with the Father and the Son in honour and dignity implies that He is like them a person and that He is God, although this last term is not explicitly used of Him. But he possesses the same 'substantiality' as the other two:

> But to be stainless is a quality which belongs essentially (*substantialiter*) to none except the Father, Son and Holy Spirit; for holiness is in every created being and accidental quality, and what is accidental may also be lost.[85] [d]

So the Spirit is not a creature. Belonging to the Trinity, He possesses the absolute incorporeality that is the privilege of the Trinity alone: He is indeed explicitly mentioned after the Father and the Son in two of the three passages in the *Treatise on First Principles* which affirm that,[86] the third of which uses according to Rufinus the word Trinity,[87] a rare term in the Greek writings of Origen, but nevertheless attested.

The question of the origin of the Holy Spirit does not seem to have been clear to Origen from the rule of faith. The *Commentary on John* advances the question a little. We saw above why what Rufinus translated by '*natus aut innatus*' was rendered by Jerome as *utrum factus sit aut infectus*'.[88] The rule of faith comes no nearer to teaching that the Spirit is a Son of God. He is the inspirer of the Scripture, both the Old Testament and the New: here we find again the same concern that his statement about the Father voiced, to counter the Marcionites and the Gnōstics who separated the two Testaments.

In the study of the Trinity which opens the *Treatise on First Principles* the Holy Spirit is dealt with in chapters 3 and 4.[89] While the pagan

---

[84] §4.
[c] Translated Butterworth p. 5.
[85] *PArch* I, 5, 5;   [d] Translated Butterworth p. 50.
[86] I, 6, 4; II, 2, 2.
[87] IV, 3, 15 (27).
[88] See p. 174.
[89] I, 3, 1–4, then with the two other Persons, from I, 3, 5 to I, 4, 2.

philosophers know something of the Father and the Son – Origen is here alluding to the second hypostasis of Middle Platonism – they have no notion of the Holy Spirit: so Origen does not see any relationship between Him and the third hypostasis of Middle Platonism, the Soul of the World; in our interpretation of Origen above we likened this to the human soul of Christ. In this connection the Holy Spirit is called a *subsistentia*, an expression which means in Rufinus's Latin an individual substance, an individual being, as distinct from *substantia* which has a general sense, as the translator himself explains in the first book that he added to his translation of Eusebius's *Ecclesiastical History*.[90] The same statement that the Holy Spirit is a *subsistentia* is found in an earlier passage:[91] 'The Holy Spirit is an intellectual being (*subsistentia*) and exists with an existence of his own (*proprie subsistit et extat*)'. As Origen has not got a word to express person other than *hypostasis* or *ousia*, the fact that the Spirit is person is thus clearly stated, at least through Rufinus, by the expression *subsistentia intellectualis*. Origen goes on to reproduce texts from both Testaments speaking of the Holy Spirit, notably the gift of the Holy Spirit by the apostles after baptism by the laying on of hands. The baptismal formula invoking the three persons shows 'the great authority and dignity which the Holy Spirit has as a substantial being'[92] and so does even more the text about blasphemy against the Holy Spirit which will not be remitted, while blasphemy against the Son may be.[93]

Origen did not find it stated in the rule of faith whether the Holy Spirit was born or not born, whether He was a Son or not, but neither did he find it stated in the Scriptures that He was made or created. It did not escape him that the word Spirit is often used in the Bible, sometimes even to denote the nature of God.[94] So he puts forward the principle, following 'some of our predecessors' speaking of the New Testament – but he also extends this statement to the Old – that 'wherever the spirit is mentioned without an adjective specifying what spirit, the Holy Spirit must be understood'.[95] In communicating the knowledge of God to men and to angels the three Persons work together: 'All knowledge coming from the Father through the revelation of the Son is known in the Holy Spirit'. So the Spirit is, as it were, the spiritual 'milieu' in which knowledge is produced. And the Spirit knows the Father for He it is that gazes on the profundities of God.[96] We shall return in a moment in connection with the *Commentary on John* to the knowledge which the Holy Spirit has, because there is a contradiction, but only an apparent one, between two texts.

[90] I, 29, or X, 30 (GCS Eusebius II).
[91] *PArch* I, 1, 3.
[92] *PArch* I, 3, 2.
[93] Matt. 12, 32.
[94] *PArch* I, 1, 1, and 4.
[95] I, 3, 4.
[96] 1 Cor. 2, 10.

Next Origen speaks, as we have seen, of the trinitarian appropriations, attributing to the Father the gift of being, to the Son the gift of rationality, to the Spirit the gift of sanctity: He is to be found therefore in the saints and it is He who is preparing the Church, purified of her sins, to become a holy people. One might think, because of this noblest function and also because of the passage about blasphemy against the Spirit, of a hierarchical Trinity in which the Spirit predominates: but Origen refuses to place the Spirit above the Father and the Son:[97] see the discussion above about the Son, which deals with what Jerome and Justinian thought they found. 'A unique source of deity (the Father) governs the universe by his Word and his Reason (the Son) and sanctifies by the Spirit (the breath) of his mouth everything that is worthy of sanctification.'[98] Or again in the *Commentary on John*[99] the 'matter of the charisms', which is identified with the Holy Spirit, is produced (*energoumenēs*) by God, procured (*diakonoumenēs*) by Christ and subsists (*hyphestoses*) according to the Holy Spirit. So the charisms are the Holy Spirit in person.

Another chapter of the *Treatise on First Principles* is devoted to the Holy Spirit.[100] Its first concern is to affirm against Marcion and Valentinus, who are specifically mentioned, that there is only one Holy Spirit who inspired both the Testaments, just as there is only one Father and one Son. But while in the old covenant the Spirit was only given to the prophets, now, after the coming of the Saviour, it is poured out abundantly over the whole Church and teaches how to read the Scriptures in their spiritual sense. This Holy Spirit distributes the charisms, for in Him is found 'all the nature of the gifts': this expression 'nature' has the same meaning as as that of 'matter' (*hylē*) which we have just noted in the *Commentary on John*[101] and the charisms correspond to a certain extent to what scholastic theology was to call actual graces, that is graces attached to an act or to a function. Origen then attacks, without specifically naming them, the Montanists who attribute the name of Paraclete to 'I know not what vile spirits', that is to the demons who produce unconscious esctasy which they unworthily confuse with the Holy Spirit. Then he studies the word Paraclete which, applied to the Spirit, seems to him to mean comforter and, applied to Christ, to mean intercessor.

Another important passage about the Holy Spirit is to be found in the *Commentary on John*.[102] Its starting point is in John 1, 3: 'All things were made by him (= the Word)'. Three opinions are then put forward: either

[97] See above p. 192 what we say about the inverse hierarchy supposed by Jerome and Justinian, contradicted by Pamphilus and Athanasius.
[98] *PArch* I, 3, 7.
[99] II, 10 (6), 77.
[100] II, 7.
[101] II, 10 (6), 77.
[102] II, 10 (6), 73–88.

the Holy Spirit owes his existence to the Word, being included in these 'all things'; or He does not so owe it, being without origin; or He has not really an existence of his own (*ousia idia*) different from that of the Father and the Son: this last solution is modalist, and Origen embraces the first one. So there are three subsistant realities (*hypostases*, identical with *ousia idia*), the Father, the Son and the Holy Spirit, and – this is his answer to the second hypothesis – only the Father is without origin. The Spirit is then the highest of the beings that come from the Father by the Son: that is why He is not called a Son. Only the Son is son by nature and the Holy Spirit needs the intermediary function of the Son to subsist individually, and also to be wise, intelligent, just and all that He is and share in all the *epinoiai* of the Son. One cannot make of the word *egeneto* in John 1, 3 ('was made') a pretext for claiming that the Spirit is for Origen a creature: that would be to forget what we have said above[103] about the interchangeability before Nicaea of the verbs *gignomai* and *gennāo* as well as their derivatives with one n or two, to signify creation or generation.

At first sight this passage seems to contradict a text from the *Treatise on First Principles* of which we have not yet spoken.[104] Origen rejects the idea that the Holy Spirit knows because the Son reveals: but the reason for this rejection is that it suggests a Holy Spirit that passes from ignorance to knowledge. It would be stupid to call Him Holy Spirit and to attribute to Him, even for a moment, any ignorance; or to say that He was not previously Holy Spirit but became such by progress. In that case He would not have been included in the unity of the Trinity with the Father and the Son. In fact He was always Holy Spirit.

It is perfectly possible to reconcile these two passages. The point of the second is that the Holy Spirit is such from all eternity and did not begin to be such nor to possess the knowledge of it. But that is compatible with the statement of the other passage: the Holy Spirit derives his existence, his knowledge and everything that He is from the Father by the Son. That is so from all eternity, like the generation of the Son and there has never been any change in Him. We are clearly dealing here with the divine act that gives Him his existence and not simply with his manifestation to men with the 'economy'.

The *Commentary on Romans* contains a lot of expositions of the functions and the Holy Spirit and his gifts.[105]

In his *Treatise on the Holy Spirit* Basil who, in spite of his reservations, is generally favourable towards Origen, writes:

---

[103] See p. 174.
[104] I, 3, 4.
[105] For example X, 1 (PG 14). All the passages of the Epistle to the Romans which speak of the Holy Spirit are commented on in this writing.

However, the man did not have ideas on the Spirit that were absolutely healthy: yet in many places he too, moved by the force of custom, spoke of the Holy Spirit in terms than conform to piety.[106]

Unfortunately Basil does not tell us what inspired this judgement and the texts which he quotes favourably are orthodox. We may wonder whether Basil was truly conscious of the progress on the doctrine of the Holy Spirit occasioned by the reaction to the Pneumatomachoi and effected by him and the other Cappadocians, progress based on laborious research which is Origen's. Awareness of the development of dogma is a relatively recent thing.

*   *   *

We explained above the subordinationism for which Origen was blamed, which is also found in the other Ante-Nicenes, by showing that it was not in contradiction with orthodoxy because it does not express an inequality of power – the Father communicates to the Son and the Son to the Spirit all that they are except the fact of being Father or Son – but rather expresses realities which orthodoxy of necessity recognises, origin and mediation. We have indeed spoken of clumsy texts, but these are in fact very few. The most troublesome is the following: 'We say that the Saviour and the Holy Spirit exceed all creatures without possible comparison, in a wholly transcendent way but that they are exceeded by the Father by as much or even more than they exceed the other beings, and not the first comers.'[107] Origen is here opposing those who exaggerate the honour paid to the Son, ignoring John 14, 28 'The Father is greater then I', an expression which Origen takes of the Word and not of the God-Man, as certain post-Nicenes like Hilary of Poitiers will also do. It is explicitly a matter of 'glory' (doxa) and not of power. If the Father exceeds the two others in glory, it is because He is their Father, and the Alexandrian finds the justification for this in John 14, 28. Of course later orthodoxy would not express it like that, it would avoid anything that could express a superiority of the Father over the other two: this subordinationism is, however, of a totally different kind from that of the Arians and when this word is used attention must be paid to its different meanings, or else we shall cast into heresy the whole Church of the martyrs, for virtually all the Fathers of that period can be accused of subordinationism.

Except for the application to Christ's humanity of the pre-existence of souls which we are now going to study more completely as we deal with the origins of humanity, Origen's doctrine of the Trinity and the Incarnation constitutes, if it is read in its historical context, a clear advance on previous times. Some have seen in Origen 'the common

[106] XXIX, 73 (SC 17 or 17bis).
[107] ComJn XIII, 25, 151.

ancestor of the Arian heresy and of the Cappadocian orthodoxy' which overcame Arianism. That is a striking formula, brilliant and paradoxical, to be sure. But if Origen had an influence on Arius – and influences from the school of Antioch bore on the heresiarch also, coming from his teacher Lucian of Antioch and through him from Paul of Samosata – that influence came from misunderstood fragments of Origen, not from his doctrine as a whole.[108]

[108] Such is the conclusion that emerges, very disputable in any case, from R. Lorenz, *Arius judaizans? Untersuchungen zur dogmengeschichtlichen Einordnung des Arius*, Göttingen. 1980: the Arian conception of the Son comes, not only from Origen's doctrine of the Logos, but from his conception of the pre-existent soul of the Word!

11

The Church of the
Pre-Existence[a] and the Fall

For Origen the essence of the divine creation consisted in the rational beings, the non-rational creatures having been made by God at a second stage as it were, after the fault of the first ones: their importance is secondary and relative to man.[1] The creation of the angels and demons was originally indistinguishable from that of man since they are differentiated only by the depth of their original fall. Origen's angelology and demonology are fairly well developed but we shall not give a complete exposition of them: on the first point the reader may consult J. Daniélou's *Origène*,[2] of which this is one of the best parts.

One principle dominates Origen's cosmology: at the end is like the beginning. The end will consist in the submission of all to God, as Paul says: God will then be all in all.[3] So it is by starting at the end that Origen will try to understand the beginning. All that is said, of course, 'more by way of discussion and enquiry than of certain and exact definition':[4] we are still engaged in a research theology. On the other hand many points studied by Origen show that this similarity between end and beginning must not be taken too strictly to mean a perfect identity and equality: beginning and end are similar because of the submission of all to God, but that does not exclude the possibility of progress between the beginning and the end.

Origen raises several times the question of successive worlds. He does so hypothetically: otherwise these successive worlds, implying indefinite possibilities of new falls would be incompatible with the final end which is the apocatastasis. What does he mean by that? He does not say exactly.

[a] *'The Pre-Existence'*
It has been suggested to me that this word, which I use to translate Fr Crouzel's term 'La Préexistence' cannot be used absolutely in English, but only in such expressions as 'the pre-existence of souls'; and that I should say instead 'the pre-existent state', 'the pre-existent world', 'the pre-existent age', 'the pre-existent dispensation'. Well, which? I prefer to copy Fr Crouzel's all-embracing term rather than to take it upon myself, in each context, to decide which alternative is appropriate. If this is a neologism in English, then let it be introduced as a technical term of which the meaning is at least as clear as the concept for which it stands.
[1] Such is the essential argument of G. Dorival for refusing to see metempsychosis in the *Peri Archon*, in spite of Jerome: 'Origène, a-t-il enseigné la transmigration des âmes dans des corps d'animaux?', in *Origeniana Secunda*, Rome, 1980, pp. 11–32.
[2] Pp. 219–247.
[3] 1 Cor. 15, 23–28; *PArch* I, 6, 1–2.
[4] Ibid.

From what he says himself we may distinguish first the intelligible (*noētos*) world of the ideas, reasons and mysteries contained in the Word, then the world of the pre-existent intelligences (*noeros*), next the present world, finally that of the resurrection. Moreover, the words *kosmos* and *aiōn*, *mundus* and *saeculum*, world and age, stand in his work for notions lacking in precision.

This chapter will contain two parts: first the hypothesis of the pre-existence of the souls, and then that of the original fall that occurred in this pre-existence.[5]

The pre-existence of the souls

We have seen that the world, co-eternal with God, as clearly explained in the *Treatise on First Principles* I, 4, 3–5, is that of the 'ideas' and the 'reasons' and not that of the intelligences. The latter began to be, and that is the reason for their congenital 'accidentality'.[6]

So all the rational creatures, those which would later become angels, men, demons, were created together and absolutely equal. They were absorbed in the contemplation of God and formed the Church of the pre-existence, united like the Bride to the Bridegroom with the pre-existent intelligence that was joined to the Word and had been created with them. We shall see later why Origen preferred to call them intelligences rather than souls.[7]

We saw when we were expounding the trichotomic anthropology that these intelligences were led by their *pneuma* and clothed in ethereal bodies, the body being an essential characteristic of the creature as opposed to the Trinity; also that they were all created after the image of God, not only those which would become men, but also those who would be the angels, and even those who, denying their participation in God but without being able to destroy it, would be the demons.

This theory of the pre-existence, which included the humanity of the Christ, is for Origen, following the consistent line of his theology when

[5] Most studies of Origen deal with the pre-existence and the fall: the ancient expositions need to be treated with caution and there are few general accounts of more recent date. However, in addition to the articles indicated in the course of this chapter, we may mention a few others which touch on particular points; and with them we are more or less in agreement: G. Bürke, 'Des Origenes Lehre vom Urstand des Menschen', *Zeitschrift für katholische Theologie* 72, 1950, 1–39; U. Bianchi, 'Presupposti platonici dualistici di Origene, *De Principiis*,' in *Origeniana Secunda*, pp. 33–56; A. Castagno Monaci, 'L'idea della preesistenza delle anime e l'esegesi di Rm 9, 9–21', Ibid. 69–78; G. Sfameni Gasparro, 'Doppia creazione e peccato di Adamo nel *Peri Archon;* Fondamenti biblici e presupposti platonici dell' esegesi origeniana', Ibid. 57–67.

[6] *PArch* II, 9, 2.

[7] These intelligences are generally denoted by the plural *noes* from *nous*. This form belongs to the *koine* and later Greek. But as far as Origen is concerned this plural; is only attested by texts written after him, wrongly quoted by P. Koetschau in his edition GCS V of the *Peri Archon* as representing his thought. We have never found in the Greek works of Origen the word *nous* in the plural. As he declines this word according to the Attic declension and not the *koine*, unless he is quoting the New Testament, he would certainly not have used the plural *noes* but *noi*.

he is not relying directly on Scripture, a hypothesis, but a favoured hypothesis which constantly governs his thought even when he does not mention it specifically. And it does not seem that he ever accorded the least probability to the other two solutions current among Christians of the problem of the origin of the souls: these we shall expound shortly.

Where does this hypothesis come from and what are the reasons for it? The answer to the first question is in no doubt: it comes from Platonism. That is true, but it seems that the reasons for the pre-existence were not the same in Origen as in Plato. Indeed there is in Origen's work scarcely any clear allusion to the contemplation of the ideas in the pre-existence and to the reminiscence that would permit man to recover those ideas through the perceptible beings that share in them, in the course of his earthly existence. Although for Origen the perceptible beings are the images of divine mysteries, among which are the ideas contained in the Word, there are few clear and indisputable allusions in his work to reminiscence. Twice, however, there is reference[8] to an instruction received from God before entering the earthly body, an instruction which the soul clothed in its earthly body remembers: but it is not a matter of recognising in perceptible creatures the ideas in which they participate, but of being instructed in divine things: that is expressed more by way of question asked than of statement made and may also be a consequence of the doctrine of the image of God.[9]

In fact the reasons which caused Origen to put forward this hypothesis are Christian ones: it was first the problem of the origin of the soul and this was posed in his day; and then the controversy with the Valentinians and the Marcionites. In the preface to the *Treatise on First Principles*[10] Origen shows how uncertain the rule of faith was in his time about the origin of the soul:

> In regard to the soul, whether it takes its rise from the transference of the seed, in such a way that the principle or substance of the soul can be regarded as inherent in the seminal particles of the body itself; or whether it has some other beginning and whether this beginning is begotten or unbegotten, or at any rate whether it is imparted to the body from without or no; all this is not very clearly defined in the teaching.'[b]

Pamphilus comments on this text in his *Apology for Origen*.[11] He observes that there are in the Church a great many opinions on this subject and he lists them. Some hold that the souls are created by God and inserted by Him into the body as it is formed in the maternal womb: but this opens the way to accusing God of injustice, in view of the inequality

---

[8] ComJn XX, 7, 52; PEuch XXIV, 3.

[9] In spite of M. B. von Stritzky, 'Die Bedeutung der Phaidros interpretation für die Apokatastasislehre des Origenes', *Vigiliae Christianae* 31, 1977, 282–297.

[10] I, pref. 5.

[b] Translated Butterworth, p. 4.

[11] IX: PG 17, 604 C–607 A.

of human conditions. This solution is called creationism, but that term leads to confusion for in any case for a Christian the soul is created by God: here it simply expresses the point that it is the object of an immediate and direct creation. For their opponents, called Traducianists, there is also a creation but indirect and mediate: they suppose that the soul derives with the body from the paternal seed. The fact is that in the predominant, though not the universal, opinion of antiquity, the child comes entirely from the paternal seed, the mother being as it were the recipient or the soil in which the seed grows. This second alternative is also open to grave objections. If the soul is truly that breath which the Lord in the beginning breathed into Adam,[12] then how can it come with the body from the seed of the father? Does not this then mean that it will die with the body, a conclusion that our faith cannot accept? For the immortality of the soul and the final retribution are professed by the rule of faith,[13] as we find it in the Preface to the *Treatise on First Principles.* Pamphilus adds that we cannot treat as heretics those who hold these two opinions, in spite of the grave objections that are made to them, because nothing certain is said on the subject in Scripture or in the apostolic preaching and that we cannot accuse Origen of heresy because of his doctrine of the pre-existence, when he said what seemed best to him.

Indeed, since this point was not defined in the rule of faith, Origen thought, in conformity with the guiding intention of the *Peri Archōn*, that it was left to the theological investigation which could on the double basis of Scripture and reason formulate hypotheses. This opinion could not be charged with heresy in his time because the rule of faith contained nothing on the subject and it provided a way of escape from the objections raised against the two other possible hypotheses. Furthermore, two polemical issues are at stake. The original equality of all the rational creatures, who would only be differentiated as the result of the fault following the free decisions of each, is a reply to the Valentinian conception of different kinds of souls, a view that belies individual responsibility, the 'pneumatics' being saved without merit and the 'hylics' damned without culpability, free will only playing its part after a fashion in the case of the 'psychics'. The hypothesis of the pre-existence also had in Origen's eyes the advantage of providing him with an argument against the most difficult objection advanced by the Marcionites against the goodness of the Creator God: the inequality of human conditions at birth. Is it by the action of a good God that a child is born blind or afflicted with other infirmities which it could not have deserved, that some are born in civilised countries, among the Greeks of course, and others in barbarous regions? Origen's reply will be that the condition in which a man comes into this world is the consequence of the seriousness

[12] Gen. 2, 7.
[13] *PArch* pref. 5.

of an original fault committed in the pre-existence: he even speaks of a preliminary divine judgement preceding birth, analogous to the Last Judgement.[14] He had no difficulty in finding Scriptural support, especially the story of Jacob and Esau, the one loved, the other hated by God at birth.[15]

In the centuries immediately following the Alexandrian the origin of souls did not become much clearer, but the pre-existence came to be seen as not only mythical but even heretical. It was opposed at the beginning of the 4th century by Peter of Alexandria. At the same period, as we saw, Pamphilus of Caesarea explained and excused it but did not adopt it. The compilers of the *Philocalia of Origen*, Basil of Caesarea and Gregory of Nazianzus would discreetly excise from their quotations of the *Treatise on First Principles*, and especially from the chapter on free will, passages where it is too bluntly expressed. It was bitterly attacked during the first Origenist crisis, but they got no further on the underlying question. Rufinus confesses himself embarrassed and ignorant about the origin of the soul in the *Apology* that he addressed to Pope Anastasius.[16] The only thing he says is 'what the Church teaches clearly, that God is the creator of souls and bodies'. Augustine himself always hesitated about this subject: this can be seen in a letter to Jerome[17] in which he shows himself concerned about the evil and inequality of human conditions and his *Retractations*[18] contain evidence of similar difficulties.

The original fault in the pre-existence

So the pre-existence of souls is only to be understood along with the original fault that occurs within it, for it is only when this is also taken into account that it can counter the Marcionite attacks on the Creator God by showing that the different situations in which rational creatures find themselves result from decisions of their own free will. Note also that Origen's doctrine of original sin is not confined to what we are now discussing and contains statements which were at the time traditional and long would so remain: the impurity of the child at birth is for him the reason why baptism is necessary and justifies infant baptism in particular; this impurity is linked with the carnal act that brought him into existence, etc. So it is only one explanation among others of the original fault that is linked with the pre-existence.

The rational creatures were, remember, absorbed in the contemplation of God as the blessed will be in the final restoration. They formed a unity, a Church, whose Head and Bridegroom was the Christ in his pre-existent

[14] *PArch* II, 9, 8.
[15] Mal. 1, 2–3 taken up again in Rom. 9, 11: thus *PArch* III, 1, 22.
[16] §6: CChr XX.
[17] 131 in the correspondence of Jerome: CUFr VIII.
[18] I, 1, 3; II, XLV (LXXI); II, LVI (LXXXIII): CSEL, XXXVI.

humanity. The fall would disrupt this Church and put an end to this unity. The reason for the fall is expressed in two ways, both closely associated with the practice of the spiritual life. The first is *satietas*, being satiated with the contemplation of the divine.[19] This Latin term translates the Greek *koros:* it does not mean that the divine infinity can in some way surfeit a creature, but as Marg. Harl[20] has shown in an analysis of the word, *koros* and *satietas* express the boredom of contemplation, something like the 'accidie' which is for eastern monks one of the great temptations of the monastic life, boredom with the spiritual and finally with everything. A second explanation[21] derives from an etymology that was classical among the Greeks, but probably mistaken,[22] linking *psychē*, soul, with *psychos*, cold. God is fire and warmth. Moving further away from God the intelligences got cold and became souls. So we are talking about a decline in fervour and charity. The reduction from intelligence into soul is a matter of degree, for not all fell to the same level. Hence the diversity of rational creatures in their different orders, angels, men, demons, and within each order a continuous diversity. The original fall is thus not the immediate cause, but the motive for the diversity of the perceptible world which God created after it.

In any case the fall is due to the free will which is one of the essential characteristics of the rational creature and which, in Origen's consistent doctrine, God respects and never coerces, though He appeals to it constantly. In the exposition of the rule of faith given in the preface to the *Treatise on First Principles*[23] we read:

> This also is laid down in the Church's teaching, that every rational soul is possessed of free will and choice . . . There follows from this the conviction that we are not subject to necessity, so as to be compelled by every means, even against our will, to do either good or evil. For if we are possessed of free will, some spiritual powers may very likely be able to urge us on to sin and others to assist us to salvation; we are not, however, compelled by necessity to act either rightly or wrongly, as is thought to be the case by those who say that human events are due to the course and motion of the stars, not only those events which fall outside the sphere of our freedom of will but even those that lie within our own power.[c]

In the face of the pagan determinism represented by astrology and the philosophies inspired by it, in the face also of the gnostic determinism that assigns to each man's proper nature the cause of salvation or

---

[19] *PArch* I, 3, 8 and I, 4, 1.

[20] 'Recherches sur l'origénisme d'Origène: la satiété (koros) de la contemplation comme motif de la chute des âmes': *Studia Patristica* VIII (*Texte und Untersuchungen* 93), 1966, 374–405.

[21] *PArch* II, 8, 3–4.

[22] See P. Chantraine, *Dictionnaire etymologique de la langue grecque: Histoire des mots*, vol. III, Paris, 1968, pp. 1294–1296.

[23] §5.

[c] Translated Butterworth p. 5.

damnation, Origen was to remain in all his thought a tenacious upholder of human free will, one of the controlling ideas of his theology and, in dialogue with the divine action one of the actuating forces of his cosmology. He devoted to it one of the major chapters of the *Treatise on First Principles*[24] preserved in Greek by the *Philocalia:* after a discussion on philosophical lines he strives to set aside the objections that can be made to it on the basis of Scriptural texts: this chapter had a considerable influence and the *De libero arbitrio* of Erasmus was in large measure inspired by it.[25]

Was the fall universal, affecting all the intelligences? One at least certainly escaped, the one that was united to the Word, for Origen says it was impeccable, transformed into the Word, as the iron plunged in fire becomes fire.[26] But have not others escaped the fall? Most authors say no, starting from an *a priori:* the fall must have been as universal as the final apocatastasis. We shall see in the last chapter of this volume whether it is true to say that Origen believes clearly in a universal apocatastasis. As for the universality of the fall, that seems to be contradicted by certain passages of the *Treatise on First Principles* which, as Manlio Simonetti[27] has shown, suggest that some intelligences escaped the fall.[28] Among the angelic creatures who have not sinned, some, Origen thinks, have been incarnated like the Christ, not as the consequence of a fault, but to serve men and to help in the mission of the Redeemer. The *Commentary on John*[29] puts forward a hypothesis of this kind about John the Baptist and, on the basis of an apocryphal writing, *The Prayer of Joseph*, about several patriarchs of the Old Testament. Jerome's *Commentary on Ephesians*,[30] inspired in large measure by Origen's, reproduces on Eph. 1, 4 the same opinion about the prophets and saints of the Old Testament, sent on earth and placed in earthly bodies without sin to help in the Redemption.

1. Are all the angels in this situation for Origen or only the higher ranks of them, the others having sinned, but less profoundly than the men and the demons? It is difficult to say. The *Treatise on First Principles*[31] states that the angels got their respective functions higher or lower, of command or of obedience, according to their own merits: the contrary would imply a partiality unworthy of the Creator. Origen's insistence on merit is surprising, but it comes from his opposition to Valentinus. In any case it presupposes that there is a diversity of merit among the angels. Does this

---

[24] III, 1: or *Philoc* 21; on the same subject *Philoc* 22–27.
[25] A. Godin, *Erasme lecteur d'Origène*, Geneva, 1982, pp. 469–489.
[26] *PArch* II, 6, 4–6.
[27] 'Due note sull'angelologia origeniana' *Rivista di cultura classica e medievale*, 4, 1962, 169–208.
[28] *PArch* I, 5, 5; I, 6, 2; I, 8, 4; II, 9, 6; IV, 2, 7.
[29] II, 29–31 (24–25), 175–192 especially 186–190.
[30] PL 26, 446–447.
[31] I, 5, 3; I, 9, 1.

arise because some have progressed beyond a state once common to them all, as certain texts do not deny, or does it arise from different degrees of fall? A homily on Numbers, relying on 1 Cor. 6, 3 'Know you not that we shall judge the angels?', shows the guardian angels being judged with their human wards at the Last Judgement, and that implies that they could sin.[32] Perhaps even the duties of the guardian angels, that some are in charge of individuals, some of nations, some of churches, some even of the different natural kingdoms, reflect a kind of merciful punishment because of the primitive fall.

With the angels mention must be made of the stars. For the *Treatise on First Principles*,[33] following the philosophical tradition, but always hypothetically, shows the stars as animate and rational beings, whose souls pre-existed and who have been subjected to the indignity of visible bodies for the service of men. They also would be capable of sinning. Is their entry into a body the consequence of a fault, as quite a few ancient or modern interpreters of Origen seem to think, or did it happen simply for the service of men, without demerit on their part? The Rufinian text seems to prefer the second solution.

2. At the other extreme from the angels are the demons whose names are parallel to those of the angelic orders, Thrones, Dominations, Principalities, Powers, etc.[34] They also can be guardians, guardians in reverse, trying to make those they have taken charge of sin, whether individuals or nations. At their head is their chief, Satan, the Devil, the Evil One, in whom Origen sees the 'Principle' of the fall following Job 40, 14 (19) in the Septuagint: 'He is made to be the first of the works (*plasma*) of God, to be the laughing-stock of his angels.'[35] This word *plasma*, literally 'modelling', denotes the creation of the perceptible world which, as we shall see, was to follow the fall. Or in other words: 'He is the first terrestrial, having been the first to fall from the higher realities and having desired a life other than the best, he was worthy to become the beginning neither of the production (*ktisma*) nor of the creation (*poiēma*) but of the modelling (*plasma*) of the Lord, made to be the laughing-stock of the angels.'[36] That does not mean that Satan and his demons have earthy bodies as men have: their bodies are 'by nature something subtle like a light breath'[37] just as the bodies of the angels are ethereal.[38] The fall of Satan,[39] bringing down all the others is figured in the prophet Ezekiel[40]

[32] *HomNb* XI, 4.
[33] I, 7, 2–5.
[34] *PArch* I, 5, 2.
[35] *ComJn* I, 17, 95.
[36] *ComJn* XX, 22 (20), 182: note the series *ktisma, poiēma, plasma* noted p. [230–231].
[37] *PArch* I, pref. 8.
[38] *ComMt* XVII, 30 (GCS X).
[39] *PArch* I, 5, 4–5.
[40] 28, 11–19.

by the Prince of Tyre and in Isaiah[41] by the King of Babylon. Origen thus inaugurates a tradition: the affirmation of the greatness of Satan before the fall when he bore 'the seal of the likeness', that is to say shared in the image of God; the pride which brought about the catastrophe; the name Lucifer, *Eosphoros*, 'bringer of the dawn', denoting the morning star and applied also to Christ. This angelic origin of Satan is also affirmed by the rule of faith according to the preface of the *Treatise on First Principles:*[42]

> In regard to the devil and his angels and the opposing spiritual powers, the Church teaching lays it down that these beings exist, but what they are and how they exist it has not explained very clearly. Among most Christians, however, the following opinion is held, that this devil was formerly an angel, but became an apostate and persuaded as many angels as he could to fall away with him; and these are even now called his angels.[d]

And when the rule of faith mentions the free will with which the rational soul is endowed, it affirms of the latter:[43]

> It is engaged in a struggle against the devil and his angels and the opposing powers; for these strive to weigh the soul down with sins.[e]

The chapter of the *Treatise on First Principles* on free will is followed by a long passage[44] on the wars that the diabolic powers wage against men.

So the demons were originally, like the angels and the men, *logika,* rational beings, in the predominantly supernatural sense that that word normally has in Origen: they shared in the divine Logos, the Word and Reason of God. But by the free choice of their will they rejected this participation in the Logos and became *aloga,* beings without reason, thus assimilating themselves in a way to the animals, becoming spiritual beasts so to speak. That is why the adverse images which, because of sin, conceal the participation of man in the image of God, are called both diabolical and bestial.[45] Because of their malice the demons cannot understand spiritual realities and are ignorant of everything concerning salvation.[46] Similarly Origen sometimes gives a supernatural significance to existence, participation in God who revealed Himself to Moses as 'the One who is'.[47] Having renounced this participation in the source of their being, the demons have become in a sense *ouk ontes,* 'non-beings'.[48] The possibility

---

[41] 14, 12–22.
[42] §6.
[d] Translated Butterworth p. 4.
[43] §5.
[e] Translated Butterworth p. 72.
[44] III, 2–4.
[45] See our *Théologie de l'Image de Dieu chez Origène,* pp. 181–215.
[46] See our *Origène et la 'connaissance mystique'* pp. 421–425.
[47] Ex 3, 14.
[48] *ComJn* II, 13 (7), 98.

of the demons being converted is not as clear in Origen as is usually
asserted: we shall come back to this in the final chapter on the restoration
or apocatastasis. In the *Treatise on First Principles*[49] Origen puts the
question without answering it, leaving open two possibilities: either
conversion is possible because they still have free will; or 'on the contrary
would not the lasting and inveterate malice change in some way through
habit into nature?' The reason behind the second alternative is that free
will is more and more enslaved by bad habits which tend to become
'second nature'. That really is an opinion of Origen's and not of the
translator Rufinus for it is found several times in the works that are
preserved in Greek.[50]

> 3. The third order of rational creatures is composed of those spirits who are
> judged fit by God to replenish the human race, these are the souls of
> men.[51]

It is because they have been implicated in the primitive fall in a less
grave way than the demons and because there is for them some hope of
cure that they have been put into this perceptible and terrestrial world as a
place of correction.

4. This perceptible and terrestrial world was thus the result of a kind of
second creation comprising the inanimate beings, the vegetables and the
animals. The beginning of Book II of the *Treatise on First Principles* is
about the world and its different areas, land, sea, air, sky, etc. We need
not expound here what these complicated texts contain: they have the
character of discussion and are adapted to ancient astronomy. Origen is
struck by the variety of this perceptible world, created in this way to suit
the needs of the rational creatures which the original fall has made very
different from each other for some have fallen lower than others. But to
this very varied world God has nevertheless given a unity. The human
body, ethereal in the pre-existence, has become terrestrial, analogous to
this perceptible world in which man must now live: we shall say no more
on this point which has already been dealt with. Underlying this
conception of the world there is an idea of matter which comes from
Greek philosophy. The matter of which the world is composed is a kind
of amorphous substratum, capable of receiving different qualities and
changing them, for it is not permanently involved in any: however it
cannot exist without being informed by qualities. But, unlike the
philosophers, Origen refuses to admit that this matter is uncreated, for
everything was made by God out of nothing.[52] This conception of matter
with the quality that informs it explains not only the changes which occur

---

[49] I, 6, 3.
[50] *ComJn* XX, 21 (19), 174: *HomJr* XVIII, 1; *FragmMt* 141 (GCS XII/1).
[51] *PArch* I, 8, 4.
[52] *PArch* II, 1, 4; IV, 4, 6–7; and many other texts.

in nature, but also the sameness and difference which exist between the ethereal body of the pre-existence and the terrestrial body, as well as that, as we shall see later, between the terrestrial body and the risen body.

There is thus a link between sin and earthly corporeality. Of what kind is it? Platonist influence is undeniable but how big a part does it play? Must we see somehow in the thinking of Origen a necessary link which would even impose itself in a way on God, thus implying a dualism?[53] All that seems an exaggeration. First, those who have sinned most profoundly, the demons, are not put into earthly bodies, nor attached like men to the perceptible world: if the devil is called the First Terrestrial, that is because he was the source of the fall which caused the creation of the perceptible world, but not because he bore a terrestrial body. So there is no necessary link between sin and terrestrial materiality. If man has been put in that situation, it is in accordance with God's plan, because he can still be cured, and being placed in the perceptible world, which he enters by means of the earthly quality his body has taken on, is a trial, a merciful chastisement, a prelude to the Redemption. To understand how in Origen's view life in the perceptible constitutes a trial of our love for God we must go back to the conception of sin which we have several times expounded in this volume, especially in relation to virginity and marriage.[54] While it is good in itself, for it has been created by God and is the image of the divine mysteries, the perceptible puts man into a state of temptation, for he is always tempted to treat the perceptible as the absolute he is seeking, a false and deceptive absolute for it is only an image of the true absolute. Such is, as we have several times seen, the essence of sin for Origen, an act of idolatry which puts the perceptible in God's place, and an adultery in terms of the theme of the mystical marriage. If man, with the help of divine grace which comes to him through Christ the Redeemer, overcomes this temptation, he offers to God, in union with Christ, a love that saves him.

So there is no question of a necessary link between the original fall and the perceptible world, but of a free decision by God, the only thing compatible with the divine freedom, for any necessity, even the most tenuous that can be imagined, would in fact deprive Him of his divinity. If we take the word dualism in its usual philosophical sense it means a doctrine which causes everything to be derived from two principles, of which each is irreducible to the other. It is clear that such a term cannot be applied to Origen's synthesis because of its author's very strong conception of the divine absolute and of creation out of nothing. Can one

[53] Such is the opinion expressed by U. Bianchi in the article mentioned in note 5. It was one of the main subjects of the colloquium held at Milan from 17 to 19 May 1979 between historians of religion and patristic scholars. The papers and discussions were published: *Archē e Telos: l'antropologia di Origene e di Gregorio di Nissa, Analisi storico-religiosa* (ed. U. Bianchi and H. Crouzel, Milan, 1981.

[54] See pp. 137–140.

see dualism in the thought of Plato himself? Even that seems disputable because of some uncertainties that remain and are illustrated by the divergent views of the historians of philosophy. Supposing that one can call Plato a dualist, one would then have to say that Origen took over in part a structure that was dualist in origin, but that his conception of God excludes all dualism. Nor can one say that Origen's doctrine is monist, reducing everything absolutely to a single principle, for it is marked profoundly by the fundamental paradox of Christianity, that of an almighty God freely creating a creature endowed with free will, that is to say called to accept God's will but able to oppose it. The interplay of the divine action and human freedom is one of the fundamental features of the synthesis expounded in the *Treatise on First Principles* and underlying all the Alexandrian's work. It is held in tension between dualism and monism.

It is also said quite frequently that for Origen the fall is something ineluctable, which was bound to happen: we think this statement lacks foundation. First, is it legitimate to pass in this way from the plane of fact on which Origen takes his stand – affirmatively about what the 'Church's preaching' delivers to him, hypothetically about his own speculations – to the plane of law? Since some of the rational creatures, in addition to the soul of the Christ, did not fall, this conclusion cannot be accepted. But supremely, to consider the fall ineluctable is to deny the free will of the creatures, who would not then be free, but in reality manipulated, and so would lack the respect which it is so often asserted that God shows towards them. If what is involved in the fall is a necessity that comes from God, then a quite unworthy idea of God is being put forward, for it would imply that he pretends to respect the freedom of men when in fact He does not do so, and it would attribute to the good God – and this is one of the charges Origen is constantly bringing against the Marcionites – the responsibility for evil. If it is suggested that this necessity does not come from God, that is to take away his divinity, imposing on Him, as on his creatures, a Destiny which determines them. Nothing is more contrary to the profound thought of our theologian.

To conclude this exposition of the fall, the motive for God's creation of the perceptible world, it would be tempting to sketch a parallel between Origen's conception and that of his principal adversaries, the Valentinians.[55] The two lower planes of the world, according to them, the Intermediate State, the kingdom of the Creator God, the Demiurge, and of the souls, and the Kenoma, place of the void, the domain of the cosmocrator, the devil, and the bodies, result from a drama played out in the Pleroma, the Paradise of the Aeons. This drama, which might irreverently be called, from the title of a children's book by the Countess of Ségur, 'The

[55] See in Irenaeus, *Adversus haereses* I, 1–9 (SC 264) the account of the doctrines of the Valentinian Ptolemy.

Misfortunes of Sophie', is as follows: Sophia, Wisdom, the last of the Aeons, was seized with an irrepressible desire to see the Father, the supreme God, which endangered the whole Pleroma by threatening to overturn its hierarchy. This inconceivable *hybris* was in the end detached from Sophia in the form of a misbegotten Aeon to which she gave birth, Sophia-Achamoth; she was expelled from the Pleroma that order might be restored. Such is the Valentinian version of the fall. From Achamoth will emerge the Intermediate State with its Demiurge and the Kenoma with its Cosmocrator, as well as the angelic and human creatures that populate them. Achamoth intervenes directly in the creation of the Pneumatics, by breathing, without the knowledge of the Demiurge, into some of the creatures the latter had made seeds coming from the Pleroma to which she belongs. In the eschatology when Achamoth, their mother, is finally received into the Pleroma and united with the Saviour, that is the masculine Aeon who was begotten to 'form' her and save her, the pneumatics will also be received there and united, as feminine elements, to the Saviour's angels.

Mythical as it is, Origen's version of the fall has little in common with this mythology. First, the fall is for him the work of rational creatures and not the result of a drama that took place in a transcendent world and of which one of the consequences would be the creation of human beings. Again, free will plays practically no part in the Valentinian gnōsis as events unfold. It is not present in the creatures, who do not yet exist, nor yet in Sophia, the initiator of the drama, for that irrepressible desire to see the Father is not a free act of will; nor is the process by which the Demiurge creates; perhaps to some extent the breathing in of the pneumatic seeds by Achamoth is one, but as in the distinction of the three natures, every thing is conceived to make the least possible room for free will.

⁕   ⁕   ⁕

The hypothesis of the pre-existence of the souls and the version of the fall that is linked with it, are certainly the most vulnerable parts of Origen's thought, and, as we have seen, they were soon contested by the Alexandrian's adversaries; they were not upheld, but only explained, by his defenders. However that was to be developed and would become one of essential points of later Origenism, as much in the 4th as in the 6th century. This is in part understandable on account of the polemic against the heretics of the 3rd century, Valentinians and Marcionites, and of the Middle Platonism which formed the universe of philosophical discourse in which Origen thought. All the elements in it are not valueless, especially the conception of sin.

One might wonder what is the connection between this supposed
prehistory of man and the narratives of creation in the Book of Genesis.
Unfortunately we no longer have, except for a few fragments and
information derived from later authors, the *Commentary on Genesis*
which would explain allegorically the first chapters of the book: we have
to be content with the first homily on the book which is probably less
explicit than the Commentary would have been, and also with scattered
allusions. As has been said about the trichotomic anthropology and the
image of God, chapter 1 of Genesis figures the creation of the pre-existent
intelligences, the mention of male and female applying not to a sexuality
that did not yet exist but to the pre-existent Christ with his Bride, the
Church of the pre-existence, the gathering of the intelligences. Chapter 2
speaks of the creation of the body, but there is a grave inexactitude about
this: if it is talking about the terrestrial and sexual body consequent on the
fall, how could Origen find this in chapter 2 which is before chapter 3 in
which the fall occurs? According to the evidence of Procopius of Gaza, as
we have seen,[56] the *Commentary on Genesis* interpreted it of the
'dazzling' body which clothed the pre-existent intelligence and then the
two creations, that of chapter 1 and that of chapter 2, ought to be
considered as concomitant, a creature not being able to exist without a
body. But in that case what was Origen doing with verses 21 to 25 of
chapter 2, about the creation of woman and her union with the man
through the care of God, a passage which took an important place in
Origen's conception of marriage as in that of the whole primitive Church.
Did he interpret it only of 'the great mystery'[57] of the union of Christ and
his Church and only indirectly of that of the man and the woman, its
image? In the *Commentary on Genesis* it was necessary for chapter 3 to
figure the fall and for the 'garments of skins' of verse 21, according to
Procopius of Gaza, to represent the earthly 'quality' which would
henceforth hide the 'dazzling body' which clothed the pre-existent
intelligence. Now it is only at that moment that one can speak of a second
creation concerning the perceptible world and likewise a sexed body:
Origen himself remarks that it is only after the departure from Paradise
that Scripture mentions that 'Adam knew his wife'.[58] To complicate the
picture still more let us add that it is by no means sure that Origen, even
as he allegorised them, did not see in Adam and Eve historical persons.
Certain expressions seem to show this and, in any case, for Origen as for
Paul, the allegorisation of a story is not incompatible with belief in its
historicity. The loss of the *Commentary on Genesis* prevents us
answering these questions, but we can be sure that Origen would have
extricated himself from all these difficulties with his usual skill.

[56] See pp. 91–92.
[57] *Eph* 5, 32.
[58] Gen. 4, 1: *Fragm 1 Cor.* XXIX *JThS* IX, 370.

12

The Church of the Present Age

In Origen's view the history of the Church is co-extensive with that of the rational beings: we have already been made aware of this several times. It began with the creation of the pre-existent intelligences. Their unity then constituted the Church of the pre-existence, united, as the Bride with the Bridegroom, with Christ in his pre-existent humanity. Its heavenly location is often called by Origen the heavenly Jerusalem, mother of the Logos, mother of the intelligences, higher worlds which seems indistinguishable from the 'bosom of the Father'. But the precosmic fall breaks this unity. The angels remain in the bosom of the Father, seeing the face of God, so forming the heavenly part of the Church in which they will be joined by the blessed, since, in Origen's view, unlike that of some of his contemporaries, the righteous go to Paradise even before the Resurrection: the rest of the Church, cast upon the earth, is broken by sin into a thousand pieces. But the Church is reconstituted after a fashion in the old Israel. Although she does not yet have the Bridegroom with her and the age is as it were a period of betrothal, the Bridegroom manifests Himself to her from time to time by theophanies in the primitive humano-angelic state of the pre-existence. But most of the time he uses messengers, the 'Bridegroom's friends', patriarchs, prophets and angels, to foster in the yet infant Church the love and desire for Him. All that is fully worked out in the *Commentary on the Song of Songs.*

At last comes the moment fixed by the Father for the Incarnation:

> And He left, for the sake of the Church. He, the Lord, who is the Bridegroom, the Father beside whom He dwelt when He was in the form of God; He left also his Mother, for He was also the Son of the Jerusalem above. He clove to his wife who had fallen down here and they became here on earth two in one flesh.[1]

The woes of Jeremiah are a prophecy of the Incarnation:

> He leaves his Father and his Mother, the Jerusalem above, He goes towards the earthly place and says: I have abandoned my home, I have left my inheritance.[2] His inheritance is the place where He lived with the angels, it

---

[1] *ComMt* XIV, 17 (GCS X); [a] Trans. J. Patrick, ANCL, IX, Edinburgh, 1897, p. 506.
[2] Jer. 12, 7.

was his condition among the holy powers. I have given my beloved soul into the hands of his enemies.[3] He has delivered up his soul into the hands of the enemies of that soul, into the hands of the Jews who killed him.[4]

As we have seen it is the God-Man who is directly the subject of the kenosis, and the Word only indirectly. And as for Jeremiah it is tragedy. The major part of the Synagogue, which was then the Church, rejected Him, had Him put to death, deceived Him with her adulterous lover, the Devil. In the bosom of the Church the Jews were replaced by those coming from the nations. Henceforth the Bride has the Bridegroom with her, but still partially, 'in a glass, darkly' and she yearns for the perfect union 'face to face',[5] the final and complete marriage. This will occur at the end of the ages.

> It is true: in the resurrection of the dead, people will no longer take husbands and wives, but will be like the angels in heaven.[6] But that is also true which is said, as in a parable about a marriage different from those on earth: The kingdom of heaven is like a human king who celebrated the wedding of his son,[7] and then: the kingdom of heaven will be like ten virgins, who, taking their lamps, etc.[8] So the King's Son will, at the resurrection of the dead, contract a marriage which is above every marriage which the eye has seen or the ear heard, or the heart of man conceived.[9] And this venerable, divine and spiritual marriage will be celebrated with ineffable words which it is not possible for man to pronounce[10] . . . a marriage of which it cannot be said: The two will be one flesh,[11] but more exactly: The Wife and the Husband are a single spirit.[12]

The three periods which follow the pre-existence correspond respectively to the Old Testament, the temporal Gospel and the eternal Gospel. In affirming that these two forms of the Gospel differ in the *epinoia*, a human way of looking at things,[13] Origen professes that they are identical in the *hypostasis*, the substance, and the *pragma*, the reality, terms which are usually the opposite of the *epinoia;* and the study we have made of the paradoxical situation of the New Testament, still image and at the same time reality,[14] shows Origen's acute sense of the essential dimension of the time of the Church here below, which we call sacramentalism: the divine realities are already given to us, but in realities which are themselves perceptible, under the veil of an image.

[3] Ibid.
[4] *HomJr* X, 7.
[5] 1 Cor. 13, 12.
[6] Matt. 22, 30.
[7] Matt. 22, 2.
[8] Matt. 15, 1.
[9] 1 Cor. 2, 9.
[10] 2 Cor. 12, 4.
[11] Gen. 2, 24.
[12] 1 Cor. 6, 17; *ComMt* XVII, 33 (GCS X).
[13] *ComJn* I, 8 (10), 44.
[14] Cf, pp. [151–155].

A more circumscribed notion of the sacrament was only to emerge in the High Middle Ages. One might say that for Origen the fundamental sacrament is the Christ, a man in whom 'resides bodily the fulness of the Deity,'[15] and after Him there are two other 'sacraments', not quite so fundamental, the Church, a human society which is the body of Christ, and the Scripture, a human book which expresses the Word of God. But here we are using languages which is not yet Origen's. Of the seven religious acts to which mediaeval theology will attach the name of sacrament five belong to his doctrine: baptism, eucharist, penance, marriage and orders. We have already spoken of marriage, we shall deal with orders through an exposition of the priesthood, and then we shall show briefly what he says about the three other sacraments.

The ecclesiastical hierarchy
Origen developed very strongly a doctrine of the Church seen mainly in its spiritual aspect. J. Chênevert has devoted a book to this, based on the *Commentary on the Song of Songs*, where it is chiefly though not exclusively found, and H. J. Vogt has also studied it in part of his work. On the visible Church, Origen's work also provides much information, although this is not developed on its own account but arises haphazard from the exegeses. An idea of its importance can be gained from A. Vilela's book, *La condition collégiale des prêtres au IIIe siècle.*[16]

The starting point of this information is especially the allegorical exegesis of the Levitical priesthood in the homilies on the Hexateuch. This not only pre-figures clerical functions in the Church, but, as constantly happens in Origen's work, has a whole spectrum of mutually enriching meanings: Christ's priesthood, the common priesthood of his body the Church, whence the priesthood of believers, the visible ministerial priesthood of the Church, the invisible priesthood of perfection, the heavenly priesthood of Christ and his angels. On the priesthood of believers one of the most characteristic passages is to be found at the end of the *Contra Celsum:*[17] the Christians do not take up arms because they are priests and thus share in the role which pagans ascribe in their priests. It is by their prayers that they contribute to the safety of the state.

The ministerial hierarchy is represented by the bishops, priests and deacons. Origen's homilies often criticise severely the faults of the clergy

[15] Col. 2, 9.
[16] In A. Vilela's book (Paris, 1971) 114 pages are devoted to Origen, 16 to Clement, 26 to Tertullian, 86 to Cyprian, 32 to Hippolytus: Origen and Cyprian are thus the principal sources. J. Chenevert, *L'Église dans le Commentaire d'Origène sur la Cantique des Cantiques*, Brussels/Montreal/Paris, 1969; H. J. Vogt, *Das Kirchenverständnis des Origenes*, Cologne/Vienna, 1976. On the priesthood Th. Schaeffer, *Das Priester-Bild im Leben und Werk des Origenes*, Frankfurt, 1977.
[17] VIII, 73.

who do not always live up to the very exacting ideal of holiness which ought in Origen's view to be theirs: the visible hierarchy is in fact the image of the hierarchy of holiness and ought consequently to share in that. He reproaches them, but without failing as a priest himself to take his share of the blame, with showing pride and arrogance, assuming the airs of lords, being authoritarian, of having career ambitions rather than regarding the ministry as a service, of being sometimes contemptuous of the humble and poor, of vacillating between an excessive rigour and a no less excessive indulgence.[18] Episcopal elections, made by the people – of which Origen hardly approves[19] – and by neighbouring bishops, are often manipulated by money, even at this time when martyrdom was a frequent occurrence, and by nepotism and family interests. The portrait is far from flattering, but it would not do to generalise from it about the period: addressed to Christians, the homilies tend to emphasise faults, as opposed to the *Contra Celsum* which was addressed to pagans. We may, however, conclude that even in those heroic times there were clergymen who did not live up to their vocation.

The requirements formulated for the clerical life are almost all monastic: separation from the world, poverty, total consecration to God. Separation from the world is required, not fully effective like of anchorites, because priests are before everything else pastors, but in a spiritual sense. They are present in the midst of the people, but they must not have a worldly spirit: they must bear with them everywhere their consecration to God. For:

> It is not in a place that the sanctuary must be sought, but in the actions of life, in morals. If these are in accordance with God's will, if they are in line with his precepts, then it matters little whether you are at home, or on the forum, it even matters little if you are at the theatre: If you are serving the Word of God then you are in the sanctuary, be in no doubt about it.[20]

As for the matrimonial situation of members of the clergy the only law to be found in Origen as in his contemporaries is that of 1 Tim. 3, 2 and 12, Tit. 1, 6, the 'law of monogamy': the bishop, the priest, the deacon must be 'the husband of one wife only', which means in the general understanding of the time, that they cannot re-marry if widowed and that men already married twice cannot be ordained. This 'monogamy' is contrasted with a 'bigamy' or a 'polygamy' of a successive kind, not with simultaneous bigamy which Roman law officially prohibited. Several attempts have been made to represent Origen as a partisan of celibacy or rather of ecclesiastical abstinence,[21] which was only required by a specific law at a later date, after the beginning of the 4th century (Council of

---

[18] All this is detailed by A. Vilela, *op.cit.*, pp. 65–79.
[19] *HomGn* III, 3; *HomNb* XXII, 4.
[20] *HomLv* XII, 4.
[21] The continence imposed on clerics who were married before their ordination.

Elvira): but to sustain that view texts have to be slightly twisted, especially the *Homily on Leviticus VI*.[22] Origen turns physical procreation, which was a duty for the priests and levites of the old law, into a spiritual procreation by an allegorical exegesis of a kind very common with him. But it is to force what he says somewhat to conclude that this spiritual procreation rules out physical procreation: in any case he does not clearly say so.

In the Latin of Rufinus and Jerome the word *sacerdos* is applied both to the bishop and the priest, the latter being subordinate to the former. The bishops and priests are sometimes regarded as equivalent to the apostles, the priests also to the seventy-two disciples. In the eucharistic assembly the bishops and priests are seated, the deacons stand to maintain order: the presbyterium is like the senate of a city. Bishops and priests have the right to maintenance from the contributions of the faithful, so that they can devote themselves entirely to their task. A lot more information on the life of the clergy is given in the course of the exegeses.

Baptism[23]

The Church's rite of baptism is placed by Origen, like the other sacraments, in a series of symbolisms, corresponding to the triple distinction of the Old Testament as shadow, the temporal Gospel as image, and the eternal Gospel as reality. There is in fact an Old Testament baptism pre-figured by the passage of the Red Sea under the leadership of Moses, figure of the law, contrasted with the crossing of the Jordan under Jesus, the son of Navē, Joshua, figure of 'my Jesus'. In the one case the salt water of the Red Sea is the harshness of the law with its literal precepts, in the other the fresh water of Jordan is the gentleness of the Gospel. The principal manifestation of this Old Testament baptism was that of John which is not to be confused with that of Jesus, administered in the Spirit and in fire. John's baptism is conferred beyond Jordan in that Transjordania which always represents for Origen the old covenant, since the Jordan, which stands for the Incarnation of Christ, has not yet been crossed. It is a perceptible baptism, turned towards the old realities, only signifying penitence.[24]

The baptism of Jesus, of course, is also perceptible, it is a baptism in water. But it is also by the realities in which it shares a baptism of Spirit and a baptism of fire.[25] These realities are multiple. A curious text seems to allow us to suppose that there is a 'real presence' of the Holy Spirit in

---

[22] §6.
[23] See C. Blanc. 'Le baptême d'après Origène', *Studia Patristica* XI (*Texte und Untersuchungen* 108), 1972, 113–124; H. Crouzel, 'Origène et la structure du sacrament', *Bulletin de Littérature ecclésiastique*, 63, 1962, 81–104.
[24] *ComJn* VI, 44 (26), 228–230; *FragmJn* LXXXI (GCS IV).
[25] *ComJn* VI, 43 (26), 223–224.

the water of baptism: 'Let us see whether the water is not distinguished from the Spirit by the *epinoia* only (that is to say, in a human way of looking at things) and not in its *hypostasis* (substance, its own reality)'.[26] We have already met this distinction in the case of the temporal Gospel and the eternal Gospel, a single reality in their *hypostasis*, differing only in the way man looks at them, the *epinoia*. There is an echo here of John 7, 38–39: '. . . from his bosom shall flow rivers of living water. He said that of the Spirit which those who believed in Him were about to receive,' and through this text of several others, of the Old Testament, representing the Spirit by flowing water.[27]

This gift of the Spirit, which effects the remission of sins and gives life, is associated in Rom. 6, 3 with the death and the resurrection of Christ to whom the baptised are conformed. The Passion was called baptism by Jesus Himself.[28] That is why martyrdom, being conformed in action to the death and resurrection of Christ, is the supreme baptism of which the baptism in water is a sacramental image. It would scarcely be in accordance with Origen's outlook to represent the baptism of blood as a kind of substitute for the baptism in water, as we used to hear it described in catechisms in days gone by: that would be somehow to subordinate the mystery to the image. Figuring the resurrection of Christ, baptism is the beginning of a 'first resurrection'[29] which takes effect 'in a glass, darkly', in contrast to the second resurrection, the final one, which will be 'face to face'. This expression 'first resurrection' comes from Apoc. 20, 5, in the pericope Apoc. 20, 1–6, which was the basic text for millenarian (or chiliastic) notions: by interpreting it in the light of Rom. 6, 3ff. Origen was certainly trying to disentangle it from that kind of interpretation, in a way that is perfectly in accordance with his capital distinction between the temporal Gospel and the eternal Gospel.

Baptism is also the image of another mysterious reality which we shall study more completely in the chapter on the eschatology, the baptism of fire, that is the eschatological purification, our Purgatory, of which Origen is the first great theologian and which he finds particularly indicated in 1 Cor. 3, 12–15. This will be given at the moment of Judgement and will purge the last stains: but for that it is necessary to have passed through the first baptism. We cannot resist the pleasure of quoting on this subject, in Jerome's version, a magnificent passage:

> Thus the Lord Jesus will stand in the river of fire beside the flaming sword,[30] and whoever, at the end of this life, wants to pass into Paradise

[26] *FragmJn* XXXVI (GCS IV).
[27] Isa 43, 20; 44, 3; 55, 1; 58, 11; Ezek 47, 1–12; Joel 3, 1; 4, 18; Zech 13, 1; 14, 8; Prov. 18, 4.
[28] Mark 10, 39; *ComMt* XVI, 6 (GCS X).
[29] H. Crouzel, 'La "première" et la "seconde" résurrection des hommes d'après Origène', *Didaskalia* 3, 1973, 3–19.
[30] Gen. 3, 24, the sword that kept Adam and Eve out of the Garden of Eden.

and still needs purification, He will baptise in this river, and then will let him go on to the place he desires; but he who does not bear the sign of the first baptisms will not be baptised in the bath of fire. First one must be baptised by water and the Spirit to be able to show, when one reaches the banks of the river of fire, that one has lived in accordance with the baths of water and the Spirit and that one deserves to receive the baptism of fire in Christ Jesus.[31]

This symbolism has both mythological and biblical overtones: we are reminded of the rivers surrounding Hades, which must be crossed in the boat of the ferryman Charon if the Elysian Fields are to be reached. But Christ is both the minister of this baptism and the river in which the baptised are plunged: in the same way Origen was to represent the fire of Purgatory as God Himself, 'a devouring fire'.[32] It is 'in Christ Jesus' that this baptism is received. The Saviour is figured both by Jesus, the son of Navē, Joshua, who baptised the Hebrews in the Jordan and by the river itself, for it is 'the river that rejoices the city of God'.[33] The mention in the text of two baptisms, distinguishing baptism from confirmation, seems to be due to the translator Jerome. As for the painful character of this baptism it is emphasised elsewhere: 'Blessed is he who is baptised in the Holy Spirit and does not need to be baptised in fire. Thrice wretched him for whom the baptism of fire is necessary. But Jesus is the one and the other baptism.'[34]

So in Origen's terms the baptism of John is a mere symbol, a shadow; that of the Church is an image, and that means that it is both symbol and mystery; the eschatological baptism of fire and the final conforming to the resurrection of Christ are mystery. Or in scholastic terms, the baptism of John is a mere *sacramentun*, a sign; that of the Church is both *sacramentum* and *res*; and the eschatological baptism is *res*, reality.

Two elements come together in the baptism of water. In fact, 'it is no longer simply water, for it is consecrated by a mystical invocation (= an epiclesis)'.[35] This epiclesis is the invocation 'in the name of the Father and of the son and of the Holy Spirit' which causes the water to share in 'the power of the Holy Trinity' and confers upon it 'an ethical and contemplative virtue',[36] giving the grace to live as a Christian and to contemplate God and his mysteries. Now this action the baptismal water effects *by itself*, if the subject, of course, is properly disposed: 'The bath

---

[31] *HomLc* XXIV, 2: see also *ComMt* XV, 23 (GCS X), but leaving aside the uncomprehending correction '*kai blepei*' made by Klostermann from the Latin translation. It is baptism itself which is 'through a glass, darkly' in contrast with Purgatory which gives pure 'face to face': Origen applies this contrast to all the realities of the temporal Gospel and the eternal Gospel, and not only to knowledge, as Paul does.

[32] Deut. 4, 24; 9, 3.

[33] Ps. 45, 5.

[34] *HomJr* II, 3.

[35] *FragmJn* XXXVI (GCS IV).

[36] Ibid.

of water is the symbol of the purification which washes the soul clean of all the stains of wrong-doing; it does so nonetheless by itself (*kath' hauto*) for the one who yeilds himself to the divine power which comes from the invocations of the adorable Trinity, origin and source of the divine charisms'.[37] It is not an anachronism to observe that this text clearly expresses what later theology will call the *ex opere operato*, that is to say the fact that the sacrament is effective by the action of grace, not by the action of him who receives it (the *ex opere operantis*), although the latter, in consequence of human freedom, must dispose himself to receive it, as our text also says: 'for him who yields himself (*tō emparechonti heauton*) to the divine power'.

The Eucharist[38]

A correct interpretation of Origen's doctrine of the Eucharist is difficult, more so than that of baptism, for, while affirming clearly the real presence of Christ in the eucharistic elements, Origen gives to the gospel texts on which he is commenting a whole spectrum of meanings, in which those which express the real presence are cheek by jowl with very different ones. Likewise several levels of meaning must be distinguished. The lowest is a purely literal sense, according to Origen's understanding of 'literal sense' to which we drew attention in the chapter on exegesis, the raw material of the expression without regard to what constitutes for the modern exegete the literal meaning, namely the intention of the speaker: that is how the Jews understood it and that is why they were scandalised over the discourse about the Bread of Life which they saw as an invitation to cannibalism.[39] But for Origen this literal sense is false and it is quoted among the few examples in the gospels of the 'letter which kills'.[40] In fact, in Origen's terms, the eucharistic texts of the New Testament do not really have a valid literal sense: this literal sense is a misunderstanding.

The eucharistic meaning of these texts is thus a first allegorical sense, situated in the setting of the temporal Gospel, which is both the realisation and the prophecy of the mystery: by its perceptible elements, the bread and the wine, it is yet the symbol of a higher reality, the Logos Word of God and food of the intelligences. Several texts affirm these two meanings which are not mutually exclusive, but on the contrary constantly co-exist. The bread and wine are body and blood of Christ and refer to a more divine truth, the Word, no longer as body and blood, but as Word which God addresses to men. A celebrated text bears witness to the veneration shown to the Eucharist and the care taken by the faithful

[37] *ComJn* VI, 33 (17), 166: text quoted by Basil, *On the Holy Spirit*, XXIX, 73 (SC 17 and 17b).
[38] See L. Lies *Wort und Eucharistie bei Origenes*. Innsbruck/Vienna/Munich, 1978; H. Crouzel, art. cit. (note 23).
[39] John VI, 60; *HomLv* VII, 5.
[40] *HomLv* VII, 5.

not to lose a particle of the 'body of the Lord', but also expresses surprise that the same respect is not shown to the Word of God by receiving it and meditating upon it.[41]

These two meanings, both of which Origen considers allegorical on different levels, have been judged in various ways by the commentators. For some the interpretation by the Logos-Word in fact suppresses the real presence although it is affirmed; for others, without suppressing it, it misinterprets it. We can scarcely understand either position although we do not see how interpretation by the Word should misrepresent the other, when they are mutually enriching. The relationship between the bread-body of Christ and the Logos-Word is the same as that between the flesh of Christ and his divinity. However fundamental the humanity of Christ may be for the Christian, it is always related to the divinity of the Word which makes us know the Father.

Some explanation needs to be given of the expression 'typical and symbolical body' used by Origen.[42] Understood in terms of the later theology of the 12th century, it would completely suppress the real presence. But that is not so in the case of the patristic theology inspired by Platonism. To repeat the enlightening words of A. von Harnack:[43] 'Today we understand by symbol something which is not what it means, while in earlier times they meant by symbol something which in some way is what it stands for and besides the heavenly reality was always hidden in and behind this appearance, without ever being entirely confused with it on earth'. That Eucharist is 'a typical and symbolical body' means for Origen, especially in his conception of the temporal Gospel, that it is at once mystery and image, an affirmation of the real presence of Christ – the mystery – under the veil of a sign – the bread and wine.

It must also be noted that in superimposing on the meaning of the bread-body of Christ that of the very Person of Jesus, the Word Incarnate, Origen remains faithful to the double meaning which pervades the whole of the Johannine discourse on the Bread of Life.[44] Jesus starts from the reaction of the multitude to the miracle of the Feeding of the Five Thousand and points to Himself as the Bread of Life come down from Heaven. The strictly eucharistic sense underlies all this, of course, but it is particularly present from verse 51 on when there is reference to eating the flesh of Christ and drinking his blood. In fact one cannot speak of two meanings, for the sacramental Eucharist is only such because it

[41] *HomEx* XIII, 3.
[42] *ComMt* XI, 14 (GCS X).
[43] *Lehrbuch der Dogmengeschichte.* I. Tübingen, 1909, p. 476: Fr. translation taken from K. Rahner, 'La doctrine d'Origène sur la pénitence', *Recherches de Science Religieuse* 1950, p. 449.
[44] John VI, 26–65.

renders the very Person of Jesus present in perceptible form, God and man. This can be said both of John and of Origen.

The *Commentary on Matthew*[45] deals with the Eucharist at length, in a way that seems to us today clumsy in some of its expressions, but it would show a lack of historical sense to be too critical of what is one of the very first attempts to reflect on this sacrament. The author wishes to insist that the fruitful reception of the Eucharist depends on the dispositions shown to be necessary in 1 Cor. 11, 27–32. Whatever the 'simpler' people may think, it does not automatically sanctify all those who communicate, but only those who receive it with a pure conscience. Two sentences which seem to us unfortunate[46] would seem to say, if taken out of context, that the action of the Eucharist is null and the sacrament useless; only the right disposition would be fruitful. But in their context they enunciate a correct thought: the Eucharist puts him who receives it unworthily into a state of weakness, of lethargy, of spiritual death. On the other hand if the soul is well disposed, the bread is effective 'in proportion to the faith':[47] it increases the contemplative faculty of the soul, which sees what is useful to it, namely the mysteries. So the sacrament is in itself a real action, debilitating if the state of the soul is bad, illuminating if it is good. There is lacking, to be sure, an expressly formulated distinction between the operation of the sacrament itself and the dispositions which are the necessary condition of its supernatural action, between the *ex opere operato* and the *ex opere operantis*, but all that is at least indicated.

Like several of his predecessors, Justin or Irenaeus, Origen distinguishes in the bread and wine two elements, the matter which follows the course of all bodily food, and the other element, whether it be 'the prayer (*euchē*) pronounced over it', whether it be, following 1 Tim. 4, 5, 'the word of God and the invocation (*enteuxis*) or whether again it be the word that comes from Him, the Christ, the word Christ uttered at the last Supper.[48] In another passage[49] he speaks of 'these loaves . . . on which are invoked (*epikekletai*, the epiclesis) the names of God, of Christ and of the Holy Spirit'. Passages from the homilies indicate that the liturgy of the word was followed by the liturgy of the Eucharist in the Sunday service.[50] Others, echoing a practice of the primitive Church preserved in the East, require abstinence from marital relations before receiving the sacrament.[51]

[45] XI, 14 (GCS X).
[46] 'Thus it is not the fact of not eating the bread sanctified by the word of God and the invocation which in itself deprives us of some good, nor the fact of eating it which gives us good in plenty. For the cause of the deprivation is malice and sin, the cause of plenty is justice and its deeds.'
[47] Rom. 12, 6.
[48] The first two formulae are in *ComMt* XI, 14 (GCS X), the third in *CCels* VIII, 33.
[49] *Fragm 1 Cor.* XXXIV, *JThS* IX, p. 502, 1, 13.
[50] *HomEx* XI, 7; *HomLv* XIII, 5.
[51] *Fragm 1 Cor.* XXXIV, *JThS* IX, p. 502, 1, 8; *SelEz* 7, 2 (PG 13, 793B).

Few texts insist on the sacrificial character of the Eucharist, except in relation to the sacrifice of thanksgiving which is the first meaning of the word *eucharistia*. The link between the Saviour's death and the Eucharist is fairly often suggested, rarely expressed clearly: in fact several of these texts manifest the discipline of secrecy, and the practice of the Church in concealing certain points in its worship explains Origen's reserve in speaking of the sacrament and his preference for the Word of God, food of souls.

The link between the Eucharist and the Church is also not often expressed. Of course, the eucharistic bread and the Church are both of them the body of Christ, and they are linked by their relationship to the physical body of the Saviour. For if the eucharistic body is a figure of the physical body, figure in the realistic meaning given by Origen to 'type or symbol', the physical body is also a figure of the Church, 'the true and most perfect body of Christ',[52] true in the Platonist sense which makes it the opposite of image, not the opposite of error or falsehood.

Penance[53,b]

A passage from the *Treatise on Prayer*[54] has occasioned a fairly considerable literature about penance in Origen:

> But consider the person inspired by Jesus as the apostles[55] were and who can be known by his fruits as someone who has received the Holy Spirit and become spiritual by being led by the Spirit as a son of God to do everything according to the Word (or reason). This person forgives whatever God forgives and retains sins that cannot be healed, serving God like the prophets by speaking not his own words but those of the divine will. So he, too, serves God, who alone has authority to forgive.

The priests of the Old Testament offered expiatory sacrifices only for sins that could be pardoned:

> Therefore, it is the same way that the Apostles and those like the Apostles, since they are priests according to the great High Priest, have received knowledge of God's healing and know, since they are taught by the Spirit, for what sins sacrifice must be offered and when and how; and they know for what sins it is wrong to do this . . . I do not know how some arrogate to

---

[52] *ComJn* X, 36 (20), 236; cf. 35 (20), 228.

[53] The literature on penance in Origen is considerable. We mention K. Rahner 'La doctrine d'Origène sur la pénitence', *Recherches de Science Religieuse* 37, 1950, 47–97, 252–286, 422–456; also H. J. Vogt op. cit. (note 16).

[54] XXVIII, 8–10 (GCS II).

[55] John 20, 22.

[b] 'La pénitence': it is important to remember that in French the same word stands for both 'penance' and 'penitence'. Given that the section forms a series with others about 'Baptism' and 'The Eucharist' I have concluded that in the title the sacrament is meant and have translated 'penance'. I have done the same in nearly all cases in the text, sometimes with misgivings, and the reader will do well to remember that to the author and to French readers the idea of penitence as a sentiment may well be present as well as that of penance as a sacrament.

themselves powers that exceed the priestly dignity; perhaps they do not thoroughly understand priestly knowledge. These people boast that they are able to forgive adultery and fornication, supposing that through their prayers for those who have dared these things even on into death is loosed. For they do not read that 'there is a sin which is unto death. I do not say that one is to pray for that'.[c]

In this passage Döllinger[56] and Harnack[57] read: 'Any spiritual man, not only the priest, has power to forgive sins: there are irremissible sins including idolatry and the sins of the flesh'. According to these scholars Origen is here associating himself with the protest of Hippolytus and Tertullian against the famous edict of Callistus (always supposing that it is Callistus, meant in the *Elenchos* attributed to Hippolytus, who is the Pontifex Maximus in Tertullian's *De Pudicitia*).

But this interpretation has little foundation. First, none but a priest is meant in this passage: the only person who worthily exercises the power of the keys in accord with the divine intention is the priest who is a spiritual man and remits sin as God does and wills, and who has the knowledge required for this function. To go on and see in this, taking the meaning that appears at first sight, an affirmation that some sins are unforgiveable, is to set this text against all the other writings of Origen, where passages about penance are numerous. In fact, following Philo, he declares *aniata*, incurable, in other passages, sins which in the end are remitted: either he wishes to express an impossibility in human terms only which does not exist for God or, which is more likely, the word should be translated as a participle, 'not cured'.[58] Origen is here criticising priests or bishops who claim to forgive sins by their prayer alone, by a remission, *aphesis*, by grace alone, without expiation through public penance which alone displays repentance and makes the sinner fit to receive pardon, thus transforming a 'sin unto death' into one that is no longer unto death. We shall see the proofs of this interpretation. In any case the vast literature on this subject and the strong arguments produced in the last seventy years have rendered the thesis of Döllinger and Harnack highly improbable. But to that end this text must be set in the whole of Origen's penitential doctrine.

Several Greek texts of Origen's, not to mention innumerable Latin ones, show as susceptible of pardon sins which are supposed to be irremissible. Two of these are particularly important for they are

---

[c] Trans. R. A. Greer, in series *Classics of Western Spirituality*, New York and London, 1979, pp. 151–157. Lightly amended at the suggestion of the Author.

[56] *Hippolytus and Kallistus oder die römische Kirche in der ersten Hälfte des dritten Jahrhunderts*, Ratisbon, 1853, pp. 254–268.

[57] *Lehrbuch der Dogmengeschichte I*, Tübingen, 1909, pp. 448–449, note 1.

[58] See H. Crouzel, 'Notes critiques sur Origène', II: Le sens de *aniatos* dans le *Traité de la Prière* XXVIII, 8, *Bulletin de Littérature Ecclésiastique*, 59, 1958, 8–12.

[59] XXVIII. 7 (6) 51–60 (GCS IV).

contemporary with the *Treatise on Prayer:* it cannot even be said that Origen changed his mind at a given moment. Thus in Book XXVIII of the *Commentary on John*[59] Lazarus raised from the dead is a figure of apostasy remitted by the apostles, that is by the Church. To the same period belong also the fragments on the First Epistle to the Corinthians, fragments of homilies, it would seem. One of these,[60] shown to be authentic by the use, in its most delicate nuances, of Origen's trichotomic anthropology, which is scarcely to be found in his successors, deals with the excommunication by Paul of the man guilty of incest in 1 Cor. 5, 1–5: at the end of the fragment Origen sees him pardoned by Paul in 2 Cor. 2, 6–11, as do all the early Fathers except the Montanist Tertullian of the *De Pudicitia* whose basic thesis would be contradicted by this interpretation. Another of these fragments[61] is the true key to the much disputed passage in the *Treatise on Prayer:* 'The pagan repents when he wishes and receives the remission (*aphesis*) of his sins, but he who has committed fornication after receiving the faith, even if he repents afterwards, does not receive the remission (*aphesis*) of his sins, but he can cover them (*epikalypsai*). Blessed, it is said, are those whose sins are remitted (*aphethēsan*), those who come from paganism; and those whose sins have been covered (*epekalyphthēsan*), those who have sinned after receiving the faith and who have covered them by their good works, for example, incontinence by great temperance.'

Indeed, the priests who are blamed in the *Treatise on Prayer* remit (*aphienai*) fornication and adultery by their prayer alone in an *aphesis* of total grace, proper only to baptism, and to the supreme baptism, martyrdom. The baptised cannot receive again this baptismal *aphesis* unless he is martyred. He can only 'cover' his faults by penance or at least by different good works, setting these virtuous acts against sins previously committed. Sins committed after baptism must be expiated, the expiation being the sign of a true conversion which alone makes it possible to receive pardon.

In a homily, Origen[62] lists seven ways of obtaining the remission or pardon of sins. The first two, baptism and martyrdom, relate to what is called in the previous passage *aphesis.* The next four are concerned with good works which, as we have seen, 'cover' the sin and each is supported by texts from the New Testament: almsgiving;[63] forgiving offences;[64] converting the sinning brother;[65] superabundant charity.[66] None of these four is what we should call a sacramental penance. But the seventh is:

[60] XXIV, *JThS* IX, p. 364.
[61] XXVI, *JThS* IX, p. 366.
[62] *HomLv* II, 4.
[63] Luke, 11, 41.
[64] Matt. 6, 12 and 14–15.
[65] James, 5, 20.
[66] Luke 7, 47.

'There is still a seventh, a hard and laborious one, a remission of sins by penance when the sinner washes his bed with his tears and his tears are for him his bread day and night,[67] when he does not blush to admit his sin to the Lord's priest and to seek a remedy . . .' On this occasion Origen quotes James 5, 14–15, the text on which is based the unction of the sick: he applies it to penance, seeing in the sick man concerned a spiritual invalid.

Does not this seventh form of penitence apply to public penance, decided by the bishop for very grave faults and available only once? Fr. Galtier, in an article reaching conclusions which have not been very well received by critics,[68] shows by texts from the homilies that Origen seems often to fear that public penance, as it came to be extended to lesser,[69] though still serious, offences, would be used too often and would lose something of its significance; and that he went on to envisage for that kind of fault a penance that would be more frequent than public penance,[70] carried out indeed with the help of the priest,[71] but in which the penitent would be counselled to choose his own physician:[72] thus it would not be reserved to the bishop or to his duly appointed representatives as in the case of public penance. We are talking about a penance for sins which we should today consider mortal but which are not the grave sins for which recourse to public penance was necessary: it comprises confession to the priest, seen in the role of a doctor, and prescription by him of the means of cure, of expiation, whether by good works or by practice of physical penance, but the whole taking place in private. If we project onto this practice of which Origen speaks the later idea of sacramental penance, can it be said that this penance is sacramental or must this term be reserved for public penance? Personally, we see no reason why it should not be considered sacramental. If the essential gospel text which is held to institute this sacrament is John 20, 23: 'To those whose sins you remit, they shall be remitted, to those whose sins you retain, they shall be retained', it is the intervention and judgement of the priest, heir of the apostolic mission, which constitutes the sacrament and these are just as much present here as in public penance. Whether Origen is here showing a practice current in the Church of his time or an attitude which as pastor he wished to promote, it is impossible to decide because evidence outside his own works is lacking.

As a corollary there are in Origen various attempts to arrange sins in

---

[67] Ps. 6, 7; 41, 4.
[68] 'Le rémission des péchés moindres dans l'eglise du troiséme an cinquiéme siecle' 'Recherches de Science Religieuses, 13, 1923, pp. 97–129, Origen 97–104.
[69] HomJos VII, 6; ComMt XVI, 8 (GCS X).
[70] HomLv XV, 2.
[71] HomNb X, 1.
[72] HomPs 37, II, 6 (PG 12, 1386).

order of gravity here is one of them:[73] 'I think there is a difference between carnal and earthly . . . If you sin unto death,[74] you are no longer carnal, but earthly. If you sin but not unto death, you are not entirely earthly, you have not fallen from Christ's grace, but they you are carnal.' The later distinction between mortal and venial sins is here, using different expressions, exactly indicated: the second does not take away the grace of Christ, the first does, giving death to the soul.

✻   ✻   ✻

If the reader finds this chapter devoted to the Church of the present age somewhat scanty, he must not forget that the four chapters devoted to Origen's spiritual doctrine, dealing respectively with anthropology, knowledge, the mystical themes, and the ascetic and moral life, also fall under the term 'The Church of the present age', for they are about the daily life of the Christian. The distinction between the spiritual teaching of Origen and his speculative theology, justified as it is, is clearly not a separation and we have been able to see several times in relation to the three sacraments their moral and spiritual effects.

---

[73] *Fragm 1 Cor.* XIII, *JThS* IX, p. 242.
[74] 1 John 5, 16.

13

The Church of the Age to Come

Along with the pre-existence of souls the point in Origen's synthesis that has been subjected to the strongest attacks is his eschatological doctrine: as nearly always with Origen these attacks have been unfair, especially where they are about the resurrection and the famous 'apocatastasis', that is the final restoration. On the first point all posterity right down to the most recent times has judged Origen by the misconception of Methodius of Olympus about the *eidos sōmatikon*, without taking the trouble to study in detail his own declarations about it, numerous but scattered through his work. Sometimes the point of absurdity has been reached where Methodius and his successors are held to be right in spite of what Origen says, as though Methodius were a better witness to Origen's thought than the author himself. As for the apocatastasis, scholars have struck to certain statements in the *Treatise on First Principles*, interpreted rigidly, without taking account of other declarations in the same book and in other works; instead of explaining the *Treatise on First Principles* by reference to his work as a whole, they have interpreted the work as a whole according to the 'system' they have drawn from the Treatise; and they have defined that 'system' by leaving aside all the nuances and refusing to take seriously the numerous discussions between alternative theses assuming arbitrarily that Origen was committed to one of them.

Death and Immortality[1]

A doctrine that is found fairly frequently in Origen – the most complete exposition of it is in the *Dialogue with Heraclides*[2] – is that of three kinds of death. On the lines of the Stoic distinction of good, bad and indifferent, Origen distinguishes a 'death to sin' which is good, a 'death in sin', which is bad and an indifferent death, neither good nor bad in itself, which he also calls 'physical' or 'common' death. This last is not an evil in itself, for, rejecting the Aristotelian doctrine of three kinds of good – goods of the body, goods of the soul and external goods[3] – against which

---

[1] See our article 'Mort et immortalité chez Origène', *Bulletin de Littérature Ecclésiastique* 79, 1978, 19–38, 81–96, 181–196.
[2] §§24–27.
[3] *Nicomachian Ethics* I, 8–9, 1098B–1099B.

he often argues,[4] Origen, following Platonism, only admits as goods or evils those which affect the soul. Death in sin is the opposite of the divine life which shares in the divine Spirit and in the Christ who is Life. Death to sin consists essentially in conformity to the death of Christ which is accompanied by conformity to his resurrection (Rom. 6). As for indifferent death, the opposite of that is indifferent life, the life we share with the animals. This death is inevitable for all who are composed of a soul and a body. It is the 'shadow of death'.[5] Indeed between physical death and death in sin there is the relationship of image and reality: true death is the death of the soul, belonging to the supernatural order of the mystery; physical death belongs to the natural order and is its shadow.

For physical death the classical definition is often found: separation of soul and body. It belongs to the composite character of the human being, for every composite can be dissolved. But it only affects the body which becomes inert. Death deprives the body of life, but not the soul. These ideas are by no means original as regards the philosophy of Plato.

There is a link between death in sin and physical death. This can be understood in the light of conceptions expressed in the *Treatise on First Principles* about the hypothesis of pre-existence and the precosmic fall. According to Procopius of Gaza's evidence about what was in the *Commentary on Genesis*, it was after the fall that the 'dazzling' body of the pre-existence exchanged its heavenly, incorruptible and immortal quality for one that was earthly, corruptible and mortal, a change figured by the garments of skin[6] with which God clothed out first parents.

Now the earthly and carnal condition, though it is not sin in itself, for it was created by God who originates no evil, is nevertheless linked with sin in that its creation followed the fall and that it is an opportunity for temptation. We have expounded this several times when describing the nature of sin in Origen's thought, the fact of staying with the perceptible which is only the image of the good things of the end-time and not going on to the mysteries to which it points.

The relation between sin and physical death is affirmed in many texts: the latter is the result of the fall, the wages of sin. In some instances it is not clear whether physical death or death in sin is meant, but this very uncertainty reveals the link. The death to which our earthly body is condemned clouds all our earthly life. 'Wretched man that I am, who will deliver me from this body of death?',[7] cries Paul; and Origen comments, 'That is why the saints do not celebrate their birthdays. Only those who live the life of the body consider themselves happy to be living in this

---

[4] Thus ComPs 4 in *Philoc* 26. Also Gregory Thaumaturgus *RemOrig* II, 11–12; III, 28; VI, 75–77; IX, 122.

[5] Ps. 22 (23), 4.

[6] Gen. 3, 27.

[7] Rom. 7, 24; *HomJr* XX (XIX), 7.

body of death. Even if we know that the future glory will be beyond compare with the present life and its woes, we see with fear the day of death approaching and we should like to escape it.

Frequently the physical death of Christ is likened to the death to sin of the Christian who is conformed to Christ's death. Thus physical death, the chastisement, as we have just seen, of sin, takes on a redemptive value. This it acquires thanks to the sacrifice of Christ. Already in the Old Testament the death penalty imposed for a grave crime expunged the pain of the sin, for 'God does not punish twice the same offence':[8] so it was already a redemptive punishment. It is above all the death of Christ which is the source of the death to sin of all those who are baptised into his death and consequently mortify their earthly members. In Christ Himself death does not touch the Word but the human nature that is joined to Him[9] and his death was like all human deaths except that He freely and voluntarily took it upon Himself for the sake of his friends: He went down into Hades, 'free among the dead',[10] stronger than death, dominating it instead of being dominated by it, in order to deliver those who had been conquered by it. By the death of Christ is destroyed the death that is Christ's enemy, death in sin. Such is the great paradox of the Redemption. This death to sin, this happy death which means to us being brought to life with Christ, Origen finds in several expressions of Paul's: 'I am crucified with Christ: it is no longer I who live, but Christ Jesus within me'.[11] Far be it from me to glory except in the cross of our Lord Jesus Christ, by which the world has been crucified to me and I to the world.'[12] 'You are dead and your life is hid with Christ in God.'[13]

We have seen that martyrdom is the most perfect imitation of Christ in his death, and hence in his resurrection. It shares in Christ's work of redemption. It obtains the remission of sins, not only for the martyr but for others, and it puts to flight the powers of the devil. The saving efficacy of the martyr's deed is so great in Origen's eyes that during the period of religous peace which marked the reign of Philip the Arabian, Origen in his homilies actually comes to regret for this reason the end of the persecutions: however, they were to be resumed on a grand scale by the man who assassinated and succeeded Philip, Decius. There could be in this the first sign of a reflection on the death of the Christian, as a configuration to the death and resurrection of Christ, a supreme baptism in the form of an action when it is motivated by the sentiments of martyrdom. This reflection is scarcely outlined in two texts. One

[8] Nah. 1, 9 in LXX: *HomLv* XI, 2 and XIV, 4.
[9] *HomJr* XIV, 6.
[10] Ps. 87 (88), 6; *ComCt* III (GCS VIII, p. 222, 1, 26); *SerMt* 132 (GCS XI); *ComMt* XVI, 8 (GCS X).
[11] Gal. 2, 20; *HomNb* VII, 3; cf. XII, 3.
[12] Gal. 6, 14.
[13] Eph. 3, 3.

distinguishes 'martyrdom in the open', that is execution, from 'martyrdom in secret', the inner feelings which go to make the martyr and which can be present though no execution takes place.[14] The second passage is found in a homily:[15] 'I have no doubt that there are in this congregation those, known to God alone, who are already martyrs by the testimony of their conscience, ready, if need be, to shed their blood for the name of our Lord Jesus Christ'. The word testimony, *testimonium*, no doubt stands for *martyrion*, both testimony and martyrdom. On this point Cyprian was to be more explicit than Origen:[16] Martyrdom is a gift of God, not available to all; but God sees our inner thoughts and for those who have not had the opportunity of martyrdom he nevertheless crowns the desire and the acceptance.

The text of the *Dialogue with Heraclides*[17] to which we alluded above distinguishes two kinds of immortality. In the case of physical death the human soul enjoys an absolute immortality. But it can also be immortal in relation to the death in sin, that means impeccability if 'it is stregthened in blessedness'. If one who is going towards God shares in the very immutability of God,[18] if the righteous man, even here below, tends to a certain impeccability, then the opinion attributed to the *Treatise on First Principles* according to which the blessed in the Beatitude could still fall is in reality only a hypothesis in a discussion. It would be possible to distinguish in Origen a natural immortality and an immortality of grace, the former being the image of the latter.

The main reason for natural immortality according to the *Dialogue with Heraclides* is the necessity, in the name of divine justice, of the final retribution. Several other reasons are formulated in the *Treatise on First Principles*.[19] Man's desire to know God, to understand his works and the way they are made, cannot be satisfied here below. God having put this desire into man, it cannot be a vain one, it must receive its fulfilment. That implies the immortality of the human faculty of knowing, that is of the higher part of the soul, intelligence, governing faculty or heart, seat of the personality. This reasoning is based on the idea which will later be expressed in the following form: '*desiderium naturae nequit esse inane* – a natural desire cannot be in vain'. Another attempt at proof is found at the end of the *Anacephaleosis* which closes the same book.[20] The demonstration relies on the idea of participation which has in Origen the strongly existential character of the Platonic notion. The human soul shares in the same intelligible and divine realities as the angelic powers: although there

[14] *ExhMart* XXI (GCS I).
[15] *HomNb* X, 2.
[16] *De Mortalitate* XVII (CSEL III).
[17] §§24–27.
[18] *Hom 1 K* (1 Sam) I, §4 (GCS VIII).
[19] II, 11, 4.
[20] IV, 4, 9–10.

are differences of degree in this, as for eyes and ears which see and hear with different degrees of intensity, while remaining similar, human intelligences and angelic powers are of the same nature. Now the latter are incorruptible and immortal: the same is also true of human souls. But the intellectual light in which the whole rational creation shares is the nature of the three Persons. Origen's reasoning then moves to a second form of the same argument. Every substance that draws a share from the eternal light is itself incorruptible and immortal, with different degrees in this sharing. To maintain that human intelligence capable of understanding God could receive death in its substance would be to blaspheme against God in the image of Whom man was created and against the Son who is Himself that image after which man was created. This demonstration implies belief in God, common to most of the pagan philosophers of the time, and also, for the first argument, belief in the existence of angelic powers. It is probably addressed to certain Christians of the time, the Thnetopsychites, who supposed that the soul dies with the body and is raised with it: we mentioned them in connection with Origen's life.[21]

The immortality of the soul, as opposed to common death, is thus part of the very nature of the rational being: a gift of God, of course, but inherent in the creation of man as in that of the angels, linked with sharing in the image of God, of which the content is, to use language which is not Origen's, both natural and supernatural. The natural character of this first kind of immortality is defended by Origen against the Valentinian Heracleon who denies it because he confuses the two immortalities,[22] failing to see that a substance mortal and corruptible cannot become immortal and incorruptible. The mortal body 'will put on' immortality at the resurrection without change of substance but only of quality. When we turn to that incorporeal substance which is the soul, there is no 'substratum' common to corporeal and incorporeal nature, while there is one beneath the various forms of corporeal nature. If the soul were mortal and corruptible, it could not receive immortality and incorruptibility: to possess them it must have them in its very substance, for it is simple and not made up of substance and qualities. On the other hand the body, mortal and corruptible here below, can 'put on' immortality and incorruptibility, for these are qualities that can be added to its substance.

These notions of substance and quality belong to the conception of matter common to the Platonists, the Aristotelians and the Stoics: we shall explain them more fully when dealing with Origen's doctrine of the risen body. If the body is normally called clothing of the soul, Origen paradoxically calls the soul clothing of the body, for at the resurrection

[21] See pp. 31–33.
[22] ComJn XIII, 61 (59), 427–430.

the soul will clothe the body with the qualities of immortality and incorruptibility which belong to the soul's nature.[23]

But the Christ is also said in the same passage to be the 'clothing of the soul'. In fact it is He who clothes the soul with the second immortality – and clothes the body through it: this is an immortality of grace which suppresses the death in sin and is of the order of the 'True life'. This 'true life', the soul, unlike the Persons of the Trinity, we repeat, does not possess substantially but accidentally, because it is given by God, and the soul possesses it in the measure that its free will receives it.

Here below every man is a sinner, even the most righteous and the most holy. The progress of the spiritual man gives him a consciousness more and more acute of his own sins. In the Trinity alone holiness is a matter of substance: that of the creature is a matter of accident, subject to progress or relapse. Impeccability on earth only exists in a progressive manner: he who approaches God shares in his immutability. The man in the parable of the Good Samaritan, who represents Adam, is left half dead, for common death has only affected half his being. He has been stripped of his garments: he has lost the immortality that was linked to his virtues.[24] This second immortality is a gift of divine grace, coming from the Trinity, but especially linked with the Person of the Son, for it is the gift of Life, and Life, like Resurrection, is a title (*epinoia*) of the Christ, mingling with his divine nature. The Christ is Resurrection, that is immortality to sin, and blessedness. He is not Resurrection for the wicked, who nevertheless will rise again, but on the other hand, He is it already for those who are in the 'first resurrection',[25] the one that happens here below through baptism and the Christian life, without however, conferring a complete immortality to sin. Numerous are the texts which thus attribute to Christ the gift of immortality. Sometimes it is not made clear whether it refers to exemption from the one death or the other. But in the continual cross-fertilisation which is one of the major features of Origen's vocabulary, mixing with one or more literal meanings one or more allegorical meanings, sometimes highlighted sometimes kept in the background like musical harmonies, both acceptations are certainly included.

Between death and resurrection
Several questions arise for Origen. Is the soul – during this interval – absolutely without a body? Where is the soul located before the resurrection? What activity does it pursue? Finally, what is the nature of the eschatological purification which Origen sees in 1 Cor. 3, 15–17?

---

[23] *PArch* II, 3, 2.
[24] *FragmLc* 168 (GCS IX[2]).
[25] H. Crouzel, 'La "première" et la "seconde" résurrection des hommes d'après Origène', *Didaskalia* 3, 1973, 3–19.

To say that the soul is absolutely without a body between death and resurrection would be to contradict a statement that is three times repeated in the *Treatise on First Principles:*[26] only the Trinity is without a body. Rational creatures, although incorporeal as souls, are always clothed with a body, even the angels and the demons, as well as the pre-existent and resurrected intelligences. When dealing with the trichotomic anthropology we saw how ambiguous the concept of body is, denoting sometimes the earthly body alone, sometimes earthly and ethereal bodies taken together, not to mention passages in which incorporeality has a purely moral sense. The body is often the mark of creaturely status, representing accidentality as opposed to the substantiality of the three Persons. Here we find the same ambiguity. Certainly most references in Origen show the soul without a body between death and resurrection. There is, however, one exception: it is preserved by Methodius of Olympus in his *Aglaophon* or *On the Resurrection,* which we possess in its entirety only in an old Slav version, and in Greek only by the note in the *Bibliotheca* of Photius who mentions this work.[27] Relying on the physical character shown in the parable of the Rich Man and Lazarus[28] – the tongue, the finger, the bosom of Abraham, the recumbent position, all that before the resurrection since the rich man's brothers are still alive on earth – and on the appearance of Samuel to Saul at the witch of Endor[29] he attributes to the soul between death and resurrection a certain corporeal envelope expressed as, following a Middle and Neo-Platonist notion, the 'vehicle' (*ochēma*) of the soul, the envelope made of corporeal *pneuma* which for the Platonists formed the joint between the body and the soul and lived on after death, surrounding the soul and explaining how phantoms appeared.[30]

As for the place where the deceased dwell before the resurrection, there is no agreement in the primitive Church. Tertullian, for example, thinks that only the martyrs are admitted to Paradise at this stage, the rest having to wait, whether righteous or sinners, in the place which the Old Testament called Sheol, the New Testament by a Greek term Hades, the Latins *inferus, infernus* or *infernum,* in the singular or the plural: the righteous there find consolation, the wicked retribution. It does not correspond to what we call Hell, denoted by the word Gehenna, but rather to what is sometimes called in French 'les Enfers', for example when one speaks of Christ's descent into 'les Enfers' after his death. So in Origen's work we must not confuse Hades, the place of the dead

---

[26] I, 6, 4; II, 2, 2; IV, 3, 15.
[27] *Aglaophon* III, 17; *Bibl.* 234, 300B.
[28] Luke 16, 19–31.
[29] 1 K (1 Sam), 28, 3–25.
[30] H. Crouzel 'Le thème platonicien du "véhicule de l'âme" chez Origène', *Didascalia* 7, 1977, 225–237.

described in the parable of the Rich Man – who suffers there – and Lazarus – who is happy there – with Gehenna, the place of torment.[31]

In Origen's famous homily on Saul's visit to the witch of Endor and the conjuring of Samuel,[32] Hades is the place where the saints of the Old Testament went after death, for, on account of the sin committed when humanity began, they could not go to Paradise, where grew the tree of life, guarded by the Cherubim with the flaming sword. It is from there that Samuel comes up to show himself to Saul. John the Baptist goes down there after his death, precursor there also of the coming of Christ. After the death of Christ, while his spirit is returned into the hands of his Father, and his body is placed in the tomb, his soul, joined to the Word and empowered with the very Power of God, is led away like other souls to Hades, from which He was to deliver the captive souls, after, Origen supposes, placing the Good Thief in Paradise. These saints of the old covenant Christ will lead to Paradise at his own glorious Ascension: thus He has re-opened for them the way which the sin of Adam had closed. Henceforth the righteous of the new covenant will not go to Hades, but, allowing for what we shall say below about the eschatological purification, directly to Paradise, before the resurrection. The reply of Jesus to the Good Thief is the main argument. Not least in Origen's entitlement to glory is the fact that he, first among Church writers, opened Paradise to the righteous at their death in spite of all the contemporary – and later – trends that kept them, either in Hades, as we saw in the case of Tertullian, or even in the vicinity of the body, as we saw when relating Origen's life.[33] And that should earn him pardon for the hesitations and contradictory positions he took up with regard to the eternity of Gehenna.

As for the place of the rejected, both before and after the resurrection, Origen uses the New Testament expressions, Gehenna of fire, eternal fire, inextinguishable fire, outer darkness. The rule of faith, as Origen expresses it in the preface of the *Treatise on First Principles*,[34] states that the soul 'after its departure from this world will be rewarded according to its deserts; for it will either obtain an inheritance of eternal life and blessedness, if its deeds shall warrant this, or it must be given over to eternal fire and torments, if the guilt of its crimes shall so determine'.

Two problems arise from the New Testament expressions that Origen uses: Of what does this fire consist? Why is this fire, which is constantly said by him to be, as the New Testament says, eternal or inextinguishable, sometimes – though not always – considered by him to be remedial, and so due to cease when the damned has been corrected?

[31] H. Crouzel, 'L'Hadès et la Géhenne chez Origène', *Gregorianum* 59, 1978, 291–331.
[32] GCS III.
[33] See p. 33.
[34] *PArch* I, pref. 5.

This fire must be distinguished from the fire of eschatological purification which is, as we shall see, God Himself, 'a devouring fire'.[35] Eternal fire is different from our material fire, for the latter goes out, the former does not. It is invisible and burns invisible realities. But there is analogy between the two: the sufferings of men who die by fire gives some idea of what that fire can make them suffer. The *Treatise on First Principles*[36] attempts a psychological explanation of that fire: it is a fire which each sinner lights for himself and which is fed by his own sins. Origen often says that our deeds leave their marks on our souls and that at the Day of Judgement those marks will be revealed and all will be able to read them. The sinner seeing on himself the marks of all his wicked deeds will feel the pricks of conscience and this remorse will constitute the fire that punishes him. It is also possible to start from the passions with which a man burns here below. Sinners caught in the net of these passions at the moment when they are leaving the world, without having in any way amended their lives, feel them at their most acute. A third approach is attempted, unconnected with fire, starting from the punishment of dismemberment and citing the destruction of the inner harmony of the soul. These images constitute a theological effort to approach by way of analogy the mystery of the penalty of damnation. The flagellation of a naked body compared with that of a clothed one gives some idea, Origen says, of the sufferings to be borne compared with those of our present life: this image[37] suggests that the damned when resurrected will feel sensual pain.

The second problem is more difficult. Thus Origen continually uses the expressions 'eternal fire' (*pyr aiōnion*) and inextinguishable fire (*pyr asbeston*) and yet he ventures to suggest several times the idea that the punishment will be remedial, and therefore should have an end; at other times he asks the question without answering it, as if the Scripture did not seem to him clear enough on this point. We shall take up the problem in a more general way at the end of this chapter in connection with the 'apocatastasis': for the moment we shall go no further than texts relating to eternal fire. In the *Homilies on Jeremiah* there are to be found preserved in Greek passages which point in both directions. Homily XX (XIX), 4 would suggest that the truth about the punishments would lie in their remedial character: however, it is not impossible that there is a certain irony in this passage, as this expression seems to show: 'How many of those whom one thinks wise . . .' According to Homily I, 15, God not only destroys the work of the devil, He annihilates it, sending the straw into an inextinguishable fire and the tares to the fire. But since the torment of eternal fire could not corrupt people, what God

[35] Deut. 4, 24 and 9, 3.
[36] II, 10, 4–5.
[37] *SelPs*, 6, after Pamphilus in PG 12, 1177–1178B.

annihilates by the fire seems to be the devil's work in man and we get back to the remedial character. On the other hand Homily XVIII, 1, describing Jeremiah's visit to the potter's workshop,[38] implies that the state in which a man is when death takes him is in a certain way definitive, like that of the vessel fired in the kiln. We shall see several more examples of the pendulum swinging like this, often in the course of the same work.

The essential reason why the expression *pyr aiōnion* does not seem to imply for Origen necessarily eternity as we understand it is that the adjective *aiōnios* translated by eternal keeps all the ambiguity of the word from which it comes, *aiōn*. In both Testaments, alongside the meaning 'eternity' conceived as a duration without end, there is also found the one which we translate in French by 'siècle' (and in English by 'world'), a long period of time, in particular, the duration of the present world. In the *Treatise on First Principles*[39] in Rufinus's version, Origen defines, in connection with the eternal generation of the Son, the adjectives *sempiternum* and *aeternum:* 'that which has not had a beginning to its existence and that which can never cease to be what it is'. On this point Origen has no hesitation and we have seen him use several times over the formula which Athanasius would popularise: 'There was not a moment when the Son was not'.[40] And the generation of the Son is not only eternal but also continuous: a double affirmation which brings us close to the notion of eternity conceived not only as a time without beginning or end, but as a recapitulation of everything in a timeless present.

But when we are talking of rational creatures, the *aiōn* often represents a very long time, but one which has an end. According to the *Commentary on Romans:*[41]

> eternity signifies in Scripture sometimes the fact that we do not know the end, sometimes the fact that there is no end in the present world, but there will be one in the next. Sometimes eternity means a certain length of time, even that of a human life.

And Origen gives Scriptural examples of these different meanings. He is ready to assign to the life of the blessed an infinite duration, but the sense of the words *aiōn* and *aiōnios* in Scripture does not seem to him sufficiently clear, for reasons which we shall expound in connection with the apocatastasis, in the matter of the punishment of the damned: those hesitations and affirmations persist in both senses.

It is the same with the 'outer darkness' mentioned in the two parables of the Wedding Guests and the Talents:[42] it stands either for the state of

[38] Jer. 18, 1–16.
[39] I, 2, 11.
[40] *PArch* I, 2, 9 (Rufinus); IV, 4, 1 (Rufinus and Athanasius); *ComRm* I, 5 (PG 14) (Rufinus); Cf. [p. 244].
[41] *ComRm* VI, 5 (PG 14).
[42] Mt. 12, 13; 25, 30; cf. 8, 12.

ignorance of the damned or for the dark body which will be theirs in the resurrection.[43] Does it represent a definitive or a temporary state? In the *Commentary on John*[44] Origen formally admits that he does not know. In the *Commentary on Matthew*[45] he cautiously suggests a remedial punishment.

When speaking of baptism we saw that it was for Origen the sacramental image of another baptism, the baptism of fire, which John the Baptist says will be given by Jesus:[46] this is for Origen the fire of eschatological purification, our Purgatory.[47] It is also found figured by other images: the theme, inspired perhaps by the Valentinian gnōsis, of the 'customs officers of the Beyond' represented by the publicans, the fallen angels, who, posted at the frontiers of this world, strip those passing of what belongs to them, the demons;[48] or again the exegesis of Luke 12, 58–59, the prison from which there will be no escape before paying the last farthing.[49] But the main Scriptural passage is 1 Cor. 3, 11–15: on the foundation which is Jesus Christ we can build with imperishable materials, gold, silver, precious stones, or with perishable, wood, hay, straw. When the Day comes the work of each will be put to the test: if it lasts the builder will receive his reward; if it is consumed he will be harmed, but he will be saved as through the fire. This text is explained thirty-eight times in what is extant of Origen's work: sometimes it is applied to the apostolic worker, orthodox or heretic, but most often to all the deeds of the Christian. The gold, silver and precious stones represent virtuous deeds; the wood, hay and straw faults which are not of the most grave and in which the personality and the will are not completely engaged. The Day is the Day of Judgement: this will happen either when our life is over, or at the End of the Ages. The fire which consumes is, we repeat, in most of the texts, God Himself, 'a devouring fire',[50] for God does not consume perceptible materials but spiritual realities, our sins. It is also Christ, according to an *agraphon*:[51] 'Those who approach me approach the fire, those who depart from me depart from the Kingdom'. This identification of God with the purifying fire is all the more remarkable in that it would be found in the intuitions of certain later mystics relying on the experience of their inner purifications, for example, St Catherine of Genoa, in her celebrated *Treatise on*

[43] *PArch* II, 10, 8.
[44] XXVIII, 8 (7), 61–66 (GCS IV).
[45] *ComMt* XVII, 24 (GCS X); *SerMt* 69 (GCS XI).
[46] Matt. 3, 11 and parallels.
[47] H. Crouzel, 'L'exégèse origénienne de 1 Cor. 3, 11–15 et la purification eschatologique' in *Epektasis: Mélanges patristiques offerts au Cardinal Jean Daniélou* (ed. J. Fontaine and Ch. Kannengiesser), Paris, 1972, 273–283.
[48] *HomLc* XXIII.
[49] *HomLc* XXXV.
[50] Deut. 4, 24 and 9, 3.
[51] An *agraphon* is a saying attributed to Jesus but not found in the New Testament.

Purgatory: the purifying fire for her is none other than the divine love, source of great joy and of great suffering, for it renders the soul conscious of its impurity and so purifies it. Thus it is God, or Christ, who will purify what has been built in wood, hay or straw, by painfully consuming the building. But sometimes Origen also speaks in this context of a fire which is proper to each sinner, and has been lighted by his sins.

At the end of the section devoted to penance[52] we gave an example of the way Origen grades sins, distinguishing those which cause us to lose the grace of Christ from those which do not. Homily XIII on Jeremiah,[53] preserved in Greek, sets out clearly the problems to which Purgatory is the answer. Would it be in conformity with the justice of God to damn one who leaves this life full of good deeds, but also burdened with sins? But would it be fair in such a case to admit him to blessedness without purification? But several passages show that this doctrine is not very familiar to some of Origen's hearers, who are persuaded that if they have not committed idolatry or fornication they will go straight to heaven regardless of the rest. As for the painful character of this purification, we have seen it stated in connection with the baptism of fire: it is also mentioned in comment on 1 Cor. 3, 11–15, and Origen does not hesitate to say that he fears this purification for himself. Commenting on Paul's desire to die that he might be with Christ,[54] he cries:

> For my part, I cannot speak thus, for I know that, when I go hence, my wood will have to be burned in me.[55]

The apostles themselves had to pass through the river of fire, to pass near the flaming sword – necessarily, since the fire is God and his Christ – and they did it without coming to any harm:

> But if there is a sinner like me, he will come to this fire like Peter and Paul, but he will not be able to cross it like Peter and Paul.[56]

What is the activity of the righteous in blessedness with the Lord, after suffering or not suffering this ultimate purification? Although separated from the earthly body, these souls are none the less active. A fragment of the *Commentary on the Psalms,*[57] starting from the frequent identification in Greek literature as well as in the Scriptures of death with sleep, shows that in death as in dreaming the soul acts without the medium of the body. Its main activity is, of course, that to which, according to the *Treatise on First Principles*[58] the *cursus studiorum* of the school of souls

[52] Cf. pp. 229–233.
[53] §§5–6.
[54] Phil. 1, 23.
[55] *HomJr* XX, 3.
[56] *HomPs* 36, III, 1 (PG 12, 1337B).
[57] *SelPs* 3, 6: PG 12, 1128BC.
[58] II, 11, 6–7.

led, the contemplation of the works of God, then the 'contemplation and comprehension of God, essential food of rational creatures', knowledge which is identified, after Gen. 4, 1, with love in union. This activity will be pursued in a more perfect manner still after the resurrection. But before that moment comes, will the saints, in Origen's view, take any interest in their brethren still on earth? He often speaks of their intercession with God, starting from two texts of the Old Testament: the dead Samuel prophesies for Saul at the house of the witch of Endor[59] and of Jeremiah it is written: 'He who is the friend of his brethren and prays much for the people and for the whole holy city, Jeremiah, the prophet of God'.[60] Origen cites these two examples several times[61] to show that the saints in heaven do not remain idle, but are full of charity for their brethren still in this world, whom they help with their prayers and intercessions. Several texts emphasise the intervention of the martyrs, co-redeemers with Christ, on behalf of their brethren. The saints of the Old Testament also go before us in the front rank in our battles with the evil powers. The blessed, says Paul, suffer with those who suffer, rejoice with those who rejoice. With Christ Himself they share the woes of believers. The angels themselves are invisibly present in the churches at the assemblies of the faithful and thus, when the latter gather together, a double Church is present, angelic and human: the souls of the dead are there also.

In a celebrated homily[62] Origen is not afraid to say, thinking of Christ in his total body, that the joy of Christ and the saints will not be complete until the whole Body is reconstituted in the heavenly Jerusalem:

> My Saviour weeps for my sins. My Saviour cannot rejoice while I remain in iniquity . . . The Apostles themselves have not yet received their joy, but are waiting for me to share in their merriment. On their departure hence the saints do not immediately receive the full reward of their merits, but they wait for us, although we are slow, although we are lazy. Not for them the perfect joy so long as they are suffering for our errors and weeping for our sins.

These expressions, paradoxical in Origen's own thought, are intended to emphasise the powerful solidarity which unites Christ to all the members of his Body. This sermon, read to the chapter in the Abbey of Clairvaux, stirred various movements, and Bernard, caught between the offence taken by some and the admiration of others, had the next day to explain himself before his monks.[63] Through him, says H. de Lubac,[64]

[59] 1 K (1 Sam) 28, 3–25.
[60] 2 Macc. 15, 14–16.
[61] See the article 'Mort et immortalité . . .' (note 1), pp. 193–196: for this and what follows.
[62] HomLv VII, 2.
[63] Sermon 34 de diversis: PL 183, 630ff.
[64] Exégèse Médiévale I/1, Paris, 1959, 281–284.

this homily would, five centuries later still, inspire Pascal's *Mystère de Jésus*.

The Resurrection of men[65]

When we were talking of baptism we said that Origen, in an attempt to reduce the attraction of the millenarian content given to Apoc. 20, 1–6, by interpreting the passage literally, followed Rom. 6 in using the term 'first resurrection'[66] to mean the change produced by baptism and the Christian life that ensued: we have there an imperfect resurrection or rather one that is in the making, 'through a glass darkly'. Jesus is Resurrection in that he is the author both of this first resurrection and of the second. In correlation with this Origen describes as 'living' those who have not sinned gravely after baptism and thus pass in all innocence from the first resurrection to the second, and as 'dead in Christ' those who have gravely sinned and repented. This second distinction was misunderstood by Methodius of Olympus[67] who sees in the 'dead' sinners who are not repenting and thus attributes to Origen the idea of universal salvation.

But here we are concerned with the 'second resurrection' which is 'face to face' and total. Many points would have to be looked at it if we were attempting a complete exposition: for example, the relation between the resurrection of Christ and that of men; the resurrection as a work of God, who is alone capable of raising from the dead. Origen sees the resurrected as divided into different orders or classes,[68] according to the merits of their earthly life: he finds that figured by various texts, notably by the descriptions of the Hebrews' camp in the Book of Numbers. And this diversity is found in passages which at the time affirm their unity. He mentions the resurrection unto damnation, taking Theodotion's reading of Daniel, 12, 2, and sees in the 'outer darkness' the dark and murky bodies of those raised and damned, which torments cannot rot away. The reason for this resurrection of the damned is that the soul is not punished without the body, an argument which reproduces the main reasoning of Athenagoras in the second part of his *Treatise on the Resurrection*. We saw in the preceding section what Origen thought of the pains of Gehenna.

Several texts of the Old Testament directly prophesy the resurrection, and others do when spiritual exegesis is used.[69] Among the former are Job

---

[65] H. Crouzel, 'La doctrine origénienne du corps ressuscité', *Bulletin de Littérature Ecclésiastique* 81, 1980, 175–200, 241–266. Likewise: 'Fonti prenicene della dottrina di Ambrogio sulla risurrezione dei morti', *La Scuola Cattolica*, 102, 1974, 373–388.

[66] See the article cited in note 25.

[67] *Aglaophon* III, 21: Greek text in Photius, *Bibl.* 234, 301B.

[68] H. Crouzel, 'Différences entre les ressucités selon Origèn' in *Jenseits-vorstellungen im Antike und Christentum: Gedenkschrift für Alfred Stuiber, Jahrbuch für Antike und Christentum*, Ergänzungsband 9, Münster i.W., 1982, 107–116.

[69] H. Crouzel, 'Les prophéties de la Resurrection chez Origène', in *Forma Futuri: Studi in onore del Cardinale Michele Pellegrino*, Turin, 1975, 980–992.

19, 25–26 LXX and, following a rather curious reasoning, the end of the same Book; and Daniel 12, 1–3 according to Theodotion. Among the latter are the faith of Abraham preparing to sacrifice Isaac according to Heb. 11, 17–19; the description of the Israelite camp in the Book of Numbers 1–2. As for the prophecy of Ezekiel about the dry bones that recover their life,[70] Origen, in accordance with the explanation that the prophet himself gives and in contradiction of the opinions of other Fathers, such as Methodius – who criticises Origen's interpretation – and Ambrose, refuses to see in this a prophecy of the resurrection in the literal and individual sense: since it represents according to Ezekiel the resurrection of the people of Israel after the exile, it is only a prophecy of the resurrection in the spiritual and collective sense, figuring that of 'the true and most perfect Body of Christ, his holy Church'.[71] The rite of circumcision is likewise a figure of the resurrection, just as chastity and virginity are its living witness here below. Finally, in the symbolic arithmetic which is at the root of many of the Alexandrian's exegeses, the resurrection, that of Christ and consequently that of men, is associated with two numbers, three because Jesus was raised on the third day, and eight because the resurrection of Jesus took place on the morrow of the seventh day, Sunday.

But the point that was most fiercely attacked by Methodius of Olympus and Peter of Alexandria at the turn of the 3rd and 4th centuries was Origen's conception of the raised body. Unfortunately his two opponents misunderstood it, caricatured it and then criticised their caricature. And many of their successors, right down to the 20th century, instead of looking for the Alexandrian's teaching in his own works, where it is widely scattered, have sought to save themselves this trouble and have been content to reproduce the accusations of Methodius, thus perpetuating his misconceptions.

To understand a doctrine it is necessary to be clear about the problem it was answering and about its main concerns. At the root of Origen's conception of the risen body, is what Paul says in 1 Cor. 15, 12–58, but especially the comparison of the seed and the plant developed in verses 35 to 44. The mystery of the relation between the earthly body and the glorious body lies in their identity and their dissimilarity: as between the seed and the plant there is identity and difference. Such is the central intuition which Origen develops with the help of various philosophical doctrines. In this task he is concerned about opinions that he considers erroneous, with shortcomings which he is anxious to overcome. In fact he wants to affirm the reality of the resurrection of bodies in the face of infidels and heretics who deny it. But he perceives acutely that the

---

[70] Ezek 37, 1–14.

[71] ComJn X, 35–36, 230–238; ComPs I, 6 §§13 and 15 in Methodius, *Aglaophon*, I, 21 and 23, or Epiphanius, *Panarion* 64, 13 and 15 (GCS Methodius and GCS Epiphanius II).

conceptions many Christians hold of this mystery are largely responsible for this denial. Opponents are shocked on grounds of common sense, and confusing these crude pictures with faith in the resurrection itself, reject everything. Incredibility and what we should today call 'integrism' are paradoxically joined: to be able the better to despise the Christian religion its detractors understand it in the most startling way, rejecting every other approach.

So Origen begins by opposing the doctrine of the resurrection current among many Christians of his own day, those who are usually called millenarians or chiliasts. We have mentioned their belief in a thousand-year reign of Christ and the martyrs in the earthly Jerusalem before the final resurrection. As regards the state of the body after this resurrection, they imagine that it will be identical with the earthly body so that people will eat and drink, marry and procreate, and that the heavenly Jerusalem will be like a city here below. The spiritual body will differ in nothing from the psychic body and everything in the Beyond will be like life in this lower world. For, being anthropomorphites, the millenarians take literally the biblical anthropomorphisms. They suppress all difference between the terrestrial body and the glorious body, keeping only the identity. An illustration of this is afforded by the first part of the *Treatise on the Resurrection* by Athenagoras.[72] Apparently quite ignorant of the transient character of the material constituents of the body, of which Origen on the contrary has a very clear idea, he raises the following problem: if an animal eats a man and subsequently a man eats that animal, to whom at the resurrection will belong the parts of the first man that passed this way into the second? He solves this problem by calling in aid the theory of digestion of the physician Galen and by confusing the physical and moral aspects of the question: a man and an animal can only assimilate food that is natural to them and all food that is unnatural will be rejected; now man is an unnatural food for man; so the second man will not be able to assimilate what comes from the first and will reject it. This shows the level of the conceptions that Origen is contesting. Now the pagans, men like Celsus, identify that kind of thing with the Christian doctrine of the resurrection which becomes for that reason an object of their derision. Origen scents that similar notions underlie the Sadducean rejection of the Resurrection reported in Matt. 22, 23–33 where they raise the objection about the woman with seven husbands. And as the Sadducees are for him figurative of the heretics, the latter are in the same position, those of whom Origen says in the *Dialogue with Heraclides*[135] that all heretics deny the resurrection: in saying this he goes somewhat too far, as is shown by the very orthodox *Treatise on the Resurrection* by

[72] Ed. Schoedel, Oxford 1972.
[73] 6, 5.

Tertullian,[74] composed at a time when, without having yet broken with the Great Church, its author was not afraid to rely openly on the revelation of the Paraclete, as the Montanists did.

In our exposition of Origen's doctrine we begin with the difference. The main text is the conversation of Jesus with the Sadducees.[75] The risen will be like the angels in heaven. But does not this comparison endanger the corporeal character of the resurrection? That would be true for Christians today, accustomed to consider the angels as 'pure spirits', incorporeal. It is not true for Origen for his dominant opinion – we noted it when speaking of the body in connection with the trichotomic anthropolgy – is that the angels, like the demons, have a body, but of a more tenuous nature than ours. Now the bodies of the risen will be like those of the angels: 'those who are considered worthy of the resurrection of the dead become like the angels in heaven (not only in the absence of sexual activity), but also because their bodies of humiliation are transfigured and become like the bodies of the angels, ethereal, a dazzling light (*augoeides*)'.[76] As this text shows the blessed at the resurrection do not put on another body of an ethereal nature but it is their earthly bodies themselves which become ethereal: the 'substance' remains the same, only the 'quality' changes, from earthly to heavenly. So the glorious bodies are described as 'dazzling' (*augoeide*) and ethereal. The doctrine of the ether which is expressed here is of philosophical origin, found in Plato as well as Aristotle. For Origen the ether denotes a part of the sky, above that of the air which is one of the four common elements, and it also means the nature of the bodies to be found there, the purest state which corporeal nature can receive. The stars are ethereal. But Origen refuses to apply this term to God, who is not corporeal. He applies it to the glorified body of Jesus and to the bodies of men raised from the dead. In two passages,[77] however, he opposes the doctrine that Aristotle developed in his early writing *On Philosophy,* making the ether a fifth element – the 'quintessence' – over and above the classical four. Origen does not reject the ether as a quality that can clothe substance, but as another body, which would not conform with the identity of the risen body with the earthly one. If the risen body is to be ethereal, that is because it must inhabit ethereal places and 'it is necessary that the soul, when it finds itself in corporeal places, should be using a body adapted to that place'. If we had to live in the sea, we should have to have marine bodies.[78] Several times 2 Cor. 5, 4 is quoted in this connection; 'For while we are still in this tent, we sigh with anxiety; not that we would be unclothed, but that

[74] *CChr* II.
[75] Matt. 22, 29–33.
[76] *ComMt* XVII, 30 (GCS X).
[77] *PArch* III, 6, 7; *ComJn* XIII, 21, 126.
[78] *ComPs* I, 5 from Methodius I, 22 or Epiphanius 14, 7–8 (see note 71).

we would be further clothed, so that what is mortal may be swallowed up by life'. For Origen the tent is the body which is the same in the present life and the risen life: but the 'habitation' of the body changes. The latter possesses in this life the qualities of mortality and corruptibility, and in the other world those of immortality and incorruptibility. The change does not affect the substance of the body – you cannot 'doff' that – but the qualities with which it is clothed to live in a new environment. The clothing is not the body but the qualities which inform it.

Origen further reads in Matt. 22, 29–33, that in the resurrection neither men nor women will marry. According to the *Commentary on Matthew*[79] the conception of the resurrection underlying the Sadducean objection is that each will be raised to a life like today's. Relations with other human beings will continue as in the past, husband to wife, father to son, brother to brother. Now the Creator only makes what is useful; that is the postulate that governs Origen's reply. In the world of becoming there are generation and corruption; so there are sexual relations, procreation, relations of parents to children, brothers to brothers. But all that was then necessary will not be necessary in the world to come. To suppose with the Sadducees that there is sexual life there, is to re-establish in the new world all the realities of this one, necessarily accompanied by their woes. With an implacable logic, but one that is carried too far, Origen reaches the point of ruling out in the world to come the permanence of those relationships, including those of family, which have marked our life in this lower world, without realising that by doing this he is hurting at the deepest point the very personality of the risen, such as it was formed in this life, and that he is endangering the identity of the man here below with what he will be in the future world, not simply in terms of the body but in terms of spiritual personality.

If the Creator only makes what is useful, since there will no longer be sexual activity in the next world, we might conclude from this passage that not only the sexual organs, but all those connected with becoming – that is, in fact, everything about the human body – will no longer exist in the risen body. Origen does not say that clearly anywhere. He seems to suggest it, but not very plainly, in two texts of which it is not the main point. However, the absence from the risen body of organs and limbs connected with becoming, an absence that results from a principle invoked by Origen rather than from clear statements, was to become one of the points in Origen's doctrine of the resurrection that would be most severely criticised during the Origenist quarrels. Methodius of Olympus would ask as a joke what was to be the outward shape of the glorious body in Origen's view, 'round, polygonal or cubic'.[80] Jerome would

---

[79] XVII, 29–33.
[80] *Aglaophon* III, 15 (GCS).

attack Origen through his defender, Bishop John of Jerusalem, and would remark that the transfigured Lord had not lost his limbs to appear 'in the roundness of the sun or of a sphere'.[81] Justinian would attribute to Origen the idea that the glorious bodies are spherical.[82] This absurdity probably arises from a misconception about a passage in the *Treatise on Prayer*[83] in which spherical heavenly bodies were understood to mean the resurrected, when they really referred to the stars. It is also possible that the Palestinian monks who originated the document promulgated by the emperor had taken seriously the ironical questions asked by Methodius and Jerome about the outward form of the glorious bodies without their limbs.

In enunciating the principle that the Creator makes nothing useless, Origen behaved in a rather off-handed manner towards the mystery, when more restraint and an avowal of ignorance would have been more acceptable: it is to be noted, however, that while he drew certain regrettable conclusions about human relationships, he did not dare go any further on the subject of the presence or absence in the glorious body of organs and limbs related to becoming. It was his detractors who pushed his logic to absurdity. But, except on this point, his general opinions on the identity and the difference of the earthly body and the resurrection body constitute an expression of the mystery, rather than an explanation of it in the strict sense, which would be impossible.

Using the data provided by the New Testament and by Greek philosophy, Origen was to try to express in three ways the identity of the earthly body and the risen body: by the Hellenic distinction between the material body and its qualities which we have already encountered several times; by the Stoic notion of 'seminal Reason'; by a corporeal 'form' (*eidos*) expressing the identity of the body with itself in spite of the perpetual flux of its material constituents.

In a passage on the *Treatise on Prayer*[84] of which the very technical form contrasts with the rest of the book, Origen distinguishes two kinds of *ousiai*, substances, in connection with the famous adjective *epiousios* which qualifies our Father's bread: he distinguishes a spiritual substance and a material substance. Only the latter concerns us now, for this first matter which possesses in itself no quality, which receives its qualities from outside without irrevocably becoming attached to any of them, is the basis of all the expressions he uses of the nature of the glorious body. It is found in the *Treatise on First Principles* as well as in the *Commentary on John* and the *Contra Celsum*, and the mystery of the identity and difference of the risen body in relation to the earthly one is thus expressed

[81] *Against John of Jerusalem* 29 (PL 26).
[82] Book *Against Origen* in PG 86/1, 973A and anathema 5 (of 543), Ibid. 989C.
[83] *PEuch* XXI, 3 (GCS II).
[84] *PEuch* XXVII, 8 (GCS II).

by using this doctrine of matter. There is a stable element, named substance, matter, substratum, body, nature, which is not in itself bound to any quality, but cannot subsist without a quality and can change its qualities by the will of the Creator: these qualities (*poiotētes*), also called by the equivalent terms *schema* or *habitus*, terms which could be translated by 'state', are the variable element capable of transforming the animal body into a spiritual body. Thus, according to the exegesis of 2 Cor. 5, 4, although we sigh, overwhelmed by living in a corruptible body, we do not want to take it off, but to put on over it the quality of incorruptibility, the 'true life', that is to say the divine life, swallowing up everything that is mortal in us.

The Stoic notion of the 'seminal reason' or '*logos spermatikos*' enables a philosophical expression to be used of Paul's image of the seed and the plant.[85] There is identity between them since the plant is the same being as the seed at a more advanced stage of its development; there is difference, for they differ greatly in their make up, in their dimensions, in their outward appearance, etc. Paul compared the earthly body to the seed, the glorious body to the plant which emerges from it after its 'death' in the ground.[86] For Origen, as for Stoicism, there is in the seed a *logos* or a *ratio*, *logos spermatikos* or seminal reason, that is to say a force of growth, of development, as well as of individuation, which will make of the seed a plant. So there is already present in the earthly body a *logos*, a *ratio*, a force of individuation and growth which, when the earthly body is dead will germinate to give the glorious body. This *logos* or *ratio* constitutes truly, to use the terms we were studying earlier, the substance of the human body, abandoning the qualities of corruptibility and mortality to receive those of incorruptibility and immortality. This *logos* is thus already in the earthly body, the anticipated or virtual presence, better still the dynamic presence of the future body. Interpreting circumcision as a figure of the resurrection, Origen sees in the flesh that is lost that of which it is said: 'All flesh is grass and all the glory of it is as the flower of grass' and the flesh that is retained symbolises that of which the Evangelist writes: 'All flesh shall see the salvation of God'.[87] This flesh preserved is the *logos* present in our body of lowliness and destined to blossom into a body of glory. This way of expressing the identity is also found in the great works of Origen, from the *Treatise on the Resurrection*, of which only fragments remain, to the *Treatise on First Principles, Homilies on 1 Corinthians, Latin Commentary on Matthew, Contra Celsum*.

The identity of our earthly body with the glorious body is expressed in yet a third way in the long fragment of the *Commentary on Psalm 1*

[85] 1 Cor. XV, 35–44.
[86] John 12, 24.
[87] Isa 40, 6, then 5, quoted in Luke 3, 6 in *ComRm* II, 13 (PG 14).

preserved by Methodius and Epiphanius.[88] The argument from which this piece starts is difficult to rebut and modern science will not contradict that of the 3rd century: the material elements are constantly renewed in the organism and so cannot explain the unity and individuality of the earthly body; so we cannot rely on them to assure the identity of the glorious body with the earthly one, since they do not play any part in assuring the identity of the earthly body with itself at different stages of its life. The primordial question is not the mystery of the identity of the earthly body with the risen one which is only reached in a consequential way but more philosophically what assures the identity of the earthly body with itself, beneath the constant flux of its material elements. The body is like a river, says Origen, with waters ever different but always the same river!

Its unity is here expressed by a bodily 'form' (*eidos*) which must be defined. It is not a matter of hylemorphism in the Aristotelian sense, for Origen declares that it is a principle of unity proper to the body, analogous to the material substance and the *logos spermatikos* already studied, while for Aristotle it is the soul which is form (*morphē, eidos*) for the body. It 'characterises' the body and remains always the same: as proof of this the Alexandrian cites the permanence of features from childhood to old age and that of scars or blotches. He appeals to certain signs which reveal at the bodily level the permanence of a personality through all the changes that its appearance has undergone. The *eidos* here denotes a metaphysical principle which prints the characteristics of the personality on the body, both the earthly and the spiritual, a dynamic force which assimilates the materials of which it takes possession, using their qualities to impose on them its own characteristics. There are precedents for this in the Platonic idea and the Aristotelian form, also each denoted by *eidos*, but differing considerably one from the other, if only in the individual character of its *eidos*. It would not do to take this word of outward appearance in its popular sense, although the *eidos* is shown by outward signs as we have seen. If this latter sense were valid, how could Origen say that the outward form remains the same from the embryo to the old man when it changes so completely from the seed to the plant? And if it is true that Origen shows a certain tendency to deprive the resurrection body of the organs necessary in a world of becoming, the argument gains further weight.

So one can define the *eidos* in this passage as the body's principle of unity, development, existence and individuation: it shows outwardly in the features by which a person is recognised, not confusing these with outward appearance which is changing like all the material elements which succeed each other in the organism. It uses their qualities changing

---

[88] *Aglaophon* I, 20–24; *Panarion* 64, 10 and 12–16: see note 71.

them into its own qualities and imprinting its characteristics on them. So it is the *eidos* which constitutes what is essential in the body which the constantly fluid material elements could not determine. So it is the *eidos* that will be raised and which will assure the substantial identity of the earthly body with the glorious one.

This fragment on Psalm 1, 5 and the doctrine of the *eidos* takes a great place in Methodius of Olympus's book entitled *Aglaophon* or *On the Resurrection*.[89] The second participant in the dialogue, Proclus, who speaks for Origen, in the second part of his speech, preserved in Greek by Epiphanius, quotes the text and comments.[90] At the end of the dialogue in book III, Methodius, through the mouth of the reporter Eubolius, subjects this passage and this doctrine to harsh criticism. Book III is not preserved in Greek by Epiphanius who cut Methodius's text unintelligently: he presents as criticism of Origen what is really criticism of the first speaker in the dialogue, Aglaophon, there is no question of Origen either in the plea or in its refutation: on the other hand there is constant reference to Origen in the second part of the plea of Proclus, which Epiphanius quotes, and in Book III, in its refutation by Euboulius, which Epiphanius does not quote, and which we know, as we do the rest of the book, in an Old Slav version. Only in the latter, of which a German translation has been published by N. Bonwetsch, adorned with Greek fragments, mostly preserved by Photius in his notice on the book,[91] can we read the criticism of Origen by Euboulius-Methodius. Reading the commentary on our text by Proclos and the criticism of it by Euboulius we can measure the extent and gravity of Methodius's misconception of the nature of the bodily *eidos*, as Origen conceived it: he has not grasped the philosophical meaning of the term, he takes it in its popular sense of outward appearance and by doing that renders completely absurd the doctrine he is seeking to refute. He consequently considers that the glorious body is in Origen's view a different body from the earthly body, to which has been given the same outward appearance: he thus frustrates the efforts of the Alexandrian to express the identity without neglecting the difference. This fundamental misunderstanding deprives Methodius's complaints about Origen's doctrine of the resurrection body of almost all their value.

To this exposition of the raised body we must add a brief consideration of the glorious body of Christ. The Transfiguration stands as a prelude to the Resurrection: it is in Origen the symbol of the highest knowledge of God in the Son that can be had here below. But the transfigured body is not different from the usual earthly body of Jesus: if the three apostles see

---

[89] H. Crouzel, 'Les critiques adressées par Méthode et ses contemporains à la doctrine origénienne du corps ressuscité', *Gregorianum*, 53, 1972, 679–716.
[90] *Aglaophon* I, 20–26.
[91] *Bibl.* 234 (CUFr V).

the divinity through it, that is partly because Jesus wished to manifest to them his divine nature, for a divine or angelic nature is only known if he will to make himself known, and partly because they have climbed the mountain, symbol of the spiritual and ascetic ascent, and that they therefore possess 'spiritual' eyes which can receive the grace of God who reveals Himself. After the Resurrection we must distinguish between the period preceding the Ascension when Jesus appears to his disciples 'in a state intermediate between the density of his body before the Passion and the condition in which the soul appears stripped of such a body'.[92] In fact He allows Himself to be touched by his apostles, shows them his wounds: He has 'a solid and palpable body',[93] but passes through closed doors. This point also was not properly understood by Methodius. Several passages of the *Commentary on John*[94] and of the *Commentary on Matthew*,[95] and fragments preserved by Pamphilus,[96] present the Ascension with a whole panoply of angels as that of the flesh going up to heaven. There is Jesus with his risen body: the least disputable witness is the exegesis of the Word as Horseman in Apoc. 19, 11–16, clothed in a mantle sprinkled with blood, which figures his flesh and his Passion of which He keeps the marks.[97] Origen does not shrink from very realistic expressions, but these must not cause us to lose sight of the fact that, since the resurrection of men is of the same kind as the resurrection of Christ, all the speculations of the Alexandrian seeking to express both identity and difference apply *a fortiori* to Jesus. According to the *Contra Celsum*[98] the quality (*poiotēs*) of mortality in the body of Jesus has changed into an ethereal and divine quality and the flesh of Jesus has changed its qualities to be able to dwell in the ether.

The apocatastasis

This word, which means restoration, re-establishment, with the Latin equivalent *restitutio*, usually denotes the doctrine of the restoration of all things at the end of time, a doctrine attributed to Origen and to Gregory of Nyssa. The noun *apokatastasis* and the verb *apokathistēmi* are used by Origen, not very often and in various senses, some of which can be taken to symbolise the final apocatastasis, others the return of the Israelites to their own country from exile. In the first book of the *Commentary on John*[99] there is mention of 'what is called the apocatastasis', defined as the situation to which Paul refers in 1 Cor. 15–25. The expression 'what is

---

[92] *CCels* II, 62.
[93] *PArch* I, pref. 8.
[94] VI, 56–57, 288–295.
[95] XVI, 9 (GCS X).
[96] PG 17, 600AB; 600C.
[97] *ComJn* II, 8, 61.
[98] III, 41–42.
[99] I, 16, 91.

called' shows that Origen is not the inventor of this apocatastasis and that he found it in what was earlier said about the Pauline verse. In the *Treatise on First Principles* the two occasions when *apokatastasis* is used in the texts of the *Philocalia* do not refer to our apocatastasis, but three times in Rufinus's version there is reference to *restitutio omnium* or *perfecta universae creaturae restitutio* and sometimes the verb *restituere* is used in the same sense.

The main passage on which Origen's apocatastasis is based is 1 Cor. 15, 23–28, which is about the resurrection of the dead: 'But each (will be raised) in his own order: Christ the firstfruits, then at his coming those who belong to Christ. Then comes the end, when he delivers the kingdom to God the Father after destroying every rule and every authority and power. For he must reign until he has put all his enemies under his feet.[100] The last enemy to be destroyed is death. For God has put all things in subjection under his feet.[101] But when it says all things are put in subjection under him, it is plain that he is excepted who put all things under him. When all things are subjected to him, then the Son himself will also be subjected to him who put all things under him, that God may be everything to everyone.'[102]

Nothing in what we possess of Origen's work allows us to attribute to him the opinion ascribed to him by Theophilus, namely that this passing of power from the Son to the Father would mean the end of the Son's reign, as Theophilus keeps asserting throughout his *Paschal Letter* of 401.[103] This submission of the Son to the Father is interpreted by Origen of the submission to the Father of the whole rational creation, henceforth subjected to the Son: it does not mean, as the heretics claim, that the Son himself would not be subject to the Father before this final submission which coincides with the gift by the Father of perfection and blessedness.[104]

Several questions arise about the use Origen made of these Pauline verses, questions which must be answered, not from isolated texts but from his work as a whole. 1. Does Origen represent this restoration as incorporeal? 2. As pantheistic? 3. Is it for him absolutely universal, implying the return to grace of the demons and the damned, and does he attach to this universality, if there is universality, the status of dogmatic affirmation, or is it simply a great hope? 4. Whence comes Origen's insistence on this Pauline text and on the 'restoration of all things'?

1. As for an incorporeal apocatastasis, the question would seem superfluous after all we have said about the resurrection of the body.

[100] Ps. 109 (110), 1.
[101] Ps. 8, 7.
[102] H. Crouzel, 'Quand le Fils transmet le Royaume à Dieu son Père: l'interprétation d'Origène' *Studia Missionalia* 33, 1984, pp. 359–384.
[103] Letter 96 in the correspondence of Jerome, who translated this letter (CUFr V): see the article mentioned in the previous note.
[104] *PArch* III, 5, 6–7.

True, a modern might say that these ethereal bodies seem to him to lack consistency and they amount in fact to a declaration of incorporeality: but in saying that he would be substituting his own outlook for that of Origen and would scarcely deserve the title of historian. The question arises in four passages of the *Treatise on First Principles*[105] in which Origen, read in the translation of Rufinus, discusses two alternative hypotheses, that of a corporeal end for rational creatures, supported by reasons drawn from Scripture, and that of an incorporeal end for them, supported by philosophical reasons; and he comes to no conclusion, which is not unusual in this book. It is true that Rufinus seems to have somewhat telescoped this second hypothesis, as appears from the fact that fragments preserved by Jerome have nothing corresponding to them in Rufinus. But he does take account of the two hypotheses and recognises that the passages are by way of discussion. The same cannot be said for the fragments translated by Jerome: as his object is to make a collection of heretical 'pearls', he suppresses almost entirely the context of discussion, only retains the texts which speak of incorporeality and gives the impression that final incorporeality was firmly a tenet of Origen's. The resurrection of bodies is not denied, but looked upon as a provisional stage before total incorporeality. We may wonder whether Jerome did not read Origen through the opinions of his contemporary Evagrius Ponticus, for the final dissolution of the glorious body is found several times over in the *Kephalaia Gnōstica;*[106] and the texts of Justinian are mainly dictated by the Origenism of the 6th century.

Since there is the contradiction between Rufinus on the one hand and Jerome and Justinian on the other, and since, as Rufinus himself says, Origen at every point expresses the two alternatives without choosing clearly between them, the only way to find the answer is to study the other works of Origen. Sometimes the suggestion that he believed in final incorporeality has been based on a small number of texts, read without taking sufficient account of the various meanings that Origen gives to the word body: earthly corporeality, ethereal corporeality, the moral sense of incorporeality as a manner of life. Thus these passages are not significant, and there is not found outside the *Treatise on First Principles* any clear declaration that the glorious body would have a transient character: and in the Treatise itself it is only to be found in Jerome's interpretations. On the other hand in these other works it is several times either stated or implied that the state of the glorius body is final. If it is right to draw from the principles enunciated by Origen the conclusion that the glorious body will be without organs related to becoming, then it follows that all change

[105] I, 6, 4; II, 1–3; III, 6; IV, 4, 8. See J. Rius-Camps, 'La suerte final de la naturaleza corpórea según el Peri Archon de Orígenes', *Vetera Christianorum* 10, 1973, 291–304 or *Studia Patristica* XIV (*Texte und Untersuchungen* 117), 1976, pp. 167–179.
[106] See in chapter IX note 67.

is ruled out. Origen blames the Sadducees for restoring, in the conception they have of the resurrection, succession in time as we experience it here. Now, if the blessed are clothed in a glorious body that is going to disappear, either suddenly or gradually, so that they can be lost in the 'henad', that is in the divine unity, then they are still subject to becoming and to change. In the *Dialogue with Heraclides*[107] Origen forcefully declares that the risen body is sheltered from death:

> It is absolutely impossible that the spiritual should become a corpse or that the spiritual should become unconscious: if in fact it is possible for the spiritual to become a corpse, it is to be feared that after the resurrection, when our body will be raised according to the word of the Apostle: It is sown a physical body and raised a spiritual body,[108] we should all die. In fact Christ raised from the dead dies no more,[109] but those who are in Christ raised from the dead will die no more.

Although it is not quite the same problem as that raised by the discrepancies between Rufinus and Jerome and Justinian, the fact that all the works of Origen, other than the *Treatise on First Principles,* show the state of the resurrected as final nevertheless has its importance. So it is impossible to attribute to Origen with certainty an incorporeal apocatastasis, although he discussed this hypothesis in the *Treatise on First Principles* along with that of a corporeal apocatastasis.

2. Is Origen's apocatastasis pantheistic? Does it imply that the final union of the spiritual creatures with God and with each other will be effected by the dissolution of their 'hypostases', that is of their substances and personalities? We could bring forward again in this connection the texts we have just quoted on the fact that the raised will no longer know death. Origen often expresses the unity of the believer with God by 1 Cor. 6, 17: 'But he who is united with the Lord becomes one spirit with him', a replica of Gen. 2, 24, previously quoted in the same verse: 'The two shall become one flesh'. Between the believer and the Lord, as between the husband and the wife, there is both union and duality. Likewise, as we have seen, Origen defines knowledge, that of God and the divine realities, which is the only kind of knowledge he cares about by Gen. 4, 1: 'Adam knew Eve his wife', defining knowledge as union in love. We may also recall the famous image used by him of the union of the pre-existent soul of Jesus with the Word, that of the iron which, plunged in the fire, becomes fire:[110] the iron becomes fire in the sense that what touches it is burned, but nevertheless it remains iron and the image always expresses both duality and unity. There is no trace of pantheism there.

[107] §§5–6.
[108] 1 Cor. 15, 44.
[109] Rom. 6, 9.
[110] *PArch* II, 6, 6.

On the subject of the union with God and with Christ which will characterise the life of the blessed, let us quote among others two texts. The first is from the *Commentary on John:*[111]

> Then all those who have come to God by the Word who is near him will have a unique activity, to comprehend God, so as to become formed in the knowledge of the Father, all being together exactly a Son, as now the Son alone knows the Father.

In other words all the blessed, having become in a way interior to the Only Son, will know the Father as now only the Son knows Him. An equivalent text, speaking not of an only Son, but of an only Sun, after Matt. 13, 43, is found in the *Commentary on Matthew.*[112] After the resurrection the blessed will shine 'Until all end in the perfect Man'[113] and become a unique sun. Then they shall shine like the sun in the kingdom of their Father'. Since for Origen, Sun of Righteousness is one of the illuminating titles (*epinoiai*) applied to the Son, to become a unique Sun is thus to become a single Son in the Only Son. But does Origen paint a pantheistic picture of this unity of all men among themselves in the Only Son? This would be in direct contrast with Origen's criticism in the *Contra Celsum* of the Stoic pantheism. For the philosophers of the Porch history consisted in a succession of cycles, each consisting of two phases. In the first, the *diakosmēsis,* that is the organisation of the world, the latter emerges gradually from the divine fire, a God represented as material; in the second, the *ekpyrōsis,* the conflagration, the world is again absorbed little by little in the divine fire. Origen takes this view of the second phase:[114]

> The Stoics may destroy everything in a conflagration if they wish. But we do not recognise that an incorporeal being is subject to a conflagration, or that the soul of man is dissolved into fire, or that this happens to the being of angels, or thrones, or dominions, or principalities, or powers.

In the face of the materialistic pantheism of the Stoics which re-absorbs all creatures into God and, consequently, does not believe in the immortality of the soul, but only in a 'survival' – Origen denotes it by the terms *diamonē* or *epidiamonē* – which only lasts until the next conflagration, he clearly affirms that the union with God will not mean the suppression of human and angelic personalities. Further on in the same book[115] he again contrasts the Stoic conflagration with the Christian beatitude showing that the latter is, to be sure, the work of the divine Logos, but that it must be received and accepted by men in freedom: 'The Stoics say that when the element which, as they think, is stronger than the

[111] I, 16, 92.
[112] X, 2 (GCS X).
[113] Eph. 4, 13.
[114] *CCels* VI, 71, Fr. Translation by M. Borret, SC 147.
[115] *CCels* VIII, 72, Ibid.

others becomes dominant, the conflagration will take place and all things change into fire. But we believe that at some time the Logos will have overcome the entire rational nature, and will have remodelled every soul to his own perfection, when each individual simply by the exercise of his freedom will choose what the Logos wills and will be in that state which he has chosen.' Man's freedom is an essential element in the way that leads to the apocatastasis and we shall see that that must also be taken into consideration. In any case these two texts contrasting the final restoration according to Christianity and the Stoic conflagration exclude all pantheism from the former.

3. Did Origen profess a universal apocatastasis, including the return to grace of the demons and the damned? If all the texts are taken into account, or even just those in the *Treatise on First Principles,* great confusion results. We have already drawn attention to Origen's hesitations about, and arguments for and against, the eternity of Gehenna and the ambiguity of the term *aiōnios,* expressing either eternity or a long duration.

We shall treat separately the case of the Devil or the demons and that of the damned. The clearest assertion of the salvation of, the Devil, although it is not absolutely explicit, is found in the *Treatise on First Principles;*[116] the last enemy to be destroyed, Death,[117] will not be destroyed in the sense that its substance will be annihilated but that its will, hostile to God, will be converted. That Death here represents the Devil is not clearly stated, but several times in Origen's work the last enemy to be destroyed, Death, is identified with sin and the Devil. Furthermore, since Death is sin, it is something negative, or rather privative, which has no substance, that 'nothing' which according to John 1, 3, as Origen reads it, was created without the Word.[118] So there can be no question of the substance of Death unless Death is a specific creature which can be none other than the Devil, often so called by Origen. But in contrast with this text we have the most explicit declaration possible in the *Letter to Friends in Alexandria* which we studied in connection with Origen's life. Although it is only preserved in Latin this declaration is of absolutely certain authenticity, for it was reported in equivalent terms by Rufinus[119] and by Jerome[120] at the height of their quarrel. Origen complains that he is said to hold the opinion that the Devil will be saved: now not even a lunatic would say that. This is not a matter of an insincere retraction for fear of

[116] III, 6, 5.
[117] 1 Cor. 15, 26.
[118] *ComJn* II, 13 (7), 92–99.
[119] *De Adulteratione* 7: CChr XX.
[120] Against Rufinus II, 18 (SC 303): see H. Crouzel, 'A Letter from Origen to "Friends in Alexandria"' in *The Heritage of the Early Church, Essays in honour of . . . George Vasilievich Florowsky,* edited by Neiman and M. Schatkin, *Orientalia Christiana Analecta,* 195, Rome 1973, 135–150.

episcopal thunder, for on the one hand that would be inconsistent with his character as the 'Man of steel', and on the other this second position is also found outlined in the *Treatise on First Principles* and, side by side, with the other, elsewhere in his work. Origen complains that a passage which ought only to be judged in the setting of a research theology – which is what this book is – has been hardened into a categorical statement.

In another passage of this writing[121] he asks in effect whether the demons could one day be converted to goodness by the exercise of their free will or whether inveterate and permanent evil will not have become nature to them. So he accepts the possibility that if the demons are not evil by reason of their original nature, in other words have not been created evil by God, but have become evil by the choice of their free will, the habit of wickedness might block their free will, become a second nature and render impossible all conversion to good. And this second alternative is not isolated in Origen's work. That wickedness has become nature in the Devil and his son the Antichrist is said in connection with Ezekiel's prophecy about the fall of the Prince of Tyre, figure of the Devil, in the *Commentary on John:*[122] to express that Origen even coins the neologism *pephysiōmenon*, this person has thus 'natured himself'. And the converse is also true, with the difference that if the habit of evil blocks the free will, the habit of good leads on the contrary to true freedom, which for Origen is something more than free will. In fact, in contrast to the hypothesis he advances in the *Treatise on First Principles* of a possible fall among the blessed themselves on account of free will, the Alexandrian shows often enough charity becoming nature, bringing an immutability in good. That is realised to perfection, because of the perfect charity that unites it with the Word, in the human soul of Jesus who possesses good as a matter of substance, like the Trinity, and is absolutely impeccable, while being of the same nature as other souls, endowed like them with free will, those other souls which only possess good by way of accident, with the possibility of progress and of fall.[123] Free will cannot separate from charity those who have given themselves to charity[124] and he who draws near to God shares in his immutability.[125] If the soul is absolutely immortal as regards ordinary death, it is not exempt from the death of sin, but it becomes so to the degree in which it is 'established in blessedness'.[126] Origen sometimes even goes so far as to speak of the progressive impeccability of the spiritual man as a kind of limiting

---

[121] *PArch* I, 6, 2.
[122] XX, 21 (19), 174; Ezek 28, 19. C. Blanc (SC 290) translates 'naturifié'. Also *FragMt:* 141 (GCS XII/1).
[123] *PArch* II, 6, 5–6.
[124] *ComRm* V, 10 (PG 14).
[125] *Hom 1 K* (1 Sam) I, §4 (GCS VIII).
[126] *Dialogue with Heraclides* 27, 1.

concept. For beyond free will he knows, as several texts bear witness, a conception of freedom which, like Paul's *eleutheria*, is identified with adherence to the good. Other texts again can be cited for the definitive character the damnation of the Devil.

The study of certain passages about 'eternal fire' would show Origen more inclined to accept eternal punishment for the demons than for men. However, there are texts which point in that direction, such as the homily on Jeremiah XVIII, 1, about the visit of the prophet to the potter's workshop, or some of those commenting on the sin against the Holy Spirit.[127] But where this latter subject crops up elsewhere consideration of the divine mercy leads him to leave the question open.[128] Besides, the exegesis of *dichotomēsei* in Matt. 24, 51, and Luke 12, 46 – about the dishonest steward whose master returns to find him beating his subordinates and carousing with drunkards – scarcely seems to favour the possibility of conversion for the damned. The most current interpretation[129] is as follows: the 'spirit which is in man', a divine gift, the mentor of the soul, returns to God who gave it, while the soul and the body go 'with the unbelievers' into Gehenna. Since the spirit is associated with the soul as its trainer in sanctification, its preceptor in virtue, knowledge of God and prayer, one cannot see how the soul can be sanctified once it is taken away: here below the *pneuma* is never taken away from the sinner, but only put to sleep by sin and so the man keeps the possibility of returning to God.

Consequently it would be wrong to see in the texts expressing the non-eternity of Gehenna a firm statement of conviction. Origen hesitates, not seeing how to reconcile all the statements of Scripture: sometimes he makes no pronouncement, sometimes he ventures an opinion in one direction, sometimes in the other. In any case, if the affirmations of the universality of the apocatastasis which some find in his work must be taken in this sense and regarded as propositions with dogmatic status, they would be in contradiction with a point of capital importance in the synthesis presented by the *Treatise on First Principles,* free will. In fact God and his Word never force a man, they do not manipulate him, they do not make him falsely believe that he is free when he can really be manipulated. It is freely that a man submits to the Word, it is freely that he will submit to the Father in the apocatastasis. We saw this clearly affirmed in the *Contra Celsum*[130] in contrast with the Stoic conflagration. If the free will of man, accepting or refusing God's advances, plays such a role in Origen's thought, how could he become certain that all human and

[127] *ComJn* XIX, 14 (3), 88.
[128] *PEuch* XXVII, 15 (GCS II).
[129] One of the three interpretations given in *PArch* II, 10, 7 and the only one in *ComRm* II, 9 (PG 14) and *SerMt* 57 and 62.
[130] VIII, 72.

demonic beings, in their freedom would allow themselves to be touched and would adhere to God in the apocatastasis? If Origen added anything to what Paul said in 1 Cor. 15, 23–28, it could only be a great hope. Certainty about a universal apocatastasis would be in contradiction to the authenticity of the free will with which God had endowed mankind.

As the basis of this hope there is certainly Origen's imperturable faith in the goodness of God, not only of the Father of Jesus Christ, but of the Creator God of the Old Testament, who for him as for all 'churchmen', that is members of the Great Church, are One, whatever the Marcionites and Gnostics say. By all means, including allegorical exegesis, he defends this God against the charges of cruelty levelled against Him by the heretics, going so far, we repeat, as to accept the hypothesis of the pre-existence of souls to take from God the responsibility for the unequal conditions in which men are born. For this reason he usually considers the divine punishments as remedial and merciful, aimed at the amendment and conversion of those punished. He has however, glimpsed the possibility that Gehenna might have a final character for the demons, or, with more hesitation, even for men; this is not to be imputed to God who is good, but to the obduracy of the creature who will not, and even in the end cannot, let himself be touched by that goodness: the idea that wickedness can in some way become nature through habit is not absent from his work. But he did not sufficiently work this out, hindered by his own anti-marcionite and antignostic polemics. He seems to preserve the hope that the Word of God will attain such force of persuasion that, without violation of free will, it will in the end overcome all resistance.

It will be seen how extremely delicate and qualified a reply must be given to the question of the universality of the apocatastasis in Origen. It cannot be said that he held this view, or that he firmly professed it, for if there are texts pointing in that direction, too many others exist on the other side, showing other aspects which must form part of the answer. At most it can be said that he hoped for it, in a period when the rule of faith was not fixed as it would be later on.

Of course those who look for a 'system' in Origen, by neglecting three quarters of what remains of his thought, even in the *Treatise on First Principles* itself, in order to systematise the few affirmations that they retain, will scarcely be satisfied by our exposition of the Alexandrian's views on our latter end, for it brings out the numerous qualifications, hesitations, discrepancies that exist, especially over the resurrection and the apocatastasis. They will begin with the principle that the latter should be as universal as the fall in the pre-existence, from which escaped only the soul joined to the Word. But, in fact, according to passages of the *Treatise on First Principles* which they neglect other souls beside Christ's did not share in the fault. So, following their argument, why should the apocatastasis be absolutely universal when the fall was not?

The controversy between us and the supporters of a 'system' in Origen depends on the conception of historical science. To study a doctrine, is it to project upon it a kind of geometrical frame, the main lines of which accentuate certain features and leave others in shadow, something which formal teaching unfortunately does; or it is to try and set out in the best possible way – as far as human possibilities permit, and they are never adequate to the task – the different points of the doctrine as its author gives them, without neglecting the nuances, the hesitations, the antitheses, the tensions, and even – why not? – the contradictions that it contains? Living human thought is more interesting than a system. And when it is a matter of God and the divine realities, unknowable by nature, every system is revealed as gravely deficient, often heretical, because it does not grasp the antitheses that express the real, and because it is the result of a certain narrowness of spirit. A man as passionate about God and divine knowledge as Origen does not reach God by a system, but by all the means, intellectual and mystical, that are at his disposal, even if these means do not form a system ruled by rationalist logic, and in the dark places of the faith that is ours he is not ashamed to feel his way. But that groping is much more moving and interesting than the best constructed systems.

Epilogue

After an indispensable first part on the life, works and personality of Origen, we went on to expound the three main aspects of his thought and his doctrine as we studied him successively as exegete, spiritual author and speculative theologian. Of course it is impossible to keep these separate from one another, and from that flow certain imperfections of the plan we have chosen. Thus the vision of the world underlying his exegesis is the exemplarism which was explained elsewhere under the doctrine of knowledge. And many of the points studied along with his spiritual teaching could equally well have come under the title of speculative theology and provided some more material for chapter XII.

A recent book entitled *Erasme lecteur d'Origène*[1] shows in its conclusion that the great humanist had a high regard for the exegetical and spiritual writer that was Origen without neglecting the speculative theologian: In his *De libero arbitrio* was he not closely inspired by the chapter on free will in the *Treatise on First Principles?* Three short sentences of Erasmus will serve to make the point: 'A single page of Origen teaches more Christian philosophy than ten of Augustine'. This expression 'Christian philosophy' is explained thus by Erasmus when replying to the protests of Noël Beda: 'I declare that I find more heartfelt piety (*pii affectus*) in a page of Origen than in ten of Augustine.' The third is the following: 'But for my part when it comes to commenting on Scripture I would place Origen alone above ten orthodox scholars, setting aside a few points of faith.'

As for those 'few points of faith', if account is taken on the one hand of the whole of Origen's writings, where statements balance each other, and on the other hand of the still succinct character of the rule of faith in his day, the traditional accusations lose a great part of their force. The only one with a firm foundation concerns the pre-existence of souls, including Christ's, and the fall which occurred at that stage. Of course this is a hypothesis, but it is a cherised hypothesis by which Origen constantly

[1] A. Godin, Geneva 1982.

thinks. At his time it could not be called heretical, for the Church had not then any clear teaching on the origin of the soul, except that its creation, whether indirectly (traducianism) or directly (creationism), was of God; and this the doctrine of pre-existence also affirms. If care is taken to study exactly the trinitarian doctrine of Origen, it will first be seen that the unity of the Father and the Son is expressed fairly exactly by formulae that are of an order more dynamic than ontological and that in spite of a few clumsy expressions his subordinationism is not heterodox: concerning the origin and the economy, he affirms, as Athanasius and Hilary themselves were to do, both the equality of power of the Persons and a certain subordination of the Son to the Father, considered as the decision-making centre of the Trinity. Besides the clarity of his affirmations of the eternal generation of the Son forbids us to confuse the subordination of Origen with that of Arius. As for the Apocatastasis we have shown that it was not possible to attribute clearly to him any of the characteristics which would render the doctrine heretical: incorporeality, pantheism, or universalism; account must also be taken of the still embryonic state of the rule of faith on certain points.

The other accusations are based on misconceptions by his accusers. The world created by God from all eternity is not that of the pre-existent intelligences, but that of the Platonist 'ideas' and the Stoic 'reasons', plans and seeds of beings, contained in the Son and thus created by the Father in the eternal generation of his Word. When Origen says that the Son cannot see the Father, he is contesting the anthropomorphism which understood physically the word 'see': but he speculates several times on the knowledge the Son has of the Father. The risen body is not, despite Methodius's misconception, a body other than the earthly one, but there is between the two a difference of quality, their identity being maintained by a bodily *eidos*. Origen could not in the *Treatise on First Principles* uphold the metempsychosis which in several passages of the great commentaries in Greek he treats as absurd and contrary to the thought of the Church: besides there is for him nothing in common between the human soul, equal in origin to that of the angels, and those secondary creatures, the animals, which exist only to be useful to men.[2] The renewal in heaven of the sacrifice of Christ for the sake of the demons is an idea that comes from a misunderstanding by Jerome and Theophilus of Alexandria of the cosmic character of the drama of the Cross which purified everything, heaven and earth: in Book I of the *Commentary on John*,[3] exactly contemporary with the *Treatise on First Principles*, from which Jerome derives this notion by a faulty interpretation, while admitting that Origen does not actually say it – and Justinian follows

[2] This is what G. Dorival emphasises when he rejects Jerome's claim to find metempsychosis in the *PArch*: article cited in note 45 of chapter IX.

[3] I, 35 (40), 255.

Jerome[4] – it is affirmed that this sacrifice only happened once (*hapax*). In attributing to Origen the absurd idea that the glorious bodies are spherical Justinian understood of the resurrected what the *Treatise on Prayer* says about the stars. When the latter writing declares that one should not pray to the Son but to the Father through the Son, it conforms to the liturgical custom which persists to this day in many prayers: in fact in his homilies Origen often prays to the Son and sometimes even to the Son in his humanity: it is to Him that are addressed most of the doxologies that conclude the homilies.[5] There would be no end to a list of the misconceptions from which the accusations levelled against him are derived.

We have emphasised above how little canonical and historical value can be given to the anathemas of the 5th Ecumenical Council, Constantinople II, of 453, for they do not appear in the official Minutes, probably having been discussed before the formal opening of the Council, and they concern explicitly the Origenists of the 6th century, Origen being named as their symbol and standard-bearer. But this condemnation, like all the disputes that preceded it and the stories put about by Epiphanius of an alleged apostasy, have done immense wrong to his memory. They did not completely prevent the effect that his spiritual doctrine had in the high Middle Ages on the great Cistercian teachers or on those of the Renaissance, but did seriously hinder it.

Thus posterity has been seriously unjust to the memory of one of the men to whom Christian thought is most indebted. If it is a fact that the scorn shown by Celsus for the ignorance and stupidity of the Christians is not found in the same way after Origen, for example in the attacks of Porphyry, it can be seen that the enterprise of converting the intelligent inaugurated by the school of Alexandria, by Clement and then by Origen, had its effects in the educated circles of the empire, which began to take a different view of Christianity. Who can measure the influence the movement that they started must have had upon the coming to Christianity of Roman society, both with and after Constantine?

---

[4] Fragments corresponding to *PArch* IV, 3, 13: SC 269, note 80, pp. 226–231.
[5] cf. H. Crouzel, 'Les doxologies finales des homélies d'Origène selon le texte grec et les versions latines' in *Ecclesia Orans: Mélanges patristiques offerts au P. A. G. Hamman* (ed. V. Saxer), *Augustinianum* 20, 1980, 95–107.

Index of Modern Authors

Index of Ancient Authors
and other Individuals

Index of Biblical References